T0311174

"The Catholic Commentary on Sacred Scripture richly provides what has for so long been lacking among contemporary scriptural commentaries. Its goal is to assist Catholic preachers and teachers, lay and ordained, in their ministry of the Word. Moreover, it offers ordinary Catholics a scriptural resource that will enhance their understanding of God's Word and thereby deepen their faith. Thus these commentaries, nourished on the faith of the Church and guided by scholarly wisdom, are both exegetically sound and spiritually nourishing."

—**Thomas G. Weinandy, OFM Cap**, United States Conference of Catholic Bishops

"This could be the first commentary read by a pastor preparing a text and could be read easily by a Sunday School teacher preparing a text, and it would be an excellent commentary for a college Bible class. . . . The Catholic Commentary on Sacred Scripture will prove itself to be a reliable, Catholic—but ecumenically open and respectful—commentary."

—**Scot McKnight**, *Jesus Creed* blog

"This commentary series should meet a need that has long been pointed out: a guide to Scripture that will be both historically responsible and shaped by the mind of the Church's tradition. It promises to be a milestone in the recovery of a distinctively Catholic approach to exegesis."

—**Aidan Nichols, OP**, University of Oxford; Fellow of Greyfriars, Oxford

"There is a great hunger among Catholic laity for a deeper understanding of the Bible. The Catholic Commentary on Sacred Scripture fills the need for a more in-depth interpretation of Scripture. I am very excited to be able to recommend this series to our Bible Study groups around the world."

—**Gail Buckley**, founder and director, Catholic Scripture Study International (www.cssprogram.net)

"Coinciding with the Bishops' Synod on 'The Word of God in the Life and Mission of the Church,' this great project of a seventeen-volume commentary on the New Testament represents a much-needed approach, based on good scholarship but not overloaded with it. The frequent references to the *Catechism of the Catholic Church* help us to read Holy Scripture with a vivid sense of the living tradition of the Church."

—**Christoph Cardinal Schönborn**, Archbishop of Vienna

 Catholic Commentary on Sacred Scripture

Revelation

Peter S. Williamson

Baker Academic
a division of Baker Publishing Group
Grand Rapids, Michigan

© 2015 by Peter S. Williamson

Published by Baker Academic
a division of Baker Publishing Group
P.O. Box 6287, Grand Rapids, MI 49516-6287
www.bakeracademic.com

Printed in the United States of America

Library of Congress Cataloging-in-Publication Data

Williamson, Peter S.
    Revelation / Peter S. Williamson.
       pages cm. — (Catholic commentary on sacred scripture)
    Includes bibliographical references and index.
    ISBN 978-0-8010-3650-7 (pbk.)
      1. Bible. Revelation—Commentaries. 2. Catholic Church—Doctrines. I. Title.
    BS2825.53.W555 2015
    228′.077—dc23
                                                    2014040101

Printed with Ecclesiastical Permission
Most Reverend Earl Boyea
June 19, 2014

21   22   23   24   25   26   27   12   11   10   9   8   7   6

To my wife, Marsha Daigle-Williamson,
and to my mother, Beulah Pederson Williamson,
with gratitude and love

Contents

Illustrations

Editors' Preface

The Church has always venerated the divine Scriptures just as she venerates the body of the Lord. . . . All the preaching of the Church should be nourished and governed by Sacred Scripture. For in the sacred books, the Father who is in heaven meets His children with great love and speaks with them; and the power and goodness in the word of God is so great that it stands as the support and energy of the Church, the strength of faith for her sons and daughters, the food of the soul, a pure and perennial fountain of spiritual life.

Second Vatican Council, Dei Verbum 21

Were not our hearts burning [within us] while he spoke to us on the way and opened the scriptures to us?

Luke 24:32

The Catholic Commentary on Sacred Scripture aims to serve the ministry of the Word of God in the life and mission of the Church. Since Vatican Council II, there has been an increasing hunger among Catholics to study Scripture in depth and in a way that reveals its relationship to liturgy, evangelization, catechesis, theology, and personal and communal life. This series responds to that desire by providing accessible yet substantive commentary on each book of the New Testament, drawn from the best of contemporary biblical scholarship as well as the rich treasury of the Church's tradition. These volumes seek to offer scholarship illumined by faith, in the conviction that the ultimate aim of biblical interpretation is to discover what God has revealed and is still speaking through the sacred text. Central to our approach are the principles taught by Vatican II: first, the use of historical and literary methods to discern what the biblical authors intended to express; second, prayerful theological reflection to understand the sacred text "in accord with the same Spirit by whom it was written"—that is, in light of the content and unity of the whole Scripture, the living tradition of the Church, and the analogy of faith (*Dei Verbum* 12).

The Catholic Commentary on Sacred Scripture is written for those engaged in or training for pastoral ministry and others interested in studying Scripture to understand their faith more deeply, to nourish their spiritual life, or to share the good news with others. With this in mind, the authors focus on the meaning of the text for faith and life rather than on the technical questions that occupy scholars, and they explain the Bible in ordinary language that does not require translation for preaching and catechesis. Although this series is written from the perspective of Catholic faith, its authors draw on the interpretation of Protestant and Orthodox scholars and hope these volumes will serve Christians of other traditions as well.

A variety of features are designed to make the commentary as useful as possible. Each volume includes the biblical text of the New American Bible, Revised Edition (NABRE), the translation approved for liturgical use in the United States. In order to serve readers who use other translations, the most important differences between the NABRE and other widely used translations (RSV, NRSV, JB, NJB, and NIV) are noted and explained. Each unit of the biblical text is followed by a list of references to relevant Scripture passages, Catechism sections, and uses in the Roman Lectionary. The exegesis that follows aims to explain in a clear and engaging way the meaning of the text in its original historical context as well as its perennial meaning for Christians. Reflection and Application sections help readers apply Scripture to Christian life today by responding to questions that the text raises, offering spiritual interpretations drawn from Christian tradition or providing suggestions for the use of the biblical text in catechesis, preaching, or other forms of pastoral ministry.

Interspersed throughout the commentary are Biblical Background sidebars that present historical, literary, or theological information and Living Tradition sidebars that offer pertinent material from the postbiblical Christian tradition, including quotations from Church documents and from the writings of saints and Church Fathers. The Biblical Background sidebars are indicated by a photo of urns that were excavated in Jerusalem, signifying the importance of historical study in understanding the sacred text. The Living Tradition sidebars are indicated by an image of Eadwine, a twelfth-century monk and scribe, signifying the growth in the Church's understanding that comes by the grace of the Holy Spirit as believers study and ponder the word of God in their hearts (see *Dei Verbum* 8).

Maps and a glossary are located in the back of each volume for easy reference. The glossary explains key terms from the biblical text as well as theological or exegetical terms, which are marked in the commentary with a cross (†). A list of suggested resources, an index of pastoral topics, and an index of sidebars are included to enhance the usefulness of these volumes. Further resources, including questions for reflection or discussion, can be found at the series website, www.CatholicScriptureCommentary.com.

It is our desire and prayer that these volumes be of service so that more and more "the word of the Lord may speed forward and be glorified" (2 Thess 3:1) in the Church and throughout the world.

Peter S. Williamson
Mary Healy
Kevin Perrotta

Note to Readers

The New American Bible, Revised Edition differs slightly from most English translations in its verse numbering of the Psalms and certain other parts of the Old Testament. For instance, Ps 51:4 in the NABRE is Ps 51:2 in other translations; Mal 3:19 in the NABRE is Mal 4:1 in other translations. Readers who use different translations are advised to keep this in mind when looking up Old Testament cross-references given in the commentary.

Abbreviations

†	indicates that a definition of the term appears in the glossary
//	indicates where the same episode occurs in two or more Gospels
ACCS 12	Williams C. Weinrich, ed. *Revelation*, Ancient Christian Commentary on Scripture: New Testament 12 (Downers Grove, IL: InterVarsity, 2005)
Beale and McDonough	G. K. Beale and Sean M. McDonough, "Revelation," in *Commentary on the New Testament Use of the Old Testament*, ed. G. K. Beale and D. A. Carson (Grand Rapids, Baker Academic: 2007), 1081–1161
Catechism	*Catechism of the Catholic Church* (2nd ed.)
CCSS	Catholic Commentary on Sacred Scripture
DS	Denzinger-Schönmetzer, *Enchiridion Symbolorum, definitionum et declarationum de rebus fidei et morum* (1965)
ESV	English Standard Version
JB	Jerusalem Bible
Lectionary	*The Lectionary for Mass* (1998/2002 USA Edition)
LXX	†Septuagint
NABRE	New American Bible (Revised Edition, 2011)
NET	New English Translation
NIGTC	New International Greek Testament Commentary (Eerdmans)
NIV	New International Version
NJB	New Jerusalem Bible
NRSV	New Revised Standard Version
NT	New Testament
Osborne, *Revelation*	Grant R. Osborne, *Revelation*, Baker Exegetical Commentary on the New Testament (Grand Rapids: Baker Academic, 2002)
OT	Old Testament
RSV	Revised Standard Version
v(v).	verse(s)

Books of the Old Testament

Gen	Genesis	Num	Numbers	Judg	Judges
Exod	Exodus	Deut	Deuteronomy	Ruth	Ruth
Lev	Leviticus	Josh	Joshua	1 Sam	1 Samuel

2 Sam	2 Samuel	Ps	Psalm/Psalms	Joel	Joel
1 Kings	1 Kings	Prov	Proverbs	Amos	Amos
2 Kings	2 Kings	Eccles	Ecclesiastes	Obad	Obadiah
1 Chron	1 Chronicles	Song	Song of Songs	Jon	Jonah
2 Chron	2 Chronicles	Wis	Wisdom	Mic	Micah
Ezra	Ezra	Sir	Sirach	Nah	Nahum
Neh	Nehemiah	Isa	Isaiah	Hab	Habakkuk
Tob	Tobit	Jer	Jeremiah	Zeph	Zephaniah
Jdt	Judith	Lam	Lamentations	Hag	Haggai
Esther	Esther	Bar	Baruch	Zech	Zechariah
1 Macc	1 Maccabees	Ezek	Ezekiel	Mal	Malachi
2 Macc	2 Maccabees	Dan	Daniel		
Job	Job	Hosea	Hosea		

Books of the New Testament

Matt	Matthew	1 Tim	1 Timothy
Mark	Mark	2 Tim	2 Timothy
Luke	Luke	Titus	Titus
John	John	Philem	Philemon
Acts	Acts	Heb	Hebrews
Rom	Romans	James	James
1 Cor	1 Corinthians	1 Pet	1 Peter
2 Cor	2 Corinthians	2 Pet	2 Peter
Gal	Galatians	1 John	1 John
Eph	Ephesians	2 John	2 John
Phil	Philippians	3 John	3 John
Col	Colossians	Jude	Jude
1 Thess	1 Thessalonians	Rev	Revelation
2 Thess	2 Thessalonians		

Introduction

No book of the Bible stands more in need of commentary than Revelation. Revelation, also known as the Apocalypse, is manifestly different from the other, more familiar books of the New Testament. Its arcane symbolism can strike readers as strange and its wild imagery as frightening. Further, few Christians today have the biblical knowledge to catch even half of the author's several hundred allusions to the Old Testament.[1] The historical circumstances in which the book was written are unfamiliar to many. The structure of the book is difficult to discern, and its literary characteristics differ greatly from modern ways of communicating. Finally, the fact that one of its principal topics is the last judgment and the end of history raises the stakes. The sensationalist interpretations that circulate both among believers and in the secular media make informed interpretation of this book all the more necessary.

My aim is to help contemporary readers meet these challenges by seeking to offer an interpretation of Revelation that is faithful to the text, enlightened by both contemporary scholarship and traditional interpretation, in harmony with the whole of Scripture and Christian doctrine, and relevant for the Church today.

This introduction provides a brief overview of Revelation's genre, author, historical setting, structure and literary features, interpretation and message, and its relevance to Christian life today. Readers interested in more background information can consult the Suggested Resources at the back of this book or additional articles provided online in the Revelation Resources at www.Catholic ScriptureCommentary.com.

1. Estimates range from slightly more than two hundred to one thousand allusions, depending on the criteria that are used.

Genre

How does the author of Revelation present his work, and how would first-century Christian readers have classified it? Ancient books were rare and copied by hand, and the original audience of this book, the members of the seven churches in the Roman province of Asia named in 1:11, would have first laid eyes on the scroll that contained Revelation at the liturgy. I say "audience," since most would never have the opportunity to read the book themselves but would hear it read to them by a church leader or by a messenger who brought the scroll to the Christian community in their city. The mere size of the scroll would have indicated to those present that they were about to hear a book-length text, in contrast, for example, to some of the brief letters included in the New Testament canon.

The first couple of sentences indicate the book's content, presenting it as "the revelation of Jesus Christ" made known to "his servant John," who is "reporting what he saw" (1:1–2). Although the Greek word for revelation is *apokalypsis*, that word did not yet have the associations with end-times catastrophes that "apocalypse" has for people today. Paul's Letters, which were probably familiar to the churches of Asia (present-day southwestern Turkey), use this word to refer to prophetic words or visions (e.g., 1 Cor 14:6, 26; 2 Cor 12:1, 7). The next verse pronounces a blessing on those who read and listen to "this prophetic message." Those listening would thus have classified what they were hearing as a book of Christian prophecy comparable to Old Testament prophetic books such as Isaiah, Ezekiel, and Daniel.

At the same time, Revelation's earliest audience would have recognized it as a circular letter. After its unusual prologue (1:1–3), Revelation resembles other early Christian letters for a few verses. The sender identifies himself as "John," and his recipients as "the seven churches" in Asia, then extends a greeting of "grace . . . and peace." He proceeds to offer a prayer of praise and thanks to God (1:5b–6).

As the original audience listened to the scroll being read, they would have noticed both similarities to and differences from the Old Testament prophetic books with which they were familiar. One difference is that the primary revealer in this book of prophecy is the risen Lord Jesus, although he relays a message he has received from God the Father, just as he did during his earthly ministry (1:2; John 8:26; 12:49–50). He conveys this message to the prophet John through an angel and through "the Spirit" (2:7, 11, etc.), whom the early Christians recognized as the source of prophecy.

John's original audience would not have found Revelation as strange as it seems to us today because it belongs to a type of religious literature that was popular at the time. This literary genre, which originated about 200 BC and remained widespread among Jews and Christians until a century or two after Christ, was later called "apocalypse," due in part to the use of that word at the beginning of the book of Revelation. Scholars debate how best to define apocalypse.[2] An apocalypse typically explains unseen spiritual realities behind human events or looks forward to history's end. It is characterized by dreams, visions, and other highly symbolic ways of communicating. Several noncanonical †apocalypses prior to or contemporary with Revelation (*1 Enoch, 4 Ezra, 2 Baruch*, and the *Apocalypse of Abraham*)[3] illustrate the genre, and it is likely that John and some of his readers would have been familiar with these or similar works.

Author

Four times the author of Revelation refers to himself as John (1:1, 4, 9; 22:8), implying that he expects his readers to know who he is. Important early Christian authorities, including Justin Martyr (AD 165), Tertullian (220), Irenaeus (180), Clement of Alexandria (200), Hippolytus (235), Origen (254), and Athanasius (350), identify this John as the apostle John, whom they also consider to be the author of the Gospel and the Epistles that bear his name. Western Church tradition has generally followed their lead.

Revelation has some similarities to the other Johannine writings. Like the Gospel, and unlike other New Testament writings, it refers to Jesus as the Word of God (Rev 19:13; John 1:1, 14) and as the Lamb (John 1:29, 36, although Revelation uses a different Greek word for "Lamb"). Like the Fourth Gospel, Revelation speaks of "life-giving water"[4] and alludes to Jesus being "pierced" (Rev 1:7; John 19:37; see Zech 12:10). In addition, Revelation shares vocabulary with the Gospel and the Letters of John that is not common elsewhere in Scripture: to "conquer" or "be victorious," to "keep" the word or the commandments, "dwell," "sign," "testimony," and "true."

However, there are some difficulties in identifying the author of Revelation with John the apostle or with the author of the Gospel and Letters that bear his name. First, the author of Revelation never refers to himself as an apostle

---

2. See John C. Collins, "The Apocalyptic Genre," in *The Apocalyptic Imagination*, 2nd ed. (Grand Rapids: Eerdmans, 1998), 1–42.

3. For more on the relation of Revelation to other apocalypses, see Richard Bauckham, *The Theology of the Book of Revelation*, New Testament Theology (Cambridge: Cambridge University Press, 1993), 5–12; and Wilfred J. Harrington, *Revelation*, Sacra Pagina (Collegeville, MN: Liturgical Press, 1993), 1–5.

4. See Rev 7:17; 22:1; John 4:10–11; and 7:38; the precise wording differs slightly among them.

but indicates he is a prophet (1:3) and a brother among the prophets (22:9), a group he distinguishes from the apostles (18:20). When Revelation speaks of the twelve apostles of the Lamb as the foundation stones of the wall of the new Jerusalem (21:14), there is no suggestion that the author includes himself in their number.

Second, from ancient times, learned readers have found weighty stylistic reasons to question whether the author of the Gospel of John and 1 John was the same person who wrote Revelation.[5] Writing in the mid-third century, Dionysius, bishop of Alexandria, identified significant differences in the Greek writing style, phraseology, and patterns of thought between the works. In contrast to the elegant Greek of the Gospel of John, the Greek of Revelation is heavily influenced by Hebrew or Aramaic. Dionysius also pointed out that the author of the other biblical books attributed to the apostle John does not name himself, while the author of Revelation identifies himself four times, and never in the ways the Gospel or 1 John refer to their author ("the disciple whom Jesus loved," the "Elder," the "one who testifies"). Dionysius points to the commonness of the name John and concludes that the author was another John who resided in Ephesus, noting the existence in his day of two tombs bearing the name of John and venerated by the church of Ephesus.

Other prominent Church Fathers in the East—including Cyril of Jerusalem, Gregory of Nazianzus, John Chrysostom, Eusebius, and Theodoret—did not consider the apostle John the author of Revelation or even regard it as part of the canon of Scripture. Some of their uneasiness was due to problematic interpretations of the book and to the use made of it by the Montanists, members of a heretical early Christian sect.

The striking style differences noted by Dionysius continue to persuade most scholars that the author of Revelation was not the same person who wrote the Gospel and Epistles of John. However, some scholars maintain that the apostle John did write Revelation and explain the stylistic differences as due to the book's apocalyptic genre, or to the apostle John's use of a secretary (an amanuensis) in the composition of his other books, not available to him on Patmos.[6]

Unless new information is uncovered, we cannot know for sure who wrote Revelation. There is no reason to doubt what the author says about himself—

---

5. Eusebius, *Ecclesiastical History* 7.25.

6. Gordon Fee takes the second position in *Revelation: A New Covenant Commentary* (Eugene, OR: Wipf & Stock, 2011), Kindle edition, 384. Other scholars suggest that Revelation is pseudonymous, like many apocalyptic writings, and that in calling himself John, the author is (falsely) claiming to be the famous apostle. However, the absence of any claim to apostleship or acquaintance with Jesus during his earthly life makes this unlikely.

namely, that he is a Christian prophet and his name is John. His Greek style shows his native language to be Hebrew or Aramaic; his extraordinary familiarity with the Old Testament supports the impression that he is a Jewish Christian. On the basis of the similarities to the Fourth Gospel and the Letters mentioned above, we may conclude that he has at least read those works. Regardless of whether he is the apostle John, the Church receives the book of Revelation as divinely inspired and canonical Scripture.

Historical Setting and Purpose

Date

There are two leading hypotheses as to when Revelation was written. Some scholars think it was written in the mid- to late 60s of the first century, during the reign of the Roman emperor Nero (AD 54–68). For Christians, Nero was undoubtedly a symbol of the worst possibilities of Roman imperial power, since in 64 he initiated the first large-scale government persecution of Christians, resulting in the martyrdom of many, including Peter and Paul (see sidebar, "The First Martyrs of the Church of Rome," p. 216).

However, the majority of interpreters, ancient and modern, hold that Revelation was written in the mid-90s, during the reign of the emperor Domitian (81–96).[7] Irenaeus, writing in *Against Heresies* (5.30.3) around the year 180, states that John "beheld the apocalyptic vision . . . not a very long time ago, but almost in our day, towards the end of Domitian's reign." Other ancient writers, including Victorinus, Eusebius, Clement of Alexandria, and Origen, support his view.

A key question is which period better fits the circumstances depicted in the book. Some passages in Revelation depict persecution, and there seems to have been persecution of Christians by Roman

Fig. 1. A bust of the emperor Domitian (AD 81–96), regarded by some as a second Nero.

Jastrow/Wikimedia Commons

7. David Aune, a leading Revelation scholar, takes a middle position, proposing that some of the visions were written down beginning in the 60s but that the book reached its present form in the 90s. See Aune, *Revelation 1–5*, Word Biblical Commentary 52a (Dallas: Word, 1997), lviii.

authorities during Domitian's reign. Although the extent of Domitian's persecution of Christians is debated, some evidence for such a persecution exists. In AD 96, toward the end of Domitian's reign, Clement of Rome writes guardedly of "sudden and unexpected happenings and experiences that have befallen us" (*1 Clement* 1.1),[8] and some second-century Christian authors allude to persecutions by Domitian.[9] The fact that some of Domitian's pagan contemporaries regarded him as another Nero is consistent with this possibility.[10] Other details in Revelation better fit the 90s than the 60s—for instance, the prosperity of Laodicea (3:17), which suffered a major earthquake in AD 60, and the line "do not damage the olive oil or the wine" (6:6), which might allude to an edict of Domitian about vineyards in Asia in 92.[11]

This commentary will presuppose the majority view, that Revelation was written in the 90s, but will occasionally consider the possible implications of an earlier date for interpreting the book.

John's Audience

John writes to seven churches in the Roman province of Asia, a region that today comprises the southwestern part of Turkey. Ephesus was the chief city of the province, and its church was the leading church, due to both the city's prominence and its very successful evangelization by the apostle Paul and his coworkers in the mid-50s (see Acts 19, especially 19:10, 26; 20:17–38). The churches of Asia included Jewish believers but consisted primarily of Gentile converts from paganism. Although it has been common to assume that John's readers were all suffering persecution, a careful reading of the messages to the churches (chaps. 2–3) finds mention of persecution only in the †oracles to Smyrna (2:10), Pergamum (2:13, a reference to the past), and Philadelphia (3:8–10). These references suggest that at the time the book of Revelation was written, its addressees were experiencing periodic and localized persecution— not the worldwide pressure to worship the beast and persecution that the book foretells (11:7; 12:17; 13:7).

8. After recalling the martyrdoms of Peter and Paul (chap. 5) and of the Roman martyrs (chap. 6), Clement writes, "We are in the same arena, and the same contest lies before us" (7.1).

9. Eusebius reports a persecution and martyrdom of Christians in Domitian's final year (96). Melito of Sardis petitions the emperor (ca. 170–80), claiming that only Nero and Domitian persecuted Christians (*Ecclesiastical History* 4.25). Tertullian says the same. See Raymond E. Brown, *Introduction to the New Testament* (New York: Doubleday, 1997), 805–9.

10. Richard Bauckham, *The Climax of Prophecy: Studies on the Book of Revelation* (Edinburgh: T&T Clark, 1993), 410.

11. These are selected from details supplied by Osborne, *Revelation*, 9.

Christians and Jews of the first century distinguished themselves from the surrounding Greco-Roman culture by their refusal to worship anything other than the Creator God of Israel. Worship of the pagan gods was so woven into daily rituals and civic life that the refusal of many Jews and Christians to participate in these rites seemed narrow-minded and antisocial, if not downright unpatriotic. Jewish abstinence from pagan rituals enjoyed legal protection because Judaism was a recognized ancient religion, but Christians did not enjoy the same privilege. Prior to the Jewish revolt and the destruction of Jerusalem in AD 70, Roman authorities considered Christians a sect within Judaism, but afterward they gradually began to treat Christians as a distinct religious group lacking legal recognition and therefore obliged to participate like everyone else in the †imperial cult.

Theological Presuppositions

If Revelation was written in the 90s, John and his readers would have been familiar with the Synoptic traditions about Jesus, probably by possessing one or more of the †Synoptic Gospels. I have already mentioned why it is likely that John was at least familiar with the Gospel and Letters of John. It is also likely that he and his readers were familiar with some or all of the Pauline literature, since Ephesus was a major Pauline center and Paul's Letters were in circulation from quite early on (Col 4:16; 2 Pet 3:15–16). Recognizing the likelihood that John and his readers were familiar with the Old Testament and many of the New Testament writings is a tremendous key to unlocking the meaning of Revelation.

Revelation manifests faith in the sacrificial death and resurrection of Jesus and in his divine status. It likewise presupposes hope in Jesus' future glorious return and, despite its vivid symbolic presentation, reflects an †eschatological outlook similar to that of other New Testament writings. Like them, Revelation anticipates times of trial and persecution for Christians during the time of their testimony to the gospel. While Revelation's depiction of the dragon, the beast, and the false prophet adds details not found in other sources, it builds on Jewish eschatology and lines up with early Christian understanding regarding Satan and eschatological opposition attested elsewhere (Dan 7; 2 Thess 2; 1 John 2:18).

Structure and Plot

The elaborate structure of Revelation is both fascinating and bewildering at the same time. Unlike some Old Testament prophetic books that offer a loosely organized collection of oracles, Revelation provides a narrative that progresses toward the consummation of history, although by a circular rather than a direct route. After a prologue and an opening greeting, John presents his book as what was shown to him in a prophetic experience when in exile on the island of Patmos (1:9–11). The risen Jesus commands him to write what he has been shown that pertains to two time periods, "what is happening, and what will happen afterwards" (1:19).

The seven messages to the churches that follow (2:1–3:22) reveal "what is happening," the condition of the churches in Asia in John's day. The transition to the second part of the book, John's visions of the future, occurs in 4:1, when John hears the risen Lord invite him to enter heaven: "Come up here and I will show you

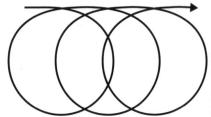

Fig. 2. Revelation's story advances by circular repetitions rather than in a straight line.

what must happen afterwards." As a spectator in heaven's throne room, John witnesses the Lamb receiving a scroll from the hand of God that represents God's plan for the world. As the Lamb opens the seven seals, human history unfolds, directed from the heavenly throne room.

Several structural markers enable John's audience to track their progress through the narrative of these chapters (6:1–22:11). First, three series of seven follow the oracles to the seven churches—the opening of seven seals, the blowing of seven trumpets, and the pouring out of seven bowls. In a schematic fashion these series of sevens reveal the events that unfold between John's vision and the end of history. The series are placed inside one another like Russian nesting dolls: the content of the seventh seal (8:1) is the blowing of the seven trumpets and the accompanying events (chaps. 8–9); the content of the seventh trumpet (11:15) is the pouring out of the seven bowls and the accompanying events (chaps. 15–16).

Two major series of visions sit on either side of the pouring out of the seven bowls. The first series begins with a second commissioning of the prophet John (chap. 10), a turning point located at the middle of the book. John is instructed to prophesy words of judgment against "many peoples, nations, tongues, and kings" (10:10–11). The other visions in this series reveal the background (the story of the woman, the male child, Michael and the dragon, 12:1–17), other principal actors (the two witnesses, the two beasts, and the Lamb's companions, 11:1–13; 13:1–14:5), and previews of history's outcome (the worship, testimony, persecution, and vindication of the Church, 11:1–13; the fall of Babylon and the harvest of the earth, 14:6–20).

After the pouring out of the seven bowls, parallel visions interpreted by angels contrast the whore Babylon and her fate (17:1–19:10) with the Bride Jerusalem and her future †glory (21:9–22:11), the fulfillment of God's purpose. Between the visions of Babylon's fall and the descent from heaven of the new Jerusalem, four visions reveal how God judges the enemies of his people and brings salvation.[12] An epilogue and a final greeting complete the work (22:12–21).

Another structural feature of Revelation is the alternation between fearsome visions of judgment on earth and consoling visions of God's throne in heaven. This oscillation serves two purposes. First, the consoling visions give relief to John's audience through his account of otherwise terrifying visions. Second, and more important, the visions of undisturbed worship and celebration in heaven despite great tumult on earth reveal a central theme of the book: God is on his throne, the Lamb is in control. With God in heaven are powerful angelic beings and the faithful †saints and martyrs, now comforted, protected, and at rest. Nothing on earth disturbs them, for the Lamb has conquered and the outcome of earth's history is secure. Indeed, they reign with Christ and exercise a role of priestly worship and intercession while God's plan for human history unfolds (7:9–17; 15:2–4; 20:4–6).

Probably the most important point to note about Revelation's structure is that its plot does not advance chronologically. Although the visions unfold one after another in an orderly manner, the story advances by a spiral rather than a straight path, like a road that circles its way up a mountain, offering diverse vistas of the terrain below. Sometimes multiple visions depict a single event. For example, the relationship between the series of seven seals, trumpets, and bowls is not strictly sequential, since the sixth item in each series seems to position the reader at the same moment just short of the end of human history, while the seventh seems to signal the end. Moreover, the forward movement of the visions is disrupted by flashbacks, such as those that recall the birth and exaltation of the Messiah (5:5, 9; 12:5) and by atemporal visions of heavenly worship in which God's victory is celebrated as already achieved (7:9–17; 11:15–18; 15:2–4; 19:5–8). Despite these nonchronological elements, the narrative of Revelation does progress from the prophet's first vision of the risen Christ (chaps. 1–3), to a vision of the heavenly throne room (chaps. 4–5), through increasingly severe chastisements of the world and trials for the Church during her time of testimony (chaps. 6–20), to the return of Christ (chap. 19) and the full arrival of God's kingdom in the final two chapters.

12. They depict (1) the victory of the †Messiah over the beast, the false prophet, and their army (19:10–21); (2) the two-stage victory of God over Satan, with the reign of the saints during the intervening "thousand years" (20:1–10); (3) the final judgment of the dead and of Death itself (20:11–15); and (4) the new creation and the new order (21:1–8).

Literary Features

Besides its intriguing structure, Revelation has other literary features that make it challenging to interpret.

Recapitulation

Like visions in other biblical books (e.g., Dan 2; 7), Revelation's visions often repeat or †recapitulate the same theme. When John's visions offer more than one account of the same event, they do not merely repeat for emphasis, like Pharaoh's dreams of seven fat and lean cows and seven fat and lean ears of corn (Gen 41:1–7). Instead, motifs that reappear add new information at each repetition. So, for example, 12:6 speaks of a woman who represents the people of God and flees to the wilderness, where she is taken care of by God for twelve hundred and sixty days. The story is repeated in 12:7–18, but this lengthier version tells of Satan's warfare against the woman, and the role of Michael and the martyrs in the victory over the devil. Chapter 13 elaborates with additional information about *how* Satan wages war against the Church: through the two beasts.

Biblical Allusions

A striking feature of Revelation is its numerous allusions to the Old Testament—more than in any other New Testament book.[13] What is unique in Revelation is that John seldom explicitly quotes the Old Testament, as other New Testament authors do (e.g., Matt 1:22–23; Rom 8:36), but weaves allusions into his reports of what he sees and hears. John's knowledge of the Jewish Scriptures is extraordinary; he must have virtually memorized them.

Revelation interprets the Old Testament prophets in light of what God has done in Christ. It confirms that their eschatological prophecies of judgment, salvation, and a transformed world began to be fulfilled through Christ's death and resurrection (e.g., Rev 5:9; 12:5) and will be completely fulfilled when Christ returns. Sometimes John signals that what he sees is the same reality that an Old Testament prophet foresaw, but that the eschatological fulfillment is different and greater than anyone imagined. For example, the new Jerusalem fulfills Ezekiel's prophecy of a future temple (Ezek 40–48; Rev 21:10–27). Likewise Revelation shows that many promises that originally applied to Israel now

---

13. Revelation alludes most to Isaiah, Ezekiel, Daniel, and the Psalms. There are also allusions to the Pentateuch and historical books, including many references to the plagues in Egypt and the exodus.

apply to eschatological Israel, the Church, which includes people from every tribe, tongue, language, and nation.

Yet not every allusion to the Old Testament indicates the fulfillment of a prophecy. In each case it is necessary to discern, by the content and context of the allusion, whether John is saying, "This *is* what Ezekiel prophesied" (e.g., the new Jerusalem is the new temple) or "This is *like* what Ezekiel prophesied" (e.g., John's prophetic commissioning in chap. 10 is similar to Ezek 3:1–4), or is simply reusing biblical language or imagery to add solemnity to his message. One of the ways Revelation alludes to the Old Testament is by using names from Israel's past, such as Balaam (2:14) or Jezebel (2:20–23) to refer to people at the time of his writing. At other times it names Old Testament places, such as Babylon, Sodom, or Egypt (11:8), to refer to non-geographical spiritual realities.

Figurative Language and Symbolism

An especially challenging feature of Revelation is its extensive use of images, symbols, and figurative language. Contemporary readers may ask, "Why doesn't the author speak plainly? How can we know what should be taken symbolically and what literally?"

Many people today are more literal in their thinking than ancient peoples, perhaps because of the esteem with which our age regards technology and the exact sciences. The literature and iconography of both Jewish and Greco-Roman culture of the era in which Revelation was written manifests a love for symbolic communication that the early Christians shared with the people of their day.

Revelation makes frequent use of similes, metaphors, and symbols. A simile compares two unlike things by the use of "like" or "as," while a metaphor attributes the qualities of one thing to another without using "like" or "as."[14] Revelation employs over seventy similes, beginning with the vision of "one like a son of man," who is described by using nine similes (1:10, 13–16). These similes illuminate particular aspects of Jesus' person and role, while conveying that the risen Jesus surpasses anything his readers have experienced. Among Revelation's many metaphors is the risen Lord's diagnosis of the spiritual condition of the church at Laodicea: "lukewarm . . . poor, blind, and naked" (3:16–17). A symbol is something that stands for something else. Although they occasionally function as mere place markers for the things they refer to, symbols can be used to communicate depths of meaning that go far beyond mere reference. The harlot

---

14. See James L. Resseguie, *The Revelation of John: A Narrative Commentary* (Grand Rapids: Baker Academic, 2009), 19. His introduction to Revelation from a literary perspective is quite helpful.

Babylon is a symbol of Rome, but also of every proud civilization that resists God, persecutes his people, and idolizes wealth and pleasure.

John draws his figures of speech from a wide range of human experience. From nature he draws comparisons to the sky, sun, moon, stars, land, and sea to refer to transcendent realities, whether good or evil. The face of the risen Christ shines "like the sun at its brightest" (1:16), while the sea represents the world of chaos and evil (13:1; 20:1). The animals of Revelation that act and speak as personal beings, whether good or evil—the Lamb, the lion, the four living creatures, the dragon, the beasts, the eagle, the locusts, the horses—all represent superhuman entities. Powerful disruptions of nature, such as earthquakes, the sun ceasing to shine (9:2), and the moon turning to blood (6:12), indicate the intervention of God, who controls the elements of nature. These †cosmic events do not necessarily refer literally to natural disasters, since Scripture sometimes uses the language of cosmic upheaval metaphorically to refer to God's dramatic intervention to bring salvation or judgment (e.g., Judg 5:4–5; Ps 18:4–20). On the other hand, Jesus prophesied that cosmic events would precede his coming, and it is likely that Revelation sometimes alludes to these.

The vast majority of John's symbols come from ordinary life and social interactions known to his readers. Items of clothing reveal the status and nature of the figures in John's visions. Familiar activities such as harvesting, winemaking, shepherding, and buying and selling are given metaphorical meanings. Colors indicate the quality of a person or thing, although the meaning varies with the context. Riding a white horse signified military victory in the Greco-Roman world. On the other hand, a bride wearing white signifies purity, while the white garments of saints and angels emphasize their participation in the resurrection or eternal life of heaven. The red color of the second horse in 6:4 and of the dragon in 12:3 indicates their readiness to shed blood.

Revelation uses numbers symbolically—that is, qualitatively rather than quantitatively. Seven and ten normally represent completeness (perhaps from seven days in a week, ten fingers and toes). On the other hand, three and a half, which is half of seven, represents partiality and incompleteness. Four represents the world—the four winds and four points of the compass—and therefore what is universal. Twelve is the number of the people of God—twelve tribes of Israel and twelve apostles of the Lamb; twenty-four (twelve plus twelve) represents God's people under both covenants. A thousand, and multiples of a thousand, indicates a very large number rather than a precise quantity; in some instances it may allude to a large military unit (as often in the OT).

Some of Revelation's numerical symbolism appears in the frequency with which key words are used in the book. For instance, "Lord God almighty" is used seven times; "the one who sits on the throne," seven times; "Christ" seven times; "Jesus" fourteen times (twice seven); "Lamb" twenty-eight times (four times seven); and the "Spirit" fourteen times. John carefully avoids multiples of seven in using words that refer to Satan (eight times), the dragon (thirteen times), the beast (thirty-eight times), and Babylon (six times).[15]

John often combines multiple symbols in his description of a single figure. Thus the Lamb (Jesus) is described as standing (resurrection) as though it had been slain (the crucifixion), having seven horns (signifying fullness of power) and seven eyes (fullness of knowledge). Descriptions in Revelation, whether of individuals or of events, are descriptions of the symbols rather than of the realities themselves.[16] Each symbolic element needs to be thought through and interpreted rather than taken as literal description. For example, the feast of the vultures in 19:17–18 is a biblical allusion likely indicating that Christ's victory at the end of history will fulfill Ezekiel's prophecy about the utter destruction of those who oppose God (Ezek 39:17–20), not a prophesy of a literal battlefield scene.

The symbolic language of Revelation engages the reader far more powerfully than it would if its message were stated in literal prose. Some readers find the visions of Revelation so objectionable or frightening that they are eager to seize upon any congenial symbolic or metaphorical interpretation. Others, however, are suspicious of any interpretation of a biblical text that is not literal. Readers who were introduced to Revelation through a literal interpretation may be reluctant to reconsider what they learned, rightly on guard against rationalist interpretation that undercuts the miracles of the Bible through allegorizing or moralizing. Often younger readers are especially resistant toward nonliteral interpretation, impressed by Revelation's dramatic narrative and concerned lest symbolic interpretation empty the text of relevance to the real world. Whatever one's predisposition, it is best to approach Revelation as objectively as possible, conscious of one's inclinations, yet open to discovering afresh what John and the Holy Spirit who inspired him are saying through the text.

Interpretation of Revelation and History

The relation of Revelation to history has been a matter of great debate since the early Church. Prominent Church Fathers held sharply divergent views (see

15. See Bauckham, *Climax of Prophecy*, 36; for a detailed consideration of Revelation's numerical symbolism, see 29–37.

16. Bruce M. Metzger, *Breaking the Code* (Nashville: Abingdon, 1993), 14, 91.

"Excursus: Interpretation of 'the Millenium' through History," p. 329). In both ancient and modern times misguided individuals have announced the imminent end of the world, basing their claims on interpretations of Revelation. In our own day, †dispensationalism, a school of interpretation followed by fundamentalist Protestants and some evangelicals, popularized in Tim LaHaye and Jerry Jenkins' Left Behind novels, interprets Revelation as predicting events in the twentieth or twenty-first century.[17] In reaction to interpretations of this sort, many interpreters, both ancient (Origen, Jerome) and modern, have avoided interpreting Revelation as predictive prophecy by drawing allegorical lessons for the moral life or by mining Revelation for its theological riches (liturgical, christological, or ecclesiological), leaving aside the question of its relation to history. However, refusing to think about the relation of Revelation to history means rejecting, in part, the message of the book. The prophet John clearly invites his readers to discern the forces of evil and the hand of God within the political and religious events of their day in the light of his prophecy and to respond appropriately. Jesus too, in his eschatological parables and prophecies, taught his disciples to interpret events in the light of prophecy, urging watchfulness and attention to the signs of the times (Matt 16:3; 25:13). Other apostolic writings say the same (e.g., Rom 13:11–14; 2 Thess 2; 2 Pet 1:19). While the New Testament urges attention to the signs of the times and promotes awareness that the end is near, it does so not to satisfy our curiosity or to titillate us with insider knowledge but to exhort one and all to conduct our lives in light of ultimate realities.

Scholars commonly distinguish between four views of the relation of Revelation to history, although in practice most interpreters combine more than one view.

The *historicist* view holds that Revelation foretells in a linear way the history of Christianity. The problem with this view is the difficulty of mapping church history onto the narrative of Revelation in a convincing manner.

The *preterist* view holds that Revelation speaks primarily, if not exclusively, of events in the first century AD. A problem for preterists who regard Revelation as inspired Scripture is that it presents the fall of Babylon at or near history's end (16:17–21; 17:16–18:24) and the defeat of the beast as brought about by the second coming of Christ (19:11–21). If the beast or Babylon simply refers to the Roman Empire or Jerusalem, as some preterists maintain, how is it that Christ has not yet returned?

17. See the Revelation Resources at www.CatholicScriptureCommentary.com for more on dispensationalist interpretation of topics such as the †rapture, Armageddon, and the millennium.

The *futurist* view, famously held by dispensationalists, holds that most of the book of Revelation (chaps. 4–19) pertains to the last few years of human history before the return of Christ. However, this view raises the question of why God would reveal this information to the seven churches of Asia in the first century, and it reduces the relevance of Revelation to all but the final generation.

Finally, the *idealist* view holds that Revelation provides images and narratives of the struggle between good and evil that have no specific relation to history; they are intended to encourage and comfort Christians engaged in the struggle. A difficulty with this view is that, even though the imagery varies and is challenging to interpret, John presents a specific narrative about how history will end (chaps. 17–20).

The approach to Revelation taken in this commentary draws insights from each of these views without adopting any one of them. Christian faith in the inspiration of Sacred Scripture maintains that the Holy Spirit, who inspired this biblical book, intends it to speak to the Christian people throughout the ages. It is therefore important to be able to understand Revelation in relation to three periods of time: the time of its writing in the first century, the end of history, and the time of the Church that lies in between.

Like other biblical books of prophecy, Revelation was intended by its inspired human author to address the situation of his contemporaries. Consequently, understanding the book's first-century historical context is essential for interpreting it correctly. However, it is also clear that Revelation claims to depict the Church's trials leading up to the return of Christ. While John regards these events as future, he considers his visions as instructive for Christians of his day, as the many exhortations throughout the book indicate. In John's view, the spiritual dynamics of the final trial are already present in the temptations and persecutions that confront the Church in his day. Other eschatological writings in the New Testament share this perspective (1 John 2:18; 4:3; 2 Thess 2:7). From our vantage point centuries later, we can see that the prophet John saw the end of history through the lens of the trial facing the first-century churches of Asia in the Roman Empire. Like other eschatological biblical prophecies, those in Revelation seem not to distinguish the author's day from that of history's end.

The principle of biblical interpretation that links the past, the present, and the ultimate future is †typology. Typology recognizes that God works in recognizable patterns throughout history and that those who oppose God follow predictable patterns. History may not repeat itself, but often it rhymes. Persons, events, places, and institutions of an earlier stage in salvation history foreshadow those in a later stage. Biblical prophets often understand the trials and crises of their day in relationship to analogous crises in the past: they envision the salvation that God will bring as resembling his famous acts of salvation known from the historical or prophetic Scriptures.[18]

Just as biblical typology shaped John's prophetic message, it also provides a key to interpreting Revelation throughout the history of the Church. When individuals, governments, and cultures behave like the enemies of God's people depicted in Revelation, readers can recognize the resemblances and respond accordingly. For example, Nero, perhaps Domitian, Hitler, and Stalin—and the empires presided over by each—behaved like the beast and are rightly recognized as its agents. Revelation links the idolatrous materialistic culture of the Roman Empire with Babylon. For those with eyes to see, the consumerist, sexually immoral, and murderous (if we consider abortion and euthanasia) secular culture of the twenty-first century bears many of the same traits. In every age Christians must discern the manifestations of these evil powers by their fruits and respond appropriately.

This does not mean that the adversaries depicted in Rev 13–20 can be *reduced* to types that share common attributes and arise from time to time in history. Rather, despite its figurative language and elusive symbolism, Revelation seems to say some specific things about the end of history that do not fit the fall of Rome or any empire since. So in addition to a general application of Revelation to trials that arise in the history of the Church, Revelation awaits a definitive fulfillment at the end of history. Jesus said, "Of that day and hour no one knows, neither the angels of heaven, nor the Son, but the Father alone" (Matt 24:36). Not only has God reserved to himself the timing of the end; he also has not revealed precisely how he will accomplish his plan, even in Revelation. It is therefore wise both to do our best to discern what is happening around us in the light of biblical prophecy and to respond faithfully, while at the same time remaining modest about our understanding of exactly how God will accomplish his purposes. My study of Revelation has left me with immense respect for all who attempt to interpret this book for Christian faith and with amazement at how the Lord is able to speak to people through it despite the difficulty of the text and the diversity of our fallible interpretations.

18. Biblical prophecies sometimes have multiple fulfillments. Ezekiel's prophecy that God would gather his people in their own land and cleanse them and bless them abundantly (36:24–38) is fulfilled in the return from exile that began in 539 BC, in the gathering of God's people through the gospel of Christ, and definitively, in the eschatological gathering of God's people in the new Jerusalem.

Message of Revelation

The content of John's prophecy can be summarized as revelation—†*apokalypsis*—about four things: (1) the condition of the churches of Asia; (2) God's sovereignty and Christ's lordship over history; (3) the conflict and tribulation before Christ's return; and (4) a preview in general terms of how God will fulfill his promises, defeat evil, and save his people. Throughout the unveiling of these realities, John weaves exhortation summoning his readers to an appropriate response.

The Condition of the Church of Asia

Chapters 2 and 3 contain Jesus' messages to seven churches of late first-century Asia Minor. In each message the risen Lord, who sees with perfect clarity, gives his evaluation of the condition of a local church, which often differs from what appears on the surface. The number seven and the geographic distribution of the churches suggest that John understood these messages as intended for *all* the churches of Asia. Churches in other times and places rightly discern their own conditions in light of these inspired messages. Indeed, each oracle concludes with the exhortation, "Let anyone who has an ear listen to what the Spirit is saying to the *churches*" (Rev 2:7 NRSV, emphasis added)—that is, pay attention to *all* the messages.

God's Sovereignty and Christ's Lordship

Revelation unveils God's sovereignty and the lordship of the risen Christ. The Christians to whom John addressed his letter were a small minority living in a time and place in which the social, cultural, religious, economic, and political forces that opposed them seemed overwhelming. They were tempted to say along with the rest of the †world, "Who can compare with the beast or who can fight against it?" (13:4). But John's visions show the true situation: the true lord and judge is "one like a son of man" who stands unseen in the midst of the churches and speaks to each. Moreover, the true throne from which human history is determined is not the throne of any king on earth but God's throne in heaven. Christ has conquered, and the blood of the Lamb allows Christians to be victorious as well. Christ holds the keys of death and the netherworld (1:18). Those who die in his faithful service enjoy healing, comfort, protection with him in heaven, worshiping in his temple as priests and sharing in his rule (7:9–17; 15:2–4; 20:4–6). From the beginning to the end of the book, Revelation declares that God and his Messiah are completely in control.

The Church's Trial before Christ's Return

Revelation lifts the veil on the conflict in which the Church is engaged and reveals its principal actors. First among the adversaries of God's people is the "huge dragon, the ancient serpent, who is called the Devil and Satan" (12:9), who seeks to destroy the Messiah and then pursues the woman and her children (12:4, 13–17). He is "the accuser of our brothers" (12:10) and the principal yet hidden enemy of the Church, as other New Testament writings also affirm (Eph 6:11–13; 1 John 5:19). It is the dragon who summons and empowers two beasts to carry out their attack on God's people. Satan's principal agent, the beast (13:1–10), bears a perverse likeness to Christ, in that it was mortally wounded, yet lives. It is a demonic power that manifests itself in a government presided over by a particular human ruler who persecutes God's people and receives the world's idolatrous submission. The second beast, also called the false prophet, speaks on behalf of the dragon and advocates a deceptive ideology or religion (13:11–17). Last to be unveiled among the adversaries of God's people is the harlot Babylon (17:1–6), a society that is the polar opposite of the Bride-Church, a civilization and culture that seduces by wealth, luxury, immorality, and idolatry, and that persecutes God's people.

The Church consists of the faithful people of God of the Old and New Testaments, depicted corporately as a woman, the mother of the Messiah (12:1–2, 5). The members of the Church are the offspring of the woman, "those who keep God's commandments and bear witness to Jesus" (12:17). Their role in the conflict is to bear witness to Jesus and remain faithful in the face of persecution and temptation. As the end of the book, Christ appears as the victorious "King of kings and Lord of lords," to destroy the adversaries of God's people (19:11–21).

Preview of Promises Fulfilled: Salvation and Judgment

The Gospels and other New Testament writings show how Jesus fulfilled the Scriptures in his birth, life, death, and resurrection. However, the arrival of the Messiah did not immediately bring the kingdom of God in its fullness and the fulfillment of *all* God's promises. Instead, Jesus taught his disciples that before the end comes there will be an interim period during which the gospel is to be preached to all nations (Matt 24:14; Luke 19:11–12; Acts 1:6–8). Revelation, the only book of prophecy in the New Testament, discloses how Scriptures not fulfilled at Christ's first coming will be fulfilled at his second coming and in the events that lead up to it. For example, Revelation teaches that God will establish his kingdom as a new paradise in a new creation free from evil and defilement. The covenant of God and his people is fulfilled in the marriage of the Lamb and his Bride; their wedding feast is the great banquet of the kingdom. God's temple is definitively established as he dwells with his people in the new Jerusalem, an eschatological holy of holies (21:16), wiping away every tear from their faces (21:4; Isa 25:8).

Meaning for Today

Nearly twenty centuries have passed since John wrote down the visions he received for his fellow Christians in Asia Minor. Although the world today is very different, many of the circumstances facing Christians of the first century are present today in different guise.

After centuries in which Christianity was the dominant religious and cultural force in Western civilization, today in many places the Church exists in a secular culture whose mass media, entertainment, and educational systems are often hostile to her beliefs and morals. In many places adherents of other religions seek to eliminate the Christian testimony by force, while governments of both secular and religious nations persecute those who "keep God's commandments and bear witness to Jesus" (12:17). Meanwhile an international, materialistic, consumerist, sexually immoral culture seduces many away from their Christian faith. While literal idolatry—the worship of pagan gods and their physical images—is less common today than in the first century, spiritual idolatry—manifest in excessive love for and ultimate trust in created things rather than in God, whether wealth, pleasure, science, technology, governments, institutions, celebrities, or leaders—is stronger than ever.

Revelation reminds Christians today, as it did its original readers, that despite appearances, Jesus Christ is Lord. God is seated on his throne, directing history toward the goal he intends.

In the midst of conflict and temptation, every Christian is summoned to conquer, to be "the victor" who will eat of the tree of life, avoid the second death, and receive a new name and all the other eschatological rewards promised in this book. Despite persecution, Christians are summoned to bear witness to the gospel in word and deed like the two witnesses (11:3–13). This entails relying on God for protection and the power of his Spirit for boldness, signs, and wonders. If testimony to Jesus costs us our lives, we are not afraid since we await a resurrection that all the world will someday see, like that of the two witnesses.

Twenty centuries after Revelation was written, we know that the consummation of all things may or may not be "soon" in the time frame of our world, but a response to the gospel is nevertheless urgent in the life of every person and society. Revelation reminds us that our ultimate hope is not merely to die and go to heaven, but rather to see the glorious return of our Lord, the resurrection, and the marriage of heaven and earth when the new Jerusalem descends like a bride. Our destiny as Jesus' disciples is the wedding feast of the Lamb in an eternal city that defies description, where we will see God face-to-face.

In closing this introduction, I wish to express my gratitude first to my parents, who from childhood taught me "the sacred writings which are able to instruct [us] for salvation through faith in Christ Jesus" (2 Tim 3:15 RSV). I am grateful to the teachers who first made Revelation intelligible to me, Stephen Clark and Ugo Vanni. I also thank the scholars and friends who took time to read part or all of the manuscript and to give me their feedback: Leslie Baynes, Peter Collins, Matthew Daniels, Mike Gladieux, Michael Gorman, Andreas Hoeck, Bishop Francis Kalabat, Donal McIlraith, and John Whiting, and especially my coeditors Mary Healy and Kevin Perrotta. Of course, any remaining errors or faults are entirely my own. Finally, thanks to my wife, Marsha Daigle-Williamson, who offered many helpful comments on the final draft and persistently exhorted me to finish this commentary lest the descent of the new Jerusalem precede its publication.

Outline of Revelation

A Revelation from Jesus Christ

Revelation 1:1–20

The last book of the New Testament is altogether unique. The Gospels tell the story of the life and teaching of Jesus in the third person. The Epistles communicate teaching and exhortation about following Christ from the apostles and other teachers of the first Christian generation. But Revelation presents its readers with a vision of the risen Lord himself, who entrusts his servant John with an urgent word of prophecy for the seven churches of Asia, and through them to the whole Church in all times and places. Thus while the whole New Testament addresses us as Jesus' disciples, in Revelation Jesus addresses us in an especially direct way.

Prologue (1:1–3)

¹The revelation of Jesus Christ, which God gave to him, to show his servants what must happen soon. He made it known by sending his angel to his servant John, ²who gives witness to the word of God and to the testimony of Jesus Christ by reporting what he saw. ³Blessed is the one who reads aloud and blessed are those who listen to this prophetic message and heed what is written in it, for the appointed time is near.

OT: Dan 2:28–47; 12:4; Amos 3:7
NT: John 5:20; 15:15; 18:37
Catechism: reading Scripture, 2653; imminence of Christ's coming, 673

The prologue tells us the title of this book, the divine origin of its content, the way it was transmitted, and the blessing that awaits all who read, hear, and heed it.

1:1–2   Although we are used to calling it the book of Revelation, or the Apocalypse, the full title of the book is **The revelation of Jesus Christ**. The Greek word translated "revelation," *apokalypsis*, literally means "unveiling." Beside this single occurrence in Revelation, the word appears seventeen times in the New Testament in reference to Christian prophecy (1 Cor 14:6, 26; 2 Cor 12:1), the disclosure of God's previously hidden plan (Luke 2:32; Rom 16:25), or the manifestation of a new order at the second coming (Rom 2:5, 8:19; 1 Cor 1:7). When Revelation was written, *apokalypsis* had not yet come to connote what people today commonly mean by "†apocalypse."

This revelation originated with God, who **gave** it to Jesus Christ for us.[1] The reason God did this was so that **his servants**, his people, would be prepared for the events that **must happen** in God's plan. By saying **soon**, John intentionally contrasts the urgency of his prophecy with the book of Daniel, where the prophet is told that his message is for the distant future (Dan 2:28–29; 12:4). John's allusion to Daniel here will be made explicit at the end of the book (22:10).

Jesus conveyed this message through **his angel** to **his servant John**, a Christian prophet.[2] The angel who mediates the revelation of this book appears and speaks in 10:8–9 and in 22:1, 6–10. John identifies himself not as the author but as the one who **gives witness** ("testified," NRSV) that this really is **the word of God** and Jesus' **testimony**. He accomplishes this by faithfully **reporting what he saw** in the visions of this book.

1:3   This **prophetic message** (literally, "prophecy") is intended to be read in the liturgical gathering of the Christian community. John pronounces a blessing on the lector who **reads** this divine message and to the members of the congregation who **listen** and **heed** (literally, "keep") its teaching. They are **blessed**, the same word found in the Beatitudes of Matt 5:3–8 and Luke 6:20–22. A beatitude pronounces someone fortunate or happy and praises the behavior that is the basis of the person's happiness. This is the first of seven beatitudes in the book of Revelation, each focusing on the conduct that characterizes a faithful disciple awaiting Jesus' glorious return.[3] Revelation is about ethics as well as †eschatology; it provides guidance about how its readers should conduct themselves. Despite our very different circumstances, we who read, listen to, and heed the message of Revelation today are also "blessed."

---

1. See John 5:20; 16:15.
2. In the OT God often refers to "my servants, the prophets" (e.g., Jer 7:25; Ezek 38:17), and that phrase occurs in Revelation as well (10:7; 11:18; see 22:6).
3. The other beatitudes are found at Rev 14:13; 16:15; 19:9; 20:6; 22:7, 14.

What Christ Means by "Soon"

BIBLICAL BACKGROUND

Prophetic language that says the end will be soon is not unique to Revelation. The prophetic books often refer to final judgment as near. Some texts say only "a brief moment" more and God's decisive salvation will be revealed,[a] using an expression similar to "a little while" in Rev 6:11; 12:12; 20:3. The prophets also speak of God's imminent salvation with the same words Revelation uses for God's intervening or Jesus' coming "soon" or "quickly," or of his being "near." "Near is the great day of the LORD, / near and very swiftly coming," says Zeph 1:14. According to Baruch, mercy "will swiftly reach you"; †Zion's neighbors will "soon see God's salvation come to you" (Bar 4:22, 24).

The New Testament has its share of urgent end-time preaching. John the Baptist and Jesus proclaim the arrival of the kingdom of God, saying, "Repent, for the kingdom of heaven is at hand!" (Matt 3:2; 4:17), and indicating that God's judgment would be soon. Judgment did in fact descend on Israel within a generation when Roman legions destroyed Jerusalem and the temple in AD 70. Although the kingdom of God *did* arrive in the person of Jesus, the full establishment of the kingdom has not yet come. Yet Jesus' resurrection marks the end of the old age and the beginning of the new (1 Cor 15:22–23), so that the †parousia could happen at any moment (see sidebar, "The Timing of Jesus' Return," p. 182). Thus St. Paul also speaks of the imminence of the end and of the need to be ready at all times (Rom 13:12; 16:20; 1 Thess 5:2–8), as does St. Peter (1 Pet 4:7).

Whatever the prophets, other biblical authors, and John may have understood when they wrote "soon," centuries later it is clear that the Holy Spirit, who inspired them, was not speaking literally in the way that human beings reckon time. Rather, it seems the Holy Spirit's intention was to stir people to action now for the sake of God's salvation and judgment that just might come to pass in their lives sooner than they expect.

a. Isa 10:25; 26:20; Jer 51:33; Hag 2:6.

The Greek does not include the word **aloud** after "reads." The NABRE translators added it since most Bible reading in the early Church took place in community gatherings (1 Tim 4:13) due to the fact that books were expensive and most people were illiterate. Communal reading had the advantage of allowing for explanation of what was read, which would have been especially valuable in reading Revelation.

The prologue concludes by stressing the urgency of responding to the message of the book, **for the appointed time is near**. The words "near" and "soon" (1:1) occur frequently in Revelation in reference to the return of Christ and other events prophesied in this book. Sometimes, as in these verses, the precise event that will happen soon is not explicitly stated. Readers are left with an encouragement to keep their eyes peeled for the fulfillment of God's plan, since it is not far off.

Reflection and Application (1:1–3)

Perhaps some misunderstanding is inevitable when God, who lives in eternity, communicates with human beings, who live in time. From God's eternal perspective, our final salvation is already present, while for us it lies in the future. C. S. Lewis describes the two perspectives this way:

> If you picture Time as a straight line along which we have to travel, then you must picture God as the whole page on which the line is drawn. We come to the parts of the line one by one: we have to leave A behind before we get to B, and cannot reach C until we leave B behind. God, from above or outside or all round, contains the whole line, and sees it all.[4]

When God tells us that our salvation will be "soon" or "in a very little while," it is a way of bridging the gap between the divine and the human points of view. Like a parent truthfully assuring an impatient child that Christmas really is not far off, God speaks to human beings from his superior perspective on time (2 Pet 3:8–9) encouraging us to persevere in hope and warning us to be vigilant. When we ourselves pass from time to eternity, we will see with perfect clarity how soon, even immediate, were his loving response to our prayers and the fulfillment of all his promises.

The time when each of us will be summoned to render an account of our life before "the judgment seat of Christ" (2 Cor 5:10) will arrive sooner than we think—perhaps unexpectedly, at the hour of our death or when the Lord returns. Consequently, the repeated warning of Revelation and the rest of the Bible that the end is near is salutary if we "listen" and "heed" (1:3).

Greeting, Praise of Christ, Prophecy (1:4–8)

---

[4]John, to the seven churches in Asia: grace to you and peace from him who is and who was and who is to come, and from the seven spirits before his throne, [5]and from Jesus Christ, the faithful witness, the firstborn of

4. C. S. Lewis, *Mere Christianity*, paperback ed. (New York: Macmillan, 1960), 147.

the dead and ruler of the kings of the earth. To him who loves us and has freed us from our sins by his blood, [6]who has made us into a kingdom, priests for his God and Father, to him be glory and power forever [and ever]. Amen.

> [7]Behold, he is coming amid the clouds,
>   and every eye will see him,
>   even those who pierced him.
> All the peoples of the earth will lament him.
>   Yes. Amen.

[8]"I am the Alpha and the Omega," says the Lord God, "the one who is and who was and who is to come, the almighty."

OT: Exod 19:6; Isa 41:4; 44:6; Dan 7:13; Zech 12:10
NT: John 19:37; 1 Tim 2:6; 6:13
Catechism: the baptized as a holy priesthood, 1140–44; prayer to the one who can save in past, present, and future, 2854
Lectionary: 1:5–8: Chrism Mass, Thursday of Holy Week; Solemnity of Christ the King (Year B); Masses for the Triumph of the Cross and the Precious Blood during Easter Season

---

This brief passage consists of four parts, the last two of which (vv. 7–8) seem to interrupt the flow of the text. One of my former teachers believes that what we have here is the script of a liturgical dialogue that took place when Revelation was read.[5] The person presiding at the liturgy "announces the subject, the audience, and the author of the communication (vv. 1–2) and pronounces a blessing (the beatitude in v. 3) on the lector and on the attentive audience (the community)."[6] The lector begins by reading the greeting of the author John (vv. 4–5a). The congregation responds with a [†]doxology praising Jesus for what he has done for us (vv. 5b–6). The lector then declares the faith of the Church in the future return of Christ, and the congregation replies, "Amen" (v. 7). Then the lector concludes by solemnly pronouncing words that identify the God who is the source and master of all that unfolds in this book and in history (v. 8). Whether or not this surmise is correct, it certainly works to read the text aloud as a liturgical dialogue. The prophetic poetry of verses 7–8 announces key ideas of the book: Jesus will return in [†]glory, and God is sovereign over all of history.

We will consider the identity of **the seven churches in Asia** where more is said about them in verse 11.   1:4–5a

John begins with a prayer-wish found in the greetings of nearly all the letters in the New Testament. He invokes on his readers a blessing of **grace** (*charis*)

---

5. Ugo Vanni, *L'Apocalisse* (Bologna: Dehoniane, 1988), 106–9.
6. Charles H. Giblin, *The Book of Revelation* (Collegeville, MN: Liturgical Press, 1991), 37.

and **peace** from God. This salutation alters slightly the common †Hellenistic greeting "rejoice" (Greek *chairein*) and combines it with the common Jewish greeting "peace" (Greek *eirēnē*; Hebrew *shalom*), since the joy of God's favor and true peace are now available in Christ.

What distinguishes this greeting is that it names the three Persons of the Trinity, whereas most of the other greetings in the New Testament only name God and Christ. However, John speaks of the Father and the Spirit in a very distinctive manner. He refers to the Father as **him who is and who was and who is to come**, drawing on God's revelation of his name to Moses in Exod 3:14–15. There God reveals himself, saying, "I am who am." The longer phrase in Revelation is probably a deliberate counterclaim to a title ascribed to the pagan god Zeus: "the one who was and who is and who will be."[7] By saying that God "is to come," John expresses a major theme of the book—that God is *coming* to save his people and to judge the wicked.

The Holy Spirit is described in a very unusual way as **the seven spirits before his throne** (see sidebar, "The Seven Spirits of God," p. 46).[8] This description probably derives from two Old Testament texts. The Septuagint of Isa 11:2–3 depicts the Spirit of the Lord resting on the †messiah to bestow seven attributes— wisdom, understanding, counsel, strength, knowledge, piety, and fear of the Lord.[9] In Zech 4 the prophet receives a vision of a lampstand with seven lamps drawing oil from one source, which symbolizes the power of God's Spirit that will enable the people to rebuild the temple: "Not by might, nor by power, but by my Spirit, says the LORD of hosts" (Zech 4:6 RSV). As in the time of Zechariah, the present stage of salvation history is one in which God is overcoming opposition and building his temple—that is, the Church—through the action of the Holy Spirit (see Eph 2:21–22; Rev 3:12; 11:1). The Spirit's activity will attain its goal in the new Jerusalem (21:3, 16, 22).

Jesus is mentioned in third place, rather than in usual Trinitarian order, because John has singled him out for a longer description, followed by a doxology focused uniquely on him, anticipating his central role in this book. Jesus is identified by four titles. The title **Christ** refers to God's anointed king descended

---

7. Osborne, also citing other scholars, *Revelation*, 60.

8. Some have interpreted the "seven spirits" as the seven angels that Jewish and Catholic tradition understand as standing before God's throne. But in Revelation the seven angels have another role (chaps. 8 and 15). Furthermore, according to Richard Bauckham, "although the term 'spirit' could certainly be used of angels (as frequently in the Dead Sea Scrolls), it very rarely has this meaning in early Christian literature and never in Revelation" (*The Theology of the Book of Revelation*, New Testament Theology [Cambridge: Cambridge University Press, 1993], 110). Besides, it would be very strange for seven angels to be placed parallel to God the Father and Jesus in bestowing grace and peace.

9. Catholic tradition subsequently identifies these qualities as the gifts of the Spirit.

The Seven Spirits Correspond to the Seven Gifts of the Spirit

Apringius of Beja, a sixth-century Latin Church Father who wrote a commentary on Revelation, interprets "the seven spirits" in relation to Isa 11.

> Here the seven spirits are introduced, which are one and the same Spirit, that is the Holy Spirit, who is one in name, sevenfold in power, invisible and incorporeal, and whose form is impossible to comprehend. The great Isaiah revealed the number of its sevenfold powers when he wrote: "the Spirit of wisdom and understanding"—that through understanding and wisdom he might teach that he is the creator of all things—"the Spirit of counsel and might"—who conceived these things that he might create them—"the Spirit of knowledge and piety"—who governs the creation with piety by the exercise of his knowledge and whose purposes are always according to mercy—"the Spirit of the fear of the Lord"—by whose gift the fear of the Lord is manifested to rational creatures. This [description reveals] the sacred character of the Spirit who is to be worshiped.[a]

a. *Tractate on the Apocalypse* 1.4, in ACCS 12:4.

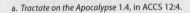

from David. He is **the faithful witness** who came into the world "to testify to the truth" (John 18:37), which he did to the point of laying down his life. The Greek word for "witness," *martys*, later came to mean "martyr," probably because of this verse and the example of other witnesses to Christ who gave their lives (e.g., Antipas in 2:13 and Stephen in Acts 22:20). A major theme of Revelation is the call for Christians to imitate their Lord as faithful witnesses, even to the point of laying down their lives if necessary (12:11). Next Jesus is called **the firstborn of the dead**, a title also mentioned in Col 1:18, to indicate that he is the first member of the human race to pass from death to eternal life (see 1 Cor 15:20). Jesus is the conqueror of death, and stands at the head of the multitude who die and rise after him. Ever since his resurrection, he is the **ruler of the kings of the earth**, holding supreme authority over every other power (Eph 1:20–23), including the Roman emperor.

John's response to the grace and peace bestowed by God, the Spirit, and especially Jesus is to offer a word of praise on behalf of his readers. It is the only doxology in the New Testament addressed solely to Jesus. Like some memorable texts from Paul's Letters (Rom 8:34; Gal 2:20; Eph 5:2, 25), it focuses on Jesus' personal love expressed in his death on the cross for our sake. In Greek, **to him who loves us** is a present participle, implying continuous or

1:5b–6

The Seven Spirits of God

Revelation mentions "the seven spirits" of God four times (1:4; 3:1; 4:5; 5:6). Richard Bauckham explains that John understands the seven spirits as a symbol for the Spirit of God on the basis of Zech 4, a key passage for John's understanding of the role of the Spirit in the world.

In a vision the prophet Zechariah sees a golden lampstand with seven lamps on it (Zech 4:2), like the seven-branched lampstand that stood in the holy place in the temple (see Exod 25:31–40; 40:4, 24–25). When Zechariah asks about the seven lamps (Zech 4:4), he is told that God will accomplish his plan "not by might, and not by power, but by my spirit" (4:6). A little later he is told that the seven lamps "are the eyes of the Lord that range over the whole earth" (4:10). John interprets this to mean that the seven lamps symbolize the seven eyes of the Lord—that is, God's own Spirit. Similarly, when John sees seven torches burning before the divine throne, he identifies them as the seven spirits of God (Rev 4:5). Like the seven lamps in Zechariah's vision, the seven spirits belong to the divine One, which is why John includes them in the Trinitarian blessing of 1:4–5.

While the allusions to Zechariah point to the relationship of the seven spirits to God, John also shows the seven spirits' relationship with the Lamb. He describes the Lamb as having "seven horns and seven eyes, . . . the [seven] spirits of God sent out into the whole world" (Rev 5:6). John's understanding of the relationship of the seven spirits to the Lamb corresponds to the common early Christian understanding that the Spirit of God is the Spirit of Christ—that the Spirit is the way in which the exalted Christ is present and active in the world (Acts 2:33; 16:6–7; Rom 8:9; Phil 1:19).[a]

a. Bauckham, *Theology of Revelation*, 115; this sidebar summarizes 110–15.

habitual action—the one who *is* loving us. Christ is the main actor in Revelation, and at the outset this expression provides a premise that must not be forgotten amid all the trials his followers will face. It is Christ's covenant love for his Bride, the Church, which will be celebrated at the wedding feast of the Lamb (19:7–9) and consummated in the new Jerusalem (21:2), that shapes all of Christ's interventions in this book. The proof of his love is what he has already done: he **has freed us from our sins by his blood**. The power of Christ's blood is a recurrent theme of Revelation (5:9; 7:14; 12:11). Here the nuance is that Christ has "freed us" (literally, "loosed us") from our sins by his death, obtaining forgiveness through his atoning sacrifice and liberating us from sin's power.[10] Having dealt thus with the evil root that afflicts the human race, Christ is in the process of eradicating all its bitter fruit. How he will do this provides the overarching story line of Revelation.

God's promise to make Israel "a kingdom of priests" in Exod 19:6 has been fulfilled in a new and greater way as a result of Jesus' death on the cross.[11] Christ **has made us into a kingdom**; "kingdom" here means not only a people that is ruled by a king, the Messiah, but also a royal people who already reign with him. Obviously, our present reign with Christ is incomplete[12] and awaits its fullness in the future establishment of God's kingdom. Israel's priestly identity was originally expressed through observance of the laws of purity and worship of the †Torah. By removing the obstacle of sin through his sacrifice, the Messiah Jesus established God's covenant people as **priests** at an entirely new level, granting access in the Spirit to **his God and Father**. John, like Paul, understands his Gentile Christian readers to be fully incorporated into this privilege of Israel (Eph 2:11–22; see sidebar, "The 'Seal' in Scripture and Tradition," p. 142).

Those baptized into Christ present priestly worship by offering their whole lives as "spiritual sacrifices" (1 Pet 2:5; see Rom 12:1) in union with Christ in the Eucharist (1 Cor 10:16–21), as well as giving alms (Heb 13:16) and interceding for the whole world (1 Tim 2:1–2). Revelation will return to speak of the royal and priestly role of Christians in 5:10 (see comments there) and 20:6, which depicts the royal and priestly role of the saints and martyrs.

John completes his doxology: may **glory and power**, praise and kingly rule, belong to Christ **forever**!

The word **Behold** here signals a prophetic announcement. Up to this point   1:7
John has been speaking in his own voice, but in the next two verses he utters prophetic †oracles as the Old Testament prophets often did. Abrupt changes in the person who is speaking are common in Hebrew prophecy and in the book of Revelation. The NABRE and some other translations lay out this verse and other portions of Revelation as poetry. They do so on the basis of parallelisms, allusions, or other content that suggests that the author intends to speak in an elevated or poetic manner.

This first prophetic message announces the principal theme of the book, the glorious return of Christ at the end of history. The fact that he is **coming**

---

10. Some ancient manuscripts say "washed" instead of "loosed"; the Vulgate, JB, and NJB follow this alternative reading, which anticipates "washed" in 7:14.

11. Following the LXX, 1 Pet 2:9 likewise draws on Exod 19:6 to affirm that Christians have become a "royal priesthood." For more on Christian priesthood in Rev 1:6; 5:10; and 20:6, see Albert Vanhoye, *The Old Testament Priests and the New Priest* (Petersham, MA: St. Bede's Publications, 1986), 279–309.

12. Other NT texts that refer to Christians reigning with Christ in this life include Rom 5:17; 6:11–12; Eph 2:6; Col 3:1–4. See also Catechism 908–12.

amid the clouds recalls Daniel's vision of "one like a son of man" (7:13) and various New Testament texts promising that Jesus will return with the clouds (Mark 14:62; Acts 1:11). His return will be public: **every eye will see him,** / **even those who pierced him.** This prophecy echoes Zech 12:10 (cited in John 19:37), which foretells Jerusalem's mourning in repentance over one they have pierced, an intense mourning that is followed by a complete purification from sin (Zech 13:1). Here, however, it is not only Jerusalem but also "all the tribes of the earth" (NRSV) who **lament him,**[13] echoing a similarly worded prophecy of Jesus (Matt 24:30). Although this mourning could be interpreted as the nations mourning in regret as they face judgment, the precedent in Zechariah and a nuance in the wording point to a much more positive outcome. The phrase that refers to those who mourn is from God's promise to Abraham: "in you *all the tribes of the earth* will be blessed" (Gen 12:3 LXX, emphasis added), an expression that the Old Testament uses only of this promise.[14] When Jesus returns, he will be greeted not only by a repentant Israel but also by many other repentant peoples, whose contrition results in purification from sin. The certainty of his glorious return is indicated by the double affirmation, **Yes. Amen.**

1:8   Another oracle follows. This time **the Lord God** himself speaks in the first person. In words that recall similar declarations in Isaiah (41:4; 44:6), God identifies himself as **the Alpha and the Omega,** the first and last letters of the Greek alphabet, indicating his authority over all of history from beginning to end and echoing his claim in Isaiah to be the first and the last (Isa 41:4; see Rev 1:17). He also identifies himself by the same title as in 1:4, **the one who is and who was and who is to come,** and by the title **the almighty,**[15] a common †Septuagint translation of "LORD of hosts." God speaks similar words directly once more, near the end of the book (21:5–6). By revealing his identity and presence at the beginning and the end, God certifies the message of this book.

John's Commissioning (1:9–11)

---

[9]**I, John, your brother, who share with you the distress, the kingdom, and the endurance we have in Jesus, found myself on the island called Patmos because I proclaimed God's word and gave testimony to Jesus.** [10]**I was caught up in spirit on the Lord's day and heard behind me a voice as**

---

13. More literally, "wail on account of him" (RSV) or "mourn over him" (NJB).
14. See Richard Bauckham, *The Climax of Prophecy: Studies on the Book of Revelation* (Edinburgh: T&T Clark, 1993), 321. The phrase also occurs in Gen 28:14; Ps 72:17; and Matt 24:30.
15. Greek *pantokratōr*, "ruler of all."

loud as a trumpet, [11]which said, "Write on a scroll what you see and send
it to the seven churches: to Ephesus, Smyrna, Pergamum, Thyatira, Sardis,
Philadelphia, and Laodicea."

NT: Acts 14:22; 2 Cor 1:7; 2 Tim 2:12

Now we hear the voice of the prophet **John**, who emphasizes his unity with   **1:9**
those who will read or hear this book by referring to himself as **your brother**
and "partner" (a literal translation, NJB) in **the distress, the kingdom, and
the endurance** that are **in Jesus**. All Christians are united to Christ and in him
to one another through faith and baptism (Gal 3:27–28). In Greek, the words
for "distress" ("tribulation," RSV), "kingdom," and "endurance" are preceded
by only one article, indicating that John understands them as inseparable
elements of Christian life. Jesus promised rewards to his disciples "with persecutions, and eternal life in the age to come" (Mark 10:30). Hardship goes
with the territory.

John recounts his reception of the prophecy contained in this book. He had
been exiled to **Patmos**, an island in the Aegean Sea about forty miles from
Ephesus, because he was evangelizing: he **proclaimed God's word and gave
testimony to Jesus.**[16] Exile was a common punishment in the Roman Empire.
John may not have remained long on Patmos. If he was exiled in the mid-90s
(see "Historical Setting and Purpose" in the introduction, pp. 21–22), he would
have been released when the emperor Domitian died in AD 96, since his successor, Nerva (96–98), gave a general amnesty to exiles.

John describes an experience of being in the Spirit.[17] While all of Christian   **1:10–11**
existence can be described as life "in the spirit" (Rom 8:9), there are times when
Christians particularly experience the Holy Spirit's presence—for instance, in
prayer or when exercising a spiritual gift or ministry (1 Cor 12:3; 14:2; Eph
5:18–20; 6:18). John's prophetic experience may have occurred in the context
of the liturgy, since it happened **on the Lord's day**, the day of Jesus' resurrection. This is the first and only use of this expression in the New Testament, and
it refers to Sunday, the Christian day of worship (see Acts 20:7). John hears
behind him a **voice as loud as a trumpet** ("loud voice like a trumpet," RSV).
Many of the messages in this book come with the "loud voice" of an angel, but
here it is Christ who is speaking.

16. Other versions translate this literally: "on account of the word of God and the testimony of
Jesus" (RSV).
17. Although the NABRE rendering "in spirit" is possible, it seems better to interpret this and the
other three uses of this phrase in Rev (4:2; 17:3; 21:10) as referring to the role of the Holy Spirit in
prophecy (see Ezek 37:1; Matt 22:43; 1 Cor 12:3).

The Spirit in Revelation

BIBLICAL BACKGROUND

While John uses the term "seven spirits" to refer to the activity of the Holy Spirit in the world (see sidebar, "The Seven Spirits of God," p. 46), he uses "Spirit," singular, to refer to the prophetic activity of the Holy Spirit in the Church. He names the "Spirit" precisely fourteen times. Seven instances occur in the oracles to the churches, indicating that the words of the risen Lord come by means of the Spirit: "Whoever has ears ought to hear what the Spirit says to the churches" (Rev 2–3). Four times John uses the phrase "in the Spirit" (RSV)[a] to indicate that the Holy Spirit is the source of his visions (1:10; 4:2; 17:3; 21:10). Twice more John refers to what the Spirit directly says, probably through prophecy (14:13; 22:17), and once he uses "Spirit" to identify the testimony of Christians to Jesus as Spirit-inspired prophecy (19:10).[b]

a. Greek *en pneumati*.
b. Bauckham, *Theology of Revelation*, 118.

The voice commands John to **Write** what he sees and send it to **the seven churches**, and then names seven cities in the Roman province of Asia. They are listed in the order that the bearer of the letter would likely carry them, starting with Ephesus, the chief city of the province, then making a circuit in a clockwise direction. Each city lies two or three days' walk from the previous one. We know there were churches at this time in other Asian cities not named here—for instance, in Colossae and Hierapolis, just a few miles from Laodicea (Col 4:13). The seven churches were probably selected as centers of communication for the churches nearby. From early on, Christian interpreters of Revelation have pointed out that "seven" symbolizes completeness, suggesting that this book was intended by the Holy Spirit for the whole Church, not only in Asia but also in the whole world.

Reflection and Application (1:9–11)

If you found yourself exiled for your Christian faith to a remote island, cut off from all your family and loved ones, how would you respond? Would you continue to pray without Mass or your parish community to support you? Would you consider yourself a partner in "the distress, the kingdom, and the endurance we have in Jesus" (1:9) with all your brothers and sisters in Christ around the world? Would you be ready to hear God speak to you, not just about *your* trying circumstances but also about his people and his purposes? The best way to know what you would do is to reflect on what you do now. Do you maintain your prayer life when there is no one else praying around you? Do you remember with your prayers and alms those who are suffering for their faith around the world?

When we face hardships, let us do our best to remember that it is not all about us, but about God and his kingdom, and pray and act accordingly.

Vision of the Son of Man (1:12–20)

[12]Then I turned to see whose voice it was that spoke to me, and when I turned, I saw seven gold lampstands [13]and in the midst of the lampstands one like a son of man, wearing an ankle-length robe, with a gold sash around his chest. [14]The hair of his head was as white as white wool or as snow, and his eyes were like a fiery flame. [15]His feet were like polished brass refined in a furnace, and his voice was like the sound of rushing water. [16]In his right hand he held seven stars. A sharp two-edged sword came out of his mouth, and his face shone like the sun at its brightest.

[17]When I caught sight of him, I fell down at his feet as though dead. He touched me with his right hand and said, "Do not be afraid. I am the first and the last, [18]the one who lives. Once I was dead, but now I am alive forever and ever. I hold the keys to death and the netherworld. [19]Write down, therefore, what you have seen, and what is happening, and what will happen afterwards. [20]This is the secret meaning of the seven stars you saw in my right hand, and of the seven gold lampstands: the seven stars are the angels of the seven churches, and the seven lampstands are the seven churches."

OT: Dan 7:7–14; 10:5–10; Zech 4:1–10
NT: Matt 17:1–8
Catechism: Jesus, the one who passed through death, 625, 635
Lectionary: 1:9–11a, 12–13, 17–19: Second Sunday of Easter (Year C)

When John turns to see the source of the loud voice he has heard, what he sees literally takes his breath away: a divine figure who resembles a human being. The figure is described in extraordinary images that appear strange if they are pictured literally. However, if the meaning of each image is sought, they reveal a great deal about this heavenly being. Only through his words in verse 18 does his identity become absolutely clear: he is the risen Jesus in the midst of his Church.

1:12–13   The **seven gold lampstands** recall both the menorah—a single, seven-branched lampstand of pure gold with seven lamps that the priests kept burning every night (Exod 25:31–40; 27:21)—and the ten gold lampstands in Solomon's temple (1 Kings 7:49). In the midst of the lampstands is **one like a son of man**. "The Son of Man" is the term by which Jesus often refers to himself in the Gospels. In Hebrew and Aramaic idiom, it simply means "human being," in contrast to an angel or animal, and it has this sense in Ezekiel and the Psalms. But the exact phrase, "one like a son of man" occurs only once in the Old Testament:

> As the visions during the night continued, I saw coming with the clouds of heaven
>
> One like a son of man.
> When he reached the Ancient of Days
>   and was presented before him,
> He received dominion, splendor, and kingship;
>   all nations, peoples, and tongues will serve him.
> His dominion is an everlasting dominion
>   that shall not pass away,
>   his kingship, one that shall not be destroyed. (Dan 7:13–14)

This mysterious text describes a humanlike figure ascending to God, "the Ancient of Days," and being given everlasting, universal kingship, something that belongs by right only to God. When Jesus was questioned at his trial by Caiaphas, the high priest, he revealed himself as this Son of Man (Mark 14:61–62).

To return to John's vision, the person speaking to John is **wearing an ankle-length robe.**[18] In the Septuagint, this word refers almost exclusively to the garment of the high priest. Although Revelation generally focuses more on Christ's kingship than on his priesthood, the priestly dimension is not absent (this dimension of Jesus' role is explored in Hebrews). As a priest, Christ communicates divine revelation to human beings (1:1), stands before God in the heavenly temple (Heb 9:12; Rev 5:6), and has consecrated his people as priests (1:6; 5:10).[19] The **gold sash around his chest** indicates his great authority; the only other figures in Revelation to wear a gold sash are the seven angels close to God's throne who are entrusted with the seven last plagues (15:6).

1:14–16   The **hair** of the one like a son of man is **white as wool or as snow**. In Dan 7:9 it is God himself, the "Ancient of Days," whose hair is "white as wool" (LXX),

---

18. Greek *podērēs*.

19. Although the death of Jesus is not explicitly presented in Revelation as a priestly offering as it is in Hebrews, the idea may be presupposed in Rev 1:5; 5:9; 7:14; 12:11 and in the symbolic depiction of the martyrs' deaths as sacrifices (6:9).

symbolizing his eternity and infinite wisdom. Here the "one like a son of man" possesses this attribute. As often in Revelation, Jesus is depicted with divine attributes.

His **eyes** are like a **flame** of fire and his **feet** like **polished brass**. These images resemble the description of the glorious angel who appears to Daniel (Dan 10:6; see also Ezek 1:7). The fiery eyes suggest penetrating vision, able to discern and judge (Sir 23:19; Rev 19:12). His **voice** is powerful, **like the sound of rushing water** (literally, "many waters," NRSV), like Niagara Falls or the waves of a Mediterranean storm pounding the shoreline.[20]

In his **right hand** he holds **seven stars**. A first-century reader might have thought of the stars as representing heavenly powers that influence earthly events. The Roman emperor was often pictured with symbols of the planets around him. Enhancing the impression of awesome power is a **sharp two-edged sword** issuing from **his mouth**. Isaiah 11:4 says that the Messiah "shall strike the ruthless with the rod of his mouth, / and with the breath of his lips he shall slay the wicked"—a text that St. Paul applies to Christ's defeat of the man of lawlessness at the end of history (2 Thess 2:8). Isaiah 49:2 says that the Lord made the mouth of his Servant a "sharp-edged sword." This description of the risen Christ combines both images, and the sword in his mouth represents the all-powerful word of God by which God created the world and brings judgment (Wis 18:1; Rev 19:13). Finally, completing the impression of heavenly †glory, John tells us that **his face shone like the sun at its brightest**. Various Old Testament texts compare the splendor of God to the sun (Ps 84:12; Isa 60:19), and Christians will recall that Jesus' "face shone like the sun" at his Transfiguration (Matt 17:2).

John's reaction to this vision of "one like a son of man" is like Daniel's when he saw a heavenly messenger (Dan 10:9): John **fell down at his feet as though dead**. The heavenly being places **his right hand** on John, expressing favor and reassurance, tells him not to be afraid, and gives him a powerful reason not to fear by disclosing his identity in solemn words: **I am the first and the last**. These are words that God uses to identify himself three times in Isaiah, distinguishing himself from the lifeless pagan idols (Isa 41:4; 44:6; 48:12). The next sentence makes his identity more explicit: **Once I was dead, but now I am alive forever and ever**. Jesus has come back from the dead, clothed with divine authority, and will never die again. The good news for us is that he has wrested control from humankind's perennial enemy: **I hold the keys to death and the netherworld**

1:17–18

---

20. The "roaring of many waters" is an image used to describe the awesome sound of the wings of the living creatures in Ezek 1:24 and of the Lord's coming in 43:2. The phrase appears again in Rev 14:2 and 19:6 to describe thunderous heavenly worship.

(literally, "Hades," the Greek word for the place of the dead that the Jews called "Sheol"). Jesus holds the keys! The Greco-Roman world knew itself to be powerless in the face of death, hoping only for some shadowy continuing existence in Hades. Although death and the netherworld will continue to exist until their final judgment at the end of history (20:14), their final defeat is confirmed by this magnificent declaration of the risen Lord.

1:19   In light of his decisive victory over death, **therefore**, the risen Lord tells John to write what he has **seen** (the vision we have just read), **what is happening** (the present situation the Son of Man is about to reveal in prophetic messages to the seven churches in chaps. 2 and 3), and **what will happen afterwards** (God's plans for the future, which the Lamb will reveal in the remainder of the book). Although these words provide a rough outline, the content of Revelation cannot be simply divided between present and future. The messages to the churches look forward to the end, and the visions of God's plan for the future often reflect the past. Both parts—chapters 2–3 and 4–21—offer guidance to the Church in her present spiritual struggle.

1:20   Before communicating messages to the churches, the risen Jesus explains the meaning of the seven stars and the seven lampstands. A heavenly being explaining visions is one of the characteristic features of †apocalyptic literature that occurs several times in Revelation (e.g., 5:5; 7:13–14; 17:1–18).

The fact that the **seven churches** are symbolized by **seven gold lampstands** is significant. A lampstand is an apt symbol for the church. Jesus called his disciples "the light of the world" and said that the proper place for a lamp is to be "set on a lampstand, where it gives light to all in the house" (Matt 5:14–15). Furthermore, while the temple in Jerusalem still stood, the menorah, a seven-branched gold lampstand with seven lamps, provided light and symbolized the radiance of God's presence (Exod 40:35–38). Analogously, the seven churches, enlightened by Christ and indwelt by the Spirit, shine in the darkness of the world with divine light, bearing witness to the truth.[21] The change from one gold menorah with seven lights to seven lampstands in seven cities symbolizes the light of the one Church shining not only in the churches of Asia but in the whole world. The location of the sacred lampstands of God's temple in the world hints that he is in the process of making the whole of creation his temple (see 11:1–2), a goal finally achieved in the new Jerusalem (21:1–22:5).

The **angels** of the seven churches refer to the bishops or to the guardian angels of the local churches (more on that in the next chapter). In either case, those in charge of the churches are entirely in the firm grasp of Jesus. The explanation

---

21. See also Matt 5:14–16; Eph 5:8–14; Phil 2:15; Rev 11:3–7; 12:11, 17; 19:10.

of these two symbols at the end of John's report of his vision sets the stage for his messages to each of the seven churches.

Reflection and Application (1:12–20)

I was dead, but now I am alive forever. The joy and hope of these words remind me of a scene from the conclusion of J. R. R. Tolkien's *Lord of the Rings*. After falling unconscious when the Ring was destroyed, Frodo's friend Samwise awakens and sees someone he thought had died months earlier: "Gandalf, you're alive! I thought you were dead! I thought I was dead! Is everything sad going to come untrue?"

The message of Revelation, epitomized in these opening words of Jesus, is a definitive "Yes! Everything sad is going to come untrue!" The revelation of the risen Lord presented in the book and the inner understanding that it evokes of who this Jesus is will enable Christians to face whatever challenges and circumstances come their way.

Seeing Jesus in Revelation. Richard Veras reflects on this awesome depiction of Jesus in light of the Gospels:

> The fiery eyes of Jesus are the eyes that looked at Peter after his denial, the eyes that looked upon the rich young man with a love greater than that sad man had for himself, the eyes that moved Zacchaeus and the Samaritan woman to follow him because the gaze of Jesus burned to the very cores of their hardened hearts. The face of Jesus, which shines like the sun, is the face of the one who called himself the light of the world.[22]

Revelation provides us with three diverse visions of Jesus—the glorious son of man and ruler (1:13; 14:14), the slaughtered Lamb (5:6), and the divine warrior (19:11)—each emphasizing different aspects of his person and work. As we study, meditate, and pray about Revelation, we also will become more deeply aware of the awesomeness of Christ.

---

22. Richard Veras, *Wisdom for Everyday Life from the Book of Revelation* (Cincinnati: St. Anthony Messenger, 2009), 3.

Words from Jesus to the Churches

Revelation 2:1–29

These next two chapters contain what are commonly called "the letters to the seven churches." Strictly speaking, rather than letters, they are prophetic messages from the risen Lord, addressed to seven churches and revealing "what is happening" as a prelude to the lengthier section of the book devoted to "what will happen afterwards" (1:19). In form these messages resemble †oracles found in the prophetic writings of the Old Testament.

These oracles to the churches are important for the interpretation of Revelation because they provide invaluable information about the circumstances facing its original readers and the world in which they lived. They confirm that Revelation was written for a specific first-century readership. They reveal a diversity of situations: some churches face poverty and persecution, while others enjoy prosperity; some tolerate false teaching, while others firmly reject it; some make fatal compromises with the surrounding culture, while some resist and remain faithful. Two churches receive only commendation and encouragement, while two churches are severely reprimanded.

Although addressed to particular churches in the first century, the oracles themselves invite all readers to consider them personally: "Let anyone who has an ear listen to what the Spirit is saying to the churches" (2:7 NRSV). This command tells readers to listen not only to the message addressed to their church but also to the messages that the Spirit addresses to all the churches. Taken together, these "letters" provide Spirit-inspired counsel for the Church in every age. Readers often find them the easiest part of Revelation to apply to their lives.

The goal of the seven messages at the outset of Revelation is to provoke readers and listeners to examine themselves and repent. One of my professors, Ugo Vanni, used to compare this summons to conversion to the penitential rite at the beginning of Mass that disposes the people of God for the liturgy. Analogously, these chapters help prepare readers to understand the unveiling of God's plan in the remainder of the book.

To the Church in Ephesus (2:1–7)

> [1]"To the angel of the church in Ephesus, write this:
>
> "'The one who holds the seven stars in his right hand and walks in the midst of the seven gold lampstands says this: [2]"I know your works, your labor, and your endurance, and that you cannot tolerate the wicked; you have tested those who call themselves apostles but are not, and discovered that they are impostors. [3]Moreover, you have endurance and have suffered for my name, and you have not grown weary. [4]Yet I hold this against you: you have lost the love you had at first. [5]Realize how far you have fallen. Repent, and do the works you did at first. Otherwise, I will come to you and remove your lampstand from its place, unless you repent. [6]But you have this in your favor: you hate the works of the Nicolaitans, which I also hate.
>
> [7]"'"Whoever has ears ought to hear what the Spirit says to the churches. To the victor I will give the right to eat from the tree of life that is in the garden of God."'"

OT: Gen 2:9; 3:22–24; Prov 3:18
NT: 2 Cor 11:13; 1 John 4:1
Catechism: the second conversion, 1428–29

All seven messages to the churches begin with a solemn introduction by Christ himself, followed by his words of rebuke or encouragement; each concludes with an exhortation to pay close attention and with the promise of a reward to those who are faithful. The structure of each letter has six distinct elements that occur in almost exactly the same order. Because of their repetition in the messages to the churches, these common structural elements will be treated in greater depth in the commentary on this first message and presupposed in the commentary on the †oracles that follow.

Each message begins by indicating the church to whom the risen Jesus is **2:1** dictating the message through the prophet John. What is unexpected is that

Common Structure of the Messages to the Seven Churches

BIBLICAL BACKGROUND

1. Address: "To the angel of the church of . . . , write"
2. Self-presentation of Christ in imagery drawn from the vision of 1:12–20
3. Jesus' disclosure of the condition of each church, beginning with "I know"
4. Specific exhortation to each church in light of Jesus' evaluation, stated as an imperative
5. General exhortation to listen to what the Spirit is saying to all the churches
6. Promise "to the victor" linked to final salvation

In two of the messages, the order of the final two elements is reversed.

John is instructed to write to **the angel of the church**. The Greek word *angelos* can mean "angel" or "messenger," and it is not clear here whether it refers to the local church's guardian angel or to its bishop.[1] In either case, however, the content of all the messages is clearly directed to the community as a whole. It is no accident that **Ephesus** is the first church named, since it was the mother church of the region, located in the leading city of the Roman province of Asia. It is natural that any communication to the churches of Asia would begin there.

In each of the seven messages, after naming the church he is speaking to, the risen Lord introduces himself, underscoring the solemnity of the communication, usually by referring to some part of the vision in chapter 1. In this first message Jesus indicates how near he is to his people and how complete is his control: he is walking **in the midst of the seven gold lampstands**, the seven churches, and he **holds the seven stars**, the guardians of the churches, whether angels or bishops, securely **in his right hand**. When Jesus introduces himself

1. Elsewhere in Revelation the word "angel" always refers to a heavenly being. Matthew 18:10 suggests that guardian angels exercise a kind of representative or mediating function between God and individual Christians. The angels of the churches may fulfill an analogous role between Christ and the churches. On the other hand, Albert Vanhoye suggests that the bishops of the churches are intended: "If one views the title 'stars' as an allusion to Dan 12:3, which speaks of stars in connection with those who teach justice, and if, on the other hand, the title 'angels' is an allusion to Mal 2:7, which gives this title to the priest by reason of his teaching function, one is led to understand that the star-angels are the leaders of the Churches . . . and also to admit . . . that these leaders, charged with passing on the Word of God, should here be seen as priests" (*The Old Testament Priests and the New Priest* [Petersham, MA: St. Bede's Publications, 1986], 288).

Ephesus

BIBLICAL
BACKGROUND

The church of Ephesus, the first of the seven to whom Revelation is addressed, played an extraordinarily important role in early Christianity. Because it was a large church, located centrally between Jerusalem and Antioch in the east and Rome in the west, Christian missionaries and travelers would naturally visit there. Church tradition and historical scholarship associate at least eleven of the twenty-seven books of the New Testament with this region.[a] The city of Ephesus was known as "the metropolis of Asia" (meaning "mother-city"). Boasting a population of about two hundred thousand (although this estimate has recently been challenged), it was the fourth-largest city of the empire and a major center of commerce, government, and religion. It was home to the temple of Artemis, a huge marble structure that was one of the seven wonders of the ancient world, and to a notable temple to the goddess Roma and many other pagan temples. Around AD 90 it became the provincial center of emperor worship when a temple was dedicated to the Flavian Sebastoi, the emperor Vespasian and his sons Titus and Domitian. To mark that occasion cities from all over Asia donated statues with inscriptions on their bases, some of which archaeologists have recovered.

Christianity also flourished in Ephesus. The account in Acts 19 suggests that it was the scene of the most successful of Paul's missionary endeavors. The church of Ephesus was large, consisting of many house churches. According to Acts 19:10, "all the inhabitants of the province of Asia heard the word of the Lord, Jews and Greeks alike." Thus Ephesus became a kind of mother church of Asia. Paul wrote to the Corinthians from Ephesus (1 Cor 16:8), and he sent his Letter to the Ephesians and 1 and 2 Timothy to the church there. The apostle John resided in Ephesus, and the Fourth Gospel and the First Letter of John may have originated here. One strand of tradition identifies Ephesus as the final home on earth of the Virgin Mary.

a. John, 1 Corinthians, Ephesians, Colossians, 1–2 Timothy, Philemon, 1–3 John, Revelation, and perhaps Luke and Acts.

in all seven messages as the one who **says this**, he employs the Greek phrase that the †Septuagint uses for "thus says the Lord." It is a solemn, awesome, yet reassuring introduction.

The third element of each message is Jesus' declaration of the condition of each church, beginning with the words **I know**. In these prophetic messages Jesus speaks as the future judge who knows **your works**. The second-person "you" or "your" is singular throughout this message, because Christ is addressing the community as a whole. The Gospel of John and other New Testament

2:2

writings (Acts 17:31; 2 Cor 5:10) teach that Jesus is the one whom God has appointed to judge the human race at the end of history: "The hour is coming when all who are in their graves will hear his voice and will come out—those who have done good, to the resurrection of life, and those who have done evil, to the resurrection of condemnation" (John 5:28–29 NRSV).

In the seven letters John's readers are given an advance warning about their standing in the eyes of their judge so that they can make whatever changes are necessary before the final judgment. This is their midterm examination. The criterion by which they will be judged is their conduct.[2] We are saved by grace but will be judged by our works, understood not as a mere counting of good deeds but as Christ's all-knowing evaluation of our thoughts, words, and deeds.

Christ begins by commending the church of Ephesus for several things: **your labor**, probably meaning their hard work in every kind of ministry, and **your endurance**, a major theme in Revelation. This term[3] occurs seven times in Revelation (1:9; 2:2, 3, 19; 3:10; 13:10; 14:12), always in the context of trials. It indicates "a life of trust and patient steadfastness in hard times."[4] It may come as a surprise that the next thing Christ commends the Ephesians for is that they **cannot tolerate the wicked** ("evildoers," NRSV). When it comes to false teaching in the Church, tolerance is not a virtue (see also 2:20). The Ephesians have **tested** itinerant teachers **who call themselves apostles** and **discovered** that **they are impostors**—literally, "false." First John 4:1 says, "Beloved, do not trust every spirit but test the spirits to see whether they belong to God, because many false prophets have gone out into the world." Christians are to measure those who claim to speak God's word by the fruit of their lives (Matt 7:15–23; 2 Tim 3) and are to evaluate their teaching by its consistency with Scripture and the apostolic tradition.[5] About fifteen years after Revelation was written, St. Ignatius, the bishop of Antioch, also commended the Ephesians for their rejection of false teachers: "I have heard of some who have come to you with false doctrine, whom you have not allowed to sow among you, but closed your ears, so that you might not receive those things which were sown by them."[6]

2:3   Christ repeats his praise for their **endurance**, observing that they have **suffered** persecution for his **name**. They have **not grown weary** and given up; they have persevered.

---

2. Rev 2:23; 9:20; 20:12–13. See also John 5:28–29; Rom 2:5–8; 2 Cor 5:10, etc.
3. Greek *hypomonē*.
4. Osborne, *Revelation*, 114.
5. E.g., see Gal 1:8–9; 1 Thess 5:19–21; 2 Tim 3:14–17; 1 John 2:24; Jude 3.
6. *To the Ephesians* 9.1.

Repent!

BIBLICAL BACKGROUND

The Greek word for "repent," *metanoeō*, literally means "to change one's mind—one's attitude or mentality." In the New Testament it is found especially in the preaching of John the Baptist, Jesus, and the apostles, where it refers to a radical change of direction, turning from sin to faith in God (see Catechism 1427). Although this word appears most often in the New Testament in relation to initial conversion, it also refers to repentance in the course of Christian life (2 Cor 7:9–11; 12:21). Other texts lack the word but convey the same idea: James 5:19–20; 1 John 1:5–2:2.

In Revelation the word "repent" appears seven times in the letters to the churches (though only four churches are thus addressed), summoning Christians to repent of defective love (2:5), incomplete works (3:3), erroneous teaching (2:15–16), idolatry (2:21–22), lukewarmness (3:16), and unwarranted self-satisfaction (3:19). The word appears four times later in Revelation to refer to the unwillingness of the wicked to repent of their idolatry and other evil conduct despite the chastisements of the seven trumpets and bowls (9:20–21; 16:9–11).[a]

a. For more on repentance, see "Reflection and Application" on 2:1–7 and 3:1–6.

After commending them for what they have done well, Jesus now identifies what is deficient: **I hold this against you**—and the defect is not small. They have **lost the love** they had **at first**. They are no longer responding wholeheartedly to the one who loves them and shed his blood for them (1:5). Their love for one another is weak. They are continuing to serve and endure, but the fervent attentiveness to Jesus and care for one another has begun to fade. This disease is fatal if unchecked (1 Cor 13:1–3). The oracle to the church of Ephesus warns that it is possible to remain doctrinally orthodox but to fail for lack of love.

2:4

After the diagnosis of their problem, Jesus offers a remedy. Instead of **Realize how far you have fallen**, the Greek literally says, "Remember then from where you have fallen." It helps to *remember* the initial fervor we had when we first discovered God's love for us. It helps to recall the generosity we demonstrated when our lives were freshly touched by his grace. Doing so helps us to **Repent**, to turn from an anemic love back to Love himself. Love is not primarily a feeling but instead a decision from deep within that expresses itself in action. We are able to love "because the love of God has been poured out into our hearts through the holy Spirit that has been given to us" (Rom 5:5). Renewal in the Holy Spirit makes it possible to do **the works you did at first**, the proof of love.

2:5

When we realize our conduct falls short, repentance, which God is eager to grant and then answer with forgiveness, leads the way home (Luke 15:10, 20).

Christ's command is not optional advice. Unless they **repent,** he **will come** and **remove** their **lampstand.** Despite its orthodoxy, the shining reputation and even the existence of the church of Ephesus are imperiled by its lack of love. Jesus' future coming spoken of here, as in the other messages, likely refers both to his coming to judge at the end of history and to his coming to judge within history. Commenting on the latter, Victorinus of Petovium (d. 303) says that to remove their lampstand means to "disperse the congregation."[7] Over the centuries the Christian communities in some places—including Ephesus—have been scattered and passed out of existence. The consequences of losing our first love are serious.

2:6   Christ returns briefly to commendation of the church of Ephesus because they **hate the works of the Nicolaitans,** which he also hates. This sect is mentioned again in verse 15, and we will discuss it there. The important point is that there is a kind of conduct that Christ detests, and he commends the Ephesians for detesting this conduct as well. Christ does not speak of hating a group of people; it is their "works" that he deplores.

2:7   Each letter to a church ends with an exhortation to listen and a promise of eternal reward to everyone who is victorious in the Christian life. The exhortation, **Whoever has ears ought to hear,** echoes what Jesus said during his earthly ministry about the parables (Matt 11:15; 13:9, 43). It is an invitation to listen carefully, to reflect, and to apply the message to one's life. Although it is the risen Jesus himself who is speaking, he speaks by means of the **Spirit** and through what John has prophesied and written. As in Acts and Paul's Letters, the Holy Spirit is the agent through whom the risen Lord acts in Christians and in the Church (e.g., Acts 2:33; 16:6–7; Rom 8:9; Phil 1:19). The members of each church must pay attention to what is said **to the churches,** not just what is specifically addressed to their own community. Although specific words are addressed to specific groups, this whole book is addressed to the whole Church.

Then comes another phrase found in all seven letters: **To the victor,** or more literally, "to the one who conquers" (ESV). The Greek word used here is the verb *nikaō,* to conquer (see sidebar, "The Importance of Conquering," p. 87). It expresses an important theme in Revelation: Christians are engaged in battle, a contest, in which it is possible either to win or to lose. If they remain faithful, even though they are killed, they are victorious. Jesus has already conquered

---

7. *Commentary on the Apocalypse of the Blessed John* 2.4–5. Victorinus wrote the first commentary on Revelation that has come down to us.

(5:5), as have the martyrs (12:11). The beast is temporarily allowed to con-quer—that is, to seem to prevail over "the holy ones" (13:7). But God's people ultimately conquer Satan and his agents by the blood of the Lamb, by their faithful testimony (12:11), and by refusing to worship the beast (15:2). At the end of the book Jesus conquers the beast (17:14) and destroys all the enemies of God's people. A final mention of "the victor" at the end of Revelation (21:7) ties the book together, describing the heritage of those who persevere through trial and temptation: "I shall be his God, and he will be my son." Faithfulness in the present will enable Jesus' disciples to conquer and to enter into their eternal inheritance.

The particular reward promised in 2:7 is **the right to eat from the tree of life**. Here Jesus refers to the marvelous tree located in the **garden**[8] of Eden that symbolized immortality. Access to this tree and its life-giving fruit was denied to the human race after the fall (Gen 2:9; 3:22, 24). Here Jesus promises eternal life to those who work hard in the service of Christ and others, endure suffering, reject false teaching like the Ephesians do, and rediscover their first love. The final vision of Revelation unveils the tree of life in the new Jerusalem (22:2). The mention at the end of the book of the rewards promised to victors in the †oracles to the churches indicates that the way readers can prevail in the great trials of the intervening chapters is to obey Christ's instructions here at the beginning.

Reflection and Application (2:1–7)

"Remember then from what you have fallen; . . . do the works you did at first" *(2:5 NRSV)*. What was it like when you first experienced God's love and began to love him and others? I was a freshman at the University of Michigan when I became convinced that Christianity is true and was baptized in the Spirit in a charismatic prayer group. My whole life changed. I started taking time daily for prayer and Scripture. I began attending prayer meetings two nights a week. I took every opportunity I could to tell people about Jesus and the power of the Holy Spirit. Some friends and I began a weekly evangelistic Bible study in my dormitory room. In addition, we met for prayer every night from 11:00 to 11:30 p.m. in the dormitory basement. I wasn't a Catholic yet, but I began join-ing my friends at daily Mass in the student chapel. I read the lives of Catholic saints, Protestant missionaries, the exploits of contemporary Christians who

---

8. Some translations say "Paradise," since *paradeisos* is the Greek word for "garden" used here and in the LXX of Genesis.

experienced Christ's power and followed him radically, and the writings of Christian authors like C. S. Lewis. I majored in history so that I could study the history of Christianity. I devoted my summers to evangelization, living in common with friends in households, and making retreats at monasteries between semesters. I gave generously of the little money I had.

What might it mean to "do the works I did at first" forty years later? For me, it means renewing my relationship with the Holy Spirit (Eph 5:18–20), praying more, watching television less, and approaching my relationship with Jesus more personally. It means taking a more aggressive stance against the things in my life that hinder my relationship with Christ. It means interceding for others more and talking more often and more directly to those who do not know Jesus and the truth of the gospel.

A marriage self-help book advises husbands to renew their love toward their wives by doing the things that express the love they would like to have. Expressing love increases love. Perhaps it is with this truth in mind that the risen Jesus says, "Do the works you did at first."

To the Church in Smyrna (2:8–11)

[8]"To the angel of the church in Smyrna, [2]write this:

"'The first and the last, who once died but came to life, says this: [9]'I know your tribulation and poverty, but you are rich. I know the slander of those who claim to be Jews and are not, but rather are members of the assembly of Satan. [10]Do not be afraid of anything that you are going to suffer. Indeed, the devil will throw some of you into prison, that you may be tested, and you will face an ordeal for ten days. Remain faithful until death, and I will give you the crown of life.

[11]"'Whoever has ears ought to hear what the Spirit says to the churches. The victor shall not be harmed by the second death.'"

OT: Isa 44:6; Dan 1:12–15
NT: Rom 2:28–29; Rev 3:9; 12:11
Catechism: martyrs refuse even to simulate idolatry, 2113
Lectionary: St. Polycarp, bishop and martyr

2:8   Smyrna, modern-day Izmir, is a harbor city located thirty-five miles north of Ephesus. It had long-standing ties with Rome as a wealthy trading partner and had erected a temple to the goddess Roma in 195 BC and the first temple in Asia for the worship of the emperor Tiberius in AD 26. It remained a center of the

St. Polycarp, the Church of Smyrna's Most Illustrious Martyr

LIVING TRADITION

As a young man, St. Polycarp (ca. 69–ca. 155) may have heard the book of Revelation the very first time it was read to the church of Smyrna. According to St. Irenaeus (d. 202), who saw and heard him during his youth in Smyrna, Polycarp talked about his conversations with the apostle John and others who had seen Christ. He was appointed bishop of Smyrna by first-generation companions of Jesus. Alongside Ignatius of Antioch and Papias, Polycarp was one of the most important of the †Apostolic Fathers, handing on the teaching and traditions of the apostles to the Church of the second century. He received a letter from St. Ignatius, as Ignatius was on his way to martyrdom in Rome (ca. 110), and he wrote a letter *To the Philippians*.[a] The Roman proconsul put Polycarp to death by fire and sword at the age of eighty-six for refusing to burn incense to the emperor. His death, recounted in *The Martyrdom of St. Polycarp*, written and circulated by the church of Smyrna, is one of the earliest accounts of Christian martyrdom. Here is an excerpt from the exchange between Polycarp and the Roman governor:

> When he was brought forward, the Proconsul tried to persuade him to deny the faith, saying: "Have regard for your age," and other suggestions such as they usually make. When the Proconsul urged him, "Take the oath and I will release you; revile Christ," Polycarp replied: "Eighty-six years I have served him, and He has done me no wrong. How can I blaspheme my King who has saved me?"[b]

a. "St. Polycarp of Smyrna," *Early Christian Writings*, http://www.earlychristianwritings.com/polycarp .html.

b. Condensed from *The Martyrdom of St. Polycarp* 9, in *The Apostolic Fathers*, trans. Francis X. Glimm, Joseph M.-F. Marique, and Gerald G. Walsh, Fathers of the Church 1 (Washington, DC: Catholic University Press, 1947), 155–56.

†imperial cult, which may have been the reason why the church of Smyrna faced persecution. This church became famous in Christian history for its martyr-bishop St. Polycarp (d. 155; see sidebar above, "St. Polycarp, the Church of Smyrna's Most Illustrious Martyr").

In addressing these persecuted Christians, the risen Lord introduces himself with titles that emphasize his divine eternity—**the first and the last** (see comments on 1:17–18) and his victory over death—**who once died but came to life**.

Jesus offers comfort by assuring the Christians of Smyrna that he knows well their **tribulation and poverty**. "Tribulation" (Greek *thlipsis*, also translated as "affliction," "hardship," "distress") is commonly used in the New Testament for

2:9

the suffering that Christians undergo on account of their faith.[9] Perhaps the economic plight of this community was a consequence of its refusal to take part in the idolatrous practices woven into the commercial life of a pagan city (see "Message of Revelation" in the introduction, p. 33). Or perhaps it was simply because these Christians came from the lower ranks of society. But no matter: in the eyes of their Lord and in the goods that last beyond the present age, they are **rich**.

Jesus also knows the **slander of those who claim to be Jews and are not**. Smyrna had a large Jewish community. Although Acts does not mention Smyrna, it bears witness to the fierce opposition the early Christians suffered at the hands of Jews who denied that Jesus was the †Messiah.[10] The preaching of the apostles produced a parting of the ways between the Jews who accepted Jesus as the Messiah and those who did not. Both Jews and Christians considered themselves to be the faithful people of the God of Israel. In these words the risen Christ denies that those who slander his disciples are really Jews.[11]

Because the Roman Empire recognized Judaism as an ancient religion, it exempted its members from the idolatrous rituals that were otherwise obligatory. But when the Jewish community excluded followers of Jesus, Christians were left without this legal protection. At times the Jewish community seems to have exploited this vulnerability, testifying against Christians, whom they regarded as heretics. Jesus had foretold this situation to his disciples (Matt 10:17–18; 24:9; John 16:2). Perhaps it was legal testimony of this kind that lies behind the word "slander," which can simply mean "speaking against." Jesus says that those who do this are an **assembly** (literally, "synagogue") allied with **Satan**, the enemy of God and his people, the accuser of the brothers and sisters (12:10). This is strong language, but the Gospel of John attributes similar language to Jesus during his earthly ministry in reference to Jewish leaders who refused to believe in him and sought to kill him (John 8:44).

2:10–11   Jesus exhorts the church of Smyrna, **Do not be afraid of anything** that **you are going to suffer**. The frequent biblical command not to fear is not about how a person *feels*, since the emotion of fear is spontaneous and to some degree involuntary, but about how believers *respond* to danger and the feelings that accompany it. In Gethsemane, Jesus felt dread at what was about to happen to him (Mark 14:33–34; Luke 22:44), but he did not succumb to fear. Courage is not the absence of fear but the strength to overcome it. Jesus urged his disciples

---

9. See Matt 24:21; 2 Cor 1:4, 8; 2:4; Col 1:24; 1 Thess 1:6.

10. E.g., Acts 13:50; 14:2, 19; 17:5; 18:12; see Rom 11:28.

11. Paul makes an analogous argument about being a Jew inwardly and spiritually in Rom 2:17–29 and describes Gentile Christians as "circumcised" spiritually in Phil 3:3; Col 2:11–14.

The Church and the Jewish People Today

LIVING
TRADITION

Despite a painful history between the two communities, significant progress has occurred in Jewish-Christian relations since the Second Vatican Council. The Council's *Declaration on the Relation of the Church to Non-Christian Religions* (*Nostra Aetate* 4) firmly rejects anti-Judaism, affirms that "the Jews remain very dear to God," and insists that "neither all Jews indiscriminately at that time, nor Jews today, can be charged with the crimes committed during [Christ's] passion. . . . Jews should not be spoken of as rejected or accursed as if this followed from holy scripture."

Recent popes have taken many steps to strengthen Jewish-Christian relations. Speaking in the synagogue of Rome, Pope John Paul II said, "With Judaism, therefore, we have a relationship which we do not have with any other religion. You are our dearly beloved brothers, and in a certain way, it could be said that you are our elder brothers."[a]

Christians believe that the Jewish people have a special place in God's plan (see Rom 11:29). Catholics look forward to Christ's "recognition by 'all Israel' [Rom 11:20–26; cf. Matt 23:39]" and "the 'full inclusion' of the Jews in the Messiah's salvation [Rom 11:12, 25; see also Luke 21:24]," something that is necessary for "the People of God to achieve 'the measure of the stature of the fullness of Christ,' in which 'God may be all in all' [Eph 4:13; 1 Cor 15:28]" (Catechism 674).

a. "The Roots of Anti-Judaism in the Christian Environment," April 13, 1986, http://www.vatican.va /jubilee_2000/magazine/documents/ju_mag_01111997_p-42a_en.html.

to seek this strength in prayer (Mark 14:38). The foundation of Christian courage is trust that God is in control, that he cares for us and those we love, and that he will save all who entrust themselves to him.

The opponent of the Christians in Smyrna is the same as the one who acted against their Lord (Luke 22:3; John 13:27): **the devil.** Acting through the civil authorities, he will throw some of the members of the church **into prison.** God, who is ultimately in control, permits this persecution so **that you may be tested** (see James 1:2–4). The **ten days** of **ordeal** (*thlipsis,* "tribulation," as in 2:10) is not meant to predict exactly the length of their incarceration, since numbers in Revelation are nearly always symbolic. It indicates a short period of time, comparable to the testing of Daniel and his friends (Dan 1:12–15). Nevertheless, it seems that the lives of these Christians are at risk, since Jesus exhorts them to remain **faithful unto death** and promises them the reward, **the crown,** of eternal **life.** In Greco-Roman athletic competitions, winners received a crown of leaves. How infinitely more valuable the crown of life! Other

Tertullian: In Persecution, God Is in Control — LIVING TRADITION

The early Christian writer Tertullian (d. ca. 220) compares persecution to an athletic competition:

> A persecution can be considered as a contest. Who sets the terms of any contest if not the one who provides the crown and the prizes? You will find the terms of the contest decreed in the Apocalypse, where he proclaims the rewards of victory, especially for those who really come through persecution victorious, and in their victorious struggle have fought not merely against flesh and blood but against the spirits of wickedness. Obviously, then, the superintendent of the games and one who sets the prize is the one who decides who is the winner in the contest. The essence, then, of a persecution is the glory of God.[a]

a. *On Flight in Time of Persecution* 1.5, in ACCS 12:22.

New Testament writings speak of a crown as the reward of endurance (see 2 Tim 4:7–8; James 1:12). The **victor**—everyone who remains faithful through such trials—will be preserved from the **second death**, which the conclusion of the book reveals to be "the lake of fire" (RSV), the lasting recompense of the wicked (20:14; 21:8). The exhortation to the Christians in Smyrna echoes Jesus' teaching in Matt 10:28: "Do not be afraid of those who kill the body but cannot kill the soul; rather, be afraid of the one who can destroy both soul and body in Gehenna."

Reflection and Application (2:8–11)

Facing persecution. As humans we can imagine what might happen to us and how we would respond. I have sometimes thought of how I would *like* to respond if I were facing imprisonment or death for my faith. Like St. Peter, I am tempted to say, "Lord, I am prepared to go to prison and to die with you" (Luke 22:33), but we know how that turned out! Of course, Peter's failure occurred before he was strengthened by the Spirit at Pentecost; eventually he *did* die for his Lord.

Only the Lord himself can grant us the strength to be faithful in times of great testing—the flesh is weak. That is why Jesus tells his disciples to pray so that they might not succumb to temptation (Matt 26:41). Beyond prayer, we can prepare for great trials by being faithful in the small things of daily life. This also requires the power of the Spirit. Humility in acknowledging that we are unable to be victorious even in small things, and learning to ask for and receive his strength for daily challenges, prepares us for greater challenges that may come in the future.

God uses trials. Although the devil and human adversaries may afflict us for their own reasons, God is in control of circumstances and uses persecution and hardship to test, purify, and strengthen us. Revelation teaches that faithful witness in the face of opposition provides the occasion for our conquering the devil by the blood of the Lamb (12:11)! Such acts of faithfulness belong to the shining garment of righteous deeds with which God is adorning the Bride of the Lamb for the great wedding feast (19:8). Many biblical texts offer wise counsel about enduring trials, including Sir 2; Heb 12; James 1; and 1 Pet 2:19–3:18; 4:12–19.

To the Church in Pergamum (2:12–17)

---

¹²"To the angel of the church in Pergamum, write this:

"'The one with the sharp two-edged sword says this: ¹³"I know that you live where Satan's throne is, and yet you hold fast to my name and have not denied your faith in me, not even in the days of Antipas, my faithful witness, who was martyred among you, where Satan lives. ¹⁴Yet I have a few things against you. You have some people there who hold to the teaching of Balaam, who instructed Balak to put a stumbling block before the Israelites: to eat food sacrificed to idols and to play the harlot. ¹⁵Likewise, you also have some people who hold to the teaching of [the] Nicolaitans. ¹⁶Therefore, repent. Otherwise, I will come to you quickly and wage war against them with the sword of my mouth.

¹⁷"'"Whoever has ears ought to hear what the Spirit says to the churches. To the victor I shall give some of the hidden manna; I shall also give a white amulet upon which is inscribed a new name, which no one knows except the one who receives it."'"

OT: Num 22:1–6; 25:1–3; 31:16; Isa 62:2; 65:15
NT: 2 Thess 2:8; Rev 1:5, 16; 12:11; 17:6; 19:15
Catechism: new name, 1025, 2159; idolatry, 2113; fame and riches, 1723; the body, 2289; money, 2424

The city of **Pergamum**, modern-day Bergama, lies forty miles to the north of   **2:12** Smyrna and fifteen miles inland. Centuries earlier it had been a proud capital of the Attalid kingdom, ruling much of what is today western Turkey. In Roman times Pergamum boasted a library of two hundred thousand volumes, second

Fig. 3. This huge altar to Zeus (117 feet by 110 feet), now at the Berlin Museum, once towered over Pergamum. It is likely that Revelation refers to it as Satan's throne (2:13).

in size only to that of Alexandria. The geographical setting of the city was striking. A walled acropolis, the location of many of its temples and civic buildings, stood on a steep hill thirteen hundred feet above the rest of the city. From there, an immense altar to Zeus the savior looked down on the city. Pergamum was a center of pagan religion in Asia. Athena, goddess of wisdom and victory, was the patroness of the city; and Dionysius, god of wine and merrymaking, was the patron of the royal dynasty. A shrine to Asklepios (or Asclepius), the god of healing, featuring a complex of medicinal baths, lay at the base of the hill. For a number of years the city was home to the famous physician Galen (d. ca. 199), the father of anatomy. The last king of the city during its era of independence deeded it to its ally Rome in 133 BC, and Rome returned the favor by making Pergamum the first capital of the province of Asia before Caesar Augustus transferred that privilege to Ephesus in 27 BC.[12] Three times Rome bestowed on Pergamum the honorary title of temple-warden of the †imperial cult.

The risen Lord presents himself to the church in Pergamum by calling attention to the **sharp two-edged sword** issuing from his mouth, which manifests power and threatens judgment (2:16; see 19:15).

2:13   Jesus begins by acknowledging the difficult circumstances under which this church lives: **You live where Satan's throne is, . . . where Satan lives**. This is probably a reference to the massive altar of Zeus, which might also be compared to a throne (see fig. 3), towering over the city on the lofty acropolis. The Greeks considered Zeus the king of the gods. Since Jews and Christians considered the pagan gods to be demons (see 1 Cor 10:20), it was natural for them to identify the king of these supposed deities with Satan. It is likely that the altar, whose artwork depicted the victory of Zeus and the Greek gods over

12. There is some scholarly debate as to whether being capital of Asia was truly transferred from Pergamum to Ephesus. There was competition among Asian cities to be recognized as preeminent, especially among Ephesus, Smyrna, and Pergamum.

Roman Persecution of Christians

BIBLICAL BACKGROUND

About 112, Pliny the Younger, proconsul of the province of Bithynia in Asia Minor, just north of the seven churches and on the south side of the Black Sea, wrote the emperor Trajan about trying the cases of people charged with being Christians. Pliny was seeking guidance, since Roman law did not directly address the matter. Pliny writes:

> So far this has been my procedure. . . . I have asked the accused themselves if they were Christians; if they said "Yes," I asked them a second and third time, warning them of the penalty; if they persisted, I ordered them to be led off to execution. First I had no doubt that, whatever kind of thing it was that they pleaded guilty to, their stubbornness and unyielding obstinacy at any rate deserved to be punished.
>
> Later . . . further varieties came to my notice. An anonymous document was laid before me containing many people's names. Some of these denied that they were Christians or had ever been so; at my dictation they invoked the gods and did reverence with incense and wine to your image, which I had ordered to be brought for this purpose along with the statues of the gods; they also cursed Christ; and as I am informed that people who are really Christians cannot possibly be made to do any of those things, I considered that the people who did them should be discharged.

The emperor Trajan replied that Pliny had acted properly. Christians were not to be searched out, but if charged and convicted they must be punished. Anyone who denied that he was a Christian and proved it by invoking the pagan gods was to be released. However, "Anonymous documents . . . should receive no attention [since] they are a very bad precedent and quite unworthy of the age in which we live."[a]

Although this correspondence took place about twenty years after Revelation was written, it gives us a fascinating glimpse into circumstances close in time and place. It illustrates how Christians were subject to demands to worship images of the emperor. It shows how the work of the beast (see Rev 13) could be carried out by civil servants who, though conscientious, held a false and idolatrous worldview.

a. Quotations from Pliny's and Trajan's correspondence are from F. F. Bruce, *New Testament History* (New York: Doubleday, 1969), 423–25.

an ancient race of giants, played a role in the imperial cult, whose provincial seat was Pergamum.

Christ commends the Christians of Pergamum for remaining faithful, holding fast to his **name** and not denying their **faith**, which they would have done by burning incense to Zeus or to the emperor. To refuse to participate in such worship was regarded as unpatriotic at best, treasonous at worst. These Christians were resisting social and legal pressure to engage in false worship despite the fact that one of their prominent members, **Antipas**, probably their bishop, **was martyred** (literally, "killed"). Jesus calls him **my faithful witness**, the same title ascribed to Jesus Christ in the opening greeting (1:5).

2:14–15   Despite the Pergamemes' faithfulness under pressure, the risen Lord has **a few things** against them concerning the conduct of some members of the community. Jesus explains that some **hold to the teaching of Balaam**, identifying their sin by labeling it with the name of an infamous Old Testament figure. According to Num 25:1–2, during Israel's sojourn in the wilderness, "the people profaned themselves by prostituting themselves with the Moabite women. These then invited the people to the sacrifices of their god, and the people ate of the sacrifices and bowed down to their god." This immorality and idolatry provoked the Lord to strike Israel with a plague (Num 25:8–9). Later Moses explains that the pagan prophet Balaam was responsible for proposing this strategy of seduction to **Balak** the Moabite king as the way to defeat the Israelites (Num 31:16). Jesus further identifies the problem in the church in Pergamum as the **teaching of [the] Nicolaitans**, mentioned earlier, in 2:6.[13] It is not a matter of their doctrine of God or of Christ but their moral teaching. Christ compares it to the **stumbling block** that Balak used to undermine the Israelites' relationship with God: **to eat food sacrificed to idols and to play the harlot** (literally, "practice immorality," RSV). To "play the harlot" here may refer either to actual sexual immorality or to participation in idolatrous rites, which the prophets often describe metaphorically as adultery (e.g., Ezek 16).

With the exception of actual adultery, sexual immorality, including prostitution, concubinage, and homosexual behavior, was common and accepted in Greco-Roman society. Ritual sexual acts and prostitution were associated with the worship of the goddess Aphrodite and other deities. Paul and other New Testament authors consistently teach against pagan sexual mores as incompatible with God's law and Christian holiness (1 Cor 6:9–20; 1 Thess 4:3–8; 1 Pet 4:3–4).

Abstaining from these practices on grounds of conscience made Jews and Christians stand out from their neighbors. Apparently those whom this prophecy calls Nicolaitans[14] taught that participation in the society's pagan worship

13. The Greek can be read either as saying that Pergamum *also* has adherents of the Nicolaitans or that the Pergamemes *thus* subscribe to the teaching of the Nicolaitans—that is, that their error is the same. I take the latter view, along with majority of commentators, the RSV, and the NRSV.

14. Some think the term "Nicolaitans" has a symbolic meaning that can be discerned from its etymology, that it derives from two Greek words, *nikaō*, "to conquer," and *laos*, "people." Thus a Nicolaitan

Food Offered to Idols and the New Testament

Pagan culture of the first century was permeated by rituals of worship toward its many gods. In particular, most of the meat that city dwellers ate was sacrificed (i.e., ceremonially offered) to an idol in a pagan temple. Either the meat was prepared, sold, and consumed on site—pagan temples were the restaurants of that day—or it was sold in the marketplace for the support of the temple and priesthood. Civic, guild, and family celebrations normally entailed sacrifices to pagan gods and took place at their temples.

Christian abstention from such rites did not endear them to their pagan neighbors. To abstain from pagan worship associated with civic life could call into question a person's loyalty to the empire. In the second century Christians were sometimes called "atheists" due to their rejection of Greco-Roman gods and were accused of "hatred of the human race," since their religious exclusivism was deemed antisocial.[a]

Besides Revelation, several New Testament writings grapple with the challenge presented to Gentile Christians by meat offered to idols. The Jerusalem council ruled that Gentile Christians should not eat such foods (Acts 15:19–20, 28–29). The apostle Paul distinguishes between eating a sacrificial meal in a pagan temple and eating food purchased in the marketplace that may have been offered to idols. Although mature Christians realize that pagan gods and the idols that represent them are not gods (1 Cor 10:19), Paul teaches that Christians should not eat in pagan temples lest they lead their less mature brothers and sisters to fall into sin (1 Cor 8). Besides that, sacrifices offered to idols are in reality offered to demons, and Christians who share in the cup of the Lord should want nothing to do with the cup of demons (1 Cor 10:20–22). On the other hand, Paul allows Gentile Christians to eat food purchased in the marketplace "without raising questions on grounds of conscience" (10:25), unless someone points out that the food had been offered to an idol, indicating the vulnerability of that person's conscience (10:27–31; see sidebar, "Idolatry: What It Is and What's Wrong with It," p. 175).

It seems that the early Christians drew the line in different places between acceptable and unacceptable foods. The two places where Revelation sternly condemns eating food sacrificed to idols (2:14, 20) are not explicit enough to indicate where the line is being drawn. If the first readers of Revelation were familiar with 1 Corinthians, it is likely they followed Paul's teaching.

a. For example, pagans call Christians "atheists" in *The Martyrdom of Polycarp* 3; 9; Tacitus charges Christians with "hatred of the human race" in *Annals* 15.44.

and sexual practices was acceptable, compromising Christian monotheism and sexual morality to accommodate the surrounding culture—a perennial temptation.

2:16   But Christ rejects this accommodation and issues a solemn warning to the community: **Therefore, repent.** Although the community is not denying the faith by its words (2:13), some of its members are denying the Lord by their deeds, and the whole church is called to account. The community is being summoned to maintain discipline, to uphold its standards in faith and morals. We *are* our brother's keeper and must warn the person who is doing wrong (Ezek 3:17–19; 33:6–9). As with Israel of old, the consequence of idolatry and immorality is divine judgment: **Otherwise, I will come to you . . . and wage war against them**. Christians who persist in idolatry and immorality will find themselves under assault by the divine warrior. This judgment **by the sword of my mouth** will come **quickly** ("soon," NRSV, RSV), whether in this life (see comments on 2:22–23), at the moment of death, or when Christ returns.

2:17   But **to the victor**—to whoever listens to what the Spirit is saying, repents, resists compromise, and holds his or her ground—Christ promises to **give** three tokens of relationship with him, which are difficult to interpret. First, **the hidden manna** may allude to Jewish traditions that the Messiah will feed his people with manna when the new age begins. Thus victors are promised a share in the future heavenly feast. Speaking of manna also makes Christians think of the Eucharist. By promising *hidden* manna, Christ may be promising to faithful Christians the interior spiritual nourishment that the Eucharist contains.[15] Second, there will be **a white amulet** (literally, a white "stone"), which probably alludes to the practice of giving stones as tickets of admission to feasts or other events. Thus the gift of a white stone symbolizes the victor's admission to the messianic banquet, "the wedding feast of the Lamb" (19:9). Finally, the **new name** known only to the recipient may refer to the believer's new identity in Christ. In Col 3:3–4 Paul writes: "You have died, and your life is hidden with Christ in God. When Christ your life appears, then you too will appear with him in glory" (see Isa 62:2; Rom 8:19, 23; 1 John 3:2). Christians discover their true identity in Christ, an identity that will be fully revealed in the life to come.[16]

---

is one who conquers the people. Another possibility is that "Nicolaitans" simply refers to the followers of a certain Nicholas, a common Greek name.

15. See Catechism 1098, 1131.

16. See Catechism 1025; 2159. The meaning of all three tokens is uncertain and hypotheses abound. Osborne lists seven possibilities for the white stone alone (*Revelation*, 148–49).

Reflection and Application (2:12–17)

Is idolatry obsolete? Modern people do not generally worship stones and statues as gods, but that does not mean they are immune from idol worship. An idol, or false god, is anything or anyone to whom we give the devotion, trust, or obedience that belongs to God alone (see sidebar, "Idolatry: What It Is and What's Wrong with It," p. 175). With that definition in mind, it is possible to identify some of the false gods in contemporary life and to consider which idols tempt us.

Money, sex, and power have long functioned as idols (pagan gods were associated with each), and they remain rivals for our hearts. Jesus said, "You cannot serve God and mammon," meaning money (Matt 6:24). Sometimes people idolize money because of excessive desire, referred to in Scripture as "greed" or "covetousness," for things they do not possess. Often, however, people pursue wealth out of anxiety to secure their future (Luke 12:16–23). The idol of lust—with all its seductive and addictive power, a distortion of natural God-given desires—is common in our sex-crazed society. The pursuit of power expresses itself in politics and business, in nations and families, and regrettably, sometimes in the Church. Often the compulsion to be in control is rooted in fear. The desire for fame or prestige shapes some people's entire lives. It is all too easy to place the approval of peers above the loyalty due to God. Jesus attributed the Jewish religious scholars' inability to believe in him to their accepting "praise from one another" rather than seeking "the praise that comes from the only God" (John 5:44).

St. Augustine viewed idolatry as rooted in a disordered love of self, undermining the love of God. Many have recognized the cult of self-worship in contemporary culture, expressed by absorption with one's career, personality, talents, problems, appearance, health, exercise, or diet. For some, sports is the idol that dominates their time and thoughts. Others seek to fill the God-shaped vacuum inside with food, alcohol, drugs, media, or entertainment. Any good thing from God—such as people we love, family life, a group we belong to, the Bible, or even the Church itself—can subtly take the place of God in our lives as that which we love first or rely on most.

Just as the Christians in Pergamum and Thyatira were tempted to combine the worship of God with service to idols, so it is for us today. God's word remains the same: "You shall not have other gods beside me" (Exod 20:3). God wants our undivided devotion, not only because he desires an intimate relationship with us but also for our own good. Everything else ultimately disappoints or debases us.

Where do our time, money, and thoughts go? What are we most tempted to love, hope in, or fear apart from God? When we discover idols in our lives, it is not enough to renounce them. We must renew our relationship with the One whose love, power, and faithfulness alone can satisfy.

Nicolaitans today? The Nicolaitan teaching that the Lord detests (2:6) can be found whenever Christian teachers compromise the gospel, relieving the tension between God's word and the idolatry of the surrounding culture. In our day it may be found in the teaching of those who allow loyalty to their government or party to rival their loyalty to God. It may be found in those who approve the pursuit of wealth or who justify luxurious lifestyles without insisting on commensurate sharing with the needy, contrary to Jesus' teaching.[17] Likewise, the teaching of the Nicolaitans is found in those who allow sexual relations apart from God's unitive and procreative intention in marriage, including those who say that premarital sex or homosexual acts are acceptable. Finally, the Nicolaitan teaching is found in those who deny that our conduct will be judged by God or who hold out the false hope that all will be saved regardless of choices in this life.

To the Church in Thyatira (2:18–29)

---

[18]"To the angel of the church in Thyatira, write this:

"'The Son of God, whose eyes are like a fiery flame and whose feet are like polished brass, says this: [19]"I know your works, your love, faith, service, and endurance, and that your last works are greater than the first. [20]Yet I hold this against you, that you tolerate the woman Jezebel, who calls herself a prophetess, who teaches and misleads my servants to play the harlot and to eat food sacrificed to idols. [21]I have given her time to repent, but she refuses to repent of her harlotry. [22]So I will cast her on a sickbed and plunge those who commit adultery with her into intense suffering unless they repent of her works. [23]I will also put her children to death. Thus shall all the churches come to know that I am the searcher of hearts and minds and that I will give each of you what your works deserve. [24]But I say to the rest of you in Thyatira, who do not uphold this teaching and know nothing of the so-called deep secrets of Satan: on you I will place no further burden, [25]except that you must hold fast to what you have until I come.

[26]"'"To the victor, who keeps to my ways until the end,
I will give authority over the nations.

17. E.g., Luke 12:15–21, 33–34; 16:19–31.

²⁷**He will rule them with an iron rod.**
    Like clay vessels will they be smashed,

²⁸**just as I received authority from my Father. And to him I will give the morning star.**
    ²⁹**""Whoever has ears ought to hear what the Spirit says to the churches.""**

OT: 1 Kings 16:31–33; 2 Kings 9:22; Ps 2:9; Jer 17:10
NT: Acts 15:28–29; 2 Cor 5:10; Rev 1:14–15; 20:12–13
Catechism: Christ as judge, 679, 682; particular judgment, 1021–22; punishments of sin, 1472–73

The commercial and manufacturing town of **Thyatira** was the least significant   2:18
of the seven cities addressed by the book of Revelation. If we are correct that
a messenger originally carried the book of Revelation to the seven churches
in the order they are listed, the messenger would have turned to the southeast
from Pergamum and traveled forty miles on the main road toward Sardis. The
modern town of Akhisar is located over the ancient site of Thyatira. According to Acts 16:12–15, Lydia, a merchant of purple goods who was Paul's first
convert at Philippi, came from there. Thyatira was known for its trade guilds;
ancient inscriptions mention "the shoemakers, the makers and sellers of dyed
cloth, and the bronze smiths."[18] The guilds were centers of social and religious
life, each having its own pagan gods as patrons, whose festive meals involved
idolatrous worship and often sexual immorality. Christians would have experienced considerable social and economic pressure to participate. Apollo, the
sun god and a son of Zeus, was the chief deity of the city.

Christ's presentation of himself as **the Son of God** introduces a title not
mentioned elsewhere in Revelation, but one well-suited to contradict the claims
made for Apollo. The fact that he has **eyes . . . like a fiery flame** shows the risen
Lord as one who sees to the heart of things with a holy, penetrating gaze (Jer
17:10). His **feet . . . like polished brass** connote power. He is a judge whose
very appearance threatens the wrongdoer and makes those who are complacent
uneasy.

Jesus begins with an impressive commendation. The church of Thyatira   2:19
possesses the virtues of **love, faith, service, and endurance**. Faith and love
are praised in every book of the New Testament; hope finds its practical manifestation in endurance, the virtue most frequently commended in Revelation;
service (Greek *diakonia*) probably refers to works of charity toward the poorer

---

18. Osborne, *Revelation*, 151. I am especially indebted to Osborne for my descriptions of the seven cities.

members of the community. The members of this church are progressing in virtue: their **last works are greater than the first**.

2:20–23   Despite this excellent record, the risen Lord expresses dissatisfaction with the church of Thyatira because they **tolerate** a false teacher. This kind of tolerance is not a virtue. A church that does not take a stand against false teaching is irresponsible, like a town that does not fence off hazards or that allows dangerous animals to wander freely, failing to protect vulnerable members of the community. What follows is a threat of judgment against the teacher and her followers. Christ calls the false teacher **Jezebel**, not because that was her actual name, but because that symbolic name reveals the nature of her wrongdoing. Jezebel was the foreign wife of King Ahab, who promoted idolatry in Israel, the worship of the pagan god Baal (see 1 Kings 16:31–33; 21:25–26; 2 Kings 9:22). This false teacher claims to speak for God; she **calls herself a prophetess**. However, she **teaches and misleads . . .** Christ's **servants**, his people, **to play the harlot** (literally, "practice sexual immorality") **and to eat food sacrificed to idols**. This probably means she teaches that these practices are *permissible*, rather than actively advocates them. As in 2:14, it is not certain whether literal or metaphorical sexual immorality is meant. The teaching of Jezebel resembles the practice of the Nicolaitans described in the previous message to the church of Pergamum (2:14–15). Christian teachers sometimes yield to the temptation to ease the tension between God's standards and those of the surrounding society by permitting conduct that the word of God condemns. This leader may have been telling Christians in Thyatira that it was acceptable to participate in pagan sacrificial feasts despite the idolatry and immoral conduct they entailed.

In the Gospels, Jesus issues the sternest warnings against whoever causes his "little ones" to sin (Matt 18:6). Here Christ says he has **given her time to repent**. Presumably she has been warned by a prophet or other church leader, perhaps by John himself. This agrees with the teaching of other texts: God delays judgment because of his mercy, desiring all to reach repentance (Rom 2:4; 2 Pet 3:9). But this woman **refuses to repent**, so judgment on her and her followers commences now: **I will cast her on a sickbed** (the Greek is present tense: "I am throwing her," NRSV) and am bringing **intense suffering** ("great distress," NRSV) on **those who commit adultery with her**. While the previous mentions of sexual immorality (2:14, 20) may be interpreted literally or figuratively, this reference to adultery is almost certainly figurative, referring to people who engage in the same idolatrous practices that she permits and practices. But a way out of judgment stands open: **unless they repent**. There is no escape, however, for those of her spiritual progeny who persist in wrongdoing: **I will**

Does God Bring Judgment in This Life?

BIBLICAL BACKGROUND

Many people think of divine judgment as something that will happen only after death, while others do not think there is such a thing as divine judgment. When bad things happen to people in this life, they view it as a random event, or as a natural consequence of poor choices—for instance, when someone who drinks and drives has an automobile accident. At the other end of the spectrum are people who view any misfortune as a sign of God's judgment. Neither of these extremes accords with what Scripture teaches.

When Jesus' disciples ask about a man born blind, "Who sinned, this man or his parents?," Jesus answers that their sin was not the cause of his blindness (John 9:1–3). Jesus also explicitly denies that the victims of a fatal accident (the collapse of the tower of Siloam) or of political violence (Pilate's execution of temple worshipers) were worse sinners than everyone else (Luke 13:1–5). Jesus regards these calamities as unrelated to the personal sins of the victims and as a wake-up call for everyone. He warns, "If you do not repent, you will all perish as they did!" Yet in some instances when Jesus heals, he associates physical infirmity with sin (Matt 9:2; John 5:14).

The Old Testament records numerous instances in which God brings judgment in this life on individuals and on Israel because of their wrongdoing (e.g., Judg 2:11–23; 2 Chron 26:19–21; Ps 107:17–20). This continues in the New Testament: Ananias and Sapphira are struck dead for lying to the Holy Spirit (Acts 5:1–10); Herod is struck down for failing to give God †glory (Acts 12:20–23).

It is helpful to distinguish between judgments that express God's definitive verdict on serious wrongdoing and remedial judgments intended to lead to conversion. Several New Testament passages refer to God sending or allowing hardships as part of his loving discipline (Heb 12:5–10; 1 Pet 4:17); in James 5:16 physical healing is linked with confession of sin. When Paul reproves the Corinthians for the disrespect they are showing toward one another and the Eucharist, he explains, "That is why many among you are ill and infirm, and a considerable number are dying" (1 Cor 11:30). Paul recommends self-examination to avoid divine judgment: "But if we judged ourselves, we would not be judged. But when we are judged by the Lord, we are disciplined so that we may not be condemned along with the world" (1 Cor 11:31–32 NRSV). Thus Paul teaches that experiencing God's judgment in this life is actually a mercy, intended to lead us to repent and be saved.

For Christians, suffering and death—provided there is opportunity for repentance—are tragic only in a limited sense, since their effects are time-limited. On the other side of the grave lies eternal life with God. The true and lasting tragedy is the refusal to repent and the consequent loss of eternal life, what Revelation calls "the second death" (20:14; 21:8).

. . . put her children to death. The future tense leaves unclear whether this refers to physical death or final condemnation. In any case, the physical illness or other distress that is about to strike this woman and her followers will demonstrate to **all the churches** that Jesus is the all-knowing judge, **the searcher of hearts and minds**, that our conduct matters, and that **each** person will receive what his or her **works deserve**. Although we are saved by God's grace, we must respond to grace with appropriate conduct and will be judged by what we do.[19]

2:24–25   But Christ distinguishes between the innocent and the guilty. He tells those who **do not uphold this teaching** (the false teaching of Jezebel) that he does not require anything more of them (**no further burden**)[20] than that they **hold fast to what you have**, probably referring to the teaching they have already received. Faithfulness to the original gospel and avoidance of novel teaching that leads in another direction are a consistent New Testament theme (2 Tim 2:14; 1 John 2:24; Jude 3). Christ refers to Jezebel's knowledge as the **deep** things **of Satan** ("secrets" is not in the Greek), either because Jezebel and her followers actually claim to disclose Satan's ways to give people mastery over them or, ironically, because they call their teaching "deep," and Christ indicates from just how far down it truly originates.

2:26–29   As in the other messages to churches, Jesus promises final reward to **the victor**. Here the person who conquers is described as the one **who keeps to my ways** (literally, "my works"), emphasizing not only orthodoxy but also orthopraxy—right conduct—**until the end**. The promise is a share in the Messiah's **authority over the nations**, in the same way it is prophesied in Ps 2:9 LXX— "You shall rule them with a rod of iron"—and is applied to Jesus in Rev 12:5 and 19:15. As is often repeated in the Gospel of John, what Jesus has **received** from the **Father**, in this case, **authority**, he gives to his faithful followers. To this the risen Lord adds that he will **give the morning star**, which is the last and brightest star (actually, the planet Venus) to be seen in the morning and the first star to be seen at night, a title Jesus applies to himself in 22:16. It seems that Jesus is promising a share in his own light, presence, victory, and rule to whoever perseveres in his teaching and his ways.

Reflection and Application (2:18–29)

Is God punishing me? When troubles come—a sickness, an accident, a miscarriage, infertility—it is common for people to wonder if God is judging them.

---

19. John 5:29; Rom 2:5–10; 2 Cor 5:10; Eph 2:8–10; Titus 2:11–14; 1 Pet 1:17; Rev 20:12–13.

20. This wording may allude to the decision of the Jerusalem council that Gentile Christians need bear no "greater burden than these necessary things: that you abstain from what has been sacrificed to idols and from blood and from what is strangled and from unchastity" (Acts 15:28–29 RSV).

Some Christians live their whole lives with a morbid sense of fear and guilt. However, most evils that befall people are not particular divine judgments for wrongdoing but are rather consequences of the evil in the world unleashed by original sin. God does not desire them but permits them and uses them to bring good to those who love him (Rom 8:28).

It is often not possible to understand why calamities occur to us or others. Besides leading us to pray for those who suffer, these can be good occasions for taking stock of our lives. This does not mean becoming scrupulous, but rather, honestly considering whether there is any sin we need to face up to, and if so, to turn from it and seek forgiveness.

If sickness comes our way, Sir 38:9–14 gives sound advice: pray for healing, repent of sin, make an offering to God, and go to the doctor (note the order). Jesus adds that when we pray we must forgive those we have anything against (Mark 11:25). James recommends that we ask the presbyters (priests)[21] for prayer and anointing, confess our sins, and pray fervently for one another (5:14–18). Hebrews 12 offers helpful advice about responding to God's fatherly discipline, whatever the cause.

Testing teachers. The church of Ephesus is commended for having tested and rejected false apostles (2:2). The church of Pergamum is told to repent because of the people among them who follow false teaching (2:15–16). The church of Thyatira is reproved for tolerating the teaching of the self-styled prophetess figuratively named "Jezebel" (2:20). Who is responsible to test teachers in the Church today? Most laypeople feel that the responsibility to deal with false teachers in their midst belongs exclusively to church leadership, whether the pastor of the parish, the bishop, or Rome. However, Jesus holds the whole community of Thyatira responsible for testing the teachers who come to them. How are we to do this?

Every Catholic is responsible for testing the teaching he or she hears, evaluating it by its faithfulness to Scripture and church doctrine and avoiding teaching that is unsound. Twice in warning about false prophets (Matt 7:15–23), Jesus says, "By their fruits you will know them." Testing teachers entails discerning whether the teaching and the conduct of ministers conforms to God's standards.

Nevertheless, Christians have different roles in this discernment process. Bishops and pastors have the final responsibility to discern and choose those they allow to minister. Laypeople, however, are responsible to discern the teaching they follow and to share any concerns that they have with their pastor,

---

21. For more explanation of this word, sometimes translated "elders," see comments below on Rev 4:4.

bishop, and if necessary with the appropriate Roman authority.[22] Those with greater knowledge bear greater responsibility. Such matters call for prudence in speech, keeping in view both the reputation of the teacher in question and the well-being of the people of God.

22. See *Lumen Gentium* (Dogmatic Constitution on the Church) 37.

More Messages to the Churches

Revelation 3:1–22

In the previous chapter, the risen Lord dictates messages to four churches in Asia Minor about their spiritual condition. The three messages in this chapter have the same theme and the same structure (see comments on 2:1–7 regarding the first message), but Jesus' message to each is unique. The churches of Sardis and Laodicea face neither the external threat of persecution nor the internal threat of false teachers. To all appearances they seem to be prospering and enjoy a good reputation. Yet Jesus' message to these two churches is almost entirely negative. Why? According to Craig Koester, "The dangers to these congregations come not from overt hostility but from the kind of comfortable conditions that lead to complacency."[1] On the other hand, Jesus' message to the third church, located in Philadelphia and struggling with fierce opponents and limited resources, is entirely positive. In all seven messages, Jesus summons all who read Revelation or hear it read to pay careful attention to what the Spirit is saying.

To the Church in Sardis (3:1–6)

---

[1]"To the angel of the church in Sardis, write this:

"'The one who has the seven spirits of God and the seven stars says this: "I know your works, that you have the reputation of being alive, but you are dead. [2]Be watchful and strengthen what is left, which is going to

---

1. Craig R. Koester, *Revelation and the End of All Things* (Grand Rapids: Eerdmans, 2001), 66.

die, for I have not found your works complete in the sight of my God. [3]Remember then how you accepted and heard; keep it, and repent. If you are not watchful, I will come like a thief, and you will never know at what hour I will come upon you. [4]However, you have a few people in Sardis who have not soiled their garments; they will walk with me dressed in white, because they are worthy.

[5]""The victor will thus be dressed in white, and I will never erase his name from the book of life but will acknowledge his name in the presence of my Father and of his angels.

[6]"""Whoever has ears ought to hear what the Spirit says to the churches."""

OT: Zech 3:3–5
NT: Matt 10:32–33; Phil 4:3; Rev 1:20

3:1   The city of **Sardis**, located about thirty-five miles southeast of Thyatira, was relatively well-to-do because of its extensive trading relationships and the fertility of the surrounding farmland. In earlier times it also had been the capital of a powerful kingdom ruled by King Croesus. Like Pergamum, the oldest part of the city was established within a fortress on a steep hill that was thought to be impregnable. Twice in Sardis's history, however, the city had been taken by surprise attack.[2] The city had a prosperous and influential Jewish community that boasted a large and beautiful synagogue.

Christ presents himself as possessing **the seven spirits of God**. Assuming that this phrase refers to the Holy Spirit (see comments on 1:5a and sidebar, "The Seven Spirits of God," p. 46), this is a striking claim, but it agrees with other New Testament passages that speak of Jesus' relationship with the Spirit. The Holy Spirit is the Spirit of Jesus.[3] Jesus is the source of the Church's life in the Spirit. He says that he has **the seven stars**, the guardians of the churches, also mentioned in the message to the church of Ephesus (2:1).

Jesus offers a devastating diagnosis of the condition of the church: **You have the reputation** (literally, "name") **of being alive**. In the eyes of Christians and pagans and, we may imagine, its own members, the church of Sardis seemed to be a vital community. Perhaps they enjoyed a rich liturgical life; perhaps they were growing in numbers and in the esteem of the wider community; perhaps they were materially well off and shared their resources with the less fortunate. But they were deceived in their self-satisfaction, their dreamy

---

2. Cyrus of Persia captured Sardis in 546 BC, when one of his soldiers scaled the cliff unobserved, entered the city, and opened the gate. The feat was repeated in 214 BC by troops of the Syrian Antiochus III.
3. See John 7:37–39; 20:22; Acts 2:33; 16:6–7; Rom 8:9; Gal 4:6; Phil 1:19.

spiritual slumber. According to Christ, in reality they **are dead**. What could be so wrong?

The next sentence indicates that their condition, though serious, is not beyond hope. **Be watchful** (or, "Wake up!") and **strengthen what is left**, what remains and is almost but not quite dead ("on the point of death," RSV). Christ explains: **for I have not found your works complete in the sight of my God**. Partial obedience is a delusion. This prophecy does not specify what is lacking; the Spirit will show each reader how this message applies. Christ prescribes a remedy similar to his call to the church of Ephesus to return to its first love (2:4–5). The church of Sardis is to **Remember** how they **accepted** the gospel with faith and how they **heard**, that is, *obeyed* it ("heard" often has this stronger sense in the Bible, e.g., Gen 22:18). Jesus urges the church: **keep it**, "hold on to that" (NJB), and **repent** (see 2:5, 16, 21–22); return to your former faith and obedience.

If you are not watchful, or "if you do not wake up" (NJB), **I will come like a thief**. The intruder they need to fear is Christ himself! These words recall Jesus' parable of the surprised householder in the Gospels (e.g., Matt 24:42–43), echoed in the Epistles (1 Thess 5:2–4; 2 Pet 3:10), about the need to stay alert for Christ's return at a moment **you will never know**. However, rather than refer primarily to Christ's second coming, this prophecy, like others in the Old Testament and in Revelation, refers to a "coming" of the Lord to judge in the present age, perhaps through persecution or other difficulties, just as other texts speak of Christ's coming in the present to comfort and restore (3:20).

However, you have a few people (literally, "names") **. . . who have not soiled their garments**. The majority of the church in **Sardis** wear dirty clothes—that is, they are in a sinful condition that must be cleansed (see Zech 3:3–5). But a few faithful members of the church will enjoy a great honor: they will **walk with** Christ **dressed in white**, as a sign that they are **worthy**. At Roman triumph celebrations, citizens wore white robes in celebration of the victory.[4] In the Bible white clothing signifies purity, victory, resurrection, or belonging to the heavenly world; all these senses are likely intended here. This honor will not be reserved exclusively for those who have kept their garments clean all along. Rather, **The victor**—whoever conquers in the spiritual battle—**will thus be dressed in white**, implying that this possibility remains open to everyone who accepts the message of the risen Lord and repents of their past sins. Furthermore, Jesus guarantees that he **will never erase his name from the book of life**—the

3:2–3

3:4–6

---

4. Osborne, *Revelation*, 179.

Fig. 4. A stone carving at Ephesus of Nike, the goddess of victory.

place where the names of all God's chosen and faithful are written.[5] Rather, Jesus will **acknowledge** him or her (literally, "**his name**") **in the presence of** the **Father and of his angels**. This is the same honor Jesus promises to those who are not ashamed to confess their relationship with him before a hostile world (Matt 10:32–33; Mark 8:38; Luke 9:26). Perhaps this is a clue that the fault of the majority in Sardis is a compromise that obscures their witness to Christ. Is this church an example of innocuous Christianity, like salt that has lost its flavor (Matt 5:13)? In any case, all are called to listen to **what the Spirit says**.

Reflection and Application (3:1–6)

I remember when, in Fr. Ugo Vanni's course on the book of Revelation, I prepared these verses for the final examination and realized with a rush of apprehension that they applied to me. Despite my reputation of being alive, I realized that death had entered in; I had fallen prey to a pattern of sin; my works were far from "complete" in the sight of God.

5. Exod 32:32–33; Ps 69:29; Isa 4:3; Luke 10:20; Phil 4:3; see sidebar, "The Catechism on the Antichrist," p. 229.

BIBLICAL
BACKGROUND

The Importance of Conquering

Jesus makes great promises to "the victor" (3:5). At the end of the book, the one who conquers inherits the new Jerusalem, life-giving water, and divine sonship (21:1–7). Other New Testament passages teach the importance of conquering. The same word, "conquer" (*nikaō*), is used six times in 1 John, always in reference to how Christians have overcome the world and the devil by their faith in Jesus, God's Son, through whom we have been begotten by God (2:13, 14; 4:4; 5:4–5).

In his farewell discourse in John, Jesus uses this verb about himself: "In the world you will have trouble, but take courage, I have conquered the world" (16:33). Paul uses it in Rom 3:4; 12:21, and an intensified form of the word in 8:37: "In all these things we conquer overwhelmingly through him who loved us." In all these uses the word "conquer" implies human struggle and prevailing in battle, but only by relying on God's strength.

Readers may be familiar with the related word, *nikē*, meaning "victory," used in the Greco-Roman world as the name of the goddess of victory (see fig. 4) and today as the brand name of a line of athletic equipment.

However, the risen Lord's message to the church of Sardis and to me was not entirely negative. He says, "strengthen what remains and is about to die" (ESV). I was comforted—something remains that is not yet dead! So the task was to remember how I had originally heard and responded to the gospel, to hold fast to that, and to repent (see "Reflection and Application" on 2:1–3:22).

To the Church in Philadelphia (3:7–13)

⁷"To the angel of the church in Philadelphia, write this:

"'The holy one, the true,
  who holds the key of David,
  who opens and no one shall close,
  who closes and no one shall open,

says this:
⁸""'I know your works (behold, I have left an open door before you, which no one can close). You have limited strength, and yet you have kept my word and have not denied my name. ⁹Behold, I will make those of the assembly of Satan who claim to be Jews and are not, but are lying, behold

I will make them come and fall prostrate at your feet, and they will realize
that I love you. [10]Because you have kept my message of endurance, I will
keep you safe in the time of trial that is going to come to the whole world
to test the inhabitants of the earth. [11]I am coming quickly. Hold fast to
what you have, so that no one may take your crown.

[12]"""The victor I will make into a pillar in the temple of my God, and he
will never leave it again. On him I will inscribe the name of my God and
the name of the city of my God, the new Jerusalem, which comes down
out of heaven from my God, as well as my new name.

[13]"""Whoever has ears ought to hear what the Spirit says to the
churches."""

OT: Isa 9:6; 22:22; 43:4; 60:14; 66:5
NT: Acts 14:27; Rev 1:18; 2:9

3:7   The church of **Philadelphia** is the second church, along with that of Smyrna
(2:8–10), that receives only encouragement and no reproof. A variety of clues
help us piece together the historical context in which this prophetic message
may have been communicated.

The city of Philadelphia lay thirty miles southeast of Sardis. Like Sardis, it was
a prosperous commercial center, located at the intersection of two important
trade routes. It seems that the Christians of Philadelphia were in conflict with
the local Jewish community, which had excluded them from participation in
the synagogue. Like the church of Smyrna, the church in Philadelphia remained
faithful to Jesus despite suffering rejection by those around them who claimed
to be God's people.

The risen Lord introduces himself with words that recall the Old Testament.
The title **holy one**, especially "Holy One of Israel," is frequently used of God
in the Old Testament (e.g., Ps 89:19; Isa 10:20; Hosea 11:9). The Greek word
translated **true** means "genuine," or "faithful." It is used in the Lord's revelation
of himself in the †Septuagint version of Exod 34:6: "The LORD, the God of
compassion and mercy, patient, very merciful, and true" (my translation). By
declaring that he **holds the key of David**, the risen Jesus is affirming that he
is the true †Messiah, David's heir.[6] The key, which symbolizes the authority to
open and close in an irreversible manner, refers to Isa 22:22. There the prophet
announces God's rejection of Shebna, the king's steward, and his replacement
by Eliakim, who will be granted "the key of the House of David," to open and

---

6. In 1:18 Jesus announces that he has the keys "to death and the netherworld." Reading that text
in light of this one indicates that the Messiah's authority over God's people extends beyond this life
(see Matt 16:18–19).

close authoritatively. The risen Messiah is telling the believers in Philadelphia who have been shut out of the Jewish community that he is the one who possesses authority to open and close the door to participation in the people of God. By alluding to Isa 22:22, Christ recalls an unfaithful steward who lost his position in the past, with the implication that this can be the fate of a Jewish community that rejects Jesus' disciples.

As in the other letters, Jesus declares that he knows what has been happening with the Christians in Philadelphia: **I know your works.** But before going on to describe the conduct of the Philadelphians, Jesus pronounces a blessing on them. The word **behold**, used three times in two verses, announces the Lord's intervention on behalf of this church. The message, **I have left an open door before you, which no one can close,** indicates that he has welcomed these members of the church, probably both Jewish and Gentile, into the messianic kingdom, and no one can exclude them (Luke 6:22; John 16:2; Col 2:18).[7] Then he returns to describe the "works" of the church that he finds pleasing. Despite their **limited strength** (other versions say "power"), meaning their low social status and limited ability to determine their own destiny in Philadelphia, these Christians **have kept** Jesus' **word**, the gospel, and have **not denied** his **name.** That is, they continue to acknowledge Jesus as the Messiah and Lord despite pressure to deny him.[8]

3:8

As in Smyrna, **the assembly of Satan** (literally, "synagogue of Satan") who **claim to be Jews and are not** probably refers to the members of the Jewish community who reject members of the local church (see comments on 2:9). In saying that they **are lying,** the risen Messiah is not saying that they deliberately deceive, but rather that they speak falsely in claiming to be God's faithful people while excluding his followers. Christ reveals what he is about to do: **behold.** By saying that he will make these Jews **come and fall prostrate** at the feet of the Philadelphian Christians, most of whom are probably Gentile, Jesus overturns the traditional Jewish understanding of the promise in Isa 60:14.

3:9

> The children of your oppressors shall come,
> > bowing before you;
> All those who despised you,
> > shall bow low at your feet.

---

7. This interpretation of "open door" corresponds to what is said in Acts 14:27 about God opening a "door of faith" to the Gentiles. However, some commentators understand this as an open door of evangelistic opportunity—the way Paul uses the phrase "open door" in 1 Cor 16:9; 2 Cor 2:12; and Col 4:3—perhaps among the local Jewish community.

8. The mention of not denying Jesus recalls his words recorded in Matt 10:32–33 and Luke 12:8–9 and may imply a contrast to the compromised members of the church of Sardis (Rev 3:5).

> They shall call you "City of the Lord,"
> Zion of the Holy One of Israel."

Jews looked forward to the day when their Gentile oppressors would come, bowing to them. Now Jesus reveals that the church of Philadelphia, comprised of Jews and Gentiles united in the Messiah, belongs to that †eschatological Israel whom God will vindicate. The day is coming, Jesus says to the Philadelphian Christians, when your Jewish opponents will know for sure that **I love you** (literally, "I loved you"). This expression indicates God's choice of the church of Philadelphia (see Rom 9:13) and his covenant relationship with them. While this promise refers to the vindication of Jesus' followers at the end of history,[9] it may imply that members of the local Jewish community would soon change their minds and turn in faith to Jesus as the Messiah, as many Jews did in the first two centuries of the Church.

3:10   Returning to his commendation of the church, Christ says that they **have kept my message of endurance**. The context and Greek wording suggest a different translation: "You have kept the message of *my* endurance." The Philadelphian Christians have embraced the pattern of Christ's sufferings on the cross, enduring hardship in union with their Lord. The reward that Jesus promises is to **keep** them **safe in the time of trial that is going to come to the whole †world**.[10] Jesus is promising to preserve his faithful in Philadelphia in the midst of a trial that is about to arrive for everyone (the Greek wording suggests an imminent event), just as the Father preserved Jesus not *from* the trial of death but *through* it (see Matt 6:13; 26:39; Heb 5:7–8). Although all must experience it, God's purpose for this trial is focused on **the inhabitants of the earth**, a phrase that Revelation uses for those who are not part of God's people (see sidebar, "Who Are the 'Inhabitants of the Earth'?," p. 130).

3:11–13   Jesus reassures the church of Philadelphia that they will not have to wait long for his **coming** to save them. He exhorts them to **Hold fast** to the faith and practice that now characterize them **so that no one may take** their **crown** of victory. Philadelphia was famous for its athletic competitions in which the victors would receive crowns of leaves honoring their success. Jesus is saying, "You are winning, you are headed for the victor's circle. Don't give up. Keep doing what you're doing, and you will win the prize." The particular reward he holds out

---

9. See Rom 11:25–26 and Catechism 674.

10. Some †dispensationalist Christians interpret this text as a promise that God's faithful will not face "the great tribulation," and will therefore be "raptured" before it arrives. But there is no mention of †rapture here, and the promise is to a church that has already endured a great deal of tribulation. See the online article on the rapture in the Revelation Resources at www.CatholicScriptureCommentary.com.

to the victorious Christians of Philadelphia, excluded from the synagogue, is that he **will make** them **into a pillar in the temple of my God,** where they will remain forever. In other words, their presence in the place where God dwells will be absolutely secure. More than that, Christ will display for everyone to see who these followers of Jesus really belong to by inscribing them with the name of his **God**, of God's **city . . . , the new Jerusalem,** and his own **name**, probably referring to Jesus' true identity manifested at his resurrection and expressed in titles such as "Son of God" (Rom 1:4), "Lord" (Phil 2:9–11), and "King of kings and Lord of lords" (19:16). This inscription symbolizes their belonging completely to God and Christ as priests (1:6; 5:10; 20:6). In ancient Israel only the high priest bore God's name (inscribed on the gold band of his turban, Exod 39:30–31). But in the new Jerusalem (22:4), and even in some way already (14:1), faithful believers bear the names of the Father and the Son inscribed on their foreheads. The new Jerusalem, **which comes down out of heaven from my God**, contrasts with earthly Jerusalem, the concern of the Jewish community, which was being rebuilt after its destruction by the Romans in AD 70.

To the Church in Laodicea (3:14–22)

[14]"To the angel of the church in Laodicea, write this:

"'The Amen, the faithful and true witness, the source of God's creation, says this: [15]"I know your works; I know that you are neither cold nor hot. I wish you were either cold or hot. [16]So, because you are lukewarm, neither hot nor cold, I will spit you out of my mouth. [17]For you say, 'I am rich and affluent and have no need of anything,' and yet do not realize that you are wretched, pitiable, poor, blind, and naked. [18]I advise you to buy from me gold refined by fire so that you may be rich, and white garments to put on so that your shameful nakedness may not be exposed, and buy ointment to smear on your eyes so that you may see. [19]Those whom I love, I reprove and chastise. Be earnest, therefore, and repent.

[20]"'"Behold, I stand at the door and knock. If anyone hears my voice and opens the door, [then] I will enter his house and dine with him, and he with me. [21]I will give the victor the right to sit with me on my throne, as I myself first won the victory and sit with my Father on his throne.

[22]"'"Whoever has ears ought to hear what the Spirit says to the churches."'"

OT: Deut 8:11–20; Prov 3:12; 8:22
NT: 1 Cor 11:32; Col 1:15–18; Heb 12:5–11

Lectionary: 3:14, 20–22: Common of Saints during Easter Season; Consecration of Virgins and Religious Profession; Mass for the Sacred Heart during Easter Season

3:14   **Laodicea**, the leading city in the Lycus Valley, lay forty miles to the southeast of Philadelphia, in the region of Phrygia. Its near neighbors were Hierapolis (clearly visible six miles to the north across the valley) and Colossae (ten miles to the east). Paul mentions Laodicea in his Letter to the Colossians as a city where his colleague Epaphras had evangelized (and probably founded the local church: Col 2:1; 4:12–16). Wilfred Harrington explains its prominence: "It was a banking center, a manufacturer of clothing and carpets of the native glossy-black wool, and the seat of a medical school noted for 'Phrygian powder' used in the making of eye salve."[11] The city was wealthy enough that when it was destroyed by an earthquake in AD 60, it declined to accept Roman aid and rebuilt itself from its own resources. Archaeological excavations have uncovered an elegant colonnade, once covered in marble, that ran through the center of the city, with covered shops on both sides, not unlike a modern mall.

Christ presents himself to the Laodiceans with titles that do not appear in the opening vision. He calls himself **The Amen**—a title for God in Isa 65:16[12] that emphasizes the certainty of his power to accomplish what he decides. In naming himself **the faithful and true witness** (echoing 1:5), he underscores the reliability of what he is about to say. Finally he identifies himself as **the source** (*archē*, "origin" or "principle") **of God's creation**, perhaps alluding to familiar texts, Col 1:18 and Prov 8:22, since the same word appears in both. These texts speak of the role of the preincarnate Christ in creation. By invoking them, the risen Lord declares his divine dignity and power and recalls what the Laodiceans had heard about him.[13]

3:15–16   Christ reproves the Laodiceans for being **lukewarm, neither hot nor cold.** The nearby city of Hierapolis was famous for its hot healing springs, while Colossae was known for its cold freshwater. Laodicea had no water source of its own but received lukewarm water from an aqueduct whose source was near Hierapolis.[14] The Lord declares that he is "about to spit you out of my mouth" (NIV). The Greek word translated **spit** (*emeō*, from which we get "emetic") literally means "vomit"; Christ is saying that the Laodiceans make him sick.

3:17   The reason turns out to be their smug complacency: **For you say, "I am rich and affluent** (literally, "I have prospered," RSV) **and have no need of anything."**

---

11. Wilfred J. Harrington, *Revelation*, Sacra Pagina (Collegeville, MN: Liturgical Press, 1993), 74–75.

12. The word "amen" appears twice in the Hebrew of Isa 65:16 but is translated "truth" or "faithfulness" since its meaning is close to that.

13. In Col 4:16 Paul asks that his Letter to the Colossians be shared with the Laodiceans.

14. Freshwater was also carried into the city from streams outside it.

Fig. 5. One can imagine, based on the impressive remains of its colonnaded main street, the material prosperity that once belonged to Laodicea.

What was the source of their deceptive self-satisfaction? Perhaps the Laodiceans enjoyed a comfortable life because of the prosperity of their city and shared in its self-sufficient attitude. Deuteronomy 8:11–20 warns that material prosperity can lead to forgetting God. Perhaps they enjoyed respectability in the eyes of their fellow citizens because they lived their faith in a moderate manner that neither offended nor challenged anyone. Perhaps the church believed that it had prospered because of its growing numbers, a healthy budget, and important people among its members. We are not told why the Laodicean Christians consider themselves rich and needing nothing, only that their self-confidence is drastically misplaced. Five stark words describe their true condition: **you are wretched, pitiable, poor, blind, and naked.**

Despite Jesus' stern warning, harsher than that given to any of the other churches, there is hope for the Laodicean Christians if they will accept the counsel that he gives. First he advises them to **buy** from him what they need. He does not mean literally to buy—what could they pay?—but rather that they come to him to acquire what they lack. The most basic thing the Laodiceans need is the humility to recognize their inability to provide for themselves. Christ employs irony in naming the three things they lack and must acquire from him,

3:18–19

Threats Reveal Hope for Pardon

LIVING TRADITION

According to Tertullian (ca. 160–ca. 220), a teacher in the early Church, the stern words of our risen Lord in the letters to the seven churches assure us that forgiveness is available:

> You have sinned, yet you can still be reconciled. You have someone to whom you can make satisfaction, yes, and one who wills it. If you doubt that this is true, consider what the Spirit says to the churches. He charges the Ephesians with "having abandoned charity." He reproaches the Thyatirenes with fornication and "eating food sacrificed to idols." He accuses the Sardians of "works that are not complete." He censures the people of Pergam[um] for teaching false doctrines. He upbraids the Laodiceans for "placing their trust in riches." And yet he warns them all to repent—even adding threats. But he would not threaten the impenitent [unless he pardoned] the penitent.[a]

a. *On Penitence* 7–8, in ACCS 12:20.

since their city was famous for wealth, textiles, and eye medicine. Since these items are also familiar biblical symbols, Christ is urging them to seek specific spiritual goods from him: **gold refined by fire** symbolizes faith in Christ that has been purified by enduring trial (1 Cor 3:12–14; 1 Pet 1:7), **white garments** symbolize pure and righteous conduct,[15] and **ointment to smear on your eyes so that you may see** symbolizes the anointing of the Holy Spirit that gives true discernment (1 John 2:27).

Then comes a wonderful line: **Those whom I love, I reprove and chastise.** All of Jesus' reproofs in his messages to the churches are motivated by his covenant love (1:5). This echoes what is said about the love of God in Prov 3:12 (and Heb 12:5–11): "Whom the Lord loves he reproves, as a father, the son he favors." The exhortation follows: **Be earnest** (literally, "be zealous") and **repent**.

3:20–22   The risen Lord concludes the seventh letter with an invitation to all who hear, whether they live in Laodicea in the first century or in North America or anywhere else in the twenty-first. **Behold, I stand at the door and knock.** The invitation is to **anyone** who **hears my voice and opens the door**—a universal offer of salvation. Bruce M. Metzger explains the image:

> Christ knocking on the door is a simple but profound picture of grace and free will in action. The scene has been unforgettably captured by Holman Hunt in his famous painting, "The Light of the World." The Lord has come and is knocking

15. Isa 61:10; Bar 5:2; Dan 12:10 RSV; Rev 19:14.

at the door, but there is no handle or latch on the outside of the door; it must be opened from within. Christ promises to enter when the resident opens the door.[16]

The promise that **I will enter his house and dine with him, and he with me** is a powerful image of intimacy. In the Middle East, sharing a meal indicates a relationship of trust and friendship. It is no accident that this text is used as a reading for a Mass for the Sacred Heart. To dine with Christ is to be united to him in his covenant and to know his love; it recalls our table fellowship with him in the Eucharist.

The risen Lord adds another extraordinary promise. Christ will give those who are victorious **the right to sit with** him on his **throne**, just as he **first won the victory** and the right to reign with his **Father on his throne**. Jesus conquered by perfectly obeying the Father in life and death (John 8:29; 17:4–5; Phil 2:5–11). The privilege of reigning with Christ is available to those who likewise win the victory; they do so by turning to him for grace, repenting, remaining faithful, and persevering, no matter what the cost. This message from the **Spirit** is for **whoever has ears**.

Jesus summons every reader to listen to the messages to all the churches and to hear what the Holy Spirit is saying to us and to our families, communities, parishes, and dioceses. If readers respond to what the Spirit is saying, they will be ready for the disclosure of the things that are to come in the next chapters—ready for the future itself.

Reflection and Application (2:1–3:22)

I doubt that any Christian can read Christ's messages to the churches with an open heart and not experience some conviction of sin. While advice about how to respond to Jesus' correction is scattered throughout the messages, the seventh message, addressed to the church of Laodicea, is particularly helpful.

Here we see the motive of Christ's stern words: he reproves those whom he loves. His desire, incredible as it may seem, is for relationship with us. He wants to come and eat and drink with us, and us with him. He knows that, despite our pretensions to the contrary, we do not have what we need. So he invites us to obtain from him everything: the gold of tested faith, a garment of righteousness, and the anointing of his Holy Spirit to enable us to see clearly.

While the Holy Spirit will guide us as we repent, it can be useful to recall the attitudes and actions repentance entails (see sidebar, "Repent!," p. 61).

---

16. Bruce M. Metzger, *Breaking the Code* (Nashville: Abingdon, 1993), 45–46.

Humility. First, we need to acknowledge our need for God. In Alcoholics Anonymous the first three of the Twelve Steps are (1) to admit that "we were powerless, . . . that our lives had become unmanageable"; (2) "to believe that a Power greater than ourselves could restore us"; and (3) to make "a decision to turn our will and our lives over to the care of God."[17] We are not all alcoholics, but the power of sin is greater than any of us can handle on our own.

Honesty. Next, we need to examine ourselves and admit the wrong we have thought, said, or done, as well as our sins of omission. This can be difficult, since our proud fallen nature does not like to admit its failings[18] and since our wrongdoing is sometimes a response to what other people have done. Nevertheless, we must accept responsibility for whatever we did, however it came about, and resist the temptation to blame others.

Sorrow for sin. This is also called "contrition" (see Catechism 1451–53). Remembering God's love for us and for the person we have wronged, as well as reflecting on God's future judgment on wrongdoing, can help us sincerely regret what we have done. Healthy, godly sorrow that leads to change differs from worldly sorrow, characterized by self-condemnation, guilt feelings, and a lack of hope (2 Cor 7:9–11).

Renunciation. This is the determination to not commit this wrongdoing again and to avoid, as much as possible, the circumstances that could tempt us in the future. This hatred of sin or determined avoidance of sin arises from genuine sorrow and helps make repentance effective.

Asking forgiveness. We must explicitly ask forgiveness from God and, unless it would cause more harm than good, from the person whom we have wronged.[19] It is best to do this simply and straightforwardly: "I was wrong for doing or saying X. Will you forgive me?" This is better than a vague "I'm sorry." While it is appropriate to pray for God's forgiveness as soon as we become aware of our fault, it is also important to confess our sin in the sacrament of Reconciliation as soon as possible if the nature of the wrong is serious (Catechism 1441–58). If we want to receive forgiveness, we must also forgive those who have wronged us (Matt 6:14–15).

---

17. "The Twelve Steps of Alcoholics Anonymous," Alcoholics Anonymous, http://www.aa.org/en_pdfs/smf-121_en.pdf.

18. Some people have the opposite problem of scrupulosity, accusing themselves of sin for very small imperfections or for inappropriate thoughts or feelings that are not deliberately chosen. Knowing that God loves us despite our faults, which he knows well, can help us face the truth about ourselves with confidence and hope (Rom 5:8–10; 8:31–39).

19. It is generally unwise and counterproductive to ask a person's forgiveness for sins of thought against him or her.

Making restitution. This is sometimes called "making amends," "satisfaction" (Catechism 1459), or "doing penance" (Catechism 1434–39). It entails making up for what we have done wrong by doing what lies in our power to restore what we have stolen or damaged, including a person's reputation, and to renew our relationship with God and with whomever else we have offended. It is fitting to demonstrate our change of heart by conduct that is opposite to what we did wrong; for example, if we have spoken harshly, we speak respectfully and graciously to and about that person.

The Worship of Heaven

Revelation 4:1–11

Having spoken to the seven churches to reveal their present condition, "what is happening" (1:19), the risen Jesus now summons John into heaven so that he may see "what will happen afterwards" (1:19), thus introducing the next section of the book. Chapters 4 and 5 belong together. Chapter 4 reveals the beautiful and majestic creator of the universe, seated on a throne and receiving the worship of his heavenly court. Chapter 5 reveals the slaughtered Lamb through whom God's plan of salvation will be made known and accomplished.

John's vision of God resembles those witnessed by three biblical prophets who preceded him: Isaiah (Isa 6:1–8), Ezekiel (Ezek 1–2), and Daniel (Dan 7:9–27). God's throne room in heaven resembles Israel's tabernacle and temple, not by accident, since according to Exodus, the earthly structures were built according to the pattern of God's temple in heaven (Exod 26:30; Heb 8:5; see sidebar, "God's Temple," pp. 186–87).

In an analogous way, John's visions of heavenly worship in Revelation inspired the liturgy of the early Church. Since Christian worship is a participation in the liturgy of heaven, it is not surprising that the heavenly worship depicted in Revelation has exercised an immense influence on Christian liturgy and hymnody ever since.

God's Throne in Heaven (4:1–6a)

¹After this I had a vision of an open door to heaven, and I heard the trumpetlike voice that had spoken to me before, saying, "Come up here and

I will show you what must happen afterwards." ²At once I was caught up
in spirit. A throne was there in heaven, and on the throne sat ³one whose
appearance sparkled like jasper and carnelian. Around the throne was a
halo as brilliant as an emerald. ⁴Surrounding the throne I saw twenty-four
other thrones on which twenty-four elders sat, dressed in white garments
and with gold crowns on their heads. ⁵From the throne came flashes of
lightning, rumblings, and peals of thunder. Seven flaming torches burned
in front of the throne, which are the seven spirits of God. ⁶In front of the
throne was something that resembled a sea of glass like crystal.

OT: Exod 19:16–20; 24:9–11; Ezek 1:26–28; Zech 4
NT: Matt 19:28 // Luke 22:30; 2 Cor 12:1–5
Catechism: heavenly liturgy, 1089–90, 1139

John sees an **open door to heaven,** indicating that God is making his heavenly   **4:1**
dwelling accessible to the prophet.¹ Simultaneously, John hears the same voice he
heard before (1:10), the voice of the risen Lord, which sounds like a trumpet and
invites him, **Come up here.** Jesus tells John he will **show** him **what must happen
afterwards.** Not only does this phrase signal a new section of the book after the
seven oracles that pertain to "what *is* happening" (following the program of 1:19);
these words also indicate that the *purpose* of John's entry into heaven is to receive
divine revelation. The content of that revelation is contained in a sealed scroll that
John will see in chapter 5, but whose contents he will not learn until chapter 10.

At once, John tells us, "I was in the Spirit" (more precise than the NABRE's   **4:2–3**
I was caught up in spirit). While Christians are summoned to live all their
lives "in the Spirit" (Rom 8:9; Gal 5:16, 25) and to pray "in the Spirit" (1 Cor
14:15; Eph 6:18; Jude 20), in Revelation the phrase "I was in the Spirit" occurs
three other times to indicate special moments of prophetic revelation (1:10;
17:3; 21:10).

The NABRE omits John's exclamation "Behold!"—"Pay attention!"—as he
reports seeing **a throne.** Revelation mentions God's throne forty times. One
scholar remarks: "From first to last John's vision is dominated by this symbol
of divine sovereignty. The final reality which will still be standing when heaven
and earth have disappeared is the great white throne" (20:11).²

---

1. Other examples of heaven opening for special events: Gen 28:17; Ps 78:23; Matt 3:16. †Dispensa-
tionalist Christians interpret the words "Come up here" in Rev 4:1 to refer to a time when Christ will
†rapture true Christians to heaven before "the great tribulation." However, nothing in the immediate
context of this verse suggests a rapture of the Church. For more, see the Revelation Resources at www
.CatholicScriptureCommentary.com.
2. George B. Caird, *A Commentary on the Revelation of Saint John the Divine* (New York: Harper
& Row, 1966), 62.

John's vision of God seated on the throne resembles Ezekiel's vision into the opened heavens (1:1, 26–28). However, unlike Ezekiel (1:26–27), John does not attempt to describe the figure sitting on the throne, except by comparison with precious jewels and light. His **appearance sparkled like jasper**, a reddish jewel (though found in other colors as well) and **carnelian**, a fiery red stone. **Around the throne was a halo**, or "rainbow," as in Ezek 1:28, **brilliant as an emerald**, typically green in color. Although some commentators assign them more specific meanings, nothing indicates that the resplendent jewels and halo are intended to reveal anything other than the majesty and splendor and beauty of God, who "dwells in unapproachable light" (1 Tim 6:16).

4:4   Around the throne John sees **twenty-four other thrones on which twenty-four elders sat**. The twenty-four elders represent the entire people of God—those of the Old and the New Covenants—in worship before God's throne. Revelation refers to these "elders" exactly twelve times.[3] In Scripture the number twelve symbolizes the people of God. The gates of the new Jerusalem are inscribed with the names of the twelve tribes of Israel, and the foundations of the city are inscribed with the names of the twelve apostles (21:12–14), suggesting that the twenty-four elders represent all God's people.

In Revelation, these elders worship, help lead antiphonal praises (5:8; 11:16; 19:4), and offer to God the prayers of his people as incense (5:8). All of these are priestly functions.[4] Their **white garments** indicate holiness fitting to ministers in God's heavenly throne room. Their **gold crowns**, like their thrones, show that they share in God's kingly rule (like the martyrs and saints in 20:4). The elders thus epitomize the fullness of the dignity that Christ has bestowed on God's people as "a kingdom, priests for his God and Father" (1:6).

While some regard the twenty-four elders as *angelic* representatives of God's people, it seems more likely that John understands them as *human* representatives of God's people already reigning with Christ (20:4).[5] It is characteristic of human beings rather than angels to sit on thrones and wear crowns. Also, the term "elder" (Greek *presbyteros*, from which "priest" is derived) is not used in the Bible of angels, but *was* familiar to John and his readers as the office of the church leaders, the presbyters, who presided at their liturgies.[6] The idea of worship led by presbyters at the front and surrounded by angels would have

---

3. Rev 4:4, 10; 5:5, 6, 8, 11, 14; 7:11, 13; 11:16; 14:3; 19:4.

4. It is possible that they are also heavenly counterparts of the heads of the twenty-four divisions of priests who served in the OT temple (1 Chron 24:1–19).

5. John and his readers were probably aware of Jesus' promise to his apostles that "in the new age" they would "sit on twelve thrones, judging the twelve tribes of Israel" (Matt 19:28).

6. See Acts 14:23; 15:2; 1 Tim 4:14; 5:17; James 5:14. During the NT period the terms "presbyter" and "bishop" were used interchangeably (see 1 Tim 3:1–2; 5:17–19; Titus 1:5–7). Within a generation,

seemed entirely appropriate and familiar to early Christians, who understood that their Eucharistic celebrations were a participation in the worship of heaven (Heb 10:19–22; 12:12).

From the throne issue **flashes of lightning, rumblings, and peals of thun-** **der**. A booming thunderstorm calls to mind God's awesome greatness, which human beings are powerless to resist. In Scripture, lightning and thunder often accompany a theophany, a manifestation of God. They occur when God bestows his covenant on Israel at Mount Sinai (Exod 19:16) and delivers his people on other occasions (Exod 9:23; 2 Sam 22:14–15). Lightning is evident when he calls Ezekiel and reveals Israel's future to him (Ezek 1:13). In Revelation, these particular divine portents recur with escalating intensity at the climax of each series of divine interventions—at the seventh seal (8:5), the seventh trumpet (11:19), and the seventh bowl (16:18). The **seven flaming torches** that **burned in front of the throne** recall the flames atop the seven-branched lampstand, the menorah, that stood in the sanctuary of the temple in Jerusalem. John's mention of **the seven spirits of God** recalls Zechariah's vision of seven lamps of a menorah fed by a single bowl of oil (Zech 4:2). There the seven lamps represent the divine Spirit and "the eyes of the LORD that range over the whole earth" (4:10b; see also v. 6). God sees and acts in the world by means of his omnipresent Spirit (see comments on 1:4 and sidebar, "The Seven Spirits of God," p. 46). The **sea of glass like crystal** in front of the throne probably alludes both to the large bronze basin of water, called the "sea," in Solomon's temple (1 Kings 7:23–26) and to the waters above the "dome" (Gen 1:7), the firmament that covers the earth and on which God's throne rests in Ezekiel's vision (Ezek 1:26). From below, the dome is visible as the sky, the translucent boundary between earth and heaven that shines with God's splendor (Ps 19:2).

4:5–6a

The opening verses of this vision evoke awe and wonder at the majesty of God. They help John's readers realize that this is a revelatory moment like that of Moses and the elders of Israel at Sinai (Exod 24:10), like that of Ezekiel (1:26–28). John is gazing on God in his heavenly throne room. What will happen next?

The Heavenly Worship (4:6b–11)

In the center and around the throne, there were four living creatures cov- **ered with eyes in front and in back. [7]The first creature resembled a lion,**

however, the letters of Ignatius of Antioch (ca. 108) distinguish between the unique role of the bishop (*episkopos*) and that of the presbyters (*presbyteroi*), or priests.

the second was like a calf, the third had a face like that of a human being, and the fourth looked like an eagle in flight. [8]The four living creatures, each of them with six wings, were covered with eyes inside and out. Day and night they do not stop exclaiming:

> "Holy, holy, holy is the Lord God almighty,
> who was, and who is, and who is to come."

[9]Whenever the living creatures give glory and honor and thanks to the one who sits on the throne, who lives forever and ever, [10]the twenty-four elders fall down before the one who sits on the throne and worship him, who lives forever and ever. They throw down their crowns before the throne, exclaiming:

> [11]"Worthy are you, Lord our God,
> to receive glory and honor and power,
> for you created all things;
> because of your will they came to be and were created."

OT: Isa 6:1–4; Ezek 1:13–15, 19–22; 10
Catechism: praise for creation, 295

4:6b–8   Between the throne and the twenty-four elders, John describes **four living creatures** that resemble the four living creatures, called "cherubim," that Ezekiel saw in his visions (1:13–15, 19–22; 10:1–22). In the Old Testament the cherubim are angelic beings who guarded the garden of Eden after the fall (Gen 3:24) and whose images were placed above the ark of the covenant, inside the holy of holies of the tabernacle and temple (Exod 25:18–22).[7] Various Old Testament Scriptures describe the Lord as enthroned upon or above the cherubim,[8] which is close but not identical to the idea here: they are described as **in the center and around the throne**. In Ezekiel's visions these creatures have wheels with eyes all around, are animated by the Spirit of God, and move in unison as the Lord's flying chariot. Here in John's vision the four living creatures also are **covered with eyes in front and in back**, indicating vigilance and boundless awareness of everything taking place in creation, but they remain stationed by God's throne, lead the praises of heaven, and in the heavenly liturgy announce important divine interventions on earth (6:1, 3, 5–7; 15:7). Instead of each creature having four faces (Ezek 1:10), here the angelic beings differ from one another, each having a single face, that of a **lion**, a **calf** (or "ox"), a **human being**,

---

7. There were two gold cherubim above the ark in the tabernacle and temple, not four. However, in Solomon's temple there were also four carved figures of cherubim on the four walls (1 Kings 6:29).
8. See 1 Sam 4:4; 2 Sam 6:2; 2 Kings 19:15; 1 Chron 13:6; Ps 80:2; 99:1; Isa 37:16.

The Four Living Creatures and the Four Evangelists

LIVING TRADITION

Christian iconography associates the four living creatures with the four Gospels. Craig R. Koester explains:

> Beginning in the late second century AD, Christian writers identified the four creatures in the heavenly throne room with the four gospel writers . . . [although first-century readers] would not have understood the creatures in this way. . . . Matthew's gospel has the human face because it begins with a genealogy that traces Jesus' human origins. Mark is identified with the lion because it begins by calling Jesus the 'son of God,' referring to his royal power. Luke is the ox, since his gospel begins in the temple where sacrifices were made. John is the eagle, since his soaring introduction of Jesus as the Word of God points to his heavenly origin.[a]

Although correlations between the four Gospels and the four living creatures were common among the Church Fathers, the Fathers differed as to which Gospel they assigned to each creature.[b]

a. Craig R. Koester, *Revelation and the End of All Things* (Grand Rapids: Eerdmans, 2001), 73n.
b. Osborne, *Revelation*, 233, offers a helpful chart of the diverse assignments of Irenaeus, Victorinus, Augustine, Athanasius, and modern Christians.

or an **eagle**. Although no explicit explanation is provided, many commentators believe the living creatures "represent the whole of animate creation . . . , perhaps detailing what is noblest, strongest, wisest, and swiftest."[9]

The living creatures that John sees also resemble the seraphim that Isaiah the prophet saw in his temple vision:

> I saw the Lord seated on a high and lofty throne, with the train of his garment filling the temple. Seraphim were stationed above; each of them had six wings: with two they covered their faces, with two they covered their feet, and with two they hovered. One cried out to the other:
>
> > "Holy, holy, holy is the LORD of hosts!
> > All the earth is filled with his glory!" (Isa 6:1–4)

Like Isaiah's seraphim, John's living creatures have **six wings**, indicating the capacity for swift flight. The fact that John's four living creatures differ from

9. Osborne, *Revelation*, 234.

Ezekiel's cherubim, which in turn differ from Isaiah's seraphim, indicates that the exalted beings closest to God cannot be depicted adequately in any one vision or in any single formulation of words.

The living creatures in Revelation never stop exclaiming **Holy, holy, holy . . .** When applied to God the word "holy" means totally other, different, transcendent. The strangeness of the four living creatures and everything else offers a faint suggestion of how totally "other" and beyond us God is. Along with the word "love," the word "holy" is the most accurate way to describe God. To proclaim him as thrice-holy indicates he is holy in the superlative degree and hints at the trinity of Persons. The creatures call him **the Lord God almighty**, God's most solemn title, pronounced seven times in Revelation.[10]

In heaven the praise of God never ceases, and the Church's liturgy on earth enters into the perpetual heavenly worship in progress. Rather than announce that God's glory fills the earth as the seraphim explain (Isa 6:3), the four living creatures ceaselessly proclaim God as eternal with the words twice used to describe God at the beginning of the book (1:4, 8): **who was, and who is, and who is to come**. The final phrase focuses on God as the one who will intervene decisively in history to bring salvation.

4:9–11   The constantly repeated refrain "holy, holy, holy" communicates the **glory and honor and thanks** that the living creatures render to God, who infinitely transcends human categories and description. He is **the one who sits on the throne, who lives forever and ever**. This perpetual exclamation of praise by the four living creatures who represent creation elicits a liturgical response from **the twenty-four elders**, presbyters, who represent God's people of the Old and New Testament. They prostrate themselves and **worship him**. Their bodily action expresses honor and submission to the maximum degree; they offer the kind of adoration that belongs to God alone. Their words proclaim God's eternity: he is the one **who lives for ever and ever**.

Another gesture and more praise addressed to God complete the liturgical action: the twenty-four elders **throw down their crowns before the throne**. Although they are themselves exalted figures who sit on thrones and wear golden crowns, the elders humble themselves before God and declare his unique worthiness **to receive glory and honor and power**. It is easy enough to understand that God should receive glory and honor, but how can the all-powerful God *receive* power from anyone else? He cannot. This is poetic shorthand meaning that God deserves to receive *acknowledgment* of his supreme power (see Rom 1:20). God is praised as the author of everything that exists: **for you created all**

10. Rev 1:8; 4:8; 11:17; 15:3; 16:7; 19:6; 21:22.

C. S. Lewis on the Reason for Praise

C. S. Lewis tells of encountering, early on in his Christian life, "a stumbling block in the demand ... made by all religious people that we should 'praise' God; still more in the suggestion that God Himself demanded it."[a] It suggested to his mind a very unappealing image of God, like that of people we know who constantly want to be admired and flattered.

Lewis came to understand the demand to worship by analogy:

> Many objects both in Nature and in Art may be said to deserve, or merit, or demand, admiration.... [Likewise, God] is that object to admire which ... is simply to be awake, to have entered the real world.... I did not see that it is in the process of being worshipped that God communicates his presence to men.... But the most obvious fact about praise—whether of God or anything—strangely escaped me.... I had never noticed that all enjoyment spontaneously overflows into praise.... The world rings with praise—lovers praising their mistresses, readers their favourite poet, walkers praising the countryside, players praising their favorite game.... I had not noticed how the humblest, and at the same time most balanced and capacious minds, praised most, while the cranks, misfits and malcontents praised least.... Except where intolerably adverse circumstances interfere, praise almost seems to be inner health made audible.... I think we delight to praise what we enjoy because the praise not merely expresses but completes the enjoyment; it is its appointed consummation.[b]

a. C. S. Lewis, *Reflections on the Psalms* (New York: Harcourt, Brace & World, 1958), 91. I heartily recommend the entire book, especially chap. 9, "A Word about Praising."

b. Ibid., selections from 92–95.

things. Everything depends on his gracious **will**, by which all persons, animals, and things **came to be and were created.**

Reflection and Application (4:10–11)

The words of the twenty-four elders point to a truth we do not often think about: we owe God gratitude, honor, and praise for our very existence, even more than we owe honor and gratitude to our parents. Do we think to praise God for the wonder of our existence and of all creation? Two psalms that can help us to do this are Ps 104 and 139.

The Lamb and the Scroll

Revelation 5:1–14

This chapter continues John's report of what he saw when he passed through the open door to heaven. After witnessing heaven's continuous adoration of God, John sees a scroll and learns of a seemingly insuperable obstacle to the fulfillment of God's plan and of his prophetic commission (1:19). The problem is resolved by the manifestation of the Lamb, the protagonist of Revelation. A series of liturgical acclamations reveal the significance of Jesus' death on the cross and his divine standing. The action begins when John notices an unusual object in the right hand of the transcendent and eternal Person seated on the throne.

John Sees a Mysterious Scroll (5:1–5)

[1]I saw a scroll in the right hand of the one who sat on the throne. It had writing on both sides and was sealed with seven seals. [2]Then I saw a mighty angel who proclaimed in a loud voice, "Who is worthy to open the scroll and break its seals?" [3]But no one in heaven or on earth or under the earth was able to open the scroll or to examine it. [4]I shed many tears because no one was found worthy to open the scroll or to examine it. [5]One of the elders said to me, "Do not weep. The lion of the tribe of Judah, the root of David, has triumphed, enabling him to open the scroll with its seven seals."

OT: Ezek 2:9–3:3; Dan 12:1–4, 9
NT: Heb 7:14

John sees a **scroll**[1] with **writing on both sides** (literally, "on the inside and **5:1** on the back," NRSV) held **in the right hand** of God. The scroll confirms the relationship of John's vision to that of Ezekiel. Immediately after Ezekiel saw God on his cherubim throne-chariot, he was commissioned to speak God's word to Israel and was handed a scroll "covered with writing front and back" (Ezek 2:9–10). Normally scrolls were written only on one side, with just a label or title on the outside. Writing on both sides of a prophetic scroll suggests the superabundant divine revelation it contains. The prophet Ezekiel was commanded first to eat and then to announce the content of the scroll (3:1–4). The prophet John will receive a similar command in chapter 10.

John may have surmised that his scroll, like the one shown to Ezekiel, contains God's plan of future judgment and salvation, although the fact that it is **sealed with seven seals** suggests it is even more important. Seals on documents in the ancient world fulfilled a variety of functions. A sealed letter would be opened only by the addressee; a sealed will would be opened only after the death of the testator in the presence of witnesses. Here the seals indicate that the scroll will remain unread until the authorized person opens it at the proper time. The fact that there are seven of them underscores the importance of the scroll, since that number implies completeness or finality.

John watches as **a mighty angel**[2] loudly proclaims a question regarding **5:2–4** the opening of the scroll in the court liturgy of the heavenly throne room. Throughout Revelation various figures of the heavenly court—angels, elders, living creatures, even the altar itself—speak or carry out symbolic actions that reveal or accomplish God's will, presumably under the inspiration of the Spirit. The angel asks, **Who is worthy to open the scroll and break its seals?** The two phrases, which refer to the same thing—opening the scroll and breaking its seals—reinforce the solemnity of the question.

What does it mean to be worthy to open the scroll? The text does not directly say. The prophet Isaiah needed cleansing from his wickedness and sin even to look on God in his heavenly temple, or risk death (Isa 6:3–6). Must the revealer be sinless? Opening the scroll and disclosing its contents is a revelatory act. In Ezekiel's vision, God himself unrolled the scroll to reveal the divine plan that became the basis of the prophet's message (Ezek 2:9–10). Must the revealer be

---

1. Greek *biblion*, also translated "book," since up to the end of the first century most books were in the form of scrolls. Codexes (codices), resembling modern books, came into use starting at about that time and gradually replaced scrolls over the next few centuries.

2. A "mighty angel" appears twice more in Revelation, once in connection with a scroll containing God's judgments in 10:1, and again in 18:21, where Babylon's destruction is solemnly decreed with a powerful gesture.

divine? Suffice it to say that no created being in the whole universe, including the angels, is found **worthy to open the scroll or to examine it** (literally, "look into it," NRSV, RSV).

This provokes **many tears** on the part of the prophet. John has been invited into heaven to see "what must happen afterwards" (4:1). He perceives that the scroll before him contains the message he is called to prophesy, a revelation that indicates what God will do to rescue his people and establish his kingdom. Daniel received a revelation of this kind and was instructed to keep it secret, to "seal the book until the end time" (Dan 12:4). The time of the end has come, but its fulfillment appears hindered by the lack of someone worthy.

5:5   **One of the elders** interrupts the prophet's weeping to explain that there *is* someone worthy to open the scroll: **the lion of the tribe of Judah, the root of David**. To readers of Israel's Scriptures, this title can refer only to one person, namely, the †Messiah, David's royal descendant, who belongs to the tribe of Judah. Jacob's blessing in Gen 49:9–10 describes Judah, the ancestor of king David, as "like a lion," a person from whom "the scepter shall never depart." Isaiah foretells the coming of a Davidic king on whom the sevenfold gift of the Spirit rests, whose reign will bring the transformation of creation itself and who is "the root of Jesse" (Isa 11:1–10).[3] The elder explains that this royal lion has **triumphed** ("conquered," RSV; *nikaō*, the same Greek word used for "victor" in chaps. 2 and 3), qualifying him **to open the scroll with its seven seals**. John's Christian readers understand at once: Christ is risen! He has triumphed over death. He is the one who is worthy. And it is his victory that makes possible the revelation and implementation of the final phase of God's plan for the world, up to now kept secret in the scroll in the hand of the one on the throne.

The Lamb Receives the Scroll and the Worship of Heaven (5:6–10)

> **[6]Then I saw standing in the midst of the throne and the four living creatures and the elders, a Lamb that seemed to have been slain. He had seven horns and seven eyes; these are the [seven] spirits of God sent out into the whole world. [7]He came and received the scroll from the right hand of the one who sat on the throne. [8]When he took it, the four living creatures and the twenty-four elders fell down before the Lamb. Each of the elders held a**

3. Since the Messiah is *descended* from David, the expression "root of David" could seem out of place. But in both Hebrew and Greek the word translated "root" can also mean "stock" or "lineage." Thus the "root of Jesse" in Isa 11:10 refers to the same person mentioned as Jesse's "shoot" in Isa 11:1 (see also Sir 47:22).

harp and gold bowls filled with incense, which are the prayers of the holy ones. [9]They sang a new hymn:

> "Worthy are you to receive the scroll
> and to break open its seals,
> for you were slain and with your blood you purchased for God
> those from every tribe and tongue, people and nation.
> [10]You made them a kingdom and priests for our God,
> and they will reign on earth."

OT: Exod 12:6; 19:6; Ps 141:2; Isa 53:7; Zech 3:9; 4:10

NT: John 1:29; 1 Pet 2:4–5, 9

Catechism: Christ exalted in heaven, 662–64, 668; Christ's human knowledge, 471–74; the baptized a holy priesthood, 1140–44, 1268, 1273, 1546–47

Lectionary: 5:6–12: For the Triumph of the Holy Cross, for the Sacred Heart during Easter Season

What John has *heard* prepares the reader for the entrance of a powerful royal figure. What John *sees* takes us aback: the lion is **a Lamb**! Not only that, but the Lamb **seemed to have been slain**. The Greek word for "slain" is used of a person killed by violence or of an animal slaughtered for secular or sacrificial purposes. In John's vision, the depiction of Christ as a lamb recalls the lamb that Abraham promised God would provide (Gen 22:8 RSV), as well as the Passover lamb, whose blood protected the Israelites from the judgment that fell on Egypt (Exod 12:3–13), and the Suffering Servant, "a lamb led to slaughter" (the same Greek root as "slain" here), "struck for the sins of his people" (Isa 53:7–8). Other New Testament passages compare Jesus to a lamb. John the Baptist says, "Behold, the Lamb of God, who takes away the sin of the world" (John 1:29). Peter writes to the Christians in Asia: "You were ransomed . . . with the precious blood of Christ as of a spotless unblemished lamb" (1 Pet 1:18–19; see 1 Cor 5:7). Revelation uses the word "Lamb" to refer to Jesus more than any other title, exactly twenty-eight times—seven times four—to emphasize his completeness (seven) and universal significance (four).[4]

The language is paradoxical—a Lamb who is slain yet **standing**. The posture of Christ is significant: he is not lying in a tomb; he is upright, fully alive, and ready for action.[5] His location is also significant: he stands **in the midst of the**

5:6

---

4. "Christ" appears seven times; "Lord," used of both Jesus and God the Father, appears twenty-one times; "the Word of God," once; "son of man," twice. Revelation uses a different Greek word for "lamb" (*arnion* instead of *amnos*), but it does not seem that this word choice is significant (*arnion* appears in the LXX of Ps 114:4, 6; Jer 11:19; 50:45 [NABRE verse numbering]).

5. The NT depicts the posture and activity of the exalted Jesus in a variety of ways. Most often he is seated at the right hand of God, reigning with him (Matt 26:64; Mark 14:62; Luke 22:69; Eph 1:20; Col 3:1; Heb 8:1; 12:2); Mark 16:19–20 adds that from there Jesus works with his disciples, confirming their words with signs. Stephen the martyr sees Jesus standing at the right hand of God (Acts 7:55–56);

throne and the four living creatures and the elders. Although some interpret this as meaning that Jesus is at the very center of God's throne, it seems that the Lamb stands in front of the throne, since 5:7 indicates that he *comes* to receive the scroll from the hand of God.

Unlike the living creatures and elders, the Lamb does not bow or prostrate himself in worship; rather, he receives worship (5:9–14). John continues to describe the Lamb in symbolic terms: he has **seven horns**, signifying the fullness of power,[6] and **seven eyes**, signifying the fullness of knowledge (see comments on 4:6). John's explanation links the Lamb's omniscience to the Holy Spirit, **the [seven] spirits of God sent out into the whole world** (an allusion to Zech 3:9 and 4:10; see sidebar, "The Seven Spirits of God," p. 46). When the Word became flesh, he set aside his divine power and knowledge in a way that we cannot fully fathom (Matt 24:36; Phil 2:6–7). However, by having obediently accepted death on a cross to redeem the human race, the risen Christ, who has the fullness of the Spirit of God, again possesses the fullness of divine knowledge and power, now in his glorified human nature.

5:7   Now the action in the heavenly throne room can commence. The Lamb **came and received the scroll from the right hand** of God, the one seated **on the throne**. The transfer of the scroll indicates that the Lamb is entrusted with implementing and revealing God's plan to save the human race and to establish God's rule over the cosmos. Other biblical texts depict this moment in other ways: Dan 7:13–14 speaks of one like a son of man coming on the clouds to God and receiving eternal kingship. The New Testament often recalls Ps 110:1, where the †Messiah is invited to sit at God's right hand and rule until his enemies are defeated (e.g., Acts 2:33–35; 1 Cor 15:25–27; Heb 1:13). The response that immediately follows this symbolic action indicates its great significance. A fresh round of worship bursts forth, praising God for the entire work of salvation accomplished through Christ.

5:8   The creatures closest to God's throne respond first: **the four living creatures and the twenty-four elders fell down** (prostrated themselves) **before the Lamb**, who now receives the kind of adoration that is appropriate only to God (John 5:22–23; Acts 2:36; Phil 2:9–11). **Each of the elders held a harp and gold bowls filled with incense**. Harps in ancient Israel had ten or twelve strings and were used to celebrate various joyous occasions, yet especially to accompany the singing of psalms and hymns in Israel's temple worship.[7] Incense was placed

---

Paul says Jesus is at God's right hand interceding for us (Rom 8:34); Rev 3:21 speaks of Jesus sitting with his Father on his throne.

6. In the OT, "horn" often symbolizes power; see Ps 18:3; 89:18; Dan 7:20–21; 8:5–9.

7. See, for instance, Ps 33:2; 43:4; 150:3. In Revelation, harps also appear in worship scenes in 14:2; 15:2.

in a gold bowl alongside "the bread of the Presence" (Exod 25:29–30; Lev 24:7 RSV; "showbread," NABRE) and was burned as a sacrifice on the golden altar of incense in the morning and the evening (Exod 30:7–8). The burning of incense signified the offering of acceptable worship to God ("a sweet-smelling aroma") and came to symbolize prayer that God accepts (Ps 141:2; Luke 1:10).[8] John explains that the bowls of incense that the elders (presbyters) are offering **are the prayers of the holy ones**. In the New Testament the "holy ones" ("saints" in other translations) refers primarily to the members of the Church made holy through faith and baptism, although it can also refer to God's faithful who have died (e.g., Matt 27:52). The striking truth that this verse reveals is that the petitions and praises of Christians arise like sweet-smelling incense in the throne room of God, the center from which God's plan unfolds. The prayers of God's people help shape the course of history (James 5:16–18).[9]

The living creatures and the elders who represent God's people (see comments on 4:4) **sang a new hymn**. Several psalms exhort God's people to sing "a new song" to the Lord perhaps in response to a recent act of salvation.[10] In Isa 42:10 the invitation to sing a new song is a response to the salvation that God will bring about at the climax of history through his servant.

5:9–10

The new hymn of heavenly worship addressed to the Lamb finally explains what made the Lamb **worthy to receive the scroll / and to break open its seals**, that is, to reveal the secret plan of God. The song explains what the Lamb has done that qualifies him to do what no one else could do. John has already mentioned it in his †doxology to Christ at the beginning of the letter (1:5b–6). The new song begins by naming a very strange achievement: **You were slain** (see 5:6). As in the translation, the Greek verb is passive: the Lamb was the object of violence. Two statements explain what the Lamb's slaughter accomplished: first, he has **purchased**—acquired, "ransomed" (NRSV)—human beings **from every tribe and tongue, people and nation** at the price of his **blood**, freeing us from sin (1:5b), Satan (12:9–11; 20:1–3, 10), and death (1:18; 21:4). One can compare this purchase to the ransoming of prisoners of war, kidnap victims, or slaves. Of course, no payment is made to the evil powers, but rather, the Lamb, by accepting death on a cross, offered himself to the Father in love (Eph 5:2; Rev 1:5), and God accepted his perfect self-gift (Heb 9:11–15; 10:12–20). This fourfold description of the redeemed indicates the universality of Christ's salvation: no ethnic group is left out. They are not ransomed to be their own

---

8. Osborne, *Revelation*, 258–59.

9. If the elders are human representatives of God's people, then this text also points to the priestly intercession of those in glory for the Church on earth (see 20:4–6).

10. Ps 33:3; 40:4; 96:1; 98:1; 144:9; 149:1; also Jdt 16:1.

masters, but **for God**. As Paul says, "you are not your own. . . . For you have been purchased at a price" (1 Cor 6:19–20). The price of our redemption never ceases to evoke wonder. As Peter says, "You were ransomed from your futile conduct, handed on by your ancestors, not with perishable things like silver or gold but with the precious blood of Christ as of a spotless unblemished lamb" (1 Pet 1:18–19). Precious indeed.

The second, climactic statement explains that Christ's death has achieved something that God promised centuries earlier: **You made them a kingdom and priests for our God.**[11] God expressed this gracious intention for his people when he first made a covenant with Israel at Sinai: "If you obey me completely and keep my covenant, you will be my treasured possession. . . . You will be to me a kingdom of priests, a holy nation" (Exod 19:5–6). This promise had an initial fulfillment in the kingdom of Israel and in Israel's temple worship. But now the slain Lamb's blood has fulfilled the promise that God's people will be "a kingdom and priests" in so superior a way that the earlier fulfillment is not even mentioned. Those who have been consecrated priests by the action of the Lamb presently worship God in his spiritual temple on earth (Eph 2:18–22; 1 Pet 2:4–5; Rev 11:1–2) and share in his kingdom (Rev 1:9). After death they worship in his heavenly temple and reign with him (7:9–17; 20:4–6). The Messiah's kingdom and priests includes both men and women, Jews and †Gentiles, whom God planned to bless from the beginning through Abraham and his offspring, Jesus (Gen 12:3; 22:18; Gal 3:6–16, 28).

As the Venerable Bede says, "Since the King of kings and the celestial Priest united us to his own body by offering himself up for us, there is no one of the [people of God] who is spiritually deprived of the office of the priesthood, since everyone is a member of the eternal Priest."[12] Although this hymn describes all of the followers of the Lamb as priests, the fact that they form a single "kingdom" (1:6; 5:10) indicates that their priesthood is exercised corporately. First Peter confirms this by speaking of the Church as a single "priesthood," using a Greek word that indicates a body of priests (1 Pet 2:5, 9).

It might seem that the Messiah's making his followers "a kingdom" refers simply to his uniting people from every nationality under his kingship. But the phrase that follows indicates that more is meant: **and they will reign**. Not only are Christ's followers his subjects; he also grants them to share in his royal

11. The wording of Rev 5:10—"a kingdom and priests"—is slightly different from that of Exod 19:6, "a kingdom of priests." The Hebrew of Exod 19:6 can be translated either way. Other ancient Greek and Aramaic translations of Exod 19:6 interpret it the way Revelation does. First Peter 2:9 follows the LXX in translating it yet a third way as "a royal priesthood."

12. *Explanation of the Apocalypse* 1.6, in ACCS 12:6.

authority. The idea that God's people will reign is not new; it is an ancient promise from the same vision in which Daniel saw "one like a son of man" come before God to receive an eternal kingdom: "the holy ones of the Most High shall receive the kingship, to possess it forever and ever" (Dan 7:13–14, 18, 22, 27).[13] The book of Revelation returns to this promise of the reign of God's holy people in 20:4, 6, and 22:5. It is noteworthy that the future reign of Christ's people will take place **on earth**. This promise attains its complete fulfillment in Rev 21–22, when the new Jerusalem descends from heaven and God's kingdom is established on a renewed earth, where his people reign with him.

Reflection and Application (5:9–10)

What does it mean that the Lamb has made his followers priests? First, the action reveals Christ's divinity, since to establish priests is a divine prerogative, not something human beings can do. Second, it tells of the extraordinary efficacy of Christ's death. Scripture reveals the radical inability of sinful human beings to draw near to God on our own. The ritual for the ordination of priests described in Leviticus involved first a sacrifice for sin that removed the obstacles to a priest entering God's presence (8:14–17), and then other sacrifices to consecrate and elevate him to a priestly relationship with God (8:18–29). However, Rev 5:9–10 indicates that one sacrifice of the slain Lamb suffices both to cleanse from sin and to transform human beings, making us fit for God's presence. Albert Vanhoye writes,

> Christ has won for mankind a profound transformation, which introduces them into a relationship with God, his Father, that is free from all obstacles. This relationship which is available to each and every one of the faithful makes them "priests," that is to say, sanctified persons who are able to approach God in order to offer him worship.[14]

> No traditional priest, whether Jewish or pagan, had ever found himself in a like situation with truly free access to God. From this point of view, therefore, no one was so truly a priest as Christians are now.[15]

How are all Christians called to function as priests? None of the three texts in Revelation that speak of the priestly dignity of Christians explicitly states what

---

13. In the LXX version of Dan 7:14, 18, and 22, the Greek word translated "kingship" (*basileia*) is the same word translated "kingdom" in Rev 5:10.

14. Albert Vanhoye, *The Old Testament Priests and the New Priest* (Petersham, MA: St. Bede's Publications, 1980), 290; see also 285–90.

15. Ibid., 289.

Baptismal and Ministerial Priesthood

LIVING TRADITION

The Catechism (1546–47) explains that there are two kinds of participation in the one priesthood of Christ.

> Christ, high priest and unique mediator, has made of the Church "a kingdom, priests for his God and Father" (Rev 1:6; cf. Rev 5:9–10; 1 Pet 2:5, 9). The whole community of believers is, as such, priestly. The faithful exercise their baptismal priesthood through their participation, each according to his own vocation, in Christ's mission as priest, prophet, and king....
>
> The ministerial or hierarchical priesthood of bishops and priests, and the common priesthood of all the faithful participate, "each in its own proper way, in the one priesthood of Christ." While being "ordered one to another," they differ essentially (*Lumen Gentium* 10, par. 2). In what sense? While the common priesthood of the faithful is exercised by the unfolding of baptismal grace—a life of faith, hope, and charity, a life according to the Spirit—the ministerial priesthood is at the service of the common priesthood. It is directed at the unfolding of the baptismal grace of all Christians. The ministerial priesthood is a *means* by which Christ unceasingly builds up and leads his Church.

it means in practice. Nevertheless, Revelation suggests that Christian worship (11:1–2; 14:1–5), prayers (5:8; 8:3), martyrdom (6:9; 12:11), and testimony (11:3–7; 12:11) express this priesthood.

Other New Testament texts say more about how the common priesthood of Christians is practiced. Romans 12:1–2 exhorts Christians to "offer your bodies," meaning your entire lives, as a "living sacrifice." The Letter to the Hebrews summons Christians to worship (10:19–25) and speaks of our having "an altar" from which the priests of the Old Covenant "have no right to eat" (13:10). It exhorts us to "continually offer God a sacrifice of praise" and "to do good and to share what you have"—acts that it describes as "sacrifices" that please God (13:15–16).

Peter urges us "like living stones" to let ourselves be built "into a spiritual house to be a holy priesthood to offer spiritual sacrifices acceptable to God through Jesus Christ" (1 Pet 2:5). These "spiritual sacrifices" likely refer both to participation in the Eucharist and to life lived in the Holy Spirit. A few verses later Peter explains God's purpose in making us "a chosen race, a royal priesthood, a holy nation, a people of his own": it is so that we "'may announce the praises' of him" who called us "out of darkness into his wonderful light" (1 Pet 2:9)—an announcement that constitutes witness as well as worship.

The Whole Universe Worships God and the Lamb (5:11–14)

[11]I looked again and heard the voices of many angels who surrounded the throne and the living creatures and the elders. They were countless in number, [12]and they cried out in a loud voice:

> "Worthy is the Lamb that was slain
> to receive power and riches, wisdom and strength,
> honor and glory and blessing."

[13]Then I heard every creature in heaven and on earth and under the earth and in the sea, everything in the universe, cry out:

> "To the one who sits on the throne and to the Lamb
> be blessing and honor, glory and might,
> forever and ever."

[14]The four living creatures answered, "Amen," and the elders fell down and worshiped.

OT: Dan 7:9–10, 13–14
NT: Phil 2:10; Heb 12:22
Catechism: the celebrants of the heavenly liturgy, 1136–39
Lectionary: Third Sunday of Easter (Year C)

John sees and hears **many angels** who form a third ring around **the throne** beyond **the living creatures and the elders**. The NABRE describes the angels as **countless in number**. The Greek literally says, "myriads of myriads and thousands of thousands." A "myriad," equal to ten thousand, was the highest number used in the Greco-Roman world. This vision of myriads of angels before the throne of God depicts the fulfillment of what Daniel sees in his vision before the one like a son of man comes on the clouds to receive eternal kingship from God (Dan 7:9–10, 13–14). These glorious creatures praise the risen Jesus **in a loud voice**. It is precisely because **the Lamb** has been **slain** that all the angels acclaim him as **worthy** of divine honors. While in 4:11 all of heaven praised God the Father for his work of creation, here all of heaven adores the human but glorified Christ, because of his work of redemption accomplished on the cross.[16]

5:11–12

The seven honors ascribed to Jesus in verse 12 are preceded in Greek by a single article, a way of indicating that they are aspects of a single reality. They

---

16. John 17 and Phil 2:9–11 make much the same point.

attribute to Christ qualities that belong to God. The first four can belong to human rulers, but characterize God in a superlative degree: **power and riches, wisdom and strength**. Wealth and wisdom are traditionally regarded as aspects of God's greatness (Ps 104:24; Prov 8:22; Hag 2:7–8). The last three express the worship due to the Lamb in view of his divine standing: **honor and glory and blessing**.

5:13–14   The adoration continues to radiate outward to involve **every creature**. The participation of the entire universe is indicated by the enumeration of its regions: **heaven . . . earth . . . under the earth**, and **sea**. This acclamation accords worship equally **to the one who sits on the throne and to the Lamb**. This is an extraordinary statement to arise from a Jewish monotheist like John, but it is the characteristic claim made about Jesus by the early Church.[17] That this expression of praise—**blessing and honor, glory and might**—is all-encompassing and befits God is indicated by its being fourfold (see "Figurative Language and Symbolism" in the introduction, p. 28) and eternal: **forever and ever**. The four living creatures confirm the adoration of God and the Lamb with their **Amen**, as do the twenty-four **elders** by their prostrate worship.

While Acts 1:9 depicts Jesus' ascension from the perspective of earth, the vision of Rev 4–5 depicts Jesus' exaltation to the fullness of divine authority from the perspective of heaven (see Eph 1:21–23).

A certain timelessness characterizes this vision: it begins in time with Christ's sacrifice and exaltation, but concludes when no opposition to God and Christ is found in heaven or on earth (v. 13). The universal praise of 5:13–14 thus anticipates the conclusion of the book and the end of history, the time when "at the name of Jesus / every knee should bend, / of those in heaven and on earth and under the earth" (Phil 2:10). According to the rest of Revelation, until that time comes human beings and superhuman entities will oppose the Lamb and his followers. The outcome, however, is never in doubt. The Lamb of God has truly conquered by his sacrificial death and resurrection.

This vision also reveals that Daniel's visions in the night of "one like a son of man" (Dan 7:9–27) were fulfilled in Jesus' resurrection and ascension. Both Daniel's and John's visions depict God seated on his throne in heaven, followed by a description of God's appearance and his heavenly servants who surround the throne (Dan 7:9–10; Rev 4:2–4). In each case an unlikely figure approaches God's throne and receives divine authority. In Dan 7:13–14 it is, "coming on the clouds of heaven One like a son of man," who receives universal and "everlasting dominion"; in Rev 5:5–7, 12–13, it is the slain Lamb. In both visions an outcome

17. John 1:1–18; 1 Cor 8:6; Phil 2:5–11; Heb 1:1–8.

Liturgy and Heavenly Worship

The Christian tradition has always understood that, as Pope John Paul II said, "the liturgy we celebrate on earth is a mysterious participation in the heavenly liturgy."[a] All genuine Christian prayer is a participation in the worship of heaven. According to Eph 2:6, we have already been raised with Christ and seated with him in the heavens (see Rom 8:30; Col 3:1–4; Catechism 1003). Baptized believers are in communion with heaven and God's throne because we have been joined to the risen Christ and have been filled with the Holy Spirit. This is true when we pray individually, but especially when we pray together (Matt 18:20) and, above all, when we participate in the Eucharist and re-present to God the sacrifice of his Son (Catechism 1366). Yet the participation in the life of heaven we now enjoy is incomplete and awaits a future fulfillment: "At present we see indistinctly, as in a mirror, but then face to face" (1 Cor 13:12). As the Catechism says, "In the earthly liturgy we share in a foretaste of that heavenly liturgy which is celebrated in the Holy City of Jerusalem toward which we journey as pilgrims [*Sancrosanctum Concilium* 8; cf. *Lumen Gentium* 50]" (1090).

To express this fact, the Christian liturgical tradition draws extensively from the depictions of heavenly worship in Revelation and from Old Testament temple worship, itself intended to mirror heavenly worship. The ways in which this is true are far too numerous to describe here and differ in the traditions of the Christian east and west, but include the following:

- prayers drawn from biblical praises like the "Holy, holy, holy" or composed with phrases taken directly from Scripture—for example, large portions of the Eucharistic prayer
- presbyters who preside at worship, who represent the people of God, and who wear special priestly vestments, often white robes
- the use of physical gestures that express honor and adoration, including standing, bowing, kneeling, prostrating oneself (at ordinations and religious consecrations), and so on
- the use of incense to worship God and to venerate people (the ministers and worshipers) and things (the altar, the book of the Gospels) that belong to God and are therefore holy
- the use of musical instruments and singing to adorn worship, to rouse hearts, and to express reverence and joy
- images and icons of Christ, the saints, and angels, recognized as present in Christian worship; in some Eastern Christian churches the screen before the sanctuary, the iconostasis, is decorated with such images

a. Angelus Address, November 3, 1996. For more, see the discussion and endnotes in Scott Hahn, *The Lamb's Supper* (New York: Doubleday, 1999), 116–29, 171–74.

is that "the kingship . . . of all the kingdoms under the heavens" is "given to the people of the holy ones of the Most High" (Dan 7:18, 27; Rev 5:10).[18]

Revelation 5 concludes with the Lamb standing before the throne, holding the scroll with the seven seals in his hand, poised to disclose and implement God's plan.

---

18. Beale and McDonough identify fourteen elements in basically the same order that Dan 7:9–28 has in common with Rev 4–5 (1098).

The First Six Seals

Revelation 6:1–17

Attention now focuses on the Lamb, who begins to open the seals one by one. Immediately, even before the scroll is unrolled and its contents revealed, calamities break out on earth.

John's audience knows that this portion of the Apocalypse is going to tell them something about the future, since the prophet was just told, "Come . . . and I will show you what must happen afterwards" (4:1; see 1:19). Although the content of the scroll in the hand of the Lamb remains unstated, insight about the present and the future bursts forth in the visions that mark the opening of each of the seven seals (chap. 6). This will be followed by visions that depict how God is taking care of his people (chap. 7), followed by visions of seven trumpets and accompanying events that announce the impending fulfillment of God's plan (chaps. 8–9). Not until chapter 10 do John's readers begin to learn something of the contents of the scroll. Meanwhile, the visions shed light on the circumstances in which John's readers find themselves—and in which we ourselves live.

This chapter describes the visions that accompany the opening of each of the first six seals. The first four visions depict calamities that are related to one another. The fifth vision is completely different, explaining God's delay in vindicating those who have been killed for their faithfulness to Jesus. The sixth depicts a set of †cosmic signs that immediately precede the final judgment and the end of history.

The Four Horsemen (6:1–8)

[1]Then I watched while the Lamb broke open the first of the seven seals, and I heard one of the four living creatures cry out in a voice like thunder,

"Come forward." [2]I looked, and there was a white horse, and its rider had a bow. He was given a crown, and he rode forth victorious to further his victories.

[3]When he broke open the second seal, I heard the second living creature cry out, "Come forward." [4]Another horse came out, a red one. Its rider was given power to take peace away from the earth, so that people would slaughter one another. And he was given a huge sword.

[5]When he broke open the third seal, I heard the third living creature cry out, "Come forward." I looked, and there was a black horse, and its rider held a scale in his hand. [6]I heard what seemed to be a voice in the midst of the four living creatures. It said, "A ration of wheat costs a day's pay, and three rations of barley cost a day's pay. But do not damage the olive oil or the wine."

[7]When he broke open the fourth seal, I heard the voice of the fourth living creature cry out, "Come forward." [8]I looked, and there was a pale green horse. Its rider was named Death, and Hades accompanied him. They were given authority over a quarter of the earth, to kill with sword, famine, and plague, and by means of the beasts of the earth.

OT: Ezek 14:21; Hosea 13:14; Zech 1:7–17; 6:1–8
NT: Matt 24:6–8; Rev 1:18; 20:14

6:1   Under normal circumstances, to break open seven seals on an ancient scroll would be comparable to opening a document that arrives in an envelope securely sealed with packaging tape. It might take a couple minutes to slit the tape and pry open the package, withdraw its contents, and examine what lies inside. In a similar way, the contents of a sealed scroll could not be read until all the seals were broken and the scroll was unrolled.[1]

But the Lamb's opening of this scroll is completely unlike opening any well-packaged document on earth. Each time the Lamb opens a seal, it sets in motion a vision. **One of the four living creatures** next to the throne, whose every movement is in perfect harmony with the will of the one seated on the throne, issues a command **in a voice like thunder**, as God himself sometimes speaks (Exod 19:19): **Come forward**. Each time one of the living creatures speaks, John, still in the heavenly throne room, sees a colored horse and rider ride forth

---

1. Some interpreters see the events that take place as the seals are opened as the contents of the scroll. They point to another kind of scroll found in Egypt, a folded contract deed in which wax seals are on the inside at each fold. As each seal is broken, more of the deed can be read. However, this rare kind of document is not what would ordinarily be understood by reference to a scroll bearing multiple seals. Also Revelation does not speak here of the scroll being read or identify the events at the opening of each seal with the scroll's contents.

with various frightening consequences on earth. The reader observes that it is the Lamb who was slain, now exalted to God's throne (3:21), who initiates the implementation of God's plan for human history by opening the seals. Christians can take comfort that the crucified and risen Lord "who loves us" (1:5) remains in control, no matter how dire the circumstances.

John's visions of four differently colored horses, each with a rider, allude to two visions of horses of similar colors in the book of Zechariah (1:7–17; 6:1–8). The historical context of Zechariah's visions is that God's people, having returned to Judah after the Babylonian exile, are suffering at the hands of pagan nations. In the first vision (1:7–17) the four riders on the colored mounts report that they have patrolled the earth and found it at peace. But an angel intercedes on behalf of God's people with the Lord, that he have mercy on Jerusalem. The Lord promises to disrupt the tranquility of the oppressing †nations and to restore his people:

> I am jealous for Jerusalem
>> and for Zion intensely jealous.
> I am consumed with anger
>> toward the complacent nations;
> When I was only a little angry,
>> they compounded the disaster.
> Therefore, thus says the LORD:
> I return to Jerusalem in mercy;
>> my house will be rebuilt there—oracle of the LORD of hosts—
>> and a measuring line will be stretched over Jerusalem. . . .
> My cities will again overflow with prosperity;
>> the LORD will again comfort Zion,
>> and will again choose Jerusalem. (Zech 1:14–17)

This promise in Zechariah foreshadows the story line of Revelation: God judges those who oppress his people, he rebuilds his temple, and he restores Jerusalem, a figurative name for the people of God.

In the second of Zechariah's visions, God sends out four teams of diversely colored horses pulling chariots, to bring his judgment on the nations that have oppressed his people (Zech 6:1–8). The chariots are identified as "the four winds,"[2] and the angel who interceded for Jerusalem is comforted that Babylon, "the land of the north," will be judged (Zech 6:8). The implication of the four

---

2. The RSV mistakenly translates Zech 6:5 to say that the four horses "are going forth to the four winds" instead of "are the four winds . . . coming forth," as other translations render it (e.g., NIV, NJB).

horses and riders in Revelation is that God is causing or allowing the world's peace to be disrupted, as a step toward his ultimate plan of saving his people and restoring Jerusalem (Rev 21–22).

6:2   The first **horse** is **white**, the color Roman generals wore in triumphal processions up the Capitoline Hill as a sign of their victory. But this rider **had a bow** in his hand, a disturbing symbol, since the cavalry known and feared for its ability to shoot a bow from charging warhorses belonged to the †Parthians, a warlike federation of tribes across the eastern frontier of the Roman Empire.[3] This rider wears **a crown**, signifying royal authority. The fact that it **was given** to him, a †divine passive verb, indicates that God has permitted him this power. The rider's goal is clearly military conquest, **victorious to further his victories** ("conquering and to conquer," RSV).[4]

6:3–4   The second horse is **red**, signaling bloodshed. This **rider was** permitted by God **to take peace away from the earth**. The consequence is that people **slaughter one another** in wars between nations, civil wars, or other forms of social unrest. To this end he is **given a huge sword**. Several civil wars wracked the Roman Empire during the first century, besides the ongoing threat of violence to its subject peoples posed by Roman power. John's vision may thus depict events that have begun to unfold by the time of his writing.

6:5–6   The third horse is **black**. Like those already mentioned, the third **rider** holds something in his hand, **a scale**. A **voice in the midst of the four living creatures**, signaling divine authorization, explains its meaning: **A ration of wheat costs a day's pay, and three rations of barley cost a day's pay.**[5] At these prices the poor would have nothing left over after eating, if they could even afford to eat. Wars often bring impoverishment, food shortages, and famine. In this case, however, not every kind of foodstuff is affected: the voice says **do not damage the olive oil or the wine**. The poor, who live on grain and even in good times have less to spend on oil and wine, experience the consequences of armed conflict the most.

6:7–8   The fourth horse is the worst and sums up the evils of the previous three. It is **pale green**, suggesting decay, and its rider is **named Death**. Strangely,

---

3. The Parthians twice defeated a Roman army, in 55 BC and AD 62, and attacked Roman territory several times in the AD 60s and 70s.

4. Some interpreters take this first rider to be Christ, since he is crowned and appears on a white horse as Christ does in 19:11. However, the close relationship with the other horses and riders here, which are not symbols of Christ, and with the similar visions in Zechariah—all argue against this view. Others take this rider as an antichrist figure, allowed for a time to conquer the people of God as the beast does in 13:7. Against this, however, is the fact that the persecution by the beast occurs toward the end of the narrative of Revelation, rather than here at the beginning.

5. Literally, the text says, "A quart of wheat for a denarius, and three quarts of barley for a denarius" (RSV). A denarius was the typical daily wage of a laborer. A quart of grain was about what one adult would consume in a day.

John reports that **Hades accompanied him** (literally, "followed with him"). In Greco-Roman thought, Hades was the shadowy place that the dead inhabit, comparable to Sheol in the Hebrew Bible. "The imagery of 'following behind' pictures Hades on foot gathering up the corpses left by Pestilence and Death as they struck victim after victim."[6] Death and Hades are **given authority** to kill by **sword** and **famine** and by other common biblical means of divine judgment: **plague**[7] and **beasts of the earth** (see Ezek 5:17; 14:21).[8] The horrible extent of Death's power is now disclosed: **a quarter of the earth**. Like other numbers in Revelation, this fraction should be taken qualitatively rather than quantitatively, figuratively rather than literally. A very substantial number of people die by these means, but those affected remain a minority of those who live on earth.

At first glance readers might interpret the calamities depicted in the vision of the four horsemen as four distinct events. However, the fact that the fourth calamity seems to sum up the negative results of the previous three, and the fact that biblical prophecy frequently lists these afflictions as God's standard means of bringing judgment, suggests that the four horsemen should be viewed together as forming a single picture of divine judgment.

Without denying the role of Satan's malice, what characterizes the specific evils mentioned here—conquest, violence, economic problems that lead to food shortages, disease, and death by all these means—are for the most part disasters that result from sinful human actions rather than divine intervention. The indication that power was "given" to these riders suggests that God has allowed the human will to power, violence, and selfishness to run its course, an expression of God's permissive rather than his positive will (e.g., Ps 81:11–17; Rom 1:24–32).

If that is the case, why do these calamities follow the Lamb's opening the seals, and why does one of the living creatures next to God's throne bid these four riders to "Come"? The reason is to make plain that those responsible for wars and all their tragic consequences do not act independently of God's plan. God uses their evil actions in two ways. First, he allows the suffering that evil produces to bring human beings to their senses. Just as an alcoholic must often

---

6. Osborne, *Revelation*, 282.

7. The Greek word translated "plague," *thanatos*, literally means "death" (as it is translated earlier in the verse), but can refer to contagious disease as a means of death, as many translations render it here and in 18:8, where NAB renders it "pestilence."

8. Similar judgments against Israel are expressed in the covenant curses (see Lev 26:17–26; Deut 32:23–25) and at the time of the exile in prophecies of Jeremiah and Ezekiel (Jer 14:12; 15:1–3; 44:13; Ezek 5:12). The judgments of Rev 6:1–8 differ, however, since they affect the whole world, rather than Israel, and do not include some of the distinctive characteristics of the covenant curses such as exile, desolation of the land, and humiliation before the Gentiles (see Lev 26:28–33; Ezek 5:14–15).

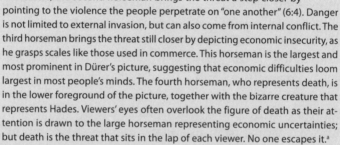

Albrecht Dürer's "Four Horsemen"

LIVING TRADITION

The famous vision of Rev 6 has captured people's imaginations and found its way into art, literature, music, and even sports. Craig R. Koester describes how Albrecht Dürer's woodcut (see fig. 6) shows the impact that the vision of the four horsemen can have on readers.

The first horseman with his bow appears in the background of the picture, furthest away from the viewers. This placement is suggestive because fear of conquest by a foreign power is often furthest away from readers' minds. If the first horseman awakens a sense of distant uneasiness, the second horseman brings the threat a step closer by pointing to the violence the people perpetrate on "one another" (6:4). Danger is not limited to external invasion, but can also come from internal conflict. The third horseman brings the threat still closer by depicting economic insecurity, as he grasps scales like those used in commerce. This horseman is the largest and most prominent in Dürer's picture, suggesting that economic difficulties loom largest in most people's minds. The fourth horseman, who represents death, is in the lower foreground of the picture, together with the bizarre creature that represents Hades. Viewers' eyes often overlook the figure of death as their attention is drawn to the large horseman representing economic uncertainties; but death is the threat that sits in the lap of each viewer. No one escapes it.ª

a. Craig R. Koester, *Revelation and the End of All Things* (Grand Rapids: Eerdmans, 2001), 82.

"hit bottom" before being willing to deal with his or her drinking problem, we human beings often refuse to repent and turn to God until our situation becomes desperate. This is a severe mercy, but often it is the only way. Second, God allows the wicked to do what they please to reveal just how wicked they are so that the justice of their final condemnation is obvious. As one writer puts it, "God will not judge them until they are fully and thoroughly deserving of it."⁹

So when do these disasters take place? As mentioned above, circumstances resembling these visions occurred in the first century. But it is also true that circumstances like these—war, violence, food shortages, famine, plague, and death—have characterized many periods of human history. The twentieth century witnessed far more deaths by war and famine at the hands of governments wielding the "huge sword" of totalitarian power than had ever occurred before.¹⁰

9. N. T. Wright, *Revelation for Everyone* (Louisville: Westminster John Knox, 2011), 66. Other biblical texts show that this is God's way of working. See Gen 15:16; Rom 1:18–32; 2:4–11; and 2 Thess 2:9–12.

10. Rudolph J. Rummel provides estimates of the numbers of deaths caused by governments in a number of books and offers a summary at "20th Century Democide," http://www.hawaii.edu/powerkills /20TH.HTM.

Fig. 6. Albrecht Dürer's "The Four Horsemen of the Apocalypse" (ca. 1497–98).

The first audience of Revelation would have recognized in the vision of the four horsemen, and in some events of the first century,[11] a fulfillment of Jesus' words to his disciples recorded in the Gospels:

> You will hear of wars and reports of wars; see that you are not alarmed, for these things must happen, but it will not yet be the end. Nation will rise against nation, and kingdom against kingdom; there will be famines and earthquakes from place to place. All these are the beginning of the labor pains. (Matt 24:6–8; see also Mark 13:7–8; Luke 21:9–11)

Thus the four horsemen are best understood as the terrible calamities that occur in the course of history as a consequence of human sinfulness. Jesus indicates that these evils will intensify before his coming at the end of history. The risen Lord allows these man-made disasters to disturb human complacency and to lead people to conversion.

Reflection and Application (6:1–8)

Unlike some later judgments in the book of Revelation (9:4; 19:19–21), nothing in the visions of the four horsemen suggests that the calamities of war, economic difficulty, famine, plague, and death will not afflict God's people. Sin and its consequences have infected our world. Even though God's people have been redeemed, we are not immune from sin's effects while the world lasts and we remain in our bodies. If this seems grim, it helps to recall that the Son of God became one of us and shared in human suffering to the point of undergoing crucifixion in order to deliver us completely from suffering and death someday (see 7:15–17; 21:4). That day, according to Revelation, is not far off. Even now the Lord is near to all who suffer and invites all to call upon him (Ps 145:18).

How then should God's people respond when calamity strikes? Our first thought needs to be for those around us who may need our physical or spiritual help. Scripture is full of exhortations to share bread with the hungry, to help widows and orphans in their affliction, and to show mercy in every way possible. Times of great trial give many opportunities to "give an explanation to anyone who asks you for a reason for your hope" (1 Pet 3:15). As regards ourselves, Hebrews 12 encourages Christians to accept hardships and difficulties, even those suffered because of our resistance to evil (12:4), as God's fatherly

---

11. For example, Parthian attacks on Roman territory in the AD 50s–70s, civil unrest in the empire in the years following Nero's death in 68, and the Roman destruction of Jerusalem in 70.

training: "'My son, do not disdain the discipline of the Lord / or lose heart when reproved by him; / for whom the Lord loves, he disciplines; / he scourges every son he acknowledges.' Endure your trials as 'discipline'; God treats you as sons. For what 'son' is there whom his father does not discipline?" (12:5–7). The Letter of James goes further: "Consider it all joy, my brothers, when you encounter various trials, for you know that the testing of your faith produces perseverance" (1:2–3; see also Jdt 8:25–27).

The Fifth Seal: The Souls of the Martyrs beneath the Altar (6:9–11)

[9]When he broke open the fifth seal, I saw underneath the altar the souls of those who had been slaughtered because of the witness they bore to the word of God. [10]They cried out in a loud voice, "How long will it be, holy and true master, before you sit in judgment and avenge our blood on the inhabitants of the earth?" [11]Each of them was given a white robe, and they were told to be patient a little while longer until the number was filled of their fellow servants and brothers who were going to be killed as they had been.

OT: Gen 4:10; Lev 17:11; 2 Macc 6:18–7:41; Job 16:18
NT: Luke 21:15–18; John 12:24–25; 15:13; Rev 12:11
Catechism: martyrs, 2473–74; intercession of, 2642; church memorials of, 1173

The vision that accompanies the fifth seal clearly does not fit the expectation of those who interpret the opening of each seal as marking a distinct historical event. Rather than describing a particular historical moment, this vision sums up the situation of the Christian martyrs throughout history in a brief symbolic narrative, a common literary feature of Revelation.[12]

At the opening of the **fifth seal**, the prophet witnesses a peculiar exchange between the martyrs and Christ or God. John sees **those who had been slaughtered**, the same word used to describe the Lamb (5:6). The reason for their deaths is explained: **because of the witness they bore to the word of God**—that is, they were killed for testifying to the gospel. The word translated "witness" is *martyria*, the ordinary word for legal "testimony"; in early Christianity it acquired the meaning of "martyrdom." Although there is no evidence to indicate that there were many martyrs in Asia by the time Revelation was written

6:9

12. Other examples include Rev 11:1–2; 12:6, 13–17.

Martyrs and Saints beneath Our Altars

LIVING TRADITION

In Catholic, Orthodox, and other ancient churches, the Mass, or Divine Liturgy, is celebrated over the relics of one or more canonized martyrs, as well as the relics of other saints. In the altars of churches of the Roman rite, the relics are kept in an altar cavity, called a *sepulchrum*. Orthodox and Byzantine Catholic priests celebrate the Divine Liturgy upon a silk cloth called the *antimension*, which depicts the burial of Christ and into which relics of martyrs and saints have been sewn.

The practice of celebrating Mass over the tombs of the martyrs began at least as early as the third century. A scholar comments on the relationship of this practice to Rev 6:9–11:

> By the fourth century, when the Eucharistic tables [began] to be erected over the tombs of the martyrs, the Christian people [were] so inclined towards this association of the sacrifice of Christ with the relics of the martyrs that [they] unwittingly establish[ed] the custom as a general rule, thus realising to the letter St. John's vision. In the churches which have not deliberately broken with tradition, every Eucharistic table is still a martyr's or confessor's tomb; the martyrs are spiritually under the altar.[a]

a. Raymond-Joseph Loenertz, *The Apocalypse of St. John* (London: Sheed & Ward, 1948), 65–66.

(only Antipas is named, 2:13), John's readers would have known of the killing of Christians in Rome, Jerusalem, and elsewhere.[13]

The significance of **the souls** of the martyrs being **underneath the altar** is that God accepts the offering of their lives as sacrifices at his heavenly altar. The symbolism relies on Old Testament understandings about sacrifice (see sidebar above, "Martyrs and Saints beneath Our Altars"). A living creature's blood was identified with its "soul" or life (Lev 17:11). When animals were sacrificed, the victim's blood was poured at the base of the altar or splashed on its sides[14] to indicate that the life or "soul" of the animal was offered to God as a gift. The understanding was that God would respond to an acceptable sacrifice by bestowing blessing, whether an answer to a prayer, forgiveness of sin, deliverance from enemies, or whatever the need might be. John's vision indicates that when, like the Lamb, Christians are killed for their testimony to God's word, their shed

---

13. See sidebar, "The First Martyrs of the Church of Rome," p. 216. For martyrdom in Jerusalem, see Acts 8:1–2; 9:1–2; 12:1–2. See Josephus, *Antiquities of the Jews* 20.9.1 for an account of the execution of James the Just (ca. AD 62).

14. See, e.g., Exod 29:16, 20; Lev 1:11; 3:2, 8, 13; 4:7, 18, 25.

blood metaphorically is poured at the base of the altar and flows beneath it, a sacred offering of their lives to God.[15]

Implicit in these few words is a rich theology of martyrdom: the blood of the slaughtered martyrs, like the blood of the slaughtered Lamb, is received by God as a sacrifice and will move him to intervene, to bless and save his people, to hear their prayers, and to bring about his reign on the earth.

The souls of the martyrs beneath the altar **cried out in a loud voice** for God to **sit in judgment and avenge** their **blood**. They ask that the evildoers who slaughtered them be brought to the bar of divine justice to receive their recompense. These words recall a second and very different Old Testament image of blood. It is expressed in God's words to Cain—"Your brother's blood cries out to me from the ground!" (Gen 4:10; see Heb 12:24)—and the biblical teaching that God requires justice for the shed blood of murder victims.[16]   **6:10**

Their cry, **How long . . . ?** echoes the cry of the psalmists and prophets (Ps 6:4; 13:2–3; 35:17; Hab 1:2) suffering affliction as they wait for God's justice. They address their cry to Christ or God, referring to him as **master**, a term for someone with absolute authority, who is **holy and true**—that is, faithful. Those held responsible for the murder of God's servants are **the inhabitants of the earth**, a phrase John uses to refer to people who do not belong to God (see sidebar, "Who Are the 'Inhabitants of the Earth'?," p. 130).

God responds to the martyrs in a manner that at first seems curious. Each **was given a white robe**. The Greek word for "robe," *stolē*, indicates a long garment worn by a person of rank.[17] In the †Septuagint it is often used to describe the apparel of priests and occasionally of angels (Ezek 10:2, 6, 7). The white color connotes victory or holiness. Each martyr was **told** (another †divine passive) **to be patient**—the Greek actually says "to wait," "rest" (see 14:13), or "be refreshed"—**a little while longer**. They are to wait **until the number** of their fellow martyrs is **filled**. This is a biblical way of saying that the answer to their prayer for justice awaits the completion of God's plan, which foresees the martyrdom of other **fellow servants** and **brothers**, fellow Christians like themselves. In other words, the martyrs will be vindicated, the scales of justice will be balanced, but not until history reaches its goal. For the Church, the present is a time of testimony and of enduring suffering. The martyrs walk in the steps of the Lamb,   **6:11**

---

15. Isaiah 6:6 mentions an altar in heaven, just as there was in the Jerusalem temple (see Exod 25:40 and Heb 8:5). The Jerusalem temple had two altars, the bronze altar on which animal sacrifices were offered that stood in front of the sanctuary, and the gold altar of incense that stood within the sanctuary. John's visions depict a single gold altar in the heavenly temple (Rev 6:9; 8:3, 5; 9:13; 11:1; 14:18; 16:7).

16. See Gen 9:5; Num 35:33; Deut 19:10; 21:1–9; Joel 4:21; Ps 9:13; Matt 23:35. Often God tempers his justice with mercy (Gen 4:13–15; 2 Sam 12:9–13).

17. See Mark 12:38; 16:5; Luke 15:22. These white robes appear again in Rev 7:9–14; 22:14.

Who Are the "Inhabitants of the Earth"?

BIBLICAL
BACKGROUND

Although the phrase itself is neutral, "the inhabitants of the earth" is always (ten times) used negatively in Revelation. The phrase refers to people who

- will be subjected to the trial coming on the earth, in contrast to God's people, who will be kept safe (3:10)
- kill Christians because of their witness (6:9–10)
- will be struck by the three woes (8:13)
- are tormented by the testimony of the two witnesses and rejoice at their death (11:10 [twice])
- worship the beast (13:8, 12)
- are deceived by the false prophet (13:14)
- drink the wine of Babylon's immorality (17:2)
- do not have their names written in the book of life (17:8).

A different Greek word is used to speak inclusively of everyone who dwells on the earth (14:6). In another place, Christians are described as "those who dwell in heaven" (13:6). The use of the neutral expression "inhabitants of the earth" as a technical term to refer to what is not of God is analogous to the frequent use of "the †world" in the Gospel and Letters of John (e.g., John 7:7; 15:17–18; 1 John 2:15–17; 3:1).

who also bore witness and whose acceptance of an unjust death was received by God as a sacred offering. God will do justice on behalf of the martyrs at the time he intends. Meanwhile, God honors and refreshes them in his presence.

Should this vision be understood literally to mean that the martyrs in heaven are praying for the punishment of their persecutors? There is nothing intrinsically wrong with praying for justice, and therefore for judgment against those who refuse to repent of murder and other crimes, since such a prayer accords with God's plan.[18] But the problem with this interpretation is that the prayer attributed to the martyrs does not correspond to Jesus' teaching about love of enemies (Luke 6:27–29, 35–36) or to his own prayer that God forgive those who were killing him, nor does it correspond to the similar prayer of the first martyr, Stephen (see Luke 23:34; Acts 7:60). In their deaths the martyrs have been conformed to Christ, whose desire is for mercy and the conversion of sinners, and to God, who takes "no pleasure in the death of the wicked, but rather that they turn from their ways and live" (Ezek 33:11).

18. See, e.g., Ps 11:5–7; 37; 75:9; 2 Macc 7.

Vengeance

**BIBLICAL
BACKGROUND**

To avenge a wrong is often confused with taking personal revenge. The two are not the same thing, even though similar words are often used. In ordinary English usage today, "vengeance" has a negative connotation, with suggestions of force, vehemence, and excess. "Vengeance" in the biblical sense is punishment that accords with justice. Most, if not all, cultures share the view that wrongs ought to be righted, that the scales of justice demand to be balanced by the punishment of wrongdoers and the rewarding of the just. The expressions "retribution" and "recompense," or more colloquially, "payback," reflect the same idea, although the last term is commonly used to justify revenge.

The Bible evaluates vengeance differently depending on who does it. God exercises judgment by right, but human avengers are often criticized. Lamech, the first human vengeance-taker, is portrayed negatively as an example of excessive and unjust vengeance (Gen 4:23–24). Vengeance-takers are among the enemies of God (Ps 8:3) and of the righteous (44:17). The reason for this discrepancy is that God has the authority to execute judgment and does so justly. Human vengeance-takers, on the other hand, lack God's authority and are prone to unjust and excessive retribution and to vindictiveness. God's disposition is different: he takes no pleasure in the death of the wicked, desiring the salvation of all (Ezek 18:32; 1 Tim 2:3–4).

According to Scripture, God is the one who avenges wrongs, and the Psalms often cry out to God to do just that. Psalm 94 begins,

> Lord, avenging God,
>   avenging God, shine forth!
> Rise up, O judge of the earth;
>   give the proud what they deserve! . . .
> They crush your people, Lord,
>   torment your very own.
> They kill the widow and alien;
>   the orphan they murder. (vv. 1–2, 5–6)

The psalm goes on to speak of the foolishness of wicked people who think that God does not see or hear and will not act (vv. 8–10), and of wicked civil authorities who perpetrate evil under the cover of law (v. 20). The psalm confidently affirms that the Lord will intervene decisively to save his people and to destroy evildoers (vv. 14–15, 23).

Scripture associates vengeance with the day of divine judgment at the end of history. Even though the word "avenge" appears only twice in Revelation (6:10 and 19:2), the punishment of the wicked and God's salvation of his people form a major theme of the book (see sidebar, "Judgment and Wrath in Revelation," p. 135).

It therefore seems best to interpret this vision as depicting symbolically the objective imbalance of unrequited justice as long as those who have murdered God's servants remain unpunished. More struggle and more martyrdom lie ahead for the followers of the Lamb, while those already killed for their testimony to the word of God wait in heaven. But this situation will not be tolerated indefinitely. Like the blood of Abel, the blood of the martyrs cries out to heaven for justice, even if their actual prayers, like those of Jesus and Stephen, appeal for mercy.

Reflection and Application (6:9–11)

Many people today, especially those living in relatively just and tranquil democratic societies, recoil at the idea of a God of vengeance, perhaps even imagining that belief in a God who avenges wrongs spawns violence.

Miroslav Volf, on the other hand, is a Croatian theologian who lived through the hellish war in Bosnia (1992–95). His friends and neighbors suffered unspeakable horrors. In his book *Exclusion and Embrace*, he argues that in the Balkans, post-Communist disbelief in a God who avenges wrongdoing led to an overflow of violence. If we live in a "sun-scorched land soaked in the blood of the innocent" and doubt that God will bring ultimate justice, then we will scarcely be able to resist taking up the sword ourselves. Injustice needs an answer.[19]

Not only does the God of the Bible assume responsibility for avenging evil himself; he also forbids personal revenge.[20] St. Paul, citing the †Torah (Deut 32:35; see Lev 19:18), instructs Christians, "Beloved, never avenge yourselves, but leave it to the wrath of God; for it is written, 'Vengeance is mine, I will repay, says the Lord'" (Rom 12:19 RSV).

The Sixth Seal: Cosmic Signs of Final Judgment (6:12–17)

> [12]Then I watched while he broke open the sixth seal, and there was a great earthquake; the sun turned as black as dark sackcloth and the whole moon became like blood. [13]The stars in the sky fell to the earth like unripe figs shaken loose from the tree in a strong wind. [14]Then the sky was divided like a torn scroll curling up, and every mountain and island was moved from its place. [15]The kings of the earth, the nobles, the military officers,

19. Miroslav Volf, *Exclusion and Embrace* (Nashville: Abingdon, 1996), 303–4.
20. God does not forbid society to avenge wrongs; rather, civil authorities are responsible to punish wrongdoers (Rom 13:1–5).

the rich, the powerful, and every slave and free person hid themselves in caves and among mountain crags. [16]They cried out to the mountains and the rocks, "Fall on us and hide us from the face of the one who sits on the throne and from the wrath of the Lamb, [17]because the great day of their wrath has come and who can withstand it?"

OT: Isa 13:10–13; 24:1–6, 19–23; 34:1–12; Hosea 10:8; Joel 2:10; 3:3–4; 4:15–16; Hab 3:6–11
NT: Matt 24:29; Mark 13:24–25; Luke 21:25–26; Acts 2:19–20

The opening of the sixth seal precipitates a vision of the time immediately before history's end, referred to as the arrival of "the great day of . . . wrath." It is as though someone has pressed the fast-forward button of the video we have been watching to the concluding few minutes when the outcome of the drama becomes clear to all the participants.

The vision John recounts is a collage of Old Testament prophecies of judgment combined with elements from Jesus' †eschatological discourse.[21] Several phrases are drawn from Isa 34:1–8, a prophecy promising "vengeance" on †Zion's enemies (Isa 34:8), indicating God's response to the injustice shown the martyrs. Although the Bible sometimes uses the language of †cosmic disaster to depict earthshaking events in the realms of politics or war,[22] on other occasions, as in the present instance (see 6:17), the Bible uses such language to speak in metaphorical terms of the end of history.[23]

An **earthquake** signals God's powerful intervention. The darkening of **the**   **6:12–14**
sun . . . as black as dark sackcloth recalls the plague of darkness against Egypt (Exod 10:21–22), also prophesied against Babylon in Isa 13:10–11. The prophet Joel foretold this darkness and the **whole moon** becoming **like blood** at the day of the Lord (Joel 3:4). Other texts speak of stars being darkened (Isa 13:10; Ezek 32:7; Joel 2:10). The **sky** being **divided like a torn scroll curling up**[24] recalls Isa 34:4: "The heavens shall be rolled up like a scroll." Above all, John's first readers would have understood these events as the fulfillment of Jesus' prophecy of the heavenly signs that will immediately precede the coming of the Son of Man:

21. See Matt 24:29; Mark 13:24–25; Luke 21:25–26.
22. For example, prophets use cosmic disaster language to foretell the defeats of Babylon (Isa 13:10–19), Egypt (Ezek 32:2–11), enemy nations of Israel (Hab 3:6–11), and Israel (Joel 2:10; 3:3–4); 2 Sam 22:8–16 (= Ps 18:7–15) does the same in reference to David's victory over his enemies (see Beale and McDonough, 1105).
23. See, e.g., Ps 102:26–27; Isa 24:1–6, 19–23; 51:6; Ezek 38:19–20; Hag 2:6–7.
24. The word translated "divided" can mean either "to separate" or "to go away." Some translations, leaning on the latter sense, say that the sky "vanished," e.g., "the sky vanished like a scroll that is rolled up" (RSV).

> Immediately after the tribulation of those days,
>
>> the sun will be darkened,
>>> and the moon will not give its light,
>> and the stars will fall from the sky,
>>> and the powers of the heavens will be shaken.
>
> And then . . . they will see the Son of Man coming upon the clouds of heaven.
> (Matt 24:29–30 // Mark 13:24–26)

Among biblical prophecies of the end, only Jesus mentions that **the stars** will fall.

6:15–17 In the previous vision the souls of the martyrs cried out to God for justice (6:10). Here, when justice is about to be executed, seven classes of people, representing the totality of human beings estranged from God, **cried out to the mountains and the rocks**.[25] The people who face judgment because they have not repented are not restricted to the wealthy or to those who wield power. Judgment falls on every class of evildoers, without partiality (Lev 19:15; Job 34:17–19). In extreme distress they hide in **caves and among the mountain crags**, begging the mountains to **fall on** them **and hide** them from God's **face**, now revealed in judgment, and from the †**wrath of the Lamb**, a solemn yet paradoxical phrase. The one who suffered as a Lamb for the sin of the world now comes as judge of all. Contrary to Israel's expectations, the fulfillment of the Old Testament promises of the coming of the †Messiah to reign and judge occurs in two phases. Christ's first coming as the Suffering Servant and Lamb of God brought the good news of grace and an offer of salvation to the human race. The Messiah's second coming will be marked by salvation for his faithful followers and judgment for those who obdurately refuse to repent in spite of the warnings and witnesses Christ has sent them.

The appeal of the unrepentant to the mountains to hide them (also mentioned by Jesus in Luke 23:30, predicting Jerusalem's destruction) echoes Hosea 10:8, which foretells divine judgment on Israel's idolatrous altars. The statement that the **great day of their wrath has come** indicates the arrival of the "day of the LORD" (Isa 13:9; Joel 2:1), the final judgment. The question, **Who can withstand it?** (literally, "who can stand?"), echoes Old Testament passages that speak of God's irresistible judgment (Ps 76:8; Nah 1:6; Mal 3:2).

If the interpretation given here of the visions that accompany the opening of the first six seals is correct, it sheds light on the interpretation of Revelation as

---

25. Some of the powerful officials named—"kings" and "nobles"—echo the LXX of Isa 34:12, which prophesies judgment on Zion's persecutors.

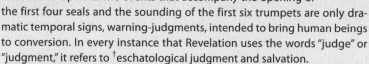

Judgment and Wrath in Revelation

Although most commentaries, including this one, refer to the calamities that occur in history at the opening of the seven seals and the sounding of the seven trumpets (chaps. 8 and 9) as "judgments," the book of Revelation never does so. Instead it reserves the terms "judge" and "judgment" for God's final judgment at the end of history. In this way John draws a sharp distinction between chastisements that God sends or allows and that only affect part of the earth and God's final judgment on evil that will bring eternal destruction upon it. The events that accompany the opening of the first four seals and the sounding of the first six trumpets are only dramatic temporal signs, warning-judgments, intended to bring human beings to conversion. In every instance that Revelation uses the words "judge" or "judgment," it refers to †eschatological judgment and salvation.

Something similar is true about the words "wrath" and "fury" when they are ascribed to God or Christ in Revelation. They are never used to describe God's attitude in sending or allowing the various calamities linked to the seals and trumpets, which have conversion as their goal. Instead, John uses these words only to refer to God's definitive destruction of evil and all who obstinately refuse to repent at the end of history.

When the Bible refers to God's wrath or fury it speaks metaphorically, ascribing human emotions to God in order to help human beings grasp that those who refuse to repent have reason to be afraid. The biblical authors do not intend to attribute to God the unwarranted or disproportionate emotional reaction that all too often characterizes human beings. God's wrath differs from human anger in that it is an expression of perfect justice and the radical incompatibility between his holiness and evil of every kind. When Scripture speaks of God manifesting his wrath it refers to his acting to render just judgment.

---

a whole. It shows that the visions of this book do not provide us with a simple preview of events arranged in chronological order. Rather, these visionary vignettes portray facts about the troubles of the time in which we live (the first four seals), about the seemingly unrequited evil that Christ's faithful witnesses endure in the present (the fifth seal), and about impending judgment (the sixth seal).

The calamities that accompany the four horsemen occur in every age and always serve as invitations to conversion. Martyrs, whose shed blood demands requital, will continue to be killed until this age comes to a close. When that day comes, it will arrive with terrifying and irresistible force against all, great or small, who persist in doing evil. Rather than present a timeline in neat chronological order, the book of Revelation instructs its readers by multiple retellings of the final period of human history, focusing on different aspects of the story in each repetition.

Reflection and Application (6:12–17)

The seven classes of human beings who are about to suffer "wrath," the consequences of their deeds, would rather die than face what lies before them. The consistent message about hell, through all the metaphorical speech about it found in Scripture, is that it is worse than death (see comments on 20:14–15 and "Reflection and Application" on 20:11–15).[26] Christian tradition has long held that meditating on the last things and our ultimate future can help us approach our lives wisely. One simple way of doing this would be to read through the Catechism's teaching on these subjects (Catechism 1005–50) or to reflect on its summary (1051–60).

---

26. For instance, see Isa 66:24; Matt 13:41–42; 24:48–51; Mark 9:47–48; 2 Thess 1:6–9; Rev 20:14–15; 21:8.

Visions of God's People

Revelation 7:1–17

The events that marked the opening of the sixth seal at the end of chapter 6 prepare the reader for the climactic conclusion of God's plan. However, before the seventh seal can be opened, two visions interrupt the revelation of present calamities and future judgment in an interlude that nourishes the hope of John's Christian readers. These visions depict God's faithful people before and after their trials. In the first (7:1–8), a kind of flashback, God acts to protect his people in advance of the distress they are about to experience or are experiencing. In the second (7:9–17), a preview of what awaits God's people on the other side of the great tribulation of this life, God shelters his people in his presence while the Lamb shepherds them and leads them to springs of life-giving water. It is our earliest and most beautiful picture of the life in heaven that awaits faithful believers after death.

Sealing of the One Hundred and Forty-Four Thousand (7:1–8)

¹After this I saw four angels standing at the four corners of the earth, holding back the four winds of the earth so that no wind could blow on land or sea or against any tree. ²Then I saw another angel come up from the East, holding the seal of the living God. He cried out in a loud voice to the four angels who were given power to damage the land and the sea, ³"Do not damage the land or the sea or the trees until we put the seal on the foreheads of the servants of our God." ⁴I heard the number of those who had been marked with the seal, one hundred and forty-four thousand

marked from every tribe of the Israelites: [5]twelve thousand were marked from the tribe of Judah, twelve thousand from the tribe of Reuben, twelve thousand from the tribe of Gad, [6]twelve thousand from the tribe of Asher, twelve thousand from the tribe of Naphtali, twelve thousand from the tribe of Manasseh, [7]twelve thousand from the tribe of Simeon, twelve thousand from the tribe of Levi, twelve thousand from the tribe of Issachar, [8]twelve thousand from the tribe of Zebulun, twelve thousand from the tribe of Joseph, and twelve thousand were marked from the tribe of Benjamin.

OT: Num 31:1–8, 48–49; Ezek 9:4–6
NT: Luke 21:16–18; 2 Cor 1:22; Eph 1:13–14; 4:30; 2 Tim 2:19
Catechism: the new people of God, 1138; the seal, 1295–96
Lectionary: 7:2–4, 9–14: Solemnity of All Saints

7:1–3   The phrase **After this I saw** indicates the sequence of John's visions, not the order in which the events unfold. The prophet sees **four angels** at the **four corners of the earth**. In the Bible as in other ancient literature, the four corners, or four points of the compass, represent the whole earth. The angels are **holding back the four winds**, linked in Zech 6:5 with the four horsemen who bring divine judgment (see comments on 6:1).[1] It is clear that chastisement is in view here since **the four angels . . . were given power to damage the land and the sea**, referring to the whole earth. The powerful angels responsible for unleashing the warning judgments are addressed by **another angel** whose extraordinary importance is signaled by the fact that he holds **the seal of the living God**. A seal is a device for impressing an emblem or other identifying mark onto something to indicate ownership. Sheep, cattle, and sometime slaves were branded with their owner's emblem or name. A seal of ownership indicated the owner's rights to and protection of what belonged to him. When soldiers enlisted in the Roman army, they were often sealed by having the name of their commanding general tattooed on their hand or forearm; other military allusions in this passage (see below) suggest this association is intended.

The angel with the seal commands the four angels **in a loud voice** to *wait* before striking **the land or the sea or the trees**—in other words, before carrying out their job of bringing judgment on the inhabited world. The trees are probably included here because of their importance for sustaining life in the ancient Mediterranean world (see comments on 8:7 and sidebar, "Do not harm . . . the trees," p. 157). Before harm is inflicted on the world, God's **servants** must be marked with his seal. In Revelation, this term usually refers to God's

---

1. In Dan 7:2; 8:8 the four winds of heaven are associated with the beasts that oppose God and his people.

faithful people (e.g., 1:1; 19:5; 22:3), except where it is specified further (e.g., "his servants the prophets," 10:7).

The seal **on the foreheads** recalls another vision in the book of Ezekiel. The prophet heard God command an angel in the likeness of a scribe to mark the Greek letter *tau*, shaped like a cross, on the forehead of all the righteous Israelites so that, when God's angels brought judgment on Jerusalem, those who disapproved of the evil done in the city would be spared (Ezek 9:3–6). Later in Revelation, John indicates that God's servants have the name of God inscribed on their foreheads (14:1; 22:4), probably a reference to the seal of God mentioned here. In contrast, the followers of "the beast" will bear the mark of the beast on their hands and foreheads (13:16; 14:9; 20:4). God's seal on his servants before the judgments begin indicates that they belong to God, are under his protection,[2] and are enlisted as his soldiers.

Who are these "servants of our God"? After John *sees* the angel who bears   7:4–8
God's seal command the other four angels not to strike until the sealing is done, the prophet *hears* **the number** of those sealed: **one hundred and forty-four thousand**, a symbolic number: twelve times twelve times one thousand. In Scripture the number twelve stands for the whole of God's people Israel, the twelve tribes descended from twelve patriarchs. Thus, when Jesus appoints twelve apostles (Mark 3:14–19), he signals a new beginning for Israel in which he gathers the people of God around himself in his Church. In Revelation both twelves that symbolize God's people—the twelve tribes of the old covenant and the twelve apostles of the new—are of enduring importance; both fulfill critical functions in the symbolic architecture of the new Jerusalem (21:12, 14). Twelve times twelve, one hundred and forty-four, seems to be a way of intensifying the meaning of twelve: the complete number of those who are truly God's people, his faithful followers. The figure one thousand, besides symbolizing a large number, was also the largest military unit under a single commander in biblical Israel's army (e.g., Num 31:14, 48, 52, 54).

The description of **twelve thousand** from each of the twelve tribes of Israel reinforces the military imagery. The repeated phrase **from the tribe of** echoes the census of men of fighting age found in Num 1:20–45. In the Old Testament, listing numbers from a tribe usually has to do with counting the people for military purposes. In the †Torah, when the Israelites went to war at God's command, God went with them and fought for them.[3]

---

2. The seal of God is specifically mentioned as protecting God's people from the chastisements accompanying the fifth trumpet (9:4), demonic torments that afflict those who are not God's people.

3. The specific figure of twelve thousand recalls an occasion recounted in Num 31:1–6, when the Lord commands that an army of exactly that number, a thousand from each of the tribes, be sent to wage war against Midian.

So who are these **one hundred and forty-four thousand marked** (literally, "sealed") **from every tribe of the Israelites** (7:4)?

Taking "Israelites" and the twelve tribes to refer to ethnic Israel, some interpreters understand this as referring to Jews or Jewish Christians gathered from all the tribes of Israel. However, there are difficulties with this view. First, why should only *Jewish* followers of Christ be identified as "the servants of our God" who are to be protected in the coming trials (see especially 9:4)? The rest of Revelation does not single out Jewish Christians. While the seven churches of Asia undoubtedly included Jewish believers in Jesus, the majority were likely Gentile Christians, as Acts and the New Testament Letters to that region suggest (Ephesians, Colossians, 1–2 Peter, 1–2 Timothy). Second, after the Assyrian conquest of Israel in 721 BC, many members of the ten northern tribes were exiled from the land and disappeared from history, assimilating with the †Gentiles among whom they lived. Finally, and most important, John, like other New Testament authors, identifies the Church, with its Jewish and Gentile members, as †eschatological Israel, the covenant people of God.[4]

For these reasons it seems best to understand "the servants of our God," represented symbolically as one hundred and forty-four thousand "from every tribe of the Israelites" (7:4), as referring to all God's faithful people, including both Jews and Gentiles who are united to Israel's Messiah. God has sealed his people in advance to indicate their belonging to him as his holy army and to protect them in the judgments and trials that lie ahead. While the vision might imply that the sealing of God's servants occurs at a particular moment, this is obviously not the case if the one hundred and forty-four thousand represent Christ's disciples through history (14:1–4). Instead, Christians receive the seal of God's protection during their lifetime when they believe the Gospel, repent, and are baptized.

The symbolic numbering of God's people as a holy army introduces an important theme of Revelation: the Church's call to bear witness is warfare, and God himself will fight for his people just as he did against Egypt at the Exodus (Exod 12:12; 14:14), against Jericho and other Canaanite cities in the conquest (Josh 6), and against the armies of Assyria in the time of Hezekiah (2 Kings 19:20–37). In Revelation, however, there is no mention of physical warfare on the part of God's people, but rather a summons for Christians to be victors (2:7, 11, 17; 21:7; etc.) in a battle against idolatry, immorality, materialism, pressures

---

4. See, e.g., Matt 19:28; Luke 22:28–30; Gal 3:27–29; 4:22–31; Eph 2:11–22; Phil 3:3; Col 2:11–13. In other texts ethnically Gentile Christians, understood as belonging spiritually to Israel by their incorporation into Christ, are exhorted not to conduct themselves like the Gentiles (Eph 4:17; 1 Pet 2:12; 4:3). For more, see sidebar, "Israel and the Church," p. 209.

Bede's Interpretation of the One Hundred and Forty-Four Thousand

LIVING TRADITION

The Venerable Bede (672–735), a doctor of the Church, Benedictine monk, and commentator on Revelation, offers this interpretation of the one hundred and forty-four thousand:

By this finite number is signified the innumerable multitude of the whole church, which is begotten from the patriarchs either by way of the offspring of flesh or by the imitation of faith. For it says, "If you are of Christ, you are the seed of Abraham" (Gal 3:29). And it pertains to the increase of perfection that this twelve is multiplied by twelve and is completed by the sum of a thousand, which is the cube of the number ten, signifying the immoveable life of the church. And for this reason rather often the church is symbolized by the number twelve, since throughout the four-squared world she subsists by faith in the Holy Trinity, for three fours make ten and two. And finally, twelve apostles were elected that they might preach the same faith to the world, signifying by way of the number the mystery of their work.[a]

a. *Explanation of the Apocalypse* 7.4, in ACCS 12:105.

to conform, deception, and persecution at the hands of Satan's agents. The hundred and forty-four thousand appear in a later vision (14:1–5) where more is revealed about their holiness as God's army and about what their service entails.

Although the Old Testament itself is not consistent in the way it lists the twelve tribes, two irregularities in the listing of the twelve tribes in this passage deserve comment. Here instead of Reuben, Jacob's firstborn, being listed first, that place is given to the tribe of Judah. This is because Christ the Lamb, a descendant of David, belongs to the tribe of Judah. The other peculiarity is that the tribe of Dan does not appear and is replaced by Manasseh. Perhaps this occurs because in the Old Testament the tribe of Dan is frequently associated with idolatry (Judg 18; 1 Kings 12:28–30), the very evil that Revelation warns so strenuously against.[5]

What kind of protection does "the seal of the living God" afford God's servants? The message given in 6:11 about more martyrs to come and the visions of persecution in the rest of the book (e.g., 12:11; 13:10) indicate that the seal's protection is spiritual rather than physical. This vision offers a paradoxical

5. St. Irenaeus (ca. 160) reports a tradition that the Antichrist would come from the tribe of Dan (*Against Heresies* 5.30.2); however, evidence is lacking to confirm that this tradition was known in the first century. Jewish †intertestamental literature spoke of the apostasy of the tribe of Dan (*Testament of Dan* 5:2; see 5:1–6). See Osborne, *Revelation*, 314n7.

The "Seal" in Scripture and Tradition

LIVING TRADITION

While St. Paul teaches that the Holy Spirit himself is the seal that marks Christians (2 Cor 1:22), as early as the second century Church Fathers referred to baptism, the sacrament that conveys the Spirit, as the seal. Just as circumcision was the sign that sealed the men of the old covenant (Rom 4:11), baptism is the sign that seals men and women of the new covenant. It is an indelible seal—like a brand, a tattoo, or circumcision (although invisible)—and therefore not to be repeated. It signifies belonging fully to Christ and enlistment in his spiritual army. Other Church Fathers understood tracing the sign of the cross on the foreheads of catechumens as sealing them—marking them as Christ's and protecting them from the devil. Still other Church Fathers regarded the anointing with oil that follows baptism as the seal that conveys the Spirit.[a]

The Catechism reflects this broad tradition of the seal by referring to the indelible mark left by baptism (1272–74, 2769) and confirmation (1293, 1295, 1304), sacraments that bestow the Holy Spirit (698):

> Christ himself declared that he was marked with his Father's seal (see John 6:27). Christians are also marked with a seal: "It is God who establishes us with you in Christ and has commissioned us; he has put his seal on us and given us his Spirit in our hearts as a guarantee" (2 Cor 1:21–22; see Eph 1:13; 4:30). This seal of the Holy Spirit marks our total belonging to Christ, our enrollment in his service for ever, as well as the promise of divine protection in the great eschatological trial (Rev 7:2–3; 9:4; Ezek 9:4–6). (Catechism 1296)

a. For a more complete account of how the Church Fathers interpreted the seal, see Jean Daniélou, *The Bible and the Liturgy* (Ann Arbor, MI: Servant, 1979), 54–69.

reassurance, comparable to Jesus' promise in Luke 21:16–18: "They will put some of you to death, . . . but not a hair on your head will be destroyed." In the final analysis, we are completely safe. Because of Christ's promise of eternal life, Christians need not fear those who can kill the body but cannot harm the soul (Matt 10:28; Luke 12:4).

So does the seal of the living God refer to the promise of eternal life? Yes, but I think it likely that for John and his first readers, it had a more specific meaning. Both 2 Corinthians and Ephesians—Pauline Letters that would likely have been familiar to the church in Asia in the 90s—refer to the Holy Spirit as a seal (Eph 1:13) with whom Christians are "sealed for the day of redemption" (Eph 4:30; see 2 Cor 1:22). The Holy Spirit himself marks Christians as God's sons and daughters (Gal 4:6), bearing his "name" (Rev 14:1; 22:4). The Spirit, as the "guarantee" (RSV) or "first installment" of our eternal inheritance (2 Cor 1:22; 5:5; Eph 1:13–14), safeguards Christians, although we must continue to choose to "live by the Spirit" (Gal 5:16–23; see Rom 8:1–14).[6]

Reflection and Application (7:1–8)

Although the Christian tradition often refers to the sacramental means by which the Spirit is bestowed—baptism and confirmation—as the seal, there is something to be gained by recovering the earlier biblical understanding of the Holy Spirit himself as the seal, because it focuses attention on the spiritual fruit that the sacraments communicate: life in the Spirit.

It is possible to receive the sacraments yet not benefit from them. Christ always makes his grace fully available, but "the fruits of the sacraments also depend on the disposition of the one who receives them" (Catechism 1128). This was the teaching of St. Thomas Aquinas:

> Aquinas points out that lack of faith, lack of authentic repentance, lack of understanding, lack of dealing with demonic activity, lack of desire and lack of intention . . . to live a new way of life can all block the fruitfulness of the sacraments even when they are validly administered. . . . When these defects and blocks are removed, the fruitfulness of the sacraments can be released. At the same time . . . what people experience in the fruitfulness of the sacraments varies according to the depth of spiritual desire for the sacramental graces.[7]

Without romanticizing the early Church, it is clear that the Christians depicted in the New Testament experienced considerably more of the grace and power of the Spirit through baptism than most Catholics do today.[8] If we desire to experience the fruit of the sacraments as the early Christians did, we must acquire the dispositions that allow the grace of the Spirit to work and remove the obstacles that hinder it.

How can this happen? What is needed is a fresh proclamation of the gospel accompanied by testimony from people who experience the action and power of

---

6. Christians who hold to a †futurist interpretation (see "Interpretation of Revelation and History" in the introduction, p. 31) understand the sealing of 7:1–8 as promising a special act of protection before the Church's final trial. Some interpreters regard the one hundred and forty-four thousand as the martyrs (see comments on 14:1–5).

7. Ralph Martin, "A New Pentecost? Catholic Theology and 'Baptism in the Spirit,'" *Logos: A Journal of Catholic Thought and Culture* 14, no. 3 (Summer 2011): 33. Martin cites Thomas Aquinas, *Summa theologica* III, qq. 66–77.

8. The following texts illustrate the first Christians' experience of the Spirit: Acts 2; 8:14–19; 10:44–48; 19:5–6; Rom 8:13–27; Gal 3:2–5.

the Holy Spirit in their lives. This proclamation must meet with a wholehearted response of faith, surrender to Christ's lordship (Acts 5:32), and persistent prayer for the grace of the Spirit (Luke 11:9–13; John 7:37–39; Eph 5:18–20). Catholics will need to rediscover what it means to resist the devil (James 4:7; 1 Pet 5:9), to get free of demonic oppression, and to put on "the armor of God" (Eph 6:10–18). Those who persevere on this path will discover that baptism, confirmation, and all the sacraments function as powerful means of grace and an efficacious seal that protects them from evil.

The Multitude from Every Nation (7:9–17)

⁹After this I had a vision of a great multitude, which no one could count, from every nation, race, people, and tongue. They stood before the throne and before the Lamb, wearing white robes and holding palm branches in their hands. ¹⁰They cried out in a loud voice:

> "Salvation comes from our God, who is seated on the throne,
>   and from the Lamb."

¹¹All the angels stood around the throne and around the elders and the four living creatures. They prostrated themselves before the throne, worshiped God, ¹²and exclaimed:

> "Amen. Blessing and glory, wisdom and thanksgiving,
>   honor, power, and might
>   be to our God forever and ever. Amen."

¹³Then one of the elders spoke up and said to me, "Who are these wearing white robes, and where did they come from?" ¹⁴I said to him, "My lord, you are the one who knows." He said to me, "These are the ones who have survived the time of great distress; they have washed their robes and made them white in the blood of the Lamb.

> ¹⁵"For this reason they stand before God's throne
>   and worship him day and night in his temple.
>   The one who sits on the throne will shelter them.
> ¹⁶They will not hunger or thirst anymore,
>   nor will the sun or any heat strike them.
> ¹⁷For the Lamb who is in the center of the throne will shepherd them
>   and lead them to springs of life-giving water,
>   and God will wipe away every tear from their eyes."

OT: Lev 23:39–43; Ps 23; Isa 25:8; 49:9–10; Ezek 37:26–28; Dan 12:1–4, 10; Zech 14:16

NT: Matt 24:21; John 6:35; 1 John 1:7

Catechism: celebrants of the heavenly liturgy, 1136–39, 2642; Church as sacrament of unity of human race, 775; heaven, 769, 1023–29

Lectionary: 7:2–4, 9–14: Solemnity of All Saints; 7:9, 14b–17: Fourth Sunday of Easter (Year C); 7:9–17: Common of Martyrs during Easter Season; 7:9–10, 14–17: Masses for Persecuted Christians

While the previous vision (7:1–8) reassures readers by means of a *flashback* indicating that God has placed his seal of protection on his people before their trials begin, this vision reassures by means of a *preview* of what awaits God's people after death. While the sealing of twelve thousand from each of the twelve tribes symbolizes the assembly of the Church militant, this vision of a great multitude rejoicing depicts the Church triumphant. They "have survived the time of great distress," or "the great †tribulation" (7:14), and are gathered around God's throne with the Lamb. The picture in verses 15–17 reveals the situation of Christ's faithful who have endured trial and washed their robes in the blood of the Lamb—namely, the blessedness of eternal life with God.

While John *heard* a symbolic number representing the totality of those en- **7:9** rolled in God's army, now he *sees* **a great multitude, which no one could count**. The four near-synonyms used to describe the origin of the people John saw—**from every nation, race, people, and tongue**—indicate the universal character of God's people, anticipated in God's promise to Abraham, "In you all the families of the earth shall be blessed" (Gen 12:3 NRSV). The innumerable multitude recalls God's other divine promises to Abraham to multiply his off-spring and to make him "the father of a multitude of nations" (Gen 17:4; 22:17).

This vision of a countless multitude of followers of the Lamb (Rev 7:17) from all nations is quite remarkable, coming from a prophet of a small embattled Church on the margins of first-century Greco-Roman society. It reveals extraor-dinary confidence in the ultimate success of the Church's mission to proclaim the Gospel to all nations. Along with statements that Jesus is coming soon, Revelation includes this vision that presupposes the passage of enough time for countless numbers of new Christians to be added to the Church. Twenty centuries later, two billion Christians, totaling nearly a third of the world's population,[9] can look back on this prophecy with amazement.

This multitude in John's vision stands in praise **before the throne and before the Lamb**, wearing **white robes**. These are the same honorary robes given to

9. "Global Christianity—A Report on the Size and Distribution of the World's Christian Popu-lation," Pew Research Religion and Public Life Project, December 19, 2011, http://www.pewforum .org/2011/12/19/global-christianity-exec/.

The Great Tribulation

"The great distress" of 7:14, often rendered "the great tribulation," alludes to a prophecy in the book of Daniel about "a time unsurpassed in distress" (12:1) that will precede the end of history.[a] According to Daniel, an adversary of God's people will arise and persecute the faithful because of their loyalty to the covenant (see 11:30–39, 44; 12:10). On one level this prophecy refers to the chaotic period recounted in the books of Maccabees between 168 and 164 BC, when the pagan ruler Antiochus IV Epiphanes defiled the temple in Jerusalem and persecuted faithful Jews (1 Macc 9:27). However, over the next two centuries faithful Jews came to view the suffering under Antiochus as a †type of a future trial at the hands of an eschatological adversary. That future trial constitutes the birth pangs that would precede the coming of God's kingdom and the eternal reign of the Messiah and the saints.

In his †eschatological discourse, Jesus alludes to Daniel's prophecy: "At that time there will be great tribulation, such as has not been since the beginning of the world until now, nor ever will be" (Matt 24:21), referring either to the destruction of Jerusalem in AD 70, to the end of history, or to both. However, Jesus seems also to have regarded his passion and death as inaugurating the eschatological tribulation (Mark 9:9–13; 10:35–45; 14:26–28) and warns his disciples to expect tribulation (Mark 13:9–13, 20; John 16:21, 33).[b] Other New Testament books, including Revelation, offer a similar perspective. On the one hand, the time of distress or tribulation has already begun (1:9; Col 1:24; 1 John 4:3); on the other, there will be

---

the martyrs in 6:11. White is the color of victory and of resurrection; here it has an additional significance that will be explained (7:14). They hold **palm branches**, a symbol of victory and of the Feast of Tabernacles, the great fall harvest festival that recalled God's provision during Israel's wilderness sojourn and that Jewish tradition understood as foreshadowing the end of history and the coming of God's kingdom.[10]

7:10–12   The countless multitude is engaged in liturgical worship, loudly crying out, **Salvation comes from our God . . . and from the Lamb**. Some translations render it a bit differently: "Salvation *belongs to* our God . . . , and to the Lamb" (NRSV, emphasis added). Like the living creatures and the twenty-four elders in 5:9–13, the multitude honors Jesus alongside God the Father, here in gratitude for salvation and victory (Greek *sotēria* means both). In response, three

---

10. Francis J. Moloney, *The Gospel of John*, Sacra Pagina (Collegeville, MN: Liturgical Press, 1998), 233–36.

an intensification of the conflict in the period immediately before Christ returns to establish his eternal kingdom (Rev 13–19; 2 Thess 4:7). Revelation identifies Daniel's three-and-a-half-year period of trial (Dan 7:25; 12:7; see sidebar, "Forty-Two Months, Twelve Hundred and Sixty Days, Three and a Half Years," p. 189) both with the entire span of the Church's earthly pilgrimage (Rev 12:6) and with the final period of the beast's ascendancy (13:5–7).

Some interpreters, including †dispensationalists, interpret "the great tribulation" as the intense hardships that those left behind at what they call the †rapture will suffer in the three and a half years before Christ's return. However, in view of the intensity of the persecution Christians have experienced at various moments in history—from the first martyrs in the Roman Empire (see sidebar, "The First Martyrs of the Church of Rome," p. 216), to martyrs under twentieth-century totalitarian regimes, and those facing martyrdom at the present time—it seems unreasonable to include only those who will suffer at the end of the age in the white-robed multitude that is comforted by God and the Lamb (7:13–17).

Reflecting Scripture, the Catechism both acknowledges that Christians already share in Christ's afflictions in the present (Catechism 618) and anticipates that "the Church must pass through a final trial," a final unleashing of evil before the end (Catechism 675).

a. Revelation 7:14 is the only instance of the exact phrase "the great distress," or "the great tribulation," in the Bible. Without the article, the Greek words rendered here as "great distress" do not refer to *the* great tribulation (e.g., Acts 7:11; Rev 2:22).

b. See Brant Pitre, *Jesus, The Tribulation, and the End of the Exile* (Grand Rapids: Baker Academic, 2005), 216–18, 377–79, 504–7; and Dale C. Allison Jr., *The End of the Ages Has Come: An Early Interpretation of the Passion and Resurrection of Jesus* (Edinburgh: T&T Clark, 1987), 115–41.

ranks of heavenly creatures—**all the angels . . . and . . . the elders and the four living creatures**—"fell on their faces before the throne" (a literal translation) and **worshiped God**. The angels confirm the acclamation of God's people with a solemn **Amen** and add a sevenfold †doxology of their own that combines attributes of God with words that describe the response God's grandeur deserves: **Blessing and glory, wisdom and thanksgiving, / honor, power, and might**. This praise is directed to the Father, like most biblical and liturgical prayers, but since it begins with an "Amen" to redeemed humanity's praise of God and the Lamb (7:10), it honors the Lamb as well.

In †apocalyptic literature it is common for a heavenly interpreter to explain the meaning of a vision to the person who is receiving it. Here **one of the elders** (see explanation at 4:4) asks the question on the mind of John and his readers: **Who are these wearing white robes, and where did they come from?** The prophet John recognizes that this is a teacher's leading question and respectfully

7:13–14

asks for an explanation.[11] The answer he receives is twofold. First, these are the people **who have survived the time of great distress**. The ESV renders more precisely the present continuous sense of the Greek participle: "These are the *ones coming out of* the great tribulation" (emphasis added), suggesting that John is watching as the martyrs and faithful Christians of all ages emerge from their struggle and enter into their heavenly rest.

This vision, like a few others (6:9–11; 15:2–4; 20:4), provides a glimpse of the salvation that awaits Jesus' disciples after the sufferings of this world and after death. However, it does not depict the ultimate future of God's people promised in the ancient prophecy (Dan 7:27), when "they will reign on earth" (Rev 5:10). In contrast to this vision of heaven, the last two chapters of Revelation show the people of God living in a new creation, in the new Jerusalem that has descended from heaven to earth (see "Reflection and Application" on 21:1–4).

The second part of the elder's explanation reveals more about the people in white robes: **They have washed their robes and made them white in the blood of the Lamb**. This echoes Dan 12:10, which says that when the time of distress comes, "Many shall purify themselves, and make themselves white" (RSV). Here, however, the language is more mysterious: how can clothes be made white by washing them in blood? The answer is that according to the law of Moses, the blood of certain sacrifices functions as a kind of ritual cleanser serving to purify people and things (Lev 8:15; 14:14, 52). These purification rites are fulfilled by Jesus' blood, a shorthand way of speaking about his sacrifice on the cross (Heb 9:11–14). First John 1:7 uses the same image: Jesus' blood "cleanses us from all sin."

Although salvation comes entirely from God, human freedom plays a necessary role. Verse 14 focuses on the action of God's people: "*They* have washed their robes and made them white" (emphasis added). How did human beings cleanse their "robes"—representing themselves and their conduct—in Christ's blood? They washed their robes in the blood of the Lamb by accepting the gospel, believing in Jesus, repenting of their sins, and being baptized. They survive "the great distress" by *persevering* in faith, repentance, and the grace of their baptism.[12]

7:15–17   At this point the heavenly interpreter's explanation breaks into what is plainly poetry.[13] In phrases drawn from the Old Testament prophets, the poem sketches

11. John says "my lord," using the Greek word *kyrios*, which in this context means "Sir" (NIV, NRSV).
12. Some scholars think that those who "have washed their robes . . . in the blood of the Lamb" refers only to the martyrs who physically share in Christ's death. But the texts from Daniel and 1 John and the fact that they constitute a numberless multitude suggests a reference to the whole Christian people rather than to the martyrs alone.
13. Even in English the poetic character of the text is apparent, but in Greek the parallelisms and repetition of connecting conjunctions make the poetic form clearer still.

the salvation of God's people in heaven. The picture, continued and expanded at the end of the book in the new Jerusalem (21:4, 6; 22:1, 3), has three elements: worship in God's presence, a complete end to suffering, and the tender care of God and the Lamb for the redeemed. **For this reason**—because they have washed their robes in the blood of the Lamb—the redeemed are privileged to **stand before God's throne / and worship him day and night**. This adoration is continuous, unlike the worship in the Jerusalem temple, which normally ceased between the evening and morning sacrifice. Moreover, the worship of the redeemed multitude is a *priestly* privilege for which the Lamb's sacrifice has qualified them (see 1:6; 5:10). They enjoy direct access and stand (the posture of a priest) before God's throne in his heavenly **temple** (Greek *naos*), the sanctuary itself, the part of the earthly temple that only the descendants of Aaron could enter. This verse confirms that God's throne room in heaven is his temple, something that was already implied in chapters 4 and 5.

The personal solicitude of God for his people is further revealed by the words that follow: **The one who sits on the throne will shelter them** (see Ezek 37:26–27). The Greek for "shelter" here means "to spread one's tent"; God himself "spreads his tent" over his multinational people, to dwell with and protect them.[14] God shelters them from every kind of suffering: no **hunger or thirst,** **. . . / nor . . . the sun or any heat** shall afflict them. Although they may have suffered these evils on earth (see Luke 6:21; 1 Cor 4:11; 2 Cor 11:27), now they are forever free of them (as Isa 49:10 promises in similar words).

All of this comes to them through the activity of the risen Christ: **For the Lamb who is in the center of the throne will shepherd them**. The divine nature of the Lamb is indicated both by his location on God's throne and by his role: the Lamb is their shepherd—another paradox. Numerous Old Testament texts speak of the Lord God as Israel's shepherd (e.g., Gen 48:15; Ps 23; 80), and Ezek 34:23 foretells a descendent of David who will shepherd Israel and make them one flock. Jesus identifies himself as the good shepherd (John 10:11, 14). In Rev 7:17, the shepherd-Lamb will lead his flock to **springs of life-giving water** ("living water," NIV, NJB, RSV; "water of life," NRSV), a rich biblical symbol that refers both to the Holy Spirit and to the eternal life that the Spirit communicates (John 7:38–39; Rom 8:11).

Perhaps the best is saved for last. **God**, fulfilling a fatherly role, **will wipe away every tear from their eyes**. Not only will all physical suffering be removed, but

---

14. The same Greek verb translated "shelter" is used to describe the incarnation of the Word: "And the Word became flesh / and *made his dwelling* [literally, 'pitched his tent'] among us" (John 1:14, emphasis added).

every emotional and spiritual wound—above all, the sorrow brought by death—will be comforted and healed. The image of "the Lord GOD" wiping away "the tears from all faces" comes from Isa 25:8, where God promises to "destroy death forever."

These images of God wiping away every tear, of no more death, and of life-giving water are repeated later in the vision of the new Jerusalem that descends from heaven (21:4–6), indicating continuity between the life after death of those coming out of the great tribulation and the ultimate reward of God's people. Nevertheless, the two situations of God's people must be distinguished: The "great multitude" of 7:9–17 worships in God's temple in heaven. The new Jerusalem comes "down out of heaven from God" (21:10) to a new earth (21:1). In contrast to this vision of celebration in the heavenly temple and several other references to God's temple in heaven,[15] John sees "no temple" in the new Jerusalem, since the presence of God with his people makes the new Jerusalem itself the holy of holies of a new temple (21:16, 22).

The pagan world of the first-century had little knowledge or hope regarding what lies beyond the grave. The gospel of the death and resurrection of Jesus brought that world the radical promise of a resurrection like Christ's at his return (1 Cor 15:22–26; 1 Thess 4:13–17). However, the apostles' teaching said little about the state of believers between death and the future resurrection. Paul speaks of being "with Christ" (Phil 1:23), of a "heavenly habitation," and of going "home to the Lord" (2 Cor 5:1–8). John's vision of the white-robed multitude rejoicing and waving palm branches, sheltered in God's presence with the Lamb as their shepherd, fills out the picture (see also 15:2–4 and 20:4–6).

This vision of the redeemed on the other side of the great trials of life in our world shows that all God's promises of salvation come to pass through the redemption won by Christ on the cross. They are available to those who "have washed their robes and made them white in the blood of the Lamb" (7:14). That slaughtered Lamb whose blood can cleanse will be their shepherd forever.

Reflection and Application (7:15–17)

Security in Christ. Revelation is often regarded as a book of doom and gloom, and it does include some frightening visions. But it is important to bear in mind the reassurance and extraordinary beauty of its consoling visions, like the two in this chapter. The first tells us that all followers of Jesus are sealed—marked as belonging to and protected by God—for the trials and hardships that lie ahead. We belong to his army of witnesses, called to conquer in a battle that the Lamb

---

15. See Rev 11:19; 14:15, 17; 15:5–8; 16:1, 17.

is waging to establish the kingdom of God on the earth. The outcome is certain. The nature of our struggle is indicated in the messages to the seven churches and will be explained more fully in chapters 12–19. God's seal protects us and the Lord is our shepherd:

> My sheep hear my voice. . . . I give them eternal life, and they shall never perish. No one can take them out of my hand. My Father, who has given them to me, is greater than all, and no one can take them out of the Father's hand. (John 10:27–29)

An end to suffering. The vision in Rev 7:9–17 of the eternal life promised us is extraordinarily comforting. Here is no empty promise that faithful Christians will be spared trial and suffering, a way of thinking that the life of Jesus and all of Christian history contradict. Rather, John foresees a countless multitude passing through the great tribulation of this age before Christ returns and standing victorious before God and the Lamb, wearing white robes, and waving palms in celebration.

This vision offers a partial yet helpful answer to an age-old question: How can a God who is good and all-powerful allow suffering to afflict the just? The vision reveals that all such affliction is time limited. There will be an irreversible end to the suffering of those who belong to God. Those who have "washed their robes and made them white in the blood the Lamb"—the Lamb who fully shared in the suffering of this world to the point of being slain—are destined to eternal joy in God's presence, where there will be no more hunger, thirst, oppressive heat, or any other evil. The Lamb will be their shepherd and quench their thirst with life-giving water. God their Father will heal their wounds and "wipe away every tear from their eyes."

For all the saints. The Church reads the two visions of this chapter on the Solemnity of All Saints, a feast that celebrates the sanctity of all God's faithful people who have gone on before us, not just the saints who have been canonized by the Church. The Lord calls every Christian to holiness, in every state of life. Hebrews 12:14 exhorts us, "Strive for . . . that holiness without which no one will see the Lord." It is a simple fact that *only* saints—holy people—reach heaven. Christ qualifies us to live in God's presence: he makes us holy through his death and resurrection, conveying the benefits to us through the sacraments. Nevertheless, we must "strive" to do our part as well through ongoing repentance, prayer, reading Scripture, and loving our neighbor as ourselves. Our part entails daily dying to self and surrendering ourselves completely to God. This process must be completed before we see the face of God. Why not begin in earnest now?

The Beginning of the Seven Trumpets

Revelation 8:1–13

After a comforting interlude that reminds readers of God's faithful care for his own and provides us with a glorious vision of the salvation that awaits God's people after death, Jesus breaks open the seventh and climactic seal that binds the scroll. The opening of the seventh seal unleashes another series of signs, heralded by seven angelic trumpet blasts. The pattern of the seven trumpets follows the pattern of the seven seals: the events accompanying the first four trumpets form a single picture (8:7–12); the events accompanying the fifth and sixth trumpets are different in kind (9:1–21); and an interlude of visions that reveal God's plans for his people precedes the sounding of the seventh trumpet (11:15).

In contrast to the chastisements associated with the four horsemen, which mainly follow from the actions of human beings (conquest and its consequences), the events that follow the first four trumpets depict grave disruptions of nature, events that insurance policies call "acts of God," since human beings are able neither to cause nor to prevent them. God's throne in heaven is the center from which the seven trumpet judgments issue, and the Lamb, the risen Christ, remains in control. But something intervenes before the angels sound the seven trumpets. The prayers of God's people are offered and heard in heaven. The Church is no merely passive observer. All that transpires is subject to the control of a God who is listening to the prayers of his people.

The Seventh Seal and Silence in Heaven (8:1–2)

¹When he broke open the seventh seal, there was silence in heaven for about half an hour. ²And I saw that the seven angels who stood before God were given seven trumpets.

OT: Num 10:1–10; Josh 6:1–20; Wis 18:14; Hab 2:20–3:16; Zech 2:17 (2:13 RSV)
NT: 1 Cor 15:52; 1 Thess 4:16

A dramatic pause interrupts the action. When the Lamb opens **the seventh**   8:1–2
seal, a half hour of **silence** replaces the loud praise that has characterized heaven up to now, signalling readers to get ready for what will happen next. In light of the act of worship that follows, it can be seen as a liturgical silence, a ritual preparation, like times of silence during the liturgies between Holy Thursday and Easter Sunday. It recalls the silence that Old Testament prophets proclaimed before God intervened in judgment (Amos 8:3–4; Hab 2:20; Zeph 1:7). It likewise recalls the words of Zechariah regarding God's coming to reestablish †Zion in order to dwell there with his people: "Silence, all people, in the presence of the Lord, who stirs forth from his holy dwelling" (Zech 2:17).

The **seven angels** who stand in God's presence are likely the archangels, the most important angels according to Jewish †intertestamental writings. They include Gabriel (Dan 9:21; Luke 1:19), Michael (Dan 12:1), and Raphael (Tob 12:15).[1] In the life of Israel, trumpets were blown to announce solemn feasts (Ps 81:3), to herald the beginning of a king's reign (1 Kings 1:34), to warn of trouble, and to summon the people to war (Num 10:8–10). A divine trumpet sounded when God manifested himself at Sinai (Exod 19:16, 19) and will again sound when he acts to save his people (Isa 27:13; Zech 9:14). When God fought for Israel against Jericho as the first step on giving them the promised land of Canaan, he commanded that seven trumpets be blown on seven successive days by seven priests (Josh 6:1–20). As God prepares to give his people their eternal inheritance, he begins again with **seven trumpets**.

The Gold Censer and the Prayers of God's People (8:3–6)

³Another angel came and stood at the altar, holding a gold censer. He was given a great quantity of incense to offer, along with the prayers

---

1. According to the Jewish apocalypse *1 Enoch* (20:1–8), the other four are Uriel, Raguel, Sariel, and Remiel.

153

of all the holy ones, on the gold altar that was before the throne. [4]The smoke of the incense along with the prayers of the holy ones went up before God from the hand of the angel. [5]Then the angel took the censer, filled it with burning coals from the altar, and hurled it down to the earth. There were peals of thunder, rumblings, flashes of lightning, and an earthquake.

[6]The seven angels who were holding the seven trumpets prepared to blow them.

OT: Exod 19:16–18; 30:7–8; Ps 141:2; Ezek 10:1–7
Lectionary: 8:3–4: Common for the Consecration of an Altar during Easter Season

8:3–6   In the Jerusalem temple, directly in front of the holy of holies stood a **gold altar,** on which a priest offered incense twice daily.[2] Here in the heavenly temple, an **angel** offers **the prayers of all the holy ones,** a practice the angel Raphael mentions in Tobit 12:15 (RSV). The previous mention of the prayers of God's people (Rev 5:8) identified the prayers with the incense in the golden bowls held by the elders, but here the incense and prayers are distinguished. The **great quantity of incense** the angel is given to mix with the prayers symbolizes the favor with which God receives his people's prayers; to him they are a pleasing fragrance. It seems the focus here is prayer for vindication (Luke 18:3, 7–8; Rev 6:10). Our prayer that "thy kingdom come, thy will be done on earth" implicitly asks for God's intervention to judge and to save. The hurling to **earth** of **burning coals from the altar** in heaven symbolizes the answer to this prayer. Albert Vanhoye comments: "This symbolical scene expresses the relationship between the prayer of Christians and the course of history: their prayer mounts up to God and has a decisive influence on the course of events."[3] This vision also recalls a similar event in Ezek 10:1–7, when an angel is told to fill his hands with coals of fire and scatter them over Jerusalem, a symbol of the judgment about to unfold.

The **peals of thunder, rumblings, flashes of lightning, and an earthquake,** which are similar to the signs that manifested God's presence at Sinai (Exod 19:16–18) and that appeared in the heavenly throne room (Rev 4:5), indicate that God is manifesting himself in the events precipitated by the opening of the seventh seal. These signs of †theophany will appear again with increasing intensity at the blast of the seventh trumpet (11:19) and at the outpouring of the seventh bowl (16:18–21).

---

2. This is what Zechariah was doing in Luke 1:8–11 when Gabriel appeared to him.
3. Albert Vanhoye, *The Old Testament Priests and the New Priest* (Petersham, MA: St. Bede's Publications, 1986), 296.

Reflection and Application (8:3–6)

Our prayers all rise to God. It is a powerful incentive for those praying to know that our prayers—whether corporate or individual—rise like sweet incense before the Lord (Ps 141:2) and are present to him when he makes the decisions that shape the course of our lives and of the history of the world. Our Father hears the prayers of his children, rescues the afflicted from trouble (Ps 34:16–23), warns wrongdoers to repent, judges those who persist in evil, and sees to it that "that all things work for good for those who love God, who are called according to his purpose" (Rom 8:28).

The First Four Trumpets (8:7–12)

⁷When the first one blew his trumpet, there came hail and fire mixed with blood, which was hurled down to the earth. A third of the land was burned up, along with a third of the trees and all green grass.

⁸When the second angel blew his trumpet, something like a large burning mountain was hurled into the sea. A third of the sea turned to blood, ⁹a third of the creatures living in the sea died, and a third of the ships were wrecked.

¹⁰When the third angel blew his trumpet, a large star burning like a torch fell from the sky. It fell on a third of the rivers and on the springs of water. ¹¹The star was called "Wormwood," and a third of all the water turned to wormwood. Many people died from this water, because it was made bitter.

¹²When the fourth angel blew his trumpet, a third of the sun, a third of the moon, and a third of the stars were struck, so that a third of them became dark. The day lost its light for a third of the time, as did the night.

OT: Exod 7:17–21; 9:23–25; 10:22; Wis 17:1–21; 18:4; Joel 2:30–31

Craig R. Koester captures the drama of this scene well:

With each successive scene, disaster strikes earth, sea, and sky. . . . The cycle is all the more ominous because the destruction unfolds in a relentlessly measured way. The effect is something like an orchestral performance in which the strings scrape dissonant chords while woodwinds shriek, trumpets blare, and cymbals crash in what seems to be wild discord—except that all the players move to the steady beat that is set by the conductor's hand: one, two, three, four.[4]

4. Craig R. Koester, *Revelation and the End of All Things* (Grand Rapids: Eerdmans, 2001), 93.

Before examining these verses in detail, some general observations can be made. These trumpet judgments strike the "inhabitants of the earth" (8:13) by harming the natural order on which human life depends; they unleash ecological disasters. They strike every aspect of creation—the land, sea, springs and rivers, and sky.

Just as the judgments that accompany the first four seals are related to one another—conquest and its consequences—the judgments that follow the first four trumpet blasts all involve natural disasters. The greater severity of these events is signaled by the fact that one-third of the world is affected by each, rather than one-quarter. As usual, these fractions should be interpreted qualitatively rather than literally.

Two biblical texts provide the background for the trumpet judgments. Besides the blowing of trumpets for seven days before Jericho was overthrown (Josh 6), the most important Old Testament precedent is the plagues that God sent against Pharaoh and Egypt at the time of the exodus. Several of the same plagues occur here—hail, water turned to blood, the pollution of drinking water, and supernatural darkness, although in Rev 8 these plagues are not confined to only one nation. They are analogous to the plagues against Egypt in that they demonstrate God's supreme power against those who oppress his people. An explanation after the sixth trumpet (9:20–21) indicates that like the plagues of Egypt, the trumpet judgments are aimed at convincing idolaters to repent and submit to God's will, although for the most part, these chastisements meet with stubborn resistance. They precede God's climactic final judgment.

After looking more closely at each trumpet judgment, we will consider what they signify.

8:7   **Fire** coming from the sky characterizes the first three judgments. Conquering armies often used fire to totally destroy a city, and fire was a potent Old Testament symbol of judgment (e.g., Amos 1). **Blood** characterizes the first two trumpet judgments. It recalls the plague of blood against the land of Egypt (Exod 7:17–21) and prophetic threats of judgment that mention blood (e.g., Isa 63:3–6; Joel 3:3). Even without these allusions, the mention of blood arouses a feeling of danger.

A forerunner of the first trumpet linking **hail**, fire, and the destruction of vegetation was the seventh plague on Egypt, when hail struck humans, animals, every plant, and every tree (Exod 9:23–25). The parallel is not exact, however, since here the damage to **the land** . . . , **the trees** . . . , and the **green grass** comes from the fire rather than from the hail. Although the effects of this judgment

BIBLICAL BACKGROUND

"Do not harm . . . the trees"

Prophecies of judgment in Revelation twice mention trees (7:1–3; 8:7). In ancient eastern Mediterranean culture, trees played a far greater role in human life than they do today, perhaps comparable to the ubiquitous role of petroleum or electrical energy in our world. Most oil for cooking and for light after dark came from olive trees. Any house having a large room had wooden beams. In summer, the shade of trees or of awnings stretched on wood frames were the primary means of shelter and relief from the sun's heat. In the cold of winter, the primary source of heat was wood fuel. In addition, tools and furniture were made of wood. Ancient warfare depended on trees for spears, bows and arrows, and siege engines. Finally, trees were direct sources of food, furnishing olives, nuts, dates, and various other fruits. So important were fruit trees to the sustenance of life that the law of Moses governing warfare forbade cutting them down (Deut 20:19–20).[a]

a. I am indebted to my friend Peter Collins, an environmental biologist, for his contribution to this sidebar.

---

are severe, they are nevertheless restrained (as in Rev 6:6 and Exod 9:31–32), since only **a third** of the land and trees are **burned up**. The fact that **all** the grass is burned indicates the universal extent of the judgment.

The disaster that turns a **third of the sea . . . to blood** recalls the first plague against Egypt, when Aaron struck the Nile with his rod and the water was turned to blood and the fish died (Exod 7:17–21). Not only is the food supply affected—**a third of the creatures living in the sea died**—but sea commerce also is dramatically disrupted by the destruction of **a third of the ships**. The immediate cause of this massive disaster at sea—**something like a large burning mountain was hurled into the sea**—raises questions.[5] Was there anything in the experience of John and his readers remotely like this? Some scholars point to the Aegean Islands during the first century, when volcanic eruptions turned the sky red and caused the sea to turn a reddish hue.[6] A large meteorite falling into the sea could suggest the image of a burning mountain.[7]

8:8–9

---

5. Another apocalyptic book describes fallen angels under judgment as "like great burning mountains" (*1 Enoch* 18:13), but the context seems unrelated.

6. Osborne, *Revelation*, 350–51.

7. Because of similarities to the depiction of the destruction of Babylon in Jer 51:25 and Rev 18:21, some take the large burning mountain here to be judgment on Babylon, but that seems to get ahead of Revelation's narrative. The trumpet judgments are partial, giving warning rather than final judgment.

8:10–11   Similarly, the **large star burning like a torch** and falling **from the sky** sounds like a meteorite.[8] It also recalls Jesus' prediction that "the stars will fall from the sky, / and the powers of the heavens will be shaken" (Matt 24:29 // Mark 13:25) before the coming of the Son of Man. Just as the "large burning mountain" struck and spoiled a third of the sea by turning it to blood, so now the large burning star strikes the sources of freshwater, **a third of the rivers** and **the springs of water**, making them bitter and poisonous.[9] **Wormwood**, although not actually poisonous, is an extremely bitter-tasting herb, so bitter that one ounce of it will alter the taste of 524 gallons of water.[10] Scripture associates it with poison, and it symbolizes the bitter consequences of wrongdoing.[11] Here drinking the **water turned to wormwood** is poisonous and causes many **people** to die.

8:12   When **the fourth angel** blows his **trumpet, a third of** all the heavenly luminaries—**the sun . . . moon . . .** and **stars**—are struck ("blasted," NJB), but in a peculiar way. Rather than dimming the light by one-third, this judgment eliminates all the light in the sky for a third of **the day** and a third of **the night**. Except for the limitation to a third of the time, this follows the pattern of the ninth plague on Egypt. Darkness as a sign of judgment has a rich biblical background.[12] In similar language Jesus prophesies darkness before the †parousia: "The sun will be darkened, / and the moon will not give its light, / and the stars will be falling from the sky" (Mark 13:24–25). Against the backdrop of total darkness of the plague in Egypt and Jesus' prediction, darkness for one-third of the day and night is best understood as symbolizing a partial judgment, intended to deliver a solemn warning.

So what is the significance of the judgments that accompany the first four trumpet blasts? Because they are presented in a series of visionary events starting with the opening of the first seal in 6:1, it is tempting to interpret them as depicting a straightforward sequence of historical events. Yet when we try to take them this way, various logical inconsistencies arise. When the sixth seal was opened, the sun went black, the moon became like blood, the stars fell, and the sky vanished (6:12–17). But here, two chapters later, when the fourth

---

8. On the strength of Isa 14:12–20, some interpreters take the falling star to refer to the fall of Babylon (but see preceding note). Other interpreters identify the star with a fallen angel, but again, that seems to get ahead of the story. The first four trumpet judgments seem to depict disruptions of the natural order rather than demonic activity.

9. It seems that the first Egyptian plague, in which the water turned into blood that killed the fish and ruined the drinking water (Exod 7:20–21), is paralleled by both the second and the third trumpet judgments.

10. David Aune, *Revelation 6–16*, Word Biblical Commentary 52b (Nashville: Nelson, 1998), 2:522.

11. See Deut 29:17–18; Prov 5:4; Jer 9:14; 23:15.

12. See, e.g., Isa 13:9–11; Ezek 32:7–8; Joel 2:2, 10; Amos 8:9; Zeph 1:15.

The Eruption of Mount Vesuvius, Portent of the End

If Revelation was written in the last decade of the first century, its author and readers would have known of the extraordinary volcanic eruption in AD 79 that destroyed Pompeii and Herculaneum, about 130 miles south of Rome. Here is one ancient account by Dio Cassius, a Roman historian:

> The whole plain round about [Vesuvius] seethed and the summits leaped into the air. There were frequent rumblings, some of them subterranean, that resembled thunder, and some on the surface, that sounded like bellowings; the sea also joined in the roar and the sky re-echoed it. Then suddenly a portentous crash was heard, as if the mountains were tumbling in ruins; and first huge stones were hurled aloft, rising as high as the very summits, then came a great quantity of fire and endless smoke, so that the whole atmosphere was obscured and the sun was entirely hidden, as if eclipsed. Thus day was turned into night and light into darkness. . . . [Some] believed that the whole universe was being resolved into chaos or fire. . . . While this was going on, an inconceivable quantity of ashes was blown out, which covered both sea and land and filled all the air. . . . It buried two entire cities, Herculaneum and Pompeii. . . . Indeed, the amount of dust, taken all together, was so great that some of it reached Africa and Syria and Egypt, and it also reached Rome, filling the air overhead and darkening the sun. There, too, no little fear was occasioned, that lasted for several days, since the people did not know and could not imagine what had happened, but, like those close at hand, believed that the whole world was being turned upside down, that the sun was disappearing into the earth and that the earth was being lifted to the sky.[a]

A second account comes from Pliny the Younger, who was, at age seventeen, an eyewitness to the eruption in which his uncle, Pliny the Elder, commander of the Roman fleet and author of the *Historia Naturalis*, perished. He writes,

> Ash was falling onto the ships, darker and denser the closer they went. Now it rains bits of pumice, and rocks that were burned and shattered by the fire. . . . Broad sheets of flame were lighting up many parts of Vesuvius; their light and brightness were the more vivid for the darkness of the night. . . .
>
> It was daylight now elsewhere in the world, but there the darkness was darker and thicker than any night. . . . Then came the smell of sulfur, announcing the flames, and the flames themselves. . . .
>
> [Then] came the dust. . . . We had scarcely sat down when a darkness came that was not like a moonless or cloudy night, but more like the black of closed and unlighted rooms. You could hear women lamenting, children crying, men shouting. . . . There were some so afraid of death that they prayed for death. Many raised their hands to the gods, and even more believed that there were no gods any longer and that this was the one last unending night for the world. . . . I believed that I was perishing with the world, and the world with me.[b]

a. Dio Cassius, *Roman History* 66.22.3–23.5, as quoted in Hershel Shanks, "The Destruction of Pompeii, God's Revenge?," in *Biblical Archaeology Review*, July/August 2010, 62.

b. Pliny the Younger, *Letters* 6.16; 6.20; as quoted in Shanks, "Destruction," 63.

angel blows his trumpet, the sun, moon, and stars are made dark (for one-third of the time) all over again (8:12). Similarly, all the green grass is burnt up in 8:7, yet in 9:4 an army of locusts will be instructed not to harm the grass.[13] These seeming contradictions confirm that the visions of the seals and trumpets do not foretell a series of events literally in a neat timeline: they must be saying something else.

When we discussed the chastisements accompanying the first

Fig. 7. "When the fourth angel blew his trumpet, a third of the sun, a third of the moon, and a third of the stars were struck. . . . The day lost its light for a third of the time, as did the night" (8:12).

four seals, "the four horsemen" (see comments on 6:7–8 and at end of chap. 6), we noted that calamities arising from human causes—death-dealing wars, famines, and epidemics—have happened many times in many places over the course of history. In the same way, it seems best to interpret the first four trumpet judgments as symbolizing natural disasters that God allows to occur in various times and places, perhaps becoming more severe toward the end of history, rather than a series of four specific historical events.[14] None of the trumpet judgments is allowed to destroy everything—the repetition of the fact that only "a third" of the sea, land, and so on, is affected indicates their limited impact. These partial judgments are tempered by mercy, to give the inhabitants of the earth an opportunity to repent, as a comment after the sixth trumpet indicates (9:20–21). The fourth seal judgment affects "a quarter of the earth" (6:8), and the first four trumpet judgments strike a third of the earth, sea, fresh waters, and light—thereby indicating an escalation as the end approaches. These two series of warning judgments, the seals and the trumpets, contrast with the seven bowl judgments that come later and bring total destruction (16:1–21).

John's readers would have noticed parallels between the calamities depicted in Rev 6 and 8 and events in Jesus' †eschatological discourse in the †Synoptic

13. Koester, *Revelation*, 97.

14. Because the Bible sometimes depicts major political or military upheavals with cosmic imagery, some have suggested that is what the first four trumpets signify. Another interpretation reads the natural disasters described as the ecological consequences of nuclear or chemical warfare stemming from such upheavals.

Gospels. Jesus begins by warning his disciples of disasters like those inflicted by the four horsemen: wars, rumors of wars, pestilences, and famines (Matt 24:7; Mark 13:7–8; Luke 21:9–10).[15] Toward the end of the discourse Jesus warns of signs in the heavens and natural disasters like (but not identical to) those announced by the four trumpets—darkness, falling stars (Matt 24:29), and "the roaring of the sea" (Luke 21:25). Both in Jesus' prophecy and in Revelation, things get worse as the end draws near.

Although natural disasters like those depicted in the trumpet judgments are limited by time and place, they are devastating to the people who are affected, bringing the world they have known to a sudden end, foreshadowing the end of history. Catastrophes like those described in Rev 8 were familiar to the first readers of Revelation at the end of the first century. Besides the eruption of Mount Vesuvius (see sidebar, "The Eruption of Mount Vesuvius, Portent of the End," p. 159), the inhabitants of Sardis and Philadelphia had suffered devastating earthquakes in living memory (AD 17), as had Laodicea (AD 60).

Large-scale disasters that prefigure the end of history have occurred in recent times as well. In 2004 a tsunami in the Indian Ocean killed over two hundred and thirty thousand people in Indonesia, Sri Lanka, India, and Thailand. Since 2004, massive earthquakes have taken the lives of hundreds of thousands of people in Sumatra, China, and Pakistan. In 2010 an earthquake killed between two and three hundred thousand people in Haiti. In 2011 an earthquake and tsunami killed over twenty thousand people in Japan and caused a nuclear accident that contaminated and forced the abandonment of hundreds of square miles of inhabited land. A Google search for "twentieth-century natural disasters" turns up a disturbing record of epidemics, famines, earthquakes, droughts, floods, and hurricanes that took the lives of millions of people,[16] although not nearly so many as lost their lives to actions of governments (see note 10, p. 124).

Readers ought *not* consider these as divine judgments visited on particular populations for some specific fault of theirs: in Luke 13:1–5, Jesus' comment on the victims of abusive government and of an accident teaches better. Rather, all such disasters foreshadow the end of history and provide a reminder of death that awaits all. They summon human beings to repent and to place their hope in the one who holds the keys of Hades and Death and who shepherds his faithful who persevere through trial (1:18; 7:14).

---

15. A difference is that Jesus includes earthquakes in this list, which he describes as the beginning of the labor pains (Matt 24:7–8).

16. For example, see "The Most Deadly 100 Natural Disasters of the 20th Century," The Disaster Center, http://www.disastercenter.com/disaster/TOP100K.html.

Reflection and Application (8:7–12)

Moral ecology. Scripture teaches that there is a link between human conduct and blessing in the natural order. According to Gen 3:17–18, alienation between human beings and their environment is a consequence of the fall: "Cursed is the ground because of you! / In toil you shall eat its yield / all the days of your life. / Thorns and thistles it shall bear for you, / and you shall eat the grass of the field." According to Gen 6:11–13, the reason for the flood was that human beings had corrupted the earth through violence. In Lev 18:25–28 God warns Israel not to engage in the immoral practices of the Canaanites that defiled the land such that it "vomited out its inhabitants." The prophet Jeremiah laments, "How long must the land mourn, / the grass of the whole countryside wither? / Because of the wickedness of those who dwell in it / beasts and birds disappear, / for they say, 'God does not care about our future'" (12:4).

St. Paul addresses this topic: "Creation was made subject to futility, not of its own accord but because of the one who subjected it, in hope that creation itself would be set free from slavery to corruption and share in the glorious freedom of the children of God. We know that all creation is groaning in labor pains even until now" (Rom 8:20–22). Paul looks forward to creation's liberation at the return of Christ, when our identity as God's sons and daughters becomes fully manifest (Rom 8:19). Other texts speak of creation's renewal when God's kingdom comes (Ps 96; Isa 11, 66).

In recent decades people have become aware of the importance of being good stewards of the environment through conserving resources and safeguarding air and water from harmful contaminants.[17] As important as this is, keeping God's word is even more important, even for the life of this planet.

A Warning Cry (8:13)

[13]Then I looked again and heard an eagle flying high overhead cry out in a loud voice, "Woe! Woe! Woe to the inhabitants of the earth from the rest of the trumpet blasts that the three angels are about to blow!"

OT: Deut 28:49; Hosea 8:1 (RSV)
NT: Matt 23:13–29; Luke 6:24–26

17. See *The Compendium of the Social Doctrine of the Church* (Washington: USCCB, 2005), 451–87, http://www.vatican.va/roman_curia/pontifical_councils/justpeace/documents/rc_pc_justpeace_doc_2006 0526_compendio-dott-soc_en.html.

St. Beatus of Liébana's Illustrations

LIVING TRADITION

Approximately two-thirds of the illustrations used in this volume are from St. Beatus of Liébana's illustrated *Commentary on the Apocalypse*. Beatus (ca. 730–800) was a Spanish monk and theologian. His commentary combined numerous quotations of Church Fathers, biblical texts, and his own comments, and was very popular in the Middle Ages. It has been preserved in thirty-one manuscripts, twenty-six of which copy his colorful illustrations (many of which are available online), but with differences reflecting the style and ability of the artists. The images included in this volume are from the Escorial Beatus of San Millán (ca. 950; see figs. 7, 8, 11, and 16) and from the Beatus of Facundas (1047; see figs. 9, 10, 13, 15, and 17–22).

As bad as things are after the four trumpet blasts, worse is yet to come. Now an alarming messenger appears **flying high overhead** (literally, "midheaven," NRSV; "midair," NIV) crying out with **a loud voice**. The messenger is an **eagle** (the same Greek word denotes vulture), an awe-inspiring bird of prey due to its size and speed, and a harbinger of destruction in Old Testament prophecies of judgment (Deut 28:49; Jer 48:40–42; Hosea 8:1 RSV). The word **woe** in Greek (*ouai*) and Hebrew (*oi*) is an exclamation, either a warning of imminent disaster or a cry of anguish, that some say resembles the sound an eagle makes. The threefold "woe" corresponds to the three **trumpet blasts** that are coming and the judgments they bring to **the inhabitants of the earth**, those who do not belong to God's people.

8:13

Reflection and Application (8:1–13)

Even great natural disasters are not hopeless calamities. Those who know God have no need to be afraid but can trust him even when troubles come (Ps 46). God's protective seal is on them (7:4). Their future holds infinite blessing in the presence of God and the Lamb (7:17). God is working out his purposes. God himself limits the effects of disasters, preserving the world until the time comes for its renewal (Gen 9:11–15). God hears the prayers of his people, not least when judgments fall on the earth. Our prayers are precious to him and are received at the throne, the center from which the direction of all history proceeds.

It is especially fitting to pray for all who experience these sufferings, whether they are believers or not, that they will turn to God and receive both physical and spiritual salvation (Ps 107; 1 Tim 4:10). Although Revelation shows that many experience judgments and do not repent, the biblical precedents of Egypt and Jericho give grounds to hope and pray for their conversion. Some of the Egyptians came to reverence God through the plagues (Exod 12:36–38). In Jericho, Rahab the harlot and her family acknowledged the superiority of Israel's God, were saved from destruction, and were joined to God's people (Josh 2:9–11; 6:25). Intercession for all people "is good and pleasing to God our savior, who wills everyone to be saved and to come to knowledge of the truth" (1 Tim 2:3–4).

The Woes Experienced by the Inhabitants of the Earth

Revelation 9:1–21

We have now reached the chapter of Revelation whose imagery is probably the most bizarre and terrifying of all. It is the stuff of our worst nightmares. If we look for a comparison in the world of cinema, Rev 9 resembles a horror movie.

In the final verse of the previous chapter (8:13), an eagle in midheaven warns that the remaining three trumpets portend great woe for "the inhabitants of the earth," a phrase that Revelation uses for those who do not belong to God's people (see sidebar, "Who Are the 'Inhabitants of the Earth'?," p. 130). Unlike the misfortunes that afflict humanity in general when the first four seals are opened, or the calamities that strike the created order when the first four angels sound their trumpets, the three woes, like the last seven of the ten plagues against Egypt (Exod 8:20–12:36), are discriminating in their effects. They strike "only those people who did not have the seal of God on their foreheads" (9:4).

When the fifth and sixth angels blow their trumpets, vast armies of strange demonic creatures afflict the inhabitants of the earth. At first glance the weird tormentors of this chapter and the sufferings they inflict resemble nothing in this world. However, readers who reflect more deeply may discern a likeness to spiritual and psychological afflictions that are all too real and common among people that we know and love.

The Fifth Trumpet (9:1–12)

¹Then the fifth angel blew his trumpet, and I saw a star that had fallen from the sky to the earth. It was given the key for the passage to the abyss.

[2]It opened the passage to the abyss, and smoke came up out of the passage like smoke from a huge furnace. The sun and the air were darkened by the smoke from the passage. [3]Locusts came out of the smoke onto the land, and they were given the same power as scorpions of the earth. [4]They were told not to harm the grass of the earth or any plant or any tree, but only those people who did not have the seal of God on their foreheads. [5]They were not allowed to kill them but only to torment them for five months; the torment they inflicted was like that of a scorpion when it stings a person. [6]During that time these people will seek death but will not find it, and they will long to die but death will escape them.

[7]The appearance of the locusts was like that of horses ready for battle. On their heads they wore what looked like crowns of gold; their faces were like human faces, [8]and they had hair like women's hair. Their teeth were like lions' teeth, [9]and they had chests like iron breastplates. The sound of their wings was like the sound of many horse-drawn chariots racing into battle. [10]They had tails like scorpions, with stingers; with their tails they had power to harm people for five months. [11]They had as their king the angel of the abyss, whose name in Hebrew is Abaddon and in Greek Apollyon.

[12]The first woe has passed, but there are two more to come.

OT: Exod 10:1–19 (especially 12–15); Joel 1–2
NT: Luke 8:31; 10:17–20; John 10:10

9:1–2   It is likely that the **star that had fallen from the sky** represents a fallen angel, probably Satan himself (Isa 14:12–14; Luke 10:18; Rev 12:7–9). God allows it (**It was given**, a [†]divine passive) to open **the passage to the abyss** and release the evil forces residing there. The reason God allows this does not appear until the end of the chapter, namely, to lead the inhabitants of the earth to repentance (9:20–21). Smoke arises from a shaft to the abyss, **like smoke from a huge furnace**, words that echo the description in Gen 19:28 of the burning of Sodom and Gomorrah.

9:3–6   **Locusts** were a familiar-enough pest in Palestine and northern Africa, but here, two Old Testament texts about plagues of locusts provide the background. Exodus 10 describes the eighth plague against Egypt as a swarm of locusts so numerous that they consumed every green thing growing in the land. Joel 1:2–2:12 describes a devastating plague of locusts, a trumpet blast, and an announcement of the "day of the LORD," God's judgment against Judah. In both cases, the purpose of the judgment by locusts is remedial rather than punitive, intended to bring about a change of attitude rather than to destroy those whose crops are smitten by it. Pharaoh is being urged to release God's people to serve

The Abyss

BIBLICAL BACKGROUND

In the †Septuagint, the abyss refers to deep waters (e.g., Gen 1:2), and sometimes the chaotic sea that God mastered when he created the world (Ps 74:13–14).

By the time of the New Testament, however, the abyss represents the place of the dead (Rom 10:7) or a place where evil spirits are confined (Luke 8:31). "Abyss" occurs seven times in Revelation, always in relationship to evil spiritual beings.[a] In this chapter demonic locusts arise from the abyss (9:2, 11). In other texts the beast comes from the abyss (11:7; 17:8), and the dragon Satan is confined there (20:1, 3).

a. Rev 9:1, 2, 11; 11:7; 17:8; 20:1, 3.

him (Exod 10:3–4, 16–17). Judah is being urged to repent of its unfaithfulness, so that God can again bless it (Joel 2:12–16).

While the purpose of this plague is also to elicit repentance (Rev 9:20–21), these locusts are entirely different from those in Exodus and Joel: they **harm not the vegetation but people**—specifically, those **who** do **not have the seal of God on their foreheads**, meaning the part of humanity that does not belong to God (9:4).[1] Ordinary locusts eat plants, but these are no ordinary locusts since they inflict **torment . . . like that of a scorpion when it stings a person**. Scorpions are common around the Mediterranean. They are related to spiders and have stingers in their tails that produce a severely painful wound, in some species sufficiently venomous to be fatal to human beings. Jesus refers to demons as "serpents and scorpions" in Luke 10:19, and that symbolism is intended here as well since the locusts arise from the abyss (9:2–3) and are ruled by the "angel of the abyss" (9:11). Nevertheless, God retains control of these scorpion-like locusts and restrains their malevolence: **They were not allowed to kill** their victims, **but only to torment them for five months**. Five months is the typical lifespan of a locust, but here it represents suffering that is time limited rather than endless. Nevertheless, the pain of this torment is so intense that those afflicted **seek death** and **long to die** but are not able to do so.

1. The fact that only those with the seal are spared from this plague lends support to the interpretation of 7:1–8 that the one hundred and forty-four thousand servants of God who receive the seal refers not to Jews, Jewish Christians, martyrs, or any other special group but rather to the whole of God's army of faithful people.

9:7–9   The next paragraph elaborates on the fearsome nature of the diabolical locusts in language largely borrowed from Joel 2:4–7.[2] In Joel a plague of locusts
is described metaphorically as an army; here in Rev 9:7–11, a demonic army
is described metaphorically as a plague of locusts. The locusts' **appearance** as
horses ready for battle would have been frightening to first-century readers.
"Roman warhorses were very large, bred for battle, taught to bite, and equipped
with razor sharp hooves."[3] The fact that they wear **what looked like crowns
of gold** indicates a claim to rule. That their **faces were like human faces, and
they had hair like women's hair** indicates personhood that resembles human
personality but is not the real thing. They are humanoids but not human. Their
teeth . . . like lions' teeth (echoing Joel 1:6) indicate their ferocity; their **chests
like iron breastplates**, their invincibility. A terrifying **sound** accompanies the
locusts' bone-chilling appearance. In ancient times **horse-drawn chariots** were
among the most effective weapons available; hearing the sound might affect
first-century people as the rumble of tanks or the screaming of jet fighters or
bombers might affect people today.

9:10–11   Verse 10 repeats that these locusts have **power to harm people for five months**
and locates this power in their scorpion-like **tails**. Their diabolical nature is confirmed by the identification of **their king** as **the angel of the abyss**. His Hebrew
name **Abaddon** means "destruction." The Greek name **Apollyon** means "one
who destroys."[4] Readers of John's Gospel may recall the words of Jesus: "The thief
comes only to steal and kill and destroy" (10:10 RSV). The destructive angel of
the abyss is a demonic power, Satan or one of his lieutenants.[5]

9:12   The diabolical locusts represent **the first woe**, with **two more to come**, enabling the reader to understand that the three woes correspond to the final
three of the seven trumpets.

---

2. "Their appearance is that of horses; / like war horses they run. / Like the rumble of chariots / they
hurtle across mountaintops; / Like the crackling of fiery flames / devouring stubble; / Like a massive
army / in battle formation. / Before them peoples tremble" (Joel 2:4–6).
3. Osborne, *Revelation*, 369.
4. Osborne points out an interesting twist: "The name of the Greek god Apollo was taken from
this term, and the locust was one of his symbols, since he was the god of pestilence and plague. Moreover, the emperor Domitian (perhaps ruler of Rome at the time of writing) viewed himself as Apollo
incarnate" (*Revelation*, 374).
5. Some biblical scholars deny the reality of supernatural evil and reinterpret Revelation accordingly.
Wilfrid Harrington writes, "To look to an influence beyond ourselves, and an influence, for that matter,
more malignant and more powerful than we, is to evade our responsibility. . . . There is an influence,
true, that weighs upon us, but it is the inherited burden of human perversity. . . . Satan is a powerful
symbol, representing the whole gamut of evil and its infectious presence in the human race" (*Revelation*,
Sacra Pagina [Collegeville, MN: Liturgical Press, 1993], 111). This interpretation represents neither the
biblical author nor the Christian tradition, which insists on the existence of a personal evil power in
addition to the problem of human sinfulness (see Catechism 2851).

The Sixth Trumpet (9:13–19)

¹³Then the sixth angel blew his trumpet, and I heard a voice coming from the [four] horns of the gold altar before God, ¹⁴telling the sixth angel who held the trumpet, "Release the four angels who are bound at the banks of the great river Euphrates." ¹⁵So the four angels were released, who were prepared for this hour, day, month, and year to kill a third of the human race. ¹⁶The number of cavalry troops was two hundred million; I heard their number. ¹⁷Now in my vision this is how I saw the horses and their riders. They wore red, blue, and yellow breastplates, and the horses' heads were like heads of lions, and out of their mouths came fire, smoke, and sulfur. ¹⁸By these three plagues of fire, smoke, and sulfur that came out of their mouths a third of the human race was killed. ¹⁹For the power of the horses is in their mouths and in their tails; for their tails are like snakes, with heads that inflict harm.

NT: Rev 16:12–14; 20:7–8

The blast of the sixth trumpet signals the final warning. The **voice** that au-   9:13–16
thorizes the event comes from the **horns of the gold altar before God**. It was
at this altar that an angel offered the prayers of the holy ones, God's people,
before the series of seven trumpets began (8:3–5).[6] Perhaps the voice is that of
the angel who made that offering and then took the censer filled with coals from
the altar and cast it down to earth. The **four angels** are probably fallen angels,
since they had been **bound** and their intention to kill **a third of the human race**
(9:15) is identified with the act carried out by an immense army of demonic
troops (9:18). These angels are located by **the great river Euphrates**. Like the
other place names in Revelation (except for the cities of the seven churches),
it bears a figurative meaning. In biblical history, Israel's great enemies Assyria
and Babylon came from across the Euphrates, the easternmost boundary of the
land promised to Israel (Gen 15:18; Deut 1:7; Josh 1:4). The Euphrates likewise
marked the eastern frontier of the Roman Empire, beyond which dwelt the
much-feared †Parthians. Whether John's audience was thinking about biblical
history or the security of the empire, mention of an army crossing the Euphrates would have been disturbing. These fallen angels are to be released at
a precisely determined moment in history: they were **prepared for this hour**.
God is allowing evil to be released in unparalleled force in a last-ditch effort

6. Israel's altars featured hornlike projections from each of the four corners, probably symbolizing God's strength.

to bring the inhabitants of the earth to their senses (9:20–21). Like the events that accompany the opening of the sixth seal (6:12), the attack that the sixth trumpet precipitates occurs just before the end of history, the completion of God's judgments and his salvation of his people. We know this because the blowing of the *seventh* trumpet will be accompanied by the announcement that the kingdom of God has come (11:15).

This judgment is more severe than the fifth trumpet judgment. The enemy is larger and more potent. Instead of locusts, they are horses and riders. In the ancient world **cavalry**, like chariots, were feared for their ability to deliver overwhelming force swiftly from a great distance. This enemy is an army of **two hundred million**, in other words, an immense multitude, multiplying the largest number in the Greek language (a *myriad*, ten thousand) by itself, and then doubling it. While the demonic locusts were not permitted to take life, the demonic cavalry is permitted to kill a third of the human race.

9:17–19   As in the vision that followed the fifth trumpet (the first woe), after an overview (vv. 13–16) John provides a close-up of the monsters that constitute the second woe. The Greek suggests that both the horses and their riders are wearing colored armor, as the Parthian cavalry was also known to do. The colors of their breastplates—**red, blue, and yellow** (more literally, "the color of fire and of sapphire and of sulfur," RSV) match the "fire, smoke and sulfur" that issue from their mouths and reveal their nature. **Fire** and **sulfur** (often translated "brimstone") rained down on Sodom and Gomorrah (Gen 19:24); in the Bible they often manifest divine judgment; in Revelation they characterize the lake of fire, to which Satan is condemned, along with his demonic and human allies (20:10–15).[7] In Scripture, **smoke** often occurs in connection with the fires of judgment that burn cities.[8]

If any doubt remained, the rest of the description makes plain that this is no ordinary human cavalry, but a demonic host. The heads of the horses are **like heads of lions**, "the most vicious beast known to the ancient people of the Mediterranean."[9] Furthermore, "they resemble the mythological Chimera, a fire-breathing Greek monster that has a lion's head, a goat's body, and a serpent's tail."[10] It is the monstrous horses, rather than their riders, that kill **a third of the human race**, a fraction that symbolizes many people, but not the

---

7. See Gen 19:24; Deut 29:22; Job 18:15; Ps 11:6; Isa 30:33; 34:9; Ezek 38:22; Luke 17:29. Fire and sulfur are mentioned four more times in Revelation (14:10; 19:20; 20:10; 21:8).

8. See Gen 19:28; Josh 8:20; Isa 14:31; 34:10.

9. Osborne, *Revelation*, 389.

10. James L. Resseguie, *The Revelation of John: A Narrative Commentary* (Grand Rapids: Baker Academic, 2009), 149.

major portion. The demons kill by means of **three plagues of fire, smoke and sulfur that came out of their mouths**. The fact that the deadly fumes issue from the mouths of the demons suggests the possibility that their weapon is false speech, propaganda that leads people to suffering and death (one can think of the "fumes" often spewed through the mass media or the internet). It turns out that the horses, like the locusts, **inflict harm** both with their mouths and with their **tails**, which are **like snakes**, another symbol of demons. Perhaps the mention of snakes in close proximity to the mention of scorpions (9:5, 10) would have caused John's readers to think of Jesus' promise of authority and protection reported in Luke 10:19: "Behold, I have given you the power 'to tread upon serpents' and scorpions and upon the full force of the enemy and nothing will harm you."[11]

Fig. 8. The sixth trumpet: "Now in my vision this is how I saw the horses and their riders. . . . The horses' heads were like heads of lions, and out of their mouths came fire, smoke, and sulfur. . . . Their tails are like snakes, with heads that inflict harm" (9:17, 19).

Reflection and Application (9:13–19)

The demonic cavalry of the sixth trumpet brings death to one-third of the earth's inhabitants, just as the horseman released at the opening of the fourth seal brought death to one-quarter of the earth's inhabitants (6:8). Although these quantities should be taken figuratively rather than literally, Revelation seems to say that the warning judgments intended to bring a sinful world to its senses will entail the death of large numbers of people. That seems a costly warning, especially for those who die! How can that be just?

First, in both Rev 6 and 9 human sinfulness, rather than God's deliberate will, is the true cause of death. Second, we know that God has a different perspective on bodily death than we do. From his eternal perspective he can see what we only know by faith, namely, that life in this world, even for those who live to a ripe old age, is only a brief entrance way into the vast banquet hall of eternal life. We also know that God is a just yet merciful judge, who both knows the extent and limits of every person's culpability and desires the

---

11. Jesus' words recall Ps 91:13 and Deut 8:15.

salvation of all. The Church teaches that no soul that God created is denied an opportunity to respond to his mercy and receive eternal life, even if we do not know exactly how.

Finally, physical death in this world is well suited as a warning to urge us to conversion, since it is a symbol of eternal death, what Revelation calls "the second death" that lasts forever. Death in this world is grievous and terrible; the death of Lazarus led Jesus to weep, and according to some interpreters, to express anger at this enemy of the human race (John 11:33–38). Nevertheless, the true tragedy is not physical death but the spiritual death that brings eternal separation from God, and it is this tragedy that the terrible warning of human death here is meant to prevent.

Humanity's Response to the Trumpet Plagues (9:20–21)

[20]The rest of the human race, who were not killed by these plagues, did not repent of the works of their hands, to give up the worship of demons and idols made from gold, silver, bronze, stone, and wood, which cannot see or hear or walk. [21]Nor did they repent of their murders, their magic potions, their unchastity, or their robberies.

OT: Deut 32:17; Ps 96:5 LXX
NT: Rom 1:28-32; 1 Cor 10:20; 2 Tim 3:13
Catechism: idolatry, 2112–14; magic and sorcery, 2115–17; exorcisms, 550, 1673

9:20   The final verses of the chapter make clear that God's intention for the trumpet judgments—indeed, all the calamities thus far—is to lead people to repentance. God's desire is always for salvation. The apostle Paul urges that Christians offer "supplications, prayers, petitions, and thanksgivings . . . for everyone . . . [because God] wills everyone to be saved and to come to knowledge of the truth" (1 Tim 2:1, 3–4).

According to John's vision, however, conversion is not the response of the vast majority. Even the most severe wake-up call possible, the death of a large number of people, does not suffice to persuade **the rest of the human race** to **repent**, to renounce their wrongdoing and turn to God (see "Reflection and Application" on 2:1–3:22). There is no need to interpret this to mean that no one repented. At the first coming of Christ, Israel as a whole did not repent and welcome the Messiah, but many Jews did (Acts 21:20). Other texts in Revelation point to the fruitfulness of the Church's witness (11:13), even if some of the "inhabitants of the earth" do not repent.

The nature of humanity's wrongdoing is telling. John depicts the world's idolatry in typical Old Testament language: they worship **the works of their hands**—infinitely inferior to the Creator God of Israel. The idols are made of named materials—**gold, silver, bronze, stone, and wood**—underscoring that idols are things, not gods. Then the clincher: they **cannot see or hear or walk**. The senselessness of idol worship is thus baldly exposed, as often in the Old Testament (e.g., Isa 44:9–20; Wis 13:10–15:17). However, John's vision discloses a deeper reality: at its root, idolatry entails **the worship of demons**. St. Paul says the same: "What pagans sacrifice they offer to demons and not to God" (1 Cor 10:20 RSV). John's words serve as a stern warning to Christians tempted to compromise with pagan religion.

The sins that the world refuses to renounce are grave violations of the precepts of the Decalogue that most pagans also recognized as wrong: **their murders, their magic potions, their unchastity, or their robberies**. The list follows the order of the Ten Commandments, but inserted between murder and adultery is "magic potions" (Greek *pharmaka*).[12] The word literally means "drugs" and, like its modern counterpart, could be used positively to mean medicine, or negatively, as in this case, to mean potions used as aphrodisiacs, abortifacients, contraceptives, or for other morally objectionable purposes. It is commonly translated "sorceries" (RSV, NRSV; "witchcraft," NJB) since the word also refers to the casting of magic spells. Such practices, though common, were looked down upon even by many pagans. The Greek word translated "unchastity" (*porneia*; "fornication," NRSV) refers to any form of sexual immorality.

Just as the worship of the true God leads human beings to a pattern of behavior that resembles God's character and conduct (Lev 19:2; 20:26; 1 Pet 1:16), so also the worship of idols and demons leads to a pattern of conduct that resembles that of the devil, who was a liar and murderer from the beginning (John 8:44). Just as worship of the true God leads to moral and spiritual freedom (2 Cor 3:16–18), so the worship of idols and the violation of the commandments leads to moral and spiritual bondage (John 8:34).

In this light the demonic torments of the fifth and sixth trumpet judgments are logical. These plagues strike only those who have not received the seal of

9:21

---

12. Michael J. Gorman suggests the possibility of an allusion to abortion in this text: "Although the NT makes no specific reference to abortion, the association of the use of drugs (*pharmakeia*) with abortion in pagan and later Christian writings suggests that there may be an implicit reference to abortion in such texts as Gal 5:20 and Rev 9:21, 18:23, 21:8 and 22:15, where words of the same group are used. . . . Thus, while a conclusive affirmation of explicit NT condemnation is impossible, the word *pharmakeia* and the contexts in which it is found suggest that Galatians and Revelation implicitly reject at least one major means of abortion in their rejection of magic, drugs and poisons" (*Abortion and the Early Church* [Downers Grove, IL: InterVarsity, 1982], 48).

the servants of God (see comments after 7:12). Sin opens a door to demonic activity. Those who practice evil, worship idols, and reject the testimony of Jesus become the prey of the demons they serve. The devils seek to torment and destroy their adherents, since that is their nature. As literature and human experience attest, a person cannot have commerce with the devil and come out ahead. For this reason the first and second woes, torment and death visited by cruel demons, are ultimately self-inflicted. The good news is that God works even through the affliction of demons to lead people to conversion and salvation (Mark 5:18–20; Luke 8:2; 1 Cor 5:4–5).

Revelation presents the deadly demonic onslaught that follows the sixth trumpet as belonging to the period shortly before the end. Other texts in Revelation also prophesy a release of evil before the end. The "beast" who gains power over the whole earth, who receives idolatrous worship and persecutes Christians, arises from the sea near history's end (13:1–8). So also, the frog-like demonic spirits emerge to gather the kings of the earth for battle when the penultimate sixth bowl of wrath is poured out (16:12–14). The release of Satan to deceive the nations and gather them against God's holy people depicts a period immediately before the final judgment (20:7–9). While some interpreters understand these as distinct events and try to place them sequentially on a timeline, it seems to others, myself included, that these diverse visions present complementary descriptions of the same final period.[13]

While it is difficult to be certain, it seems likely that at the end of the first century, John and his readers would have understood themselves to be living in a period in which the events of the first four seal judgments and trumpet judgments were already under way, and in which the release of the demonic armies of the fifth and sixth trumpets was imminent. Both at the beginning (1:1) and the end, Revelation states that the events of this book "must happen soon" (22:6). If indeed Revelation was written in the 90s (see "Date" in the introduction, pp. 21–22) the temple in Jerusalem had been destroyed, fulfilling Jesus' prophecy. Wars, famines, and natural calamities were already taking place. Incredibly cruel persecutions of Christians had occurred in Rome and elsewhere. The emperor Domitian was claiming divine titles and strengthening the †imperial cult. In Asia there was an upsurge in pressure from local authorities to participate in emperor worship. False teachers and prophets were teaching

---

13. In 2 Thess 2:8–12, St. Paul offers an analogous picture of a final wave of diabolical evil, entailing deception of the world and persecution of God's people, that will precede the return of Christ. In other texts he alludes to the misery that often afflicts idolaters and others who reject God's commandments (Rom 1:18–32; 2 Tim 3:1–4; Titus 3:3). Jesus' eschatological discourse also adverts to the unhappiness of evildoers in the final period of history (Matt 24:10, 12).

Idolatry: What It Is and What's Wrong with It

BIBLICAL BACKGROUND

Idolatry is the worship of any god other than the true God, or the worship of an image of the true God rather than God himself. Idolatrous worship entails the complete surrender of oneself to anything or anyone besides God.

Idolatry is strictly prohibited in the first commandment: "You shall not have other gods beside me. You shall not make for yourself an idol or a likeness of anything in the heavens above or on the earth below . . . ; you shall not bow down before them or serve them" (Exod 20:3–5). In the ancient world, an image was understood to manifest the presence of the god represented. Idol worship is the fundamental sin in the Bible, the cause of both moral disorder in the Gentile world (Rom 1) and Israel's exile from the land. The need for Israel to avoid and repent of idolatry is a primary theme of the Old Testament, especially stressed in Deuteronomy and Isaiah.

Several evils are inherent in idolatry. First, it fails to give God the thanks and worship that is his due (Rom 1:21–23). Second, when God's people engage in idolatry, it is a form of spiritual adultery, infidelity to God's spousal love (e.g., Hosea 2:1–13). Third, the power of idols is illusory; there is no god other than the one Creator of all. Idols are merely "the work of human hands. / They have mouths but do not speak, / eyes but do not see" (Ps 115:4–5). They are utterly powerless to help or save. Fourth, the worship of idols puts people in relationship to demons (Deut 32:17; Ps 96:5 LXX; Bar 4:7; 1 Cor 10:19–20).

The consequence of idol worship is summed up in the indictment of Israel that explained its exile: "Pursuing futility, they themselves became futile" (2 Kings 17:15 NJB). Human beings end up resembling what they worship. After speaking of the radical powerlessness of idols, Ps 115 continues: "Their makers will be like them; / and anyone who trusts in them" (115:8). In contrast, those who worship God become like him (2 Cor 3:18; Rom 8:29; Col 3:10).

In the New Testament, the understanding of idolatry is deepened. Jesus teaches that it is impossible to serve God and Mammon, meaning money or wealth. Colossians 3:5 and Eph 5:5 identify greed (or "covetousness," RSV), a term for disordered desire that can refer to lust, with idolatry. In Christian usage an idol refers to anything or anyone that rivals God for a person's love, obedience, trust, or fear (see Catechism 2113 and "Reflection and Application" on 2:12–17). In practice, an idol could be a person, a career, an avocation, a movement or political party, an ideology, or one's nation.

and modeling accommodation to the idolatrous and immoral practices of the surrounding culture (2:14–15, 20). Other late New Testament writings imply that the "last days" are close at hand (2 Tim 3:1; 2 Pet 3:3), and some Christians thought the return of Christ was past due (2 Pet 3:9). Other writings discern the activity of the devil: "The mystery of lawlessness is already at work" (2 Thess 2:7), and "The spirit of the antichrist . . . is already in the world" (1 John 4:3).

Reflection and Application (9:1–21)

Idols, demons, and human misery. Although the imagery of Rev 9 is startling, the reality it depicts is all too common. Almost daily the mass media inform us about athletes, entertainers, or politicians whose lives have been ruined through a disordered pursuit of wealth, fame, power, sex, or approval, or through addiction to drugs or alcohol. These are varieties of spiritual idolatry, of seeking first or depending on something other than God, and they often lead to other violations of the commandments. Most of us know people in our family or circle of acquaintances who suffer such things. The torments they experience take many forms: dysfunctional family life and divorce, failure in school or work, economic ruin, compulsive behavior, depression, alienation from loved ones, loneliness, self-loathing, guilt, fear, anxiety, and anger, to name only a few. The interior suffering that some people experience pushes them toward suicide, an evil that in Western countries is common even among the well-to-do. These maladies have physical, psychological, and natural causes of various kinds, but they often also entail demonic oppression.[14]

It is our job not to pass judgment on people who are suffering but to help them in every way we can, especially by our prayers, love, and testimony. Human suffering has many causes, and sometimes very faithful and holy people suffer greatly. When suffering is due to serious sin or idolatry, Jesus stands ready to save those who turn to him for mercy.

Discerning the present age. Many Christians have noted an escalation of evil over the last century. Besides the loss of faith and the increase of sexual immorality and drug addiction, the two world wars and other military conflicts have resulted in the deaths of more people than in all previous wars combined; totalitarian regimes persecuted Christians, Jews, and other minorities and murdered hundreds of millions more. To these one can add the murder of hundreds of millions of unborn children through abortion.

Some have discerned a new wave of demonic activity in these phenomena. On the eve of the twentieth century, Pope Leo XIII is reported to have received

---

14. Recent decades have witnessed a renewed appreciation of the Church's prayers for exorcism as well as for more informal prayer for deliverance from evil. For a useful pastoral treatment of the latter, see Neal Lozano, *Unbound* (Grand Rapids: Chosen, 2010).

Pain Gets Our Attention

LIVING TRADITION

C. S. Lewis, a professor of literature at Oxford and Cambridge and the most widely read Christian apologist of the twentieth century, explains how God can use suffering to benefit us:

> The human spirit will not even begin to try to surrender self-will as long as all seems to be well with it. Now error and sin both have this property, that the deeper they are the less their victim suspects their existence; they are masked evil.
>
> Pain is unmasked, unmistakable evil; every man knows that something is wrong when he is being hurt. . . . And pain is not only immediately recognizable evil, but evil impossible to ignore. We can rest contentedly in our sins and in our stupidities. . . . But pain insists upon being attended to. God whispers to us in our pleasures, speaks to us in our conscience, but shouts in our pains: it is His megaphone to rouse a deaf world.[a]

a. C. S. Lewis, *The Problem of Pain* (New York: Macmillan, 1962), 92–93.

a vision about increased satanic influence coming upon the world. A Lutheran sister, Mother Basilea Schlink, had a vision in the 1960s in which she saw the abyss being opened and evil spirits pouring out. She linked it to the sexual revolution and the social and political chaos unleashed in that period. A few years later, seeing the disorder in the Church, Pope Paul VI expressed his concern that "as if through some fissure, the smoke of Satan has entered the temple of God."[15] Before becoming Pope John Paul II, Cardinal Karol Wojtyla made this sobering statement: "We are now standing in the face of the greatest historical confrontation humanity has gone through. . . . We are now facing the final confrontation between the Church and the anti-Church, of the Gospel versus the anti-Gospel. This confrontation lies within the plans of divine providence."[16]

If it is true that we live in a time of exceptional spiritual evil, does that mean that the end of the world is near? The experience of the first-century Church, which likewise lived through an intensely evil period, and that of the Church in other times and places of great trial—all this history teaches us not to draw hasty conclusions. Nevertheless, awareness of the evil at work in our age can make us alert to discern what is happening, to reject every form of idolatry, to avoid inhaling the "fire, smoke, and sulfur" that pollutes the atmosphere, and to resist the devil (1 Pet 5:8–9).

15. Pope Paul VI, Feast of Sts. Peter and Paul, June 29, 1972.
16. From a 1976 speech to the bishops of the United States, reprinted in the *Wall Street Journal*, November 9, 1978.

The good news. The message of the New Testament and of Revelation is a message not of fear or despair in the face of evil but of courage and the hope of certain victory. That hope is grounded in the incarnation, life, death and resurrection, and glorious return of Jesus Christ. According to 1 John 3:8, "The reason the Son of God appeared was to destroy the works of the devil" (RSV). Although Rev 9 reveals demonic armies of untold number, Rev 19–20 tells of their eternal defeat.

The Open Scroll

Revelation 10:1–11

Just as an interlude of two visions followed the opening of the sixth seal—the sealing of the one hundred and forty-four thousand and the white-robed multitude in heaven (Rev 7)—so here, an interlude of two visions follows the sixth trumpet, preceding the climactic seventh trumpet (11:15). The first vision, recounted in this chapter, reveals a mighty angel bringing the scroll whose seven seals have now been opened (5:7; 6:1–12; 8:1) and commissioning the prophet John to begin a new round of prophesying.

A Mighty Angel and a Small Open Scroll (10:1–7)

[1]Then I saw another mighty angel come down from heaven wrapped in a cloud, with a halo around his head; his face was like the sun and his feet were like pillars of fire. [2]In his hand he held a small scroll that had been opened. He placed his right foot on the sea and his left foot on the land, [3]and then he cried out in a loud voice as a lion roars. When he cried out, the seven thunders raised their voices, too. [4]When the seven thunders had spoken, I was about to write it down; but I heard a voice from heaven say, "Seal up what the seven thunders have spoken, but do not write it down." [5]Then the angel I saw standing on the sea and on the land raised his right hand to heaven [6]and swore by the one who lives forever and ever, who created heaven and earth and sea and all that is in them, "There shall be no more delay. [7]At the time when you hear the seventh angel blow his

trumpet, the mysterious plan of God shall be fulfilled, as he promised to his servants the prophets."

OT: Dan 12:1–9; Amos 3:4–8; Hab 2:3–4
NT: Rom 16:25–27; Heb 10:35–39; Rev 5:2; 11:15

10:1–2a   John sees another **angel** described as **mighty**, as was the angel who introduced the scroll in 5:2: "Who is worthy to open the scroll?" This angel has divine attributes: he is **wrapped in a cloud**, just as God often appears in a cloud,[1] and he has a **halo** or "rainbow" around him like the one surrounding God's throne in 4:3 (Ezek 1:26–28). In some respects this angel resembles the risen Christ, who appeared to John in his first vision (1:15–16): his face is **like the sun** and his feet are like **pillars of fire** (see Exod 13:21–22).[2] It is most likely that this angel is the one mentioned at the beginning and the end of the book (Rev 1:1; 22:6), whom Jesus sent to communicate the contents of Revelation to John. What the angel does here (10:8–11) closely matches the description of the angel's role there. This angel is especially glorious because of who sent him and because his message is of capital importance.

The scroll he holds **had been opened**, referring to the Lamb's removal of the seven seals in chapter 6 and 8:1. Some interpreters question whether this is the same scroll that the Lamb unsealed because here it is called **a small scroll**, using a diminutive form of the word (*biblaridion* instead of *biblion*). However, at the end of the first century these words were used interchangeably, and 10:8 uses the same word employed in 5:1–9 (*biblion*) to refer to this scroll.[3] If there is a distinction between the scroll the Lamb unsealed and this scroll, it would represent the difference between the totality of God's plan and the part of it that John is commissioned to prophesy (10:8–11).

10:2b–4   The fact that the powerful angel places one foot **on the sea** and one foot **on the land** expresses the authority of what he is about to say to the whole earth. His **loud voice** is like the roar of a **lion**—another sign of God's presence in him, recalling Amos 3:8:

1. See Exod 13:20–22; 14:19; 19:18; Deut 4:11; Lam 3:44.
2. Some interpreters think the "angel" refers to Jesus himself, the messenger of God (Isa 42:19; Mal 3:1); the Greek word *angelos* means both "angel" and "messenger." However, Revelation nowhere else refers to Jesus as an angel.
3. Although some patristic Greek commentators on Revelation distinguish the meaning of the two words and interpret the two scrolls as distinct, Richard Bauckham points out that none of the diminutive forms in Revelation are diminutive in meaning, and that the only other known occurrences of *biblaridion* in Greek literature are in another work of Christian prophecy of the same general period, *Shepherd of Hermas*, where it is used interchangeably with *biblion* (*The Climax of Prophecy: Studies on the Book of Revelation* [Edinburgh: T&T Clark, 1993], 244).

> The lion has roared,
>> who would not fear?
> The Lord GOD has spoken,
>> who would not prophesy?

The **seven thunders** that **raised their voices** when the angel cries out also indicate that God himself is speaking, since in Ps 29 the "voice of the LORD" is described as thundering over the sea and land seven times. In the Bible, thunder implies God's presence (Exod 19:16, 19; Rev 4:5). There is a message in the thunder, and John assumes he is to **write it down** as he has written the rest of what he has seen and heard. But **a voice from heaven** directs him instead to **seal up** and **not write** what **the seven thunders have spoken**. This revelation that is not to be revealed may symbolize that God is not disclosing everything he has in mind to do (Dan 12:4; 2 Cor 12:4).

The powerful angel now raises **his right hand to heaven** to swear an oath, **10:5–7** invoking the eternal Creator God who is supreme over everything, and declares on his behalf that there will be **no more delay**. This vision echoes a similar vision recorded in Dan 12: an angelic messenger tells Daniel about a great time of conflict and trial ("the great tribulation"; see sidebar, "The Great Tribulation," pp. 146–47) that will immediately precede the resurrection of the dead. The angel then raises his hands toward heaven and swears an oath that the duration of the trial will be "a time, two times, and half a time" (12:7). Daniel does not understand, but is told not to concern himself about it, since the message does not pertain to his time but is "sealed until the end time" (12:9). The vision in Rev 10 of an unsealed scroll and an angel swearing "no more delay" implies that "the time unsurpassed in distress" (Dan 12:1) of three and a half years (see 11:2–3; 12:6, 14; and sidebar, "Forty-Two Months, Twelve Hundred and Sixty Days, Three and a Half Years," p. 189) is imminent or already under way, and that God will soon establish his kingdom.[4]

The mighty angel's oath informs John that **At the time** (literally, "in the days") **when** he hears **the seventh angel blow his trumpet, the mysterious plan of God** (literally, the "mystery of God") **shall be fulfilled**. So the seventh trumpet will signal the fulfillment of all God's promises to his people through **the prophets**, both those of the Old Testament and Christian prophets like John—promises of judgment against those who oppress God's people and promises of salvation and comfort in God's presence (e.g., 7:9–17; Isa 11:4–9).

---

4. The promise of "no more delay" is not a literal indication of timing; Hab 2:3–4 (RSV) makes a similar promise that Heb 10:35–38 interprets as an encouragement to Christian endurance.

The Timing of Jesus' Return

Several texts in the New Testament suggest that many in the early Church expected Christ's return in †glory to happen in their lifetime (e.g., John 21:22; 2 Pet 3:2–9), and Revelation itself says that Jesus will return "quickly" or soon (3:11; 22:20; see sidebar, "What Christ Means by 'Soon,'" p. 41). In 2 Thess 2, St. Paul's effort to calm such expectation is the clearest evidence of a pastoral problem along these lines. The imminent expectation of the kingdom sprang from the preaching of John the Baptist and Jesus himself that the kingdom of God is at hand. It probably also sprang from Jesus' †Olivet discourse, where he prophesies both the coming destruction of Jerusalem (which took place in AD 70) and the end of history (Mark 13).

The early Christians were aware that the transformation that began with Jesus' death and resurrection was incomplete. Paul expresses it: "We know that all creation is groaning in labor pains even until now; and not only that, but we ourselves, who have the firstfruits of the Spirit, we also groan within ourselves as we wait for adoption, the redemption of our bodies" (Rom 8:22–23).

Nevertheless, although some disciples expected the †parousia to occur in their lifetime, there is no evidence of disillusionment among the early Christians when Jesus did not return in the first century. Perhaps his teaching that no one knows "that day and hour . . . but the Father alone" (Matt 24:36) and the parables that emphasize keeping watch without knowing the time of the master's return helped to correct mistaken expectations (e.g., Mark 13:35–37; Luke 12:38–40). The New Testament curbs excessive speculation about the time of the end and directs Christian attention to the present, while keeping alive the expectation of Christ's return in glory and foretelling the signs that will mark its approach (Matt 24:32–33; Acts 1:11; 2 Pet 3:1–14).

Reflection and Application (10:1–7)

I remember many times, late in a day of backpacking in the Appalachian Mountains, thinking and hoping that the hill I was climbing was the last before our campsite. So many times that expectation was disappointed by the discovery of yet another peak that lay beyond the one I could see, followed often enough by yet another. The history of the Church has been something like that. The sack of Rome by Alaric and the Visigoths in 410, and subsequent sacks of Rome by barbarians in 455 and 546, led some Christians to think that the end was at hand. We too live in a time of crisis that raises hopes for Christ's speedy return. We need to remember the experience of our Christian forebearers and the fact that no one knows the day or the hour except the Father (Mark 13:32).

The very structure of Revelation reflects the Christian experience of deferred expectation by a tantalizing succession of seven seals, seven trumpets, and seven bowls, followed by seven visions, each seeming to indicate the end before the new Jerusalem finally comes down out of heaven at the end of the book.

The Catechism 673 reflects the balanced perspective of Christian tradition:

> Since the Ascension Christ's coming in glory has been imminent (see Rev 22:20), even though "it is not for you to know times or seasons which the Father has fixed by his own authority" (Acts 1:7; see Mark 13:32). This eschatological coming could be accomplished at any moment, even if both it and the final trial that will precede it are "delayed" (see Matt 24:44; 1 Thess 5:2; 2 Thess 2:3–12).

A New Prophetic Commission (10:8–11)

⁸Then the voice that I had heard from heaven spoke to me again and said, "Go, take the scroll that lies open in the hand of the angel who is standing on the sea and on the land." ⁹So I went up to the angel and told him to give me the small scroll. He said to me, "Take and swallow it. It will turn your stomach sour, but in your mouth it will taste as sweet as honey." ¹⁰I took the small scroll from the angel's hand and swallowed it. In my mouth it was like sweet honey, but when I had eaten it, my stomach turned sour. ¹¹Then someone said to me, "You must prophesy again about many peoples, nations, tongues, and kings."

OT: Jer 15:16–17; Ezek 2:8–3:3

Again John hears the **voice** from **heaven** that told him not to write what the seven   **10:8–10** thunders said, now instructing him to become an actor in the vision he is seeing: **Go, take the scroll**. The word for "scroll" here is the same one used several times in chapter 5 (see 10:2). The Greek word translated **lies open** is in the same verbal form as in 10:2, where it is translated more precisely as "that had been opened."

What happens next resembles an experience of the prophet Ezekiel:

> It was then I saw a hand stretched out to me; in it was a written scroll. He unrolled it before me; it was covered with writing front and back. Written on it was: Lamentation, wailing, woe!

> He said to me: Son of man, eat what you find here: eat this scroll, then go, speak to the house of Israel. So I opened my mouth, and he gave me the scroll to eat. Son of man, he said to me, feed your stomach and fill your belly with this scroll I am giving you. I ate it, and it was as sweet as honey in my mouth. (Ezek 2:9–3:3)

The scroll given to Ezekiel had writing on front and back, like the one John saw in 5:1 (see comments there). Ezekiel's scroll was opened before him by the hand of God or an angel; John is presented with a scroll that he saw the Lamb open seal by seal. John, like Ezekiel, is commanded to eat the scroll: **Take and swallow it**, and is told that **it will taste as sweet as honey**, just like Ezekiel's scroll. The image of the prophet eating the scroll provides a vivid image of divine inspiration; the prophet receives and assimilates God's word until it becomes part of him. He then expresses it as best he can in writing or speech aided by the Holy Spirit (1 Cor 2:13; 12:8). For both Ezekiel and John, receiving and speaking the word of the Lord is sweet as honey, echoing Jeremiah's experience: "When I found your words, I devoured them; / your words were my joy, the happiness of my heart" (Jer 15:16).

John is warned, however, that eating the scroll will turn his **stomach sour**; this also echoes Ezekiel's experience. Ezekiel reports that the message of "Lamentation, wailing woe" given him (2:10) left him "in bitterness in the heat of my spirit" (3:14 RSV). John's experience of taking and eating the scroll conforms to what the mighty angel told him: **In my mouth it was like sweet honey, but when I had eaten it, my stomach turned sour** ("bitter," NRSV, RSV). The sour or bitter effect on John may indicate that, like Ezekiel, he receives a word of judgment, or that he anticipates the hardships that await God's people in what lies ahead.

10:11   The climax of John's vision is the instruction he now receives. The wording is vague about who is speaking, but there is no doubt that John is receiving a divine commission: **Then someone said to me, "You must prophesy again."** John is being commanded to prophesy the contents of the scroll he has eaten. This new phase of his prophetic ministry will reveal the contents of the scroll that the Lamb received from God in chapter 5.

A single clue about this content is given. While Ezekiel's message was a warning to the house of Israel, John's message is to or "**about many peoples, nations, tongues, and kings**." The fourfold list points to its worldwide significance. The mention of kings indicates that the message touches on how political power is exercised on the earth.

Reflection and Application (10:8–11)

It is not only prophets like Jeremiah, Ezekiel, and John who are privileged to taste the sweetness of the word of God. Readers and even commentators may enjoy its extraordinary sweetness, as I can personally attest.

The Temple of God, the Two Witnesses, and the Seventh Trumpet

Revelation 11:1–19

Although John has just been told to prophesy a message that sours his stomach "about many peoples, nations, tongues, and kings" (10:11), the first revelation he receives is about what is going to happen to the people of God. This is similar to what occured in John's previous round of prophesying, when, before the unfolding of divine judgments, he received a two-part revelation about God's seal of protection on his servants and a vision of their blessed state on the other side of the great distress (Rev 7). Here John receives a two-part revelation of the role of the Church in God's plan by means of being commanded to perform a symbolic action (11:1–2) and being told a prophetic allegory about the Church's future (11:3–13).

At the end of the allegory, the seventh trumpet sounds (11:15), marking the days when "the mysterious plan of God shall be fulfilled" (10:7), and voices in heaven erupt in celebration that the kingdom of God has finally arrived. This chapter is one of the most challenging to interpret. I will present my understanding, mentioning some alternatives as space allows.

Measuring the Temple of God (11:1–2)

¹Then I was given a measuring rod like a staff and I was told, "Come and measure the temple of God and the altar, and count those who are worshiping in it. ²But exclude the outer court of the temple; do not measure

God's Temple

The essential meaning of "temple" to pagans, Jews, and Christians of the ancient world was similar: the house or dwelling place of a deity. For Jews and Christians, God's true dwelling is in heaven; his temple on earth is the place he has established for human beings to approach him in order to worship him and seek his help.

Most of the references to the temple in Revelation refer to God's temple in heaven. However, the theme of God establishing his temple on earth among his people appears from Genesis to Revelation. The early chapters of Genesis imply in a variety of ways that God created the world as a temple in which to dwell with the human race. Although this purpose was hindered by the sin of our first parents, when God made a covenant with Israel on Mount Sinai, he instructed Moses to build a portable temple, a tent or "tabernacle," so that he could live among his people and they could worship him (Exod 25:8–9). Israel understood God to be present in the inner room of the tabernacle, called the holy of holies, between the cherubim above the ark of the covenant (Num 7:89). The tabernacle was modeled on God's heavenly temple that was revealed to Moses on Sinai (Exod 26:30; Heb 8:5).

Solomon's temple succeeded the tabernacle as the earthly dwelling place of God. God's †glory filled the temple, and Solomon's prayer of dedication (1 Kings 8:10–13, 22–61) summarized what this meant to Israel: a close relationship with God and a place to worship him, to obtain forgiveness, and to seek his help on every occasion of communal or personal need. When the

it, for it has been handed over to the †Gentiles, who will trample the holy city for forty-two months.

OT: 1 Macc 3:45, 51; Ezek 40–42; Dan 7:25; 12:7; Zech 1:16–17; 2:5–17
NT: Luke 21:24; Eph 2:19–22; 1 Pet 2:5

11:1   After eating the scroll, the prophet John is again called to play an active part in the vision he is seeing. He is given a **measuring rod like a staff** and told to **measure** the temple and the altar, and to **count** the worshipers in the temple. This instruction recalls another of Ezekiel's visions, in which an angel uses a measuring rod to measure all the dimensions of the new temple where God will come to dwell with his people forever (40:3–43:5).

To what does the **temple of God** refer? Since none of the other fifteen uses of "temple" in Revelation speak of the Jerusalem temple, which the Romans destroyed in AD 70, it is unlikely that is its meaning here. It is also unlikely

Babylonians destroyed that temple in 586 BC, God promised through the prophets a new, more glorious temple where he would live with his people forever (e.g., Ezek 40–47).

Although the Jews built a second temple in Jerusalem (520–515 BC) after the exile, the true fulfillment of this promise began with the Incarnation: "The Word became flesh / and made his dwelling among us" (John 1:14). Other texts in the Gospel of John confirm that the human body of the incarnate Word was the true temple, the "place" on earth where God is present and available to his people (John 2:19–21; 10:38; 14:7–11). When that "temple" was destroyed by crucifixion, Jesus "rebuilt" it by rising from the dead. When he poured out his Spirit on his disciples, the Church became his body, the temple of God, the new location of God's dwelling on earth. The New Testament uses the image of a temple for the universal Church (Eph 2:19–22; 1 Pet 2:5), for the local church (1 Cor 3:16–17), and for the body of every Christian (1 Cor 6:19) because of the indwelling presence of the Holy Spirit.

The end of Revelation reveals that the final stage of God's dwelling among his people will occur when the heavenly Jerusalem, the place where God dwells, descends to earth. Then God's people will dwell with him forever, worshiping God and the Lamb and seeing his face (Rev 21:2–3; 22:3–4). Revelation depicts the new Jerusalem symbolically as a perfect cube, like the holy of holies (1 Kings 6:19–20; Rev 21:16), and explains that "its temple is the Lord God almighty and the Lamb" (Rev 21:22). No other temple will be needed, since the access of God's people to God will be complete, unrestricted, and unmediated.

that God's temple in heaven is intended (11:19; 14:17), since its "outer court" is described as trampled by the Gentiles. Finally, it is unlikely that the temple here refers to a third Jewish temple yet to be built in Jerusalem, as some †futurists think, since Revelation addresses the situation of Christians in Asia rather than that of Jews and temple worship in Jerusalem.[1]

The interpretation that seems most likely is that here the temple of God refers to the Church, God's dwelling on earth, a familiar concept to the early Christians.[2] As his temple on earth, the Church was understood to be in communion with God's temple in heaven. The **altar** refers either to the heavenly altar where the prayers of the Christian faithful are received (6:9; 8:3–5) or to the place on earth where the Church on earth offers its worship (see Heb 13:10), or to both at the same time. **Those who are worshiping** in the temple

---

1. Nothing in Jesus' words suggests that the temple in Jerusalem will be rebuilt (Matt 23:38; see Matt 24:1–31, especially 24:2, and parallels).

2. See 1 Cor 3:16; Eph 2:19–22; 1 Pet 2:5; and sidebar above, "God's Temple."

are Christians, functioning as priests (1:6; 5:10), since according to the law of Moses, only priests had the right of access to the sanctuary and altar. Although they are worshiping on earth, their worship is joined to the worship in heaven (Heb 12:22–24), since they worship God through Christ and in the Holy Spirit.

What is the point of *measuring* the temple and the altar, and of counting the worshipers? On the one hand, it suggests that the temple of God is under construction, an idea that the exclusion of the outer court in verse 2 supports. The age of the Church is the period during which God's temple is being built (1 Cor 3:9–17) by adding new members and by strengthening those in it until the descent of the new Jerusalem (see 21:3, 16, 22). At the same time, these prophetic actions, like the sealing of the one hundred and forty-four thousand (7:1–8), indicate that God keeps watch over all his people and will protect them. In a vision, Zechariah saw a young man about to measure †eschatological Jerusalem and heard the Lord promise, "I will be an encircling wall of fire for it" (Zech 2:9).

11:2   In contrast to Ezekiel's vision, in which the angel measures the entire temple, John is told to **not measure** the **outer court** (literally, "court outside the temple"). He is told to **exclude** it, using a forceful verb elsewhere translated "cast out," and then is given a reason. The outer court has been **handed over** (a †divine passive) **to the Gentiles, who will trample the holy city** for a period of time. The expression "Gentiles" here refers not to ethnicity but to those who do not belong to God's covenant people. The trampling alludes to Dan 8:10, 13, which speak of an antichrist figure who tramples "the host" of God's people.[3] The "holy city" refers to Jerusalem, but here, as in 20:9 and 21:2, Jerusalem symbolizes the people of God rather than an earthly location.[4]

Putting the imagery together, those worshiping in the temple of God and enjoying God's spiritual protection are the Church at worship. The "court outside" is the world, controlled by those who oppose God (the Gentiles). In the present period, the Gentiles trample—that is, rule over and persecute—God's people ("the holy city"). This situation is only temporary; it will last **forty-two months**, equal to three and a half years, the length of the eschatological †tribulation referred to in Dan 7:25 (see sidebar, "Forty-Two Months, Twelve Hundred and Sixty Days, Three and a Half Years," p. 189).

---

3. Zech 12:3 LXX also speaks of the Gentiles trampling Jerusalem. John may also be alluding to Jesus' prophecy recorded in Luke 21:24: "Jerusalem will be trampled underfoot by the Gentiles until the times of the Gentiles are fulfilled." If so, Jesus' words that originally referred literally to the city of Jerusalem are being interpreted spiritually to apply to Christians suffering persecution at the hands of nonbelievers.

4. At the end of Revelation the link between God's people and the "holy city" is made explicit: "I also saw the holy city, a new Jerusalem, coming down out of heaven from God, prepared as a bride adorned for her husband" (21:2). The Lord's bride is his covenant people (Isa 54:5; Eph 5:25).

Forty-Two Months, Twelve Hundred and Sixty Days, Three and a Half Years

BIBLICAL BACKGROUND

Revelation refers to the same span of time by various expressions. In 11:2 the Gentiles trample "the holy city" for forty-two months. In the next verse the two witnesses prophesy for twelve hundred and sixty days (42 x 30 = 1260). In the next chapter the woman who symbolizes the Church is nourished in the desert for the same number of days (12:6), repeated later in the chapter as "a year, two years, and a half-year" (12:14).[a] Finally, "forty-two months" occurs again in 13:5, where it refers to the period the beast is allowed to exercise authority.

According to the book of Daniel, three and a half years represents the eschatological period of persecution and †tribulation (Dan 7:25, 9:27; 12:7, 11–12). Originally this seems to have referred to a literal period of about three and a half years when the Jewish temple in Jerusalem fell into the hands of the Syrian ruler Antiochus IV Epiphanes, who replaced Israel's sacrifices with idolatrous worship (167–164 BC). However, Jewish and Christian tradition came to understand this period as a †type of the great trial at the end of history.

The number three and a half is symbolically significant because it is half of seven, a number that indicates totality. Thus three and a half years refers to a temporary period of trial that God allows (see Mark 13:20).

In Revelation, it seems that *most* of the action described as lasting the equivalent of three and a half years occurs simultaneously: God's people worship in the temple while the Gentiles "trample the holy city" (11:2); the two witnesses prophesy to those who dwell on the earth (11:3); God protects and nourishes the Church in the desert (12:6). The one apparent exception is that according to 13:5, this is the length of time the beast is allowed to wield its power.

The Fathers of the Church as well as modern scholars have differed over whether to understand the three and a half years as referring to the entire age of the Church (see comments on 12:7, 11–12) or to the period of more intense persecution when the antichrist appears at the end of history.[b] I am persuaded by a third possibility, that the three and a half years, understood as symbolizing a temporary and incomplete period, refers *both* to the entire history of the Church and in a particular way to the Church's "ultimate trial" (see sidebar, "The Great Tribulation," pp. 146–47).

a. Literally, 12:14 says "a time, times, and half a time," echoing a phrase from Dan 7:25 and 12:7.
b. See ACCS 12:155–56.

At the end, God will fully establish a new kind of temple on earth when the new Jerusalem comes "down out of heaven from God" (21:1–2). At that point another measuring takes place, this time by an angel with "a gold measuring rod," who completes what John began in 11:1 by measuring the entire city with its gates and its wall (21:15–16). All of creation will then be incorporated in a re-created Jerusalem filled with God's presence (21:22), no longer trampled by the Gentiles.

The Testimony of the Two Witnesses (11:3–6)

[3]I will commission my two witnesses to prophesy for those twelve hundred and sixty days, wearing sackcloth." [4]These are the two olive trees and the two lampstands that stand before the Lord of the earth. [5]If anyone wants to harm them, fire comes out of their mouths and devours their enemies. In this way, anyone wanting to harm them is sure to be slain. [6]They have the power to close up the sky so that no rain can fall during the time of their prophesying. They also have power to turn water into blood and to afflict the earth with any plague as often as they wish.

OT: Exod 7:17–25; Deut 19:15; 1 Kings 17:1; Jer 5:14; Zech 4:2–3, 11–14
NT: James 5:17

Many interpreters have taken 11:3–13 to refer literally to the career of two Christian prophets who will arise at the end of history to give witness to the world and to oppose the antichrist.[5] I used to hold this view myself. But as I have studied and reflected upon this brief narrative, I have come to regard it as a symbolic dramatization—an allegory or parable—of the Church's mission. My reasons will become apparent in the exposition that follows. Of course, God's word has been proclaimed by pairs of witnesses at various moments in history.[6] If the two witnesses primarily symbolize the testimony of the Church as a whole throughout history, that does not need to exclude a more literal fulfillment through a pair of witnesses who testify with particular power during the Church's final trial (see sidebar, "The Great Tribulation," pp. 146–47).

11:3   Up to this point the "voice" from heaven (10:4, 8) was unidentified, but now the content indicates that the speaker is Christ, since he says, **I will commission my two witnesses to prophesy**. Several times in the Gospels and Acts, Jesus

5. Besides Moses and Elijah, various Church Fathers suggested Enoch, Jeremiah, or the apostle John. John's original readers may have looked back to the powerful testimony of Peter and Paul, who had given their lives as martyrs in Rome in the mid-60s of the first century.
6. For example, Moses and Aaron, Joshua and Zerubbabel (see Rev 11:4–6), Haggai and Zechariah, Ezra and Nehemiah, St. Peter and St. Paul, St. Francis and St. Dominic.

describes his apostles as his witnesses.[7] The word "witness" denotes someone who solemnly attests to the truth, especially in a judicial context.

The two witnesses prophesy for **twelve hundred and sixty days**, equivalent to forty-two months (11:2; see sidebar, "Forty-Two Months, Twelve Hundred and Sixty Days, Three and a Half Years," p. 189), symbolizing the Church's testimony both during the temporary period of her earthly pilgrimage (12:14) and during her final trial (13:5–7). The witnesses wear **sackcloth**, a coarse fabric made from the hair of goats or camels, worn to signify mourning or repentance (Gen 37:34; Jon 3:8).[8] The fact that the witnesses wear sackcloth means either that they themselves have repented, that they are grieved by the sin and idolatry they see, that they preach repentance, or all of the above.

It seems that now it is John who explains about the two witnesses, although a change of speakers is not clearly marked.[9] He describes them symbolically as **the two olive trees and the two lampstands**, an allusion to a strange vision recorded in Zech 4. In Zechariah's vision there is one lampstand with seven oil lamps upon it, like the menorah that gave light in the temple, standing between two olive trees. The lampstand symbolizes the second temple, under construction despite fierce opposition (520–515 BC). The seven lamps on the lampstand receive sustaining oil from a bowl on top that in turn draws from the two olive trees standing on either side, described as "the two anointed ones who stand by the Lord of the whole earth" (Zech 4:14). The olive trees in Zechariah refer to Zerubbabel, the governor and Davidic heir, and Joshua the high priest, who were leading the effort to rebuild the temple. Zechariah's vision indicates that the Lord has anointed them for this task and that they will succeed by the power of the Spirit (4:6). The divine anointing on these two is so abundant that they are presented not merely as smeared with olive oil (the normal meaning of "anointed") but as olive trees themselves.

Just as Zerubbabel and Joshua were the Lord's anointed instruments in building the second temple, the two anointed witnesses whom Christ has authorized prepare the way for the †eschatological temple, the new Jerusalem. While in Zechariah's vision there was one lampstand, here in Revelation there are two. The only other occasion in which a lampstand is mentioned in Revelation is in chapters 1–2, where seven golden lampstands represent the Church throughout Asia and the world. A lampstand is a fitting symbol of the Church: it is the means by which the light of Christ and of his sevenfold Spirit shines in the world

11:4

---

7. As in Matt 10:18; 24:14; John 15:27; Acts 1:8.

8. The hairy garments of Elijah and of John the Baptist (2 Kings 1:8; Matt 3:4) also had this significance.

9. Biblical Greek does not use quotation marks.

(see sidebar, "The Seven Spirits of God," p. 46). The New Testament often uses the metaphor of light for Christians' witness in the world.[10] Along with many ancient and modern interpreters, I understand these two lampstands and two witnesses to represent the Church's witness to the world.

Why is the testimony of the one Church depicted as two lampstands? While it could refer, as some Church Fathers suggest, to the witness of the Old Testament and the New, or to the Church comprised of both Jews and Gentiles, it is likely the twofold witness symbolizes the Church's prophetic testimony.[11] Throughout Scripture the legal standard for judicial testimony is two witnesses.[12] This is one reason Jesus sent out his disciples in pairs (Mark 6:7, 11; Luke 10:1, 11). As in the Gospel of John (16:8–11), in Revelation the world is on trial. The testimony of two witnesses indicates that adequate testimony has been rendered and those who have heard are responsible for their choices. The content of their testimony is the gospel, described three times in Revelation as "the word of God and the testimony of Jesus Christ" (1:2; see also 1:9; 20:4 NRSV). That gospel is both an offer of grace and a solemn command to repent (14:7).

11:5–6   The two witnesses who prophesy with a superabundant divine anointing and radiate light like lampstands are engaged in a conflict with a world that rejects God's rule. Their testimony is as great and divinely endorsed as that of Moses against Pharaoh and the gods of Egypt (Exod 7:14-21; 12:12), or that of Elijah against King Ahab and the prophets of Baal (1 Kings 18). It is not just a war of words, but a power encounter between God's servants and their evil adversaries.[13] Like Moses and Elijah, the witnesses enjoy protection and the authority from God to overcome those who oppose them. Just as fire came from heaven to devour King Ahab's soldiers when they came to arrest Elijah (2 Kings 1:10–12), so **fire** comes from the witnesses' **mouths** and **devours . . . anyone wanting to harm them**. A closer parallel may be a word from the Lord to Jeremiah: "See! I make my words / a fire in your mouth / And this people the wood / that it shall devour!" (Jer 5:14). Like Elijah (1 Kings 17–18), the two witnesses have **the power to close up the sky**, inflicting drought and famine during the time of their prophesying. Like Moses and Aaron, they **have power to turn water into blood** and **to afflict the earth with any plague** (Exod 7:19–20).

Rather than provide a true-to-life picture of evangelization, this story drama-tizes the radical opposition between the Church's testimony and the surrounding

---

10. See Matt 5:14; Eph 5:8–14; Phil 2:15; Col 1:12; 1 Thess 5:5; 1 Pet 2:9.

11. For the opinions of various Church Fathers, see ACCS 12:157–60; for subsequent interpretations, see Judith Kovacs and Christopher Rowland, *Revelation* (Oxford: Blackwell, 2004), 126–30.

12. See Num 35:30; Deut 17:6; 19:15; 2 Cor 13:1; 1 Tim 5:19.

13. See 1 Cor 2:4–5; 2 Cor 10:4–5; 1 Thess 1:5; 2:13.

society and symbolizes the divine help that Christ's witnesses can expect in their struggle. The *manner* in which the Church is actually called to evangelize is exemplified by the ministry of Christ as recorded in the Gospels and that of the apostles as recorded in Acts. The Church's testimony is indeed marked by signs and wonders and by supernatural protection.[14] However, the signs drawn from biblical history of closing the heavens, turning water into blood, and striking the earth with plagues *symbolize* the Church's powerful testimony, overcoming all opposition.

The Defeat and Vindication of the Two Witnesses (11:7–12)

[7]When they have finished their testimony, the beast that comes up from the abyss will wage war against them and conquer them and kill them. [8]Their corpses will lie in the main street of the great city, which has the symbolic names "Sodom" and "Egypt," where indeed their Lord was crucified. [9]Those from every people, tribe, tongue, and nation will gaze on their corpses for three and a half days, and they will not allow their corpses to be buried. [10]The inhabitants of the earth will gloat over them and be glad and exchange gifts because these two prophets tormented the inhabitants of the earth. [11]But after the three and a half days, a breath of life from God entered them. When they stood on their feet, great fear fell on those who saw them. [12]Then they heard a loud voice from heaven say to them, "Come up here." So they went up to heaven in a cloud as their enemies looked on.

OT: Dan 7:3, 8, 21–27
NT: John 16:20

Rather than offering a straightforward preview of historical events, the concluding part of this prophecy continues to depict the end of the two witnesses' ministry and the end of the age by means of parable or allegory. To interpret it correctly, it helps to recall other symbolic narratives, such as Pharaoh's dream of the seven lean cows that ate the seven fat ones (Gen 41), or Ezekiel's vision of the dry bones that came to life (37:1–14). The meaning of each of those revelations was conveyed figuratively rather than literally.

14. Examples of signs and wonders are everywhere in the Gospels and frequent in Acts. Other texts stress their importance in the Church's work of evangelization (Mark 16:17–18; John 14:12–14; Rom 15:19; 1 Cor 12:9–10, 29–30; 2 Cor 12:12; Gal 3:2–5; Heb 2:4). Supernatural protection from harm is also attested in the Gospels and Acts (Luke 4:29–30; John 7:30; 8:20; Acts 12:6–11; 16:25–30). Miracles of the past and present are well documented in Craig S. Keener's *Miracles: The Credibility of the New Testament Accounts*, 2 vols. (Grand Rapids: Baker Academic, 2011).

11:7   When the witnesses have **finished their testimony**, the prophesying that Christ sent them to do, God allows them to be silenced, just as happened to Jesus when his hour had come.

This is the first mention of **the beast** in Revelation, but the use of the definite article "the" suggests that John expects his readers to already be familiar with this actor in the end-time drama, whether from his own previous prophesying or from oral tradition (1 John 2:18; 4:3). Many details in verses 7 and 11 indicate that John identifies "the beast" with the "fourth beast" and the "horn" referred to in Dan 7. First, it **comes up from the abyss** like the beasts in Daniel that come up from "the sea," an equivalent expression (Dan 7:3; see sidebar, "The Abyss," p. 167). In Daniel's vision a beast "made war against the holy ones and was victorious" (7:21). Echoing the †Septuagint version of Dan 7:21, John's vision foretells that the beast **will wage war against them and conquer them and kill them**. The fact that in Daniel the beast's victim is identified as the "saints" or "holy ones" (7:21, 22, 25) while in Rev 11:7 it is the two witnesses lends support to the interpretation that the two witnesses represent the people of God. Another link between this text and Dan 7 is found at the end of Daniel's vision, where it says that God's people are handed over to the beast "for a year, two years, and a half-year," which is equivalent to the period during which the "holy city" is trampled and the two witnesses prophesy (Rev 11:2–3). Revelation will return to the beast and its conquest of the people of God in 13:1–8.

11:8   The **corpses** of the two witnesses **lie** in the **main street** or square of the **great city**. The identity of this city is elusive. On the one hand, the seven other uses of this phrase in Revelation (16:19; 17:18; the rest in chap. 18) clearly indicate Babylon, which most interpreters understand to refer to Rome, as it does in 1 Pet 5:13. But here the great city is further identified as having the **symbolic names**[15] **"Sodom,"** a city known for its wickedness, **and "Egypt,"** a nation famous for the judgments God executed against it. The city is further identified as **where indeed their Lord was crucified**, which of course was Jerusalem. What does this mean? Some have proposed that Rome was understood to extend as far as its imperial power reached, so that Jesus' death at the hands of a Roman governor by a Roman mode of execution could be regarded as occurring in Rome. I, however, am inclined to think that the symbolic geography of 11:1–2 is extended here: the temple and the holy city Jerusalem refer to God's people at worship; the outer court trampled by the †Gentiles symbolizes the world system that is opposed to God and his people

15. The Greek literally says "*spiritually* called Sodom and Egypt." The NIV says "figuratively"; the NRSV, "prophetically"; and the RSV, "allegorically."

and was embodied in Sodom, Egypt, Babylon, Rome, and the earthly Jerusalem that put Jesus to death.

This interpretation sits well with the next verse, which depicts the whole world—**every people, tribe, tongue, and nation**—gazing on the corpses of the two witnesses. The viewing lasts for **three and a half days**, much less than three and a half years, yet like it in suggesting a brief and incomplete period of time. These people from all over the world treat the dead witnesses with what the ancient world considered the ultimate insult and cruelty, refusing to allow their corpses **to be buried**.

11:9

The death of the two witnesses becomes an occasion of celebration for **the inhabitants of the earth**, those who do not belong to God's people. They **gloat** ("rejoice," RSV) and are **glad** over their defeated enemies, even making a holiday of the occasion, sending **gifts** to one another. The witnesses are explicitly called **prophets** who **tormented the inhabitants of the earth**. Prophecy and righteous conduct elicit hostility and can feel like torment to those who do not want to repent (see Wis 2, especially vv. 12, 14; Jer 18:18–20; John 3:20).

11:10

Before long, however, after **three and a half days**, God vindicates his servants by raising them from the dead and, in front of everyone, bringing them up to heaven. The description of this resurrection echoes Ezekiel's vision of the †eschatological restoration of Israel, where the **breath** of God "entered into them, and they lived, and stood upon their feet, a very great congregation" (Ezek 37:10 LXX). John applies Ezekiel's vision to persecuted Christians. Their future resurrection will demonstrate to the world that they are truly God's people (see Ezek 37:12–13).

11:11–12

The result of this extraordinary vindication is that **great fear** falls upon those who witness it, like the fear that fell on the Egyptians (Ps 105:38) and the inhabitants of Canaan (Exod 15:16) at the manifestation of God's power. Then **a loud voice from heaven** summons the two witnesses with the same words that were addressed to John in 4:1: **Come up here**. The witnesses ascend **to heaven in a cloud**, the mode of transport of Jesus' ascension. The witnesses' assumption into heaven recalls not only Jesus' ascension but also the assumption of Enoch (Gen 5:24), Elijah (2 Kings 2:11–12), Moses (according to a Jewish tradition),[16] and Mary (according to Catholic and Orthodox tradition).[17] Revelation 20:4–6 speaks of a special honor of sharing in "the first resurrection" that belongs to Jesus' faithful followers. The public nature of this divine vindication is emphasized: it took place **as their enemies looked on**.

---

16. See the intertestamental work *Assumption of Moses* (likely = *Testament of Moses*).
17. Catechism 966.

The meaning of this parable-like prophecy is that the Church's witness to the world will be powerfully anointed. It will provoke fierce opposition from those who find their evildoing exposed (John 3:20), who hate and reject the Christian message. Nevertheless, the Church will remain protected by God until the time when he considers her testimony to be complete.[18] At a future time of his choosing, God will allow the beast and its followers to seemingly defeat the Church, silencing her witnesses and producing many martyrs. This seems to be another reference to the great trial and the persecution of the Church before Christ's return.[19] Circumstances like this have occurred at various times in history (see "Reflection and Application" on 17:6b–14), including several persecutions at the hands of Roman emperors.[20] The resurrection of the dead and the glorification of his people will be God's dramatic vindication of his own. On that day it will be seen by everyone, including those who once persecuted the Church.

The Response of the People of the Great City (11:13)

---

[13]At that moment there was a great earthquake, and a tenth of the city fell in ruins. Seven thousand people were killed during the earthquake; the rest were terrified and gave glory to the God of heaven.

OT: Ezek 38:19

11:13　　A **great earthquake** marks the **moment** (literally, "hour"). In Scripture, earthquakes signify a †theophany, a manifestation of God's presence, and often, as here, God's coming in judgment.[21] Still, this judgment, great as it is, is partial since only **a tenth of the city** falls in ruins and only **seven thousand people** are **killed** by the earthquake—symbolically speaking, a substantial number, but only a fraction of the total population. As noted above, here "the city" symbolizes all the inhabitants of the earth who have opposed the testimony of the Church, the two witnesses.

18. The same was true of Christ himself, who was spared from attempts on his life until the "hour," determined by the Father, came to pass (Luke 4:30; John 7:30; 8:20).
19. Other depictions of this period include Rev 13; 16:14–16; 19:19; 20:7–9.
20. Under Nero (AD 64–67), perhaps Domitian (95–96), Decius (250), Valerian (253), and Diocletian and Galerius (303–311/12).
21. The earthquake continues the echo of Ezekiel begun in Rev 11:11, where the resurrection of God's people in Ezek 37 is followed by a great earthquake. The LXX of Ezek 38:19 uses the same words, *seismos megas*, "a great shaking," for God's judgment on Gog when it tries to destroy restored Israel at the end of history.

At the conclusion of this story, in the wake of the prophesying of the two witnesses and their martyrdom and vindication, including the great earthquake, John reports a surprising outcome: **the rest** of the inhabitants **were terrified and gave glory** to God. To this point, judgments in Revelation have failed to evoke repentance on a large scale (9:20–21). Is it possible that the conclusion of this prophetic narrative promises a more positive response, namely, genuine conversion?

Some scholars think not, understanding this phrase as referring to an acknowledgment of God's power against their will.[22] However, in the Old Testament "the phrase 'give glory to God' is used when calling people to repentance (Josh 7:19; 1 Sam 6:5; Isa 42:12; Jer 13:16)."[23] More important, in Revelation, fearing and glorifying God are frequently used to indicate the ideal and proper response to God (14:7; 15:4; 19:5–7). The failure of the disobedient †nations is that they refuse to "repent and give him glory" (16:9 RSV).

Consequently, the better conclusion is that the vision indicates that, despite persecution and the murder of the Lamb's witnesses, God will in some way vindicate them publically, and this will lead to the conversion of a large number of people. Some scholars go so far as to interpret this text to mean that all unbelievers will be converted, but this does not agree with the rest of the book of Revelation, which devotes considerable attention to God's judgment of those who persist in doing evil. The good news is that very many give glory **to the God of heaven**, a phrase often used in the Old Testament to distinguish the true God from pagan deities. There may be another significance to the number seven thousand here. In 1 Kings 19:18 God promises that when judgment would fall on Israel for its apostasy, he would save seven thousand who had *not* participated in the nation's idolatry. In Rev 11:13, however, God promises that only seven thousand of the wicked city will perish, while the rest will repent.

When will the nations give "glory to the God of heaven"? On the one hand, this refers to the conversion of unbelievers throughout history in response to the testimony of Christians, often sealed by martyrdom. As Tertullian said in the second century, the blood of the martyrs is the seed of the Church.[24] Like the Lamb, Christians conquer by their willingness to lay down their lives (12:11). On the other hand, this text may foretell a wave of conversions as history draws to a close.

---

22. They cite OT texts that they interpret as pagan acknowledgment of or homage to God without conversion, such as Exod 8:19; Prov 1:24–32; Jon 1:9–10, 16; Dan 4:34.

23. Osborne, *Revelation*, 434; see 433–36 for an account of the various positions and their advocates.

24. A paraphrase of Tertullian, *Apology* 50.13.

Reflection and Application (11:3–13)

Revelation 11 depicts a twofold role of the Church in history. We are called first to worship, then to witness; first to pray and then to prophesy, to proclaim the gospel. Liturgy is not peripheral: it comes first. As we saw earlier (5:8; 8:3–5), the prayers of God's holy people offered on his altar in heaven move God to act and shape the course of history. At the same time, verbal testimony to the truth is an essential aspect of our mission, as it surely was for Christ (John 18:37).

What might Christians today learn about evangelization from this unusual prophetic narrative that depicts the Church's mission?

First, we are reminded that Christ has commissioned us to be his witnesses to the world (Luke 24:46–49; Acts 1:8). As such, we speak God's message; we "prophesy." Our message is about Jesus, but it is also entails speaking the truth about right and wrong. We are "lampstands" intended to bring light to those around us in word and deed. Our message entails a call to repentance. We must speak humbly, as people who know their need of repentance and forgiveness, earnestly desiring and praying for the conversion of all.

Second, we are reminded to speak boldly since we "stand before the Lord of the earth" and our testimony enjoys the anointing of the Holy Spirit. We are not left alone: we are empowered by the Holy Spirit, who speaks through us (Mark 13:11; John 14:16–18). We should pray for and expect divine confirmation of our message, "signs and wonders" that will demonstrate that our message is not merely a human idea but God's own word (Acts 4:29–31; 1 Cor 2:4–5).

Third, we can expect that we will encounter stiff opposition: the world will not be happy with our words and way of life. John the Baptist suffered the wrath of Herodias for his testimony (Matt 14:3–11). We need to prepare ourselves to be disliked, disapproved of, and even persecuted, realizing that "everyone who does wicked things hates the light" (John 3:20; see 2 Tim 3:12). In the face of hostility, we are called to be courageous and to endure, knowing that God himself will protect and defend us until we have finished our testimony (11:7) and that, if it be his will, we will conquer by laying down our lives (12:11).

Finally, we can look forward to divine vindication. Christ invites his faithful witnesses to reign with him in heaven. We can strive to be saints, the kind of witnesses to whom Christ will say, "Come up here" (11:12). Meanwhile, being faithful to our task of bearing witness, we can have great hope in the efficacy of God's word and God's power to reap a great harvest of men and women from all the nations who will join us in giving "glory to the God of heaven" (11:13).

The first-century Christians who faced fierce persecution at the hands of the Roman Empire would probably have been amazed to learn that their testimony would one day lead to the conversion to Christianity of the majority of those living in the Roman Empire (see "Reflection and Application" on 17:15–18). Since then, Christian testimony to the gospel has changed the course of history many times: the preaching of St. Francis, St. Dominic, and others turned back in large measure the error, worldliness, and incessant warfare of their day. The preaching of John Wesley helped prevent the excesses of the French Revolution from crossing the channel to England. The witness of William Wilberforce and other Christian abolitionists in the British Empire led to the abolition of the slave trade in 1807 and of slavery in 1833. Christian testimony achieved the same result in the United States, although the plague of a bloody civil war played its part as well.

The Seventh Trumpet and a Victory Celebration in Heaven (11:14–19)

¹⁴The second woe has passed, but the third is coming soon.

¹⁵Then the seventh angel blew his trumpet. There were loud voices in heaven, saying, "The kingdom of the world now belongs to our Lord and to his Anointed, and he will reign forever and ever." ¹⁶The twenty-four elders who sat on their thrones before God prostrated themselves and worshiped God ¹⁷and said:

"We give thanks to you, Lord God almighty,
    who are and who were.
For you have assumed your great power
    and have established your reign.
¹⁸The nations raged,
    but your wrath has come,
    and the time for the dead to be judged,
and to recompense your servants, the prophets,
    and the holy ones and those who fear your name,
    the small and the great alike,
and to destroy those who destroy the earth."

¹⁹Then God's temple in heaven was opened, and the ark of his covenant could be seen in the temple. There were flashes of lightning, rumblings, and peals of thunder, an earthquake, and a violent hailstorm.

OT: Josh 6; Ps 2; 115:13
NT: Matt 24:31; 1 Cor 15:51–52; 1 Thess 4:16–17
Catechism: the kingdom in its fullness, 1042

11:14–15   After the first two woes, which accompanied the fifth and sixth trumpets, consisting of horrible demonic torments for those who did not receive the seal of God, the audience may wonder what the **third** woe and seventh trumpet could possibly entail since it is **coming soon**. This phrase hints at the finality of the event, since the other five times it appears in Revelation it is on the lips of Christ, speaking of his glorious return: "I am coming soon."[25] The time for repentance is drawing to a close; the hour of judgment and salvation is at hand.

Now the **seventh angel** sounds his **trumpet**. Readers will recall that before the "mighty angel" commissioned John to "prophesy again" (10:1; 11), that angel raised his right hand and solemnly swore, "When you hear the seventh angel blow his trumpet, the mysterious plan of God shall be fulfilled" (10:6–7). Some identify this trumpet blast with the one that other texts say will mark Christ's return, the resurrection of the dead, and the gathering of the elect (Matt 24:31; 1 Cor 15:52; 1 Thess 4:16). In fact, the next thing that happens after the blowing of the seventh trumpet is that **loud voices in heaven** proclaim the arrival of God's kingdom in marvelous terms.

Although the †**world** refers at times to creation or the whole of the human race (John 1:9, 29), the term sometimes bears negative connotations. First John 2:16 depicts the world as the arena of temptation to disordered bodily appetites, to greed, and to pride. In the Gospel of John, Jesus speaks three times of the devil as the "ruler" of this world (12:31; 14:30; 16:11); he tells Pilate, "My kingdom does not belong to this world" (18:36).

The heavenly voices announce that the kingdom of the world **now belongs to our Lord and to his Anointed**, "his Christ" (RSV). The voices proclaim a change of ownership and government for the world that transforms its essential character. The pairing of "Lord" and "his anointed" comes from Ps 2:2, a psalm that depicts the enthronement of a descendant of David as king on Mount †Zion despite the opposition of †Gentile rulers. Although the kingdom belongs to both God and Christ, a singular subject follows: **He will reign**. God governs the world through the reign of Christ, his anointed king; God and Christ are united in their exercise of authority. The words **forever and ever** recall earlier biblical promises (Exod 15:18; Dan 2:44; 7:27), and especially Dan 7:13–14 about the "One like a son of man": "His dominion is an everlasting dominion / that shall not be taken away, / his kingship, one that shall not be destroyed." The temporal power of evil has been replaced by the eternal reign of God. The salvation that Christ brings is not merely spiritual; Christ's kingdom means

25. Rev 2:16; 3:11; 22:7, 12, 20.

the end of every kind of evil, whether physical, political, economic, social, or personal.

The prostrate adoration of **the twenty-four elders** recalls their worship before the throne in chapter 4 (see comments on 4:4). Their dignity as members of the divine council is indicated by the fact that they normally **sat on their thrones before God**. But now, as in 4:10 and 5:8, despite their own immense dignity, they **prostrated themselves and worshiped God**.

11:16

They **give thanks** with a Greek word that in Revelation appears only here, *eucharisteō*, to express praise for the fulfillment of God's plan of salvation. Although this is the standard Greek word used to express gratitude, for Christians the word acquired the specific connotation of celebrating the Eucharist.[26] The elders refer to God by his most solemn title, used seven times in Revelation: **Lord God almighty**.[27] Rather than describe God's eternal being in three terms, as the one "who is and who was and who is to come" (1:4, 8; 4:8), here the elders address God as you **who are and who were**. The significance is that now God *has* come; he has **assumed** his **great power** and **established** his **reign**. The elders' declaration celebrates the arrival of the time foretold in the writings of the prophets and the Psalms (Ps 93–99; Isa 24:23):

11:17

> The LORD reigns! . . .
> Then shall all the trees of the wood sing for joy
>   before the LORD, for he comes,
>   for he comes to judge the earth.
> He will judge the world with righteousness,
>   and the peoples with his truth. (Ps 96:10, 12–13 RSV)

Verse 18 briefly sums up the plot of the book of Revelation, concluding with God's coming to judge. Alluding to Ps 2, which speaks of the rebellion of the †nations "against the LORD and against his anointed one," it proclaims God's definitive response. The **nations raged** (Greek *orgizō*), **but** God responds in kind: his †**wrath** (Greek *orgē*) **has come**. The final judgment has arrived: **the time for the dead to be judged**.[28] This arrival of the final judgment is good news. The twenty-four elders praise God because he is about to **recompense**, literally, "reward or give wages to," his **servants**. People today tend to think

11:18

---

26. The *Didache* uses it in this sense (9.2–3; 10.2, 4), as does the NT (Matt 26:27; Mark 14:23; Luke 22:19; John 6:11, 23; 1 Cor 11:24). The use of *eucharisteō* combined with the term "elder" (*presbyteros*), normally used for those who presided over their liturgies, would have led the original audience to understand this heavenly act of thanksgiving as similar to their Eucharistic celebrations.

27. Greek *kyrie ho theos ho pantokratōr*.

28. See Isa 66:24; Dan 12:2; Matt 25:31–46; 2 Cor 5:10.

of judgment primarily in terms of its negative consequences for wrongdoers, but 11:18 and many other biblical texts celebrate judgment because it means vindication and *reward* for God's faithful people. God's servants are those who belong to him completely and obey his will. In the Old Testament it is a title of honor used of Moses, prophets, and priests (Exod 14:31; 2 Kings 9:7; Ps 134:1). In Revelation, however, the title is used more broadly.[29] The elders' praise distinguishes three groups among God's servants. First there are **the prophets**. Among many who prophesied in the early Church (1 Cor 14:5, 24, 31), some, like the author of Revelation, fulfilled a recognized ministry in the Church and were called prophets; they held a position of honor and authority second only to that of apostles (1 Cor 12:28).[30] The elders next mention **the holy ones**, the standard New Testament term for baptized Christians. Finally, the elders say, **and those who fear your name**. Some take this merely as a phrase describing "the holy ones," but the "and" placed before it suggests a distinct group. First-century Judaism recognized a class of Gentiles called "God-fearers," who had not become Jews themselves, but who honored and sought to obey the God of Israel. It is possible that this refers to a reward for just and God-fearing men and women who have not had the opportunity to be united to God through faith and baptism but who are saved nonetheless through the grace of Jesus Christ (Rom 2:6–7, 14–16).[31]

God's coming to establish his reign and judge the dead entails bad news for those who persist in doing evil, since at that time he will **destroy those who destroy the earth**. N. T. Wright explains: "The profound problems within . . . creation mean that the creator must act decisively to put things right, not because creation is bad and he's angry with it but because it's good and he's angry with the forces that have corrupted and defaced it, and which threaten to destroy it."[32] Scripture teaches a moral ecology (see "Reflection and Application" on 8:7–12). To rebel against God is to bring harm to the earth.[33]

Like the trumpets on the seventh day of Israel's march around Jericho, the seventh trumpet announces God's decisive intervention on behalf of his people. This intervention is celebrated with a liturgy in heaven that anticipates the event. It acclaims what God is about to do as already done, since the time he will act has arrived and the outcome is certain. Nevertheless, quite a bit remains to be

---

29. See Rev 1:1; 2:20; 7:3; 11:18; 19:2, 5; 22:3.

30. Other NT references to prophets include Matt 7:15–23; Acts 11:27–29; 13:1; 15:32; 21:10–14; Eph 3:5; 4:11–12.

31. See *Lumen Gentium* 16.

32. N. T. Wright, *Revelation for Everyone* (Louisville: Westminster John Knox, 2011), 105.

33. Gen 3:17–18; Jer 4:22–28; Amos 8:7–8; Rom 8:20–22. Above all, Babylon, a †type both of Rome and of the world system that "corrupted the earth" (19:2) and persecutes God's people, will be destroyed.

revealed about the way in which God will judge his adversaries and save his people. We are only halfway through the book.

The seventh trumpet also signals the third woe (11:14), the final judgment of God. However, the *content* of the third woe, symbolized by the seven bowls of divine wrath, is unpacked in the visions of judgment on Babylon, the beast and its army, and Satan, as will be described in chapters 15–20.

The dramatic proclamation of God's reign and the vision of the elders' response is marked by a momentous sign: **God's temple in heaven** is **opened**. More than that, its inner sanctum is revealed so that **the ark of the covenant** can be seen. The ark was the most important symbol of God's presence with Israel in the Old Testament and was described as his footstool on earth (1 Chron 28:2; Ps 99:5; 132:7–8). Its cover, the "mercy seat" or "propitiatory," was where the high priest sprinkled blood to atone for the sins of Israel once each year. Early in Israel's history the ark was carried into battle to signify that the Lord was fighting on behalf of his people. One of the most prominent examples was the conquest of Jericho, the previous occasion in biblical history when seven trumpets were sounded. The ark also had †eschatological significance in Jewish tradition. It disappeared from history when Babylon conquered Jerusalem and burned the temple in 586 BC (2 Kings 25:8–17). Second Maccabees 2:4–8 records a tradition that Jeremiah hid the ark in a cave on Mount Nebo, where it would remain hidden "until God gathers his people together again and shows them mercy. Then the Lord will disclose these things" (2 Macc 2:7–8). Here the appearance of the heavenly ark indicates the arrival of the time when God will gather and save his people.

11:19

Whenever the ark was brought out to go before Israel during the wilderness journey, Moses would say, "Arise, O Lord, may your enemies be scattered, / and may those who hate you flee before you" (Num 10:35). Now God is going to war against his enemies and will manifest his mighty power against them. This is confirmed by a †theophany of **lightning, rumblings, . . . thunder, an earthquake, and a violent hailstorm**, another

Fig. 9. Battle is joined: heaven is opened, the ark is revealed, the beast ascends from the abyss (11:19; 13:1).

The Virgin Mary as the Ark of the Covenant

LIVING TRADITION

The first reading for the feast of the Assumption of Mary, which describes a "woman clothed with the sun, with the moon under her feet" (12:1), begins with the mention of the ark in 11:19. This custom accords with the traditional title "Ark of the Covenant" that ancient Church Fathers such as St. Athanasius (296–373) and St. Gregory the Wonderworker (213–270) ascribe to Mary because the Word of God became incarnate in her. The traditional †typology identifying Mary as the ark of the covenant has a biblical foundation. In the Gospel of Luke, Gabriel tells Mary that the Holy Spirit will "overshadow" her (Luke 1:35), using the same Greek word that in the wilderness described the descent of God's presence on the tabernacle containing the ark (Exod 40:35 LXX).[a] For nine months the womb of the Virgin was God's dwelling, his tabernacle on the earth. The sacred objects contained in the ark—the tablets of God's word, the manna, and the rod of Aaron's priesthood—all foreshadowed Christ, who is in the most literal sense the presence of God among his people.

a. Further parallels occur in Luke's account of the Visitation (Luke 1:39–45). See the *Ignatius Catholic Study Bible: New Testament*, 2nd Catholic ed. (San Francisco: Ignatius Press, 2010).

preliminary glimpse of the final judgment like the display in 8:5. This is the third of four storm theophanies in Revelation (4:5; 8:5; 16:18–21), and the addition of the "heavy hail" (RSV) in this instance indicates escalating intensity. What will happen next?

The Woman, the Dragon, and the Male Child

Revelation 12:1–18

At the end of Rev 11 the sounding of the seventh trumpet, the celebration of the arrival of God's kingdom, and a powerful †theophany suggest that the end is at hand. But now John abruptly changes direction. In this chapter there is no mention of the consequences of the seventh trumpet or the approaching third woe. Instead, John begins a new section by reporting two signs in the sky (12:1–3; he will mention a third in 15:1). He then recounts a series of visions in chapters 12–14 that sketch the background of the Church's spiritual conflict, introduce the principal actors in the †cosmic drama under way, and preview its outcome in the final judgment (14:14–20).

A Woman Clothed with the Sun (12:1–6)

¹A great sign appeared in the sky, a woman clothed with the sun, with the moon under her feet, and on her head a crown of twelve stars. ²She was with child and wailed aloud in pain as she labored to give birth. ³Then another sign appeared in the sky; it was a huge red dragon, with seven heads and ten horns, and on its heads were seven diadems. ⁴Its tail swept away a third of the stars in the sky and hurled them down to the earth. Then the dragon stood before the woman about to give birth, to devour her child when she gave birth. ⁵She gave birth to a son, a male child, destined to rule all the nations with an iron rod. Her child was caught up to God and

his throne. ⁶The woman herself fled into the desert where she had a place prepared by God, that there she might be taken care of for twelve hundred and sixty days.

OT: Gen 3:15–16; 37:9–10; Ps 2; Song 6:10; Isa 26:16–27:1; Mic 4:10–5:4
NT: Matt 2:7–16
Catechism: Mary, Daughter of Zion, 489; Church as mother, 757; Mary, Mother of the Church, 501, 963–75
Lectionary: 11:19; 12:1–6, 10: Assumption of the Blessed Virgin Mary, Common of the Blessed Virgin Mary during Easter Season

Perhaps more than any other, this passage of Revelation has inspired art and iconography. Most Catholics are familiar with images depicting Mary as the woman in this passage, crowned with twelve stars, surrounded by the sun, with the moon at her feet. Like many of the other visions in Revelation, this one has multiple levels of meaning. On the one hand, the woman of this vision symbolizes the faithful people of God of the Old and New Testaments. On the other, she is Mary, the mother of the †Messiah, and for that reason the most exalted member of the human race after her son.

12:1   John sees a **great sign in the sky** that appears like a new constellation: **a woman clothed with the sun, with the moon under her feet** and **a crown of twelve stars**. The description emphasizes the light that surrounds this woman. The image of the sun, moon, and stars is drawn from Joseph's dream in Gen 37:7–10, where they represent his father, mother, and brothers, the patriarchs of the twelve tribes of Israel. The woman thus symbolizes Israel, who in the Bible is often personified as a woman—as daughter Zion (Isa 62:11),[1] as a mother (Ps 87; Isa 66:8–11), or as the bride of the Lord (Isa 54:5; 62:4–5). "She represents the entire story of God's people, chosen to carry forward his plans for the nations and indeed for the whole creation. That is why the sun, moon, and stars form her robe, her footstool and her crown."[2]

12:2   A closer view reveals that this glorious figure is pregnant and about to give birth. Suddenly the silence of the vision is broken by loud wailing, as the woman cries in her labor pains. Since the **child** to be born is the Messiah (12:5), these pains are the birth pangs of the Messiah, a familiar theme in †intertestamental Jewish literature based on prophetic texts that depict †Zion as laboring in childbirth.[3] The birth pangs of the Messiah were understood to be the sufferings that God's people would experience before the Messiah's coming to rescue them.

1. Zion was the hill of Jerusalem where the temple and royal palace stood. Biblical poetry often uses the name †Zion to refer to Jerusalem or to the whole people of Israel.
2. N. T. Wright, *Revelation for Everyone* (Louisville: Westminster John Knox, 2011), 108.
3. See, e.g., Isa 66:7–10; Mic 4:10–5:3.

A second and frightening sign of a **huge red dragon** now comes into view,   **12:3–4**
a creature of extraordinary power and authority, since it has seven heads, ten
horns, and seven diadems on its heads. Horns indicate power, diadems represent
kingly rule; the numbers seven and ten signify completeness. Its red color reveals
its violent character. The image of the dragon derives from Old Testament allusions to a Canaanite myth about a seven-headed sea monster that God defeated
at the dawn of creation (Ps 74:13–14) and that Isaiah prophesies will be destroyed
by God on the day of judgment (Isa 27:1).[4] With a swish of its tail the dragon
knocks **a third of the stars** out of the sky and hurls them **down to the earth**.
Since Rev 12:9 identifies the dragon as the devil, many interpret this to refer
to Satan's leading astray a third of the angels before the beginning of history.
Another possibility is that John's words allude to Dan 8:9–12 and 12:3, where
the stars represent some of God's faithful people killed by the beast who arises
at the end of history. The dragon's malice is revealed by its stance **before the
woman . . . to devour her child when she gave birth**. Herod's jealous attempt
to kill the Christ-child reflects the same mentality (Matt 2:7–16). Herod acted
under the influence of Satan, as did those who killed Christ (Luke 22:3; John
13:2, 27), as do those who persecute Christians in John's time and our own.

The mention of the woman's labor pains (see Gen 3:16) and the hostility of
the dragon, "the ancient serpent" (12:9), toward the woman's child recalls God's
words to the serpent in the Gen 3:15: "I will put enmity between you and the
woman, and between your offspring and hers; he will strike your head, and you
will strike his heel" (NRSV). This vision in Revelation resumes the story begun
in Genesis about the conflict between Satan and the human race. A second Eve
has given birth to the one who will strike the serpent's head.

The child's identity is revealed in the language of Ps 2, a psalm about God's   **12:5**
Messiah, likely sung at the enthronement of the kings of Judah:

> Kings on earth rise up
> > and princes plot together
> > against the Lord and against his anointed. . . .
> The one enthroned in heaven laughs. . . .
> Then he speaks to them in his anger,
> > in his wrath he terrifies them:
> "I myself have installed my king
> > on Zion, my holy mountain."

---

4. See comments and note on Rev 13:1. Symbols must be interpreted in their cultural contexts. In
Chinese culture, for instance, the dragon is a positive symbol, representing strength, intelligence, and
good luck; and the color red, customarily worn by brides, symbolizes joy and good fortune.

Mary, the Woman Clothed with the Sun   LIVING TRADITION

In the vision of Rev 12, Mary "represents and is the living icon of the whole Church."[a] She is the one who brought forth the divine Messiah (12:5); her soul was pierced by a sword (Luke 2:35) when her Son, the Lamb, was sacrificed. She is the mother of Christians both by being the mother of the one in whom we are born anew, and by assenting to the request of her Son on the cross, "Behold, your son" (John 19:26), indicating the beloved disciple. In tradition, this beloved disciple has been seen to represent all followers of Jesus, whom Mary has adopted.

Assumed into heaven, Mary now reigns with Christ, the martyrs, and saints (20:4–6). With all the saints she intercedes for her children on earth, "those who keep God's commandments and bear witness to Jesus" who are being pursued by the dragon (12:17).

The woman in John's vision is radiant, clothed with the light of the sun, moon, and stars, an anticipation of the †glory of God that will one day clothe all God's people in the new Jerusalem (21:9–11).

a. Donal A. McIlraith, *Everyone's Apocalypse* (Suva, Fiji: Pacific Regional Seminary, 1995), 62.

> I will proclaim the decree of the LORD,
> > he said to me, "You are my son;
> > today I have begotten you.
> Ask it of me,
> > and I will give you the nations as your inheritance,
> > and, as your possession, the ends of the earth.
> With an iron rod you will shepherd them." (Ps 2:2, 4, 5–9)

The woman's child will **rule all the nations with an iron rod**. He is the one who will one day defeat the devil and his human agents with "the rod of his mouth," his word (Isa 11:4; see Rev 19:13, 15) and rescue the human race.

At this point the relation of the woman in the vision to Mary the mother of Jesus becomes most clear. No one can deny that the Messiah was born of Mary, a particular woman of Israel. Eve, whose offspring was promised to strike the serpent's head, foreshadowed Mary, and Mary embodies faithful daughter Zion, of whose line the Messiah is born.

The woman's child is **caught up to God and his throne**. In a few words this verse telescopes the earthly life of Jesus, from his birth to his exaltation to God's throne (Mark 16:19; Eph 1:20; Heb 12:2).[5]

5. It is possible that here the Messiah's birth after a painful labor refers to his "birth" to eternal life through resurrection (Rev 1:5; Col 1:18).

Israel and the Church

In the vision of Rev 12, it is the same woman who gives birth to the Messiah (12:1–2, 5) and whose offspring "bear witness to Jesus" (12:17). Revelation, like other New Testament writings, presents the Church as †eschatological Israel, now expanded to include Gentiles joined to Israel's †Messiah in fulfillment of Old Testament prophecies.[a] Wright says it well: "John believes that since Jesus is Israel's Messiah, Israel is redefined around him."[b] In Revelation, Israel remains God's chosen people and "Jew" remains a title of honor, which is why the risen Christ denies that name to those in the synagogues of Smyrna and Philadelphia who "slander" (2:9) or exclude his disciples (3:9).

Christianity began as a Jewish sect alongside the Pharisees, Sadducees, and Essenes. Each group claimed to have the authentic understanding of what it meant to be Jewish. The parting of ways between Christianity and Judaism was a gradual process, not yet complete when John wrote Revelation. Eventually the religious heirs of the Pharisees kept the title "Jew" (the Sadducees and Essenes ceased to exist after 70 AD), while the descriptive term "Christians," first applied to Jewish and Gentile followers of Jesus in Antioch, was accepted by the Church (Acts 11:26; 26:28; 1 Pet 4:16).

It is difficult to avoid anachronism in interpreting what Revelation says about Christians and Jews. Revelation, like the rest of the New Testament, recognizes a continuity between God's people of the old and new covenant that Christians today often overlook.[c] Revelation differs from later works, like the Epistle of Barnabas, that draw a sharp line between Israel and the Church. When modern interpreters attempt to distinguish what Revelation says to Israel and to the Church, they read into it a distinction that the author is not making.[d]

a. See, e.g., Tob 13:8–18; Ps 87; Isa 2:2–3; Amos 9:11–12.
b. Wright, *Revelation for Everyone*, 109.
c. The NT word for "church," *ekklēsia*, is the same word used over a hundred times in the Greek OT (LXX) to refer to the "assembly" or "congregation" of Israel.
d. John does not address the situation of Jews who have not accepted Jesus as the Messiah as Paul does in Rom 9–11. For more on Israel and the Church in Revelation, see "Theological Presuppositions" in the introduction (p. 23) and comments on 2:9; 3:9; and 7:3–8.

The woman who escapes after Jesus' ascension to heaven refers not to Mary but to the people of God, both faithful Israel and the Church (see sidebar above, "Israel and the Church"). The description of her flight to the **desert** ("wilderness," NRSV) recalls Israel's time in the wilderness, a †type of the Church's earthly pilgrimage (1 Cor 10:1–11; Heb 4:1–11). God took supernatural care of his people in the desert, providing them with manna, water from the rock,   **12:6**

and his special protection. So now, the woman will **be taken care of**—literally, "fed" or "nourished"—in a **place** God has **prepared** for her. Christ nourishes his people (Eph 5:29) during their earthly pilgrimage by his word and the Eucharist in a sacred place, the temple of God, where they now worship under his protection (11:1).[6] The familiar time period of **twelve hundred and sixty days** identifies the duration of her sojourn in the wilderness with the period of the Church's worship and witness, and of the †Gentiles trampling the holy city (11:2–3; see sidebar, "Forty-Two Months, Twelve Hundred and Sixty Days, Three and a Half Years," p. 189).[7]

When the entire text is taken into account the woman is seen to be faithful Israel, personified as daughter Zion, who gives birth to the Messiah. At the same, the woman is the literal mother of the Messiah, Mary of Nazareth. Finally, the woman is the Church, whom God cares for during her time in the wilderness of this world and who brings forth other children (12:17). This vision illustrates Revelation's symbolic way of communicating, the multiple levels of meaning in its images, and the book's nonlinear chronology, since the story that this vision tells begins before the birth of Christ.

Reflection and Application (12:1–6)

Suffering and birth pangs. Jesus used the image of birth pangs when he spoke of the disciples' experience of his own suffering and death:

> Amen, amen, I say to you, you will weep and mourn, while the world rejoices; you will grieve, but your grief will become joy. When a woman is in labor, she is in anguish because her hour has arrived; but when she has given birth to a child, she no longer remembers the pain because of her joy that a child has been born into the world. So you also are now in anguish. But I will see you again, and your hearts will rejoice, and no one will take your joy away from you. (John 16:20–22)

Although Revelation promises a future world without suffering (21:4), in this life many good things, like childbirth, come only through suffering. A child learns to stand and walk only by trial and error that entails numerous falls. Even the Son of God "learned obedience from what he suffered" (Heb 5:8). Sirach 2 teaches that if you want to "to serve the Lord, / prepare yourself for trials.

---

6. The "place prepared" for her by God recalls the place God chose for Israel to worship (Deut 12:5–6) and the place that David prepared for the ark of the covenant (1 Chron 15), for Israel's worship.

7. The reference to the woman's three-and-a-half-year period of wilderness sojourn beginning immediately after the Messiah's ascension (12:5) indicates that Revelation uses this term to refer to the whole age of the church.

. . . For in fire gold is tested, / and worthy men in the crucible of humiliation" (Sir 2:1, 5). "At the time, all discipline seems a cause not for joy but for pain, yet later it brings the peaceful fruit of righteousness to those who are trained by it" (Heb 12:11).

Part of the mystery of suffering is its uneven distribution. Some people suffer very little while others suffer much. Why do some live in a land of plenty, where they can practice their faith in freedom, while others suffer scarcity and persecution? Even among saints and apostles, the suffering is unequal: St. Paul seems to have had to endure more than the other apostles (Acts 9:16; 2 Cor 11:23–28).

How should we approach suffering? First, there is no need to seek it; it will find us. When it does, it is perfectly appropriate to pray to be delivered from it, as Jesus did in the garden (Matt 26:39–44) and St. Paul did when he experienced his "thorn in the flesh" (2 Cor 12:7–8). When there is sickness, Scripture teaches us to seek healing (Sir 38:9–14; James 5:14–16).

If God does not remove our suffering, our call is to embrace it with courage, knowing that God allows those he loves to suffer, and that he will both sustain us and bring good from it (Rom 8:28; 1 Cor 10:13). He does not forget those who suffer, nor is he far from them (Ps 34:18; 22:25; 56:9).

St. Paul goes further, inviting us by his example to unite our sufferings to Christ's and to rejoice in them: "Now I rejoice in my sufferings for your sake, and in my flesh I am filling up what is lacking in the afflictions of Christ on behalf of his body, which is the church" (Col 1:24). St. Peter does the same: "Rejoice to the extent that you share in the sufferings of Christ, so that when his glory is revealed you may also rejoice exultantly" (1 Pet 4:13).[8]

War in Heaven (12:7–9)

---

[7]Then war broke out in heaven; Michael and his angels battled against the dragon. The dragon and its angels fought back, [8]but they did not prevail and there was no longer any place for them in heaven. [9]The huge dragon, the ancient serpent, who is called the Devil and Satan, who deceived the whole world, was thrown down to earth, and its angels were thrown down with it.

OT: Dan 10:13, 21; 12:1–7
NT: Luke 10:18–19
Catechism: The fall of the angels, 391–95; deliverance from evil, 2850–54
Lectionary: 12:7–12: Michael, Gabriel, Raphael, archangels

---

8. For more on the mystery of suffering, see John Paul II, *Salvifici Doloris* (On the Christian Meaning of Human Suffering).

These verses report how the Messiah's birth, mission, and ascension to God's throne had consequences for the dragon.

12:7–8   John reports a **war** in **heaven**, not meaning the dwelling of God or the sky, but rather a sphere above the world of human beings, where angelic beings operate and influence earthly events. This understanding of how the world works is found especially in the book of Daniel, where **Michael** is first introduced.[9] There he is depicted as a "chief prince" among the angels, the "guardian" of God's people, who battles for Israel in struggles against pagan nations and their princes (Dan 10:13, 21; 12:1) and who will battle again on behalf of God's people at the end of history (Dan 12:1–4).

The outcome of the battle between Michael and the dragon is that the dragon and its angels are defeated and lose their **place . . . in heaven**, their previous position of power (especially the power to accuse, Rev 12:10b), and are thrown down to earth. This defeat, however, does not yet render them powerless, as 12:12–17 indicates.

12:9   Now the identity of **the huge dragon** is made explicit. He is **the ancient serpent** of the garden of Eden (Gen 3), the **Devil** (*diabolos*, "slanderer"), **Satan** (a Hebrew word meaning "accuser" or "adversary"); and he is the one who is deceiving **the whole** [†]**world**.[10] The identification of the serpent of Gen 3 with the devil and Satan reflects development in Jewish understanding in the centuries before Christ (Wis 2:24).

When does this defeat of the devil and his angels take place, and how?[11] Some interpreters think it refers to the fall of the angels at the beginning of creation, an event only dimly illuminated by Scripture (Isa 14:12–15; Luke 10:18–19) but accepted by Christian tradition. Others think the defeat of Satan depicted here refers to a heavenly spiritual battle that will occur immediately before a final three-and-a-half-year [†]tribulation at the end of the age. However, John's placement of the "war in heaven" (12:7–9) between the Messiah's ascension (12:5) and the dragon's war against the Church (12:13–17) persuades many interpreters, including myself, to identify this event with the defeat of Satan that was accomplished by Christ.

The New Testament presents abundant evidence that the life, death, resurrection, and exaltation of Jesus achieved a great victory over the devil. Jesus

9. See also Eph 2:2; 6:12.

10. Satan functions as an accuser in Job 1–2 and Zech 3:1–2. The devil's work is characterized as deception in John 8:44 and Rev 20:2–3, 7–8, 10; the deceptive work of his agents is indicated in 2 Thess 2:9–10 and Rev 13:11–14; 18:23; 19:20. The NABRE interprets this deception as past ("who deceived the whole world"), but the Greek verb form and context make "is the one deceiving" preferable.

11. Christian tradition has generally identified three points at which Satan suffers loss: when the angels fell at the beginning of creation, at the time of Christ's passion and resurrection, and at the end of history.

Pope Leo XIII, Pope John Paul II, and the Prayer to St. Michael

LIVING TRADITION

In 1886 Pope Leo XIII instructed Catholics all over the world to pray to the Archangel Michael at the end of every Mass against the work of the devil. Although that requirement was removed with the liturgical reforms of Vatican II, Pope John Paul II recommended invoking Michael in prayer:

> May prayer strengthen us for the spiritual battle that the Letter to the Ephesians speaks of: "Be strong in the Lord and in the strength of his might" (Eph 6:10). The Book of Revelation refers to this same battle, recalling before our eyes the image of St. Michael the Archangel (Rev 12:7). Pope Leo XIII certainly had this picture in mind when, at the end of the last century, he brought in, throughout the Church, a special prayer to St. Michael: "Saint Michael the Archangel, defend us in battle. Be our protection against the wickedness and snares of the devil. . . ." Although this prayer is no longer recited at the end of Mass, I ask everyone not to forget it and to recite it to obtain help in the battle against the forces of darkness and against the spirit of this world.[a]

a. John Paul II, *Regina Coeli* (*Regina Caeli*, Queen of Heaven) address, April 24, 1994.

states that his exorcisms demonstrate that he has bound the strong man (Mark 3:27). Shortly before his death and resurrection he declared, "Now the ruler of this world will be driven out" (John 12:31). According to Col 2:14–15, Christ despoiled the principalities and powers and made a public spectacle of them through his cross.[12]

How does Michael fit in? As a powerful angel specially charged with the defense of God's people, Michael and the angels with him enforce the judgment against the devil won by Christ's death and resurrection. Michael's victory over Satan is achieved on the basis of the Lamb's victory (5:5–6; 12:10–11).

Celebration in Heaven (12:10–12)

[10]Then I heard a loud voice in heaven say:

> "Now have salvation and power come,
>   and the kingdom of our God
>   and the authority of his Anointed.

12. Paul refers to Jesus' death on the cross as God's secret plan to liberate the human race from Satan's power (1 Cor 2:7–8; Eph 3:9–10).

For the accuser of our brothers is cast out,
  who accuses them before our God day and night.
[11]They conquered him by the blood of the Lamb
  and by the word of their testimony;
  love for life did not deter them from death.
[12]Therefore, rejoice, you heavens,
  and you who dwell in them.
But woe to you, earth and sea,
  for the Devil has come down to you in great fury,
  for he knows he has but a short time."

OT: Job 1:6–11; 2:1–6; Zech 3:1–2
NT: Col 2:12–15; 1 Pet 1:18–19; Rev 1:5; 7:14
Catechism: martyrdom, 2473–74; resisting idolatry, 2113
Lectionary: 12:10–12: Common of Martyrs

12:10   The **loud voice in heaven,** presumably of an angel, speaks of the establishment of God's kingdom almost as though it were already completed. Only the second half of 12:12 indicates that the war is not over, even if the end is near. This inaugurated [†]eschatology is characteristic of Christian faith: through Jesus' death, resurrection, and ascension, the decisive battle has been won and Christ's reign has begun; the fierce struggle that remains is only a mopping-up action, even if it is no small conflict for those involved.

Here the heavenly proclamation celebrates the arrival of **salvation**—which in Revelation usually bears its Old Testament meaning of "victory" over evil (7:10; 19:1)—and **power,** the compelling force God exercises against his adversaries. The **kingdom of our God** is the dynamic reign of God that will replace "the kingdom of the world" (11:15). God's reign is exercised through **the authority of his Anointed,** his Christ, the royal offspring of David to whom an eternal kingship was promised (2 Sam 7:12–13; see also Dan 7:14).

The voice explains the basis of the declaration that God's kingdom has arrived: **the accuser of our brothers is cast out,** / **who accuses them before our God day and night.** The Greek for "cast out" is the same word translated "thrown down" in the verse 9. Satan's claim to power over the human race was based on accusations of wrongdoing (unfortunately true) that placed friendship with God and his blessing beyond our reach. But Satan's claim has been rendered null and void (for a reason that will be explained in the next verse), and he has lost his ability to charge us before God.

12:11   After acclaiming the accomplishment of God and Christ for bringing salvation and defeating the devil, now the heavenly voice honors Christians, "our

214

brothers," for their role in the victory. First, **They conquered him by the blood of the Lamb**. It is the sacrificial death of Christ on the cross that silences the accuser. This is why John begins the book by praising the one who "has freed us from our sins by his blood" (1:5). It is because they "have washed their robes and made them white in the blood of the Lamb" (through faith, repentance, and baptism) that a multitude past numbering survive the great trial (7:14). Colossians 2:12–15 confirms that the defeat of the powers of evil is achieved through Jesus' death on the cross and is appropriated by the believer through baptism.

Second, Christians conquer the devil **by the word of their testimony**. Like "Jesus Christ, the faithful witness" (1:5), and the martyr Antipas, whom Jesus calls "my faithful witness" (2:13), believers "testify to the truth" (John 18:37). They wield "the sword of the Spirit, which is the word of God" (Eph 6:17; see Heb 4:12). As the vision of the two witnesses illustrates (11:3–6), Christians boldly proclaim the gospel with divine power (see 2 Cor 10:3–5). Where Christ is boldly proclaimed, the powers of darkness are confounded and Satan's dominion is overthrown in the lives of those who hear with faith.

Finally, the fundamental attitude that makes their words effective is their willingness to die for the faith: **Love for life did not deter them from death**.[13] This is the commitment that Jesus asks of his disciples: "Whoever wishes to come after me must deny himself, take up his cross, and follow me. For whoever wishes to save his life will lose it, but whoever loses his life for my sake and that of the gospel will save it" (Mark 8:34–35). This is the radical love for Jesus and the hope of eternal life expressed eloquently by St. Paul[14] and shared by the saints and martyrs. These verses and Revelation as a whole emphasize martyrdom (2:10; 6:9–11; 20:4). However, it is not the martyrs alone who conquer, as the messages to the churches make clear (Rev 2–3). The martyrs in this book symbolize all who "loved not their lives even unto death" (12:11 RSV), who prioritize following Jesus above everything else, even to the point of willingness to lay down their lives (Matt 10:28–33). Their attitude is opposite to the attitude of those who worship idols or compromise with the evil of the surrounding society.

This verse is almost precisely midway in the book. One scholar calls it "the key theological sentence in the entire book."[15]

The fact that the kingdom has already begun, that Satan has been cast down, and that Christians are conquering the devil is reason to celebrate: **Therefore,**   **12:12**

---

13. Literally, "they did not love their life to the point of death."

14. See, e.g., Acts 20:24; 21:13; Gal 2:20; Phil 1:20–21; 3:8–11.

15. Gordon D. Fee, *Revelation*, New Covenant Commentary Series (Eugene, OR: Wipf & Stock, 2010), 162.

The First Martyrs of the Church of Rome
BIBLICAL BACKGROUND

The first large group of Christians to lose their lives as martyrs were those of Rome, killed by the emperor Nero between AD 64 and 67. The Roman historian Tacitus, writing in 109, says that Nero prosecuted Christians to deflect blame from himself for the great fire of Rome that occurred in 64:

> Nero fastened the guilt and inflicted the most exquisite tortures on a class hated for their abominations, called Christians by the populace. Christus, from whom the name had its origin, suffered the extreme penalty during the reign of Tiberius at the hands of one of our procurators, Pontius Pilatus, and a most mischievous superstition, thus checked for the moment, again broke out not only in Judaea, the first source of the evil, but even in Rome, where all things hideous and shameful from every part of the world find their centre and become popular. Accordingly, an arrest was first made of all who pleaded guilty; then, upon their information, an immense multitude was convicted, not so much of the crime of firing the city, as of hatred against mankind. Mockery of every sort was added to their deaths. Covered with the skins of beasts, they were torn by dogs and perished, or were nailed to crosses, or were doomed to the flames and burnt, to serve as a nightly illumination, when daylight had expired.
>
> Nero offered his gardens for the spectacle, and was exhibiting a show in the circus, while he mingled with the people in the dress of a charioteer or stood aloft on a car [chariot]. Hence, even for criminals who deserved extreme and exemplary punishment, there arose a feeling of compassion; for it was not, as it seemed, for the public good, but to glut one man's cruelty, that they were being destroyed.[a]

Among those killed were St. Peter and St. Paul. Nero's persecution is the only large-scale killing of Christians in the first century of which we have record, and it left a deep impression on Christian consciousness.[b] The Church remembers the victory of the first martyrs of the Church of Rome on June 30, and the Office of Readings for that day includes an excerpt about their martyrdom from the letter of Pope Clement *To the Corinthians* (*1 Clement*), written about the same time as Revelation.

a. Tacitus, *Annals* 15.44, trans. Alfred John Church and William Jackson Brodribb, http://classics.mit .edu/Tacitus/annals.11.xv.html.
b. It is probable that Revelation alludes to it several times (6:9–10; possibly 11:7; 17:6; 18:24; 19:2).

rejoice, you heavens, and you who dwell in them. The summons to celebrate is addressed to the angels and saints in heaven, but probably also to Christians on earth, who spiritually "dwell in heaven" while they live in this world (see comments on 13:6; also Eph 2:6; Col 3:1–4).

Nevertheless, everyone on planet earth may expect trouble: **Woe to you, earth and sea**, since **the Devil has come down to you**. Verse 9 asserts that Satan and his angels were "thrown down to earth"; here we begin to learn what that means. The final phase of history between Christ's resurrection and his return in †glory is a time of great conflict. Paradoxically, although the dragon has been "thrown down" (v. 9), "cast out" (v. 10), and "conquered" (v. 11), he is far from harmless and is capable of making things very difficult for disciples of Jesus.

For those with eyes to see, the devil's **great fury** directed against the Church is proof of his desperation: **for he knows he has but a short time**. Once again the period between Christ's victory on the cross and the final consummation is seen as a brief interlude, which it truly is, in the light of eternity.

Reflection and Application (12:10–12)

If there is no accuser . . . Some years ago the speedometer on my wife's car stopped functioning. Before she could get it repaired, she received a speeding ticket, although she had been driving no faster than the car ahead of her. She decided to go to traffic court and explain what happened in hope of getting the fine waived. As she listened to the cases of those ahead of her and observed how the judge refused every explanation, her hopes faded. But when it was her turn, and the judge called for the testimony of the policeman who had issued the ticket, no one stood up. Since no one was present to charge her, the judge dismissed the case. What came to her soon after was the thought, "This is how it will be for Christians on judgment day."

My wife's experience gives a faint hint of how important it is that "the accuser of our brothers, . . . who accuses them before our God day and night," has been "cast out" (12:10).

The continuing effects of the blood of the Lamb. Although we have been reconciled to God through Jesus' death on the cross, we know that the battle against evil in our lives does not end with conversion and baptism.

Sometimes when we sin, "the accuser of our brothers" attacks us through guilt and self-condemnation. We need to distinguish the gracious voice of the Holy Spirit, which brings conviction of sin, from the condemning voice of the evil one. Thanks be to God, we have a remedy for sin in "the blood of the Lamb," which *continues* to purify us as we persevere in following Christ: "If we walk in the light as he is in the light, then we have fellowship with one another, and the blood of his Son Jesus cleanses us from all sin" (1 John 1:7). There are a variety of ways this cleansing can occur: through our repenting and asking forgiveness as soon as we become conscious of sin, through the penitential rite at the beginning of Mass, through receiving the body and blood of Christ in Communion, and through the Sacrament of Reconciliation.

If feelings of guilt persist, we need to resist the devil and his lies (James 4:7; 1 Pet 5:9), putting our faith in the infinite value of Christ's sacrifice, remembering God's love for us (Rom 8:31–39), and knowing that "now there is no condemnation for those who are in Christ Jesus" (Rom 8:1). First John 1:9 was written for us: "If we acknowledge our sins, he is faithful and just and will forgive our sins and cleanse us from every wrongdoing."

The Dragon's Pursuit of the Woman and Her Offspring (12:13–18)

> [13]When the dragon saw that it had been thrown down to the earth, it pursued the woman who had given birth to the male child. [14]But the woman was given the two wings of the great eagle, so that she could fly to her place in the desert, where, far from the serpent, she was taken care of for a year, two years, and a half-year. [15]The serpent, however, spewed a torrent of water out of his mouth after the woman to sweep her away with the current. [16]But the earth helped the woman and opened its mouth and swallowed the flood that the dragon spewed out of its mouth. [17]Then the dragon became angry with the woman and went off to wage war against the rest of her offspring, those who keep God's commandments and bear witness to Jesus. [18]It took its position on the sand of the sea.

OT: Gen 3:15; Exod 19:4; Deut 32:11; Ps 55:7–12
Catechism: victory over Satan, 2853; Mary, Mother of the Church, 501, 963–75

This part of the vision expands on 12:6—the woman's flight to the desert, where she is cared for by God—in light of what the intervening verses have revealed about the dragon's defeat in heaven and his present fury on earth.

12:13–14   The **dragon** is not in control of its own destiny. It **saw** that it had lost its previous position and **that it had been thrown down to earth** (resuming the narrative of 12:9); now it **pursued the woman** (the Greek word translated "pursue," *diōkō*, also means "to persecute"). This is the same woman of 12:5 who gave birth to the Messiah. Here her identity as the people of God is primary, since we know of no such persecution of Mary and 12:17 describes her offspring as Christians. The same woman represents Israel before the birth and ascension of the Messiah, as well as the Church afterward; this fact indicates that John views Israel and the Church as essentially identical (see sidebar, "Israel and the Church," p. 209).

218

The woman is **given** (a †divine passive) **the two wings of the great eagle**, recalling God's deliverance of his people from Egypt (Exod 19:4) and the promise of Isa 40:31 that those who hope in the Lord will "soar as with eagle's wings." The **desert** or "wilderness" (NRSV, RSV), as mentioned at 12:6, is the place of God's provision and protection. Here the Church is kept **far from the serpent** or, as the NIV puts it, "out of the serpent's reach." The duration of this divine **care** in the desert is repeated, using different words, from 12:6—**a year, two years, and a half-year**—the same length of time identified as that of the †Gentiles' trampling the outer court and of the Church's testimony in 11:2–3, and of the oppression of God's people in Dan 7:25 and 12:7 (see sidebar, "Forty-Two Months, Twelve Hundred and Sixty Days, Three and a Half Years ," p. 189). This period, indicated variously by days, months, and years, appears to refer to the Church's whole time on earth.

Although the Church is spiritually protected from the serpent, he does not stop trying to harm her.[16] The serpent sends a **torrent of water out of his mouth** at the **woman**, intended **to sweep her away**. The imagery echoes various psalms that speak of a flood of evil coming against the psalmist David.[17] The fact that it comes from the serpent's mouth suggests that it is a flood of lies, which fits well with texts that speak of Satan as a deceiver (John 8:44; 2 Thess 2:9–16) and with the tradition that the final period of history will be characterized by satanic deception.[18] In our own day it can sometimes seem difficult to defend the truth, not so much because of the plausibility of the lies as because of their overwhelming quantity. God does not leave the woman to her own resources, but provides a supernatural rescue in response to the supernatural attack: **The earth . . . opened its mouth and swallowed the flood** that came from the dragon. This recalls events in the Old Testament when the earth opened and swallowed those who were attacking or misleading God's people (Exod 15:12; Num 16:30, 32; Deut 11:6). Here it probably means that no matter what the devil throws at the Church, God will come to her aid and preserve her: "The gates of the netherworld shall not prevail against it" (Matt 16:18). That does not mean, however, that the Church will be spared from severe trials in which her future may seem to be in jeopardy (see Luke 18:8).

12:15–16

---

16. Because the Greek noun for "dragon" is neuter, the NABRE consistently refers to the dragon as "it." However, since the Greek for "serpent" is masculine, the NABRE uses masculine pronouns ("he" and "his") for the serpent in v. 15; both terms refer to the devil.

17. See, e.g., Ps 69:2; 144:7; especially, "With Death's breakers closing in on me, / Belial's torrents ready to swallow me . . ." (Ps 18:4 NJB).

18. See 2 Thess 2:10; Rev 13:14; 18:23; 19:20; 20:8.

12:17–18   The **dragon**, having failed to destroy the woman's male child, the †Messiah (12:5, 13), expresses its anger at the **woman**, the Church, by waging **war** against **the rest of her offspring**. The distinguishing characteristics of the woman's offspring are not their baptism, church attendance, or even orthodoxy, but their obedience (they **keep God's commandments**) and their testimony to others (they **bear witness to Jesus**).

The final sentence of Rev 12 points to what will happen next: the dragon **took its position** straddling sea and land. From there it summons two evil beings to wage war against the woman and her offspring.

Fig. 10. The seven-headed serpent attacks the woman with a torrent of water, which the earth swallows, while Michael flies overhead (12:15–16).

Reflection and Application (12:13–18)

Although the context indicates that the woman and her offspring pursued by the dragon is the Church, Catholics cannot help but think of Mary, whom the Church honors with the title "Mother of the Church." Mary is the Mother of Christians on at least three counts. First, by being the mother of Jesus, the Incarnate Word, Mary is the source of the human nature of the new Adam in whom every Christian is reborn. If someone is in Christ, that person is related to Mary, since Christ was born of Mary. Second, since the time of the early Church, Christians have applied to themselves the words that Jesus addressed to the beloved disciple: "Behold, your mother" (John 19:27). It was St. Ambrose (340–397) who first called Mary "Mother of the Church." Finally, Christians are Mary's children by imitation when we say yes to God's will (Luke 1:38), when we believe, as she did, that what has been spoken by the Lord will be fulfilled (Luke 1:45) and when we "keep God's commandments and bear witness to Jesus" (Rev 12:17).

The Two Beasts

Revelation 13:1–18

The end of the previous chapter reports Satan's fury at the woman, who represents the people of God, and the dragon's departure to make war "against the rest of her offspring," namely, Jesus' obedient disciples and witnesses (12:17). The two visions of chapter 13 expand on that description of the dragon's activity to show that the devil wages war against Christians through two powerful creatures, "beasts," to whom it delegates its authority. The prophecy about the two witnesses in chapter 11 mentioned without explanation the first of these, "the beast that comes up from the abyss" and kills the two witnesses (11:7). The visions of Rev 13 reveal in greater detail the nature of these adversaries of the Church and the fact that God allows them to exercise power over his people and the entire world for a limited period of time. Revelation 16–19 will describe the role of these demonic adversaries in the conflict at the end of history.

We will consider John's visions in this chapter in the light of three questions. First, how do they draw on the prophetic-apocalyptic visions found in the Old Testament? Second, how do John and his original readers understand these visions to apply to their time? Finally, how do John's visions apply to later periods of Christian history, including the present?

The Beast from the Sea (13:1–4)

> [1]Then I saw a beast come out of the sea with ten horns and seven heads; on its horns were ten diadems, and on its heads blasphemous name[s].

²The beast I saw was like a leopard, but it had feet like a bear's, and its mouth was like the mouth of a lion. To it the dragon gave its own power and throne, along with great authority. ³I saw that one of its heads seemed to have been mortally wounded, but this mortal wound was healed. Fascinated, the whole world followed after the beast. ⁴They worshiped the dragon because it gave its authority to the beast; they also worshiped the beast and said, "Who can compare with the beast or who can fight against it?"

OT: Exod 15:11; Dan 7:1–8
NT: 2 Thess 2:1–12

13:1–4   We left the dragon standing on the shore of the sea (12:18), although there were no chapter divisions in the original text. It now becomes apparent that Satan was summoning a terrifying instrument to wield against God's people. Readers of J. R. R. Tolkien's *Lord of the Rings* may think of Sauron's deployment of the Lord of the Nazgul. The tense of the Greek participle suggests a picture of the **beast** rising from the **sea**.[1] We can imagine first the head and then the body of this terrifying creature as it emerges from the water. The sea represents the ancient chaos that was the abode of Leviathan, the great serpent-dragon (see comments on 12:3). What is immediately noticeable is that the beast, with its **ten horns and seven heads**, closely resembles its master the dragon; the only difference is that the **diadems** are on its ten horns rather than on its seven heads as is the case for the dragon (12:3). Later John will learn that the ten horns represent ten kings (17:12). The **blasphemous name[s]** are probably divine titles claimed by the creature. In Revelation, animal symbols such as the beast and the four living creatures represent powerful creatures, superior to human beings but lower than God.[2] Whatever shape this being may assume at various moments in human history, its fundamental nature is superhuman and diabolical, even though it may be embodied in human empires or individuals.[3]

The likeness of the beast to three ferocious animals—**a leopard** with **feet like a bear's** and **the mouth of a lion**—recalls a famous vision in Dan 7:3–8

1. In 11:7 the beast is described as coming from the abyss (see sidebar, "The Abyss," p. 167).
2. Other examples include the dragon, the second beast, and the eagle of Rev 8:13. The exception is the Lamb, whom Revelation depicts as receiving divine honor with God (5:12–14).
3. Its superhuman nature is indicated by its origin in the sea or abyss, its relationship with the dragon (13:1–2), and its fate, which differs from that of its human followers at the last battle (13:1–2; 19:19–20). That it is embodied in an empire follows from its antecedents, the four beasts of Dan 7. That it is embodied in a human being is evident in its †type from Daniel as well as some particular verses in Revelation (13:17; 17:8, 11).

and 17. Daniel describes four beasts—a lion, a bear, a leopard, and a fourth beast with iron teeth and ten horns—that represent four hostile empires that would arise against Israel. Daniel's beasts have seven heads among them, since the last beast has four. As in John's description of the Lamb (5:6), readers are probably not intended to form in their minds a literal composite image of these diverse characteristics, but to interpret each of the symbols individually, since no attempt is made to present a coherent picture.[4] The beast that John sees combines the traits of the previous beasts in Daniel's visions and epitomizes diabolical and human opposition to God and his people; it is "the culmination of all the evil empires of history."[5] Like its predecessors, the beast wields political and military power. John presupposes a biblical worldview in which invisible spiritual powers influence earthly political events.[6]

Fig. 11. "They worshiped the dragon because it gave its authority to the beast; they also worshiped the beast . . ." (13:4).

The dragon gives to the beast its **own power and throne**, with **great authority** (see Luke 4:5–6). Alert readers will be struck by an odd parallel between the dragon's delegation of power and authority to the beast and that of God's delegation to Christ (John 3:35; 5:21–23; Phil 2:9–11). A parallel between the beast and Christ becomes hard to miss in the next two verses. The beast was **mortally wounded** (literally, "slaughtered to death"; Greek *sphazō*, translated as "slain" when used of the Lamb in 5:6, 12). But the beast has somehow recovered, just as Jesus was raised. The result is that **the whole world** is **fascinated** (or "filled with wonder," NIV), using a word the Gospels often use for the crowd's response to Jesus' miracles (e.g., Matt 8:27; 9:33; 15:31), and **followed after** it—words often used for discipleship. Furthermore, the people of the earth **worshiped the dragon**, the source of the beast's **authority**, and **also worshiped the beast**.

4. For instance, although the beast has seven heads, its mouth is consistently referred to in the singular (13:2, 5–6).
5. Richard Bauckham, *The Climax of Prophecy: Studies on the Book of Revelation* (Edinburgh: T&T Clark, 1993), 424.
6. Deut 32:8–9; Dan 10:13, 20; Eph 2:2; 6:12.

What Does "Worship" Mean?

BIBLICAL BACKGROUND

The Greek word for worship, *proskyneō*, appears twenty-four times in Revelation, out of fifty-nine uses in the New Testament. In the †Septuagint, it translates a Hebrew word for "worship" that literally means "to bow down." In nonbiblical Greek it means "to prostrate oneself," and usually, "to adore the gods." Although the term is also used in the Bible for prostrating oneself before a human being in an extreme act of reverence (3:9), other texts indicate that prostration that amounts to worship is to be offered to God alone and not to his human or angelic servants (19:10; 22:8–9; Acts 10:25–26). This is the teaching of the first commandment: "You shall not have other gods beside me . . ." (Deut 5:7–9). To worship is not merely to express thanks for a favor received, but to acknowledge the greatness of the being who is worshiped and to express one's absolute submission.

In this light it is easy to see the evil of the worship that the world gives to the dragon and the beast, and that the false prophet (vv. 11–17) solicits for the beast. Jesus' categorical rejection of this temptation by Satan (Matt 4:9–10; Luke 4:6–8) provides the model for Christians tempted to absolutize anyone or anything other than God (see sidebar, "Idolatry: What It Is and What's Wrong with It," p. 175).

In this vision all five uses of the word "worship" depict adoration of evil beings or their images (13:8, 12, 15). The people of the world acclaim the beast with liturgical praise that perversely echoes the Song of Moses (Exod 15:11): **Who can compare with the beast or who can fight against it?** The power of this being, working through an empire or ruler, seems irresistible: the world responds with submission and worship.

Evil presents itself as good (2 Cor 11:14). Satan imitates because he cannot create. The beast attempts to counterfeit the victory of the Lamb in order to deceive. Revelation shows that these efforts are doomed to failure.

What, more concretely, might these symbols have meant to John and his first readers? (We will consider the meaning of these visions for later generations at the end of the chapter.) In Jewish and Christian apocalyptic literature, the beast represents the end-time adversary of God and his people. In Christian writings, it came to be referred to as "the antichrist" (see sidebar, "The Antichrist in the New Testament," pp. 226–27), although this term does not occur in Revelation. John and his readers discerned this adversary to be embodied in the Roman Empire, which was the dominant political, military, cultural, and economic power of their day (13:4; 17:9–10), and in the person of the emperor himself.

As to the "blasphemous names" of the beast, since the time of Caesar Augustus, it was customary for the Roman Senate to ascribe divine titles such as "Lord," "Savior," and "Son of God" to emperors after they died and to promote emperor worship as a way of reinforcing loyalty to the empire. Some emperors, including Caligula, Nero, and Domitian, assumed divine titles during their lifetime. Domitian demanded to be addressed as "My Lord and God" and even to have sacrifices offered to him in Rome.[7] The cult of the emperor was especially encouraged in the provinces and was particularly strong in Asia, the region of the Christians to whom Revelation is addressed. Emperors were believed to have received their power from the gods, especially from Zeus, also called Jupiter, the head of the Greco-Roman pantheon. Since Christians associated Zeus with Satan (see comments on "Satan's throne" at 2:13), they probably understood the worship of the dragon—that is, Satan (13:4)—as symbolizing sacrifices to Zeus on behalf of the emperor.

The beast's head that "seemed to have been mortally wounded" and then "was healed" has a variety of interpretations linked to the emperor Nero (54–68). Many pagans, Jews, and Christians of the late first century thought that Nero had not really died but had fled east to †Parthia and would return. Some scholars think that John, writing after the death of Nero in AD 68, refers to a *future* return of Nero. Others say that at the time Revelation was written, the emperor Domitian (AD 81–96) was regarded by some Romans as a second Nero. It is possible that Christians living at that time understood Domitian's rule as the beast whose mortal wound had been healed. Finally, Richard Bauckham proposes that John understood the return of Nero to have already occurred in the *past* in the restoration of imperial power that quelled the chaos in AD 69 after Nero died, the "so-called 'year of the four emperors,' in which more than one claimant was contesting the imperial title, . . . and in which the survival of the empire was put in very serious question."[8] Despite the hopes of many, Vespasian prevailed, restoring imperial power and establishing the Flavian dynasty in place of the Julio-Claudian dynasty, confirming for many the invincibility of the empire and perhaps leading them to ask, "Who can compare with the beast or who can fight against it?" (13:4).

---

7. The account of Domitian's divine pretensions comes from the Roman historian Suetonius (b. 69, d. after 122), secretary and historian to the emperor Hadrian (reign 117–138). The absence of confirming evidence that can be dated to Domitian's lifetime leads some historians to regard Suetonius's report as an exaggeration. See Steven J. Friesen, *Imperial Cults and the Apocalypse of John: Reading Revelation in the Ruins* (New York: Oxford University Press, 2001), 148–50.

8. Bauckham, *Climax of Prophecy*, 443.

The Antichrist in the New Testament

BIBLICAL BACKGROUND

The epistle known as First John reports an oral tradition accepted by the early Church regarding an †eschatological adversary called the antichrist—a figure with whom false teachers are associated: "Just as you heard that the antichrist was coming, so now many antichrists have appeared. Thus we know this is the last hour" (1 John 2:18; see 2:22; 2 John 7). Later the author clarifies that the teachers who do not acknowledge Jesus manifest "the spirit of the antichrist," which is "already in the world" (1 John 4:3).

A similar expectation was already present in Jewish †intertestamental literature, which mentions two types of anti-Messiah figures: a †Gentile ruler who opposes God and persecutes his people like the little horn of Dan 8:9–12, and a false teacher like the false prophet of Deut 18:20.[a]

In his †Olivet discourse, Jesus also warns of two types of eschatological opponents, "False messiahs [presumably rulers] and false prophets will arise, and they will perform signs and wonders so great as to deceive, if that were possible, even the elect" (Matt 24:24). Jesus may refer specifically to the antichrist in Mark 13:14, which implies, by the use of a masculine participle where a neuter form would be expected, that the "desolating abomination" is a person.

Although he does not use the term "antichrist," St. Paul describes an eschatological adversary—"the lawless one"—in 2 Thess 2:1–12. This figure will either accompany or follow a time of great apostasy (2 Thess 2:3). He "opposes and exalts himself above every so-called god and object of worship, so as to seat himself in the temple of God, claiming that he is a god" (v. 4). His "coming springs from the power of Satan in every mighty deed and in signs and wonders that lie" (v. 9), but Jesus will destroy him by "the breath of his mouth and render [him] powerless by the manifestation of his coming" (v. 8).

The Activity of the Beast and the Consequences (13:5–10)

⁵The beast was given a mouth uttering proud boasts and blasphemies, and it was given authority to act for forty-two months. ⁶It opened its mouth to utter blasphemies against God, blaspheming his name and his dwelling and those who dwell in heaven. ⁷It was also allowed to wage war against the holy ones and conquer them, and it was granted authority over every tribe, people, tongue, and nation. ⁸All the inhabitants of the earth will worship it, all whose names were not written from the foundation of the world in the book of life, which belongs to the Lamb who was slain.

⁹Whoever has ears ought to hear these words.
¹⁰Anyone destined for captivity goes into captivity.

Without using the term "antichrist," Revelation speaks of two end-time adversaries of Christ: the first beast, who makes blasphemous claims, receives worship, and wields political power to persecute Christians (11:7; 13:1–10; 17:3–14; 19:19–20); and a second beast (13:11–17), also called "the false prophet" (16:13; 19:20; 20:10), whose specialty is deception, who appears to perform signs, and who compels worship of the first beast and its image.

Many of the New Testament passages mentioned allude to the eschatological opponent of God's people in Dan 7–8 and 11 (the fourth beast and "little horn"). Probably the prophecies in Daniel originally applied to the Syrian king Antiochus IV Epiphanes, who dedicated the Jerusalem temple to Zeus and suppressed Judaism between 167 and 164 BC, approximately a three-and-a-half-year period (2 Macc 6:1–11). Since, however, his defeat was not accompanied by the inauguration of the dominion of the son of man and the eternal reign of the saints foretold in Dan 7:13–18, ancient Jewish and Christian interpreters looked for a future fulfillment (see sidebar, "Attributes of the Beast," p. 284).

Christian tradition identifies the "antichrist" of 1 John 2:18, 22 with both the figure St. Paul calls "the lawless one" and the figure Revelation calls "the beast" (see sidebar, "The Catechism on the Antichrist," p. 229).

a. Osborne, *Revelation*, 494.

> Anyone destined to be slain by the sword shall be slain by the sword.
>
> Such is the faithful endurance of the holy ones.

OT: Jer 15:2; Dan 7:7–25; 8:9–26; 11:31–36
NT: Eph 1:4; 2:6; Col 3:1–4; 2 Thess 2:1–12
Catechism: antichrist and the Church's final trial, 675–77

The duration of the beast's activity is **forty-two months**—the equivalent of   **13:5**
three and a half years, the temporary period of †eschatological trial prophesied in Daniel. While earlier references to this length of time seem to refer to the entire age of the Church (see sidebar, "Forty-Two Months, Twelve Hundred and Sixty Days, Three and a Half Years," p. 189), this instance seems to refer to the Church's final trial since verses 7–8 speak of the beast's attaining world dominance and conquering the holy ones (see also 11:7). Its **proud boasts and blasphemies,** like its blasphemous names in 13:1, probably refer to its claiming divine prerogatives and demanding worship. The little horn in Daniel likewise "spoke arrogantly" and "against the Most High" (Dan 7:8, 11, 20, 25). Paul describes the "lawless one" as exalting "himself above every so-called god and

object of worship, so as to seat himself in the temple of God, claiming that he is a god" (2 Thess 2:3–4). The fact that the beast **is given authority to act**, a †divine passive, indicates that God is in control; for a limited time God allows evil to run its course.

13:6   Besides making false divine claims, to blaspheme means to speak evil, to defame, or to speak contemptuously, which the beast does **against God**. The following phrase elaborates on this, explaining that the beast blasphemes God's **name**—that is, his person—and **his dwelling,** likely referring to God's dwelling on earth, the Church. This interpretation is confirmed by the fact that the next phrase links God's dwelling with **those who dwell in heaven**.[9] As other New Testament writings suggest, the Church is where heaven and earth overlap. The members of the Church on earth are united with God, being members of Christ, who is at the Father's right hand (Eph 1:20; 2:4-6) through the gift of the Holy Spirit (1 Cor 6:17; 12:13), a union that is actualized and experienced in their worship (Eph 5:18–20); consequently, they are understood to dwell in heaven (Eph 2:6; Col 3:1–3). At the same time, because God's Spirit dwells in them, they constitute God's temple on earth (11:1; see sidebar, "God's Temple," pp. 186–87). So the beast is depicted as railing against God and his Church.

13:7–8   More than that, it is **allowed** (literally, "granted") **to wage war against the holy ones and to conquer them**. This repeats exactly what was said in 11:7 about the fate of the two witnesses when their testimony is finished: "the beast that comes up from the abyss will wage war against them and conquer them and kill them." It echoes what is prophesied in Daniel about the time immediately before God comes to judge and establish his kingdom: "As I watched, that horn made war against the holy ones and was victorious" (7:21). The beast-antichrist can achieve this since **it was granted authority**, another divine passive, recalling Jesus' words before Pilate: "You would have no authority over me if it had not been granted to you from above" (John 19:11, literal translation). The beast's authority extends over **every tribe, people, tongue, and nation**—a four-part description indicating worldwide empire (see sidebar, "Attributes of the Beast," p. 284).

This will be a dark time in history since **all the inhabitants of the earth will worship the beast**; not every human being will worship it, but **all whose names were not written . . . in the book of life** (see sidebar, "Who Are the 'Inhabitants of the Earth'?," p. 130). Something very positive is said about the

9. The link is stronger in the RSV and NRSV, which omit the word "and" (since the best manuscripts do not include it) and place "his dwelling" and "those who dwell in heaven" in apposition. Another place where "those who dwell in heaven" *may* refer to members of the Church on earth is 12:12.

The Catechism on the Antichrist

LIVING TRADITION

Catholic teaching confirms that the Church will pass through a final trial because of the activity of the antichrist prior to Christ's return.

> Before Christ's second coming the Church must pass through a final trial that will shake the faith of many believers [cf. Luke 18:8; Matt 24:12]. The persecution that accompanies her pilgrimage on earth [cf. Luke 21:12; John 15:19–20] will unveil the "mystery of iniquity" in the form of a religious deception offering men an apparent solution to their problems at the price of apostasy from the truth. The supreme religious deception is that of the Antichrist....
> The Antichrist's deception already begins to take shape in the world every time the claim is made to realize within history that messianic hope which can only be realized beyond history through the eschatological judgment. The Church has rejected even modified forms of this falsification of the kingdom to come under the name of millenarianism [cf. DS 3839], especially the "intrinsically perverse" political form of a secular messianism [Piux XI, *Divini Redemptoris*, condemning the "false mysticism" of this "counterfeit of the redemption of the lowly"; cf. *Gaudium et Spes* 20–21]. (Catechism 675–76)

Secular messianism is evident when a government or political party promises a future or claims a loyalty that belongs to God alone.

rest of the human race whose names *are* written in this book. Their names were inscribed in the book of life **from the foundation of the world** and the book **belongs to the Lamb who was slain**.[10] These are the people "from every tribe and tongue, people and nation" whom Jesus "purchased for God" with his blood through his sacrifice on the cross (5:9). They were indeed chosen by God for eternal life. But this does not mean that their free will was overridden or that God predestines others to eternal loss, since God desires all to be saved (1 Tim 2:4). God, who lives outside of time, is able to take into account in his plan "each person's free response to grace" (Catechism 600).

John alerts his audience to the sobering implications of the beast's political power with a prophetic declaration that repeats the conclusion of the messages

13:9–10

10. The Greek word order allows for the translation "written in the Lamb's book of life, the Lamb who was slain from the creation of the world" (NIV), which has given rise to theological speculation about what this could mean. However, since in Greek the phrase translated "from the creation of the world" can also be taken to modify "written," and since we know that the death of Jesus occurred once for all at a particular time and place (see Heb 9:26; 10:10), the translation of the NABRE and most other modern versions is preferable. This interpretation is confirmed by Rev 17:8, which speaks of names written in the book of life from the foundation of the world without any suggestion that the Lamb was slaughtered at that time.

to the seven churches: **Whoever has ears ought to hear**. "Pay careful attention!" John prophesies that **anyone destined for captivity** or **to be slain by the sword** will not be able to escape his or her fate. Although John echoes phrases from Jer 15:2 and 43:11, the context is quite different. In Jeremiah the prophet speaks of judgment on Judah and Egypt at the hands of Babylon because of their sins; here the prophet speaks of captivity and martyrdom for **the holy ones**, God's people, because of the temporary triumph of evil. The common element is the inevitability of the suffering. How must Christians respond to persecution by the seemingly all-powerful beast? The answer is by **faithful endurance** or "endurance and faith" (NRSV, RSV). These closely related virtues are the ones most frequently named in the book of Revelation.

Neither here nor anywhere else does Revelation summon Christians to resist their enemies by actual physical fighting.

Reflection and Application (13:5–10)

Why does God allow the beast to wage war against the holy ones and to conquer them? Revelation does not directly answer this question. Neither do other New Testament texts that predict the increase of evil and hardship for God's people when history nears its climax.[11] Ultimately, Christians are called to trust in God's goodness as amply demonstrated through the gift of his Son. The best guide to God's attitude toward us through times of affliction remains St. Paul's words in Rom 8:28–39.

If we wish to reflect on God's purposes, it is important to remember the difference between his permissive and his deliberate will: God allows evil to flourish; he does not desire it. God's desire is for a world absolutely free of evil, namely, the new heavens and new earth that Revelation reveals he is about to establish (21:4, 27; 2 Pet 3:13).

Nevertheless, God knows how to make use of evil choices by humans and supernatural beings to advance his plan (Gen 50:20; Luke 22:3). When God allows evil to run its course and manifest its true nature, the difference between good and evil, between worshiping God and worshiping anything else, becomes clear (Rom 1:18–32). This will help some people to make better choices and find salvation. This manifestation of evil also makes the justice of God's judgment more obvious when he condemns those who choose the worship of idols and the evildoing that accompanies it (Rev 9:20–21; 11:18; 16:5–6).

11. See Matt 24:9–14; 2 Thess 2:3–12; 2 Tim 3:1–5; 4:1–8; 2 Pet 2:2–4.

Regarding Christians, the consistent teaching of Scripture is that trials, although temporarily painful, make us better if we endure them with faith and hope (13:10; 14:12; Sir 2; Heb 12:1–13). Revelation makes clear that God delights in the virtue of his people who have been faithful through trial (7:13–17; 12:11–12), that he honors those who share in Christ's ministry of testifying to the truth and who suffer for it (6:9–11; 11:3–12), and that righteous deeds like these are "a bright, clean linen garment" that will adorn the Bride of the Lamb (19:7–8). Finally, as noticed earlier, suffering in this world is strictly time-limited: "He will wipe every tear from their eyes, and there shall be no more death or mourning, wailing or pain" (21:4).

The Second Beast and Its Relationship to the First Beast (13:11–18)

[11]Then I saw another beast come up out of the earth; it had two horns like a lamb's but spoke like a dragon. [12]It wielded all the authority of the first beast in its sight and made the earth and its inhabitants worship the first beast, whose mortal wound had been healed. [13]It performed great signs, even making fire come down from heaven to earth in the sight of everyone. [14]It deceived the inhabitants of the earth with the signs it was allowed to perform in the sight of the first beast, telling them to make an image for the beast who had been wounded by the sword and revived. [15]It was then permitted to breathe life into the beast's image, so that the beast's image could speak and [could] have anyone who did not worship it put to death. [16]It forced all the people, small and great, rich and poor, free and slave, to be given a stamped image on their right hands or their foreheads, [17]so that no one could buy or sell except one who had the stamped image of the beast's name or the number that stood for its name.

[18]Wisdom is needed here; one who understands can calculate the number of the beast, for it is a number that stands for a person. His number is six hundred and sixty-six.

OT: Exod 7:11; 13:9; Deut 6:8; 2 Kings 1:10–14; Dan 3
NT: Matt 7:15; 24:24; 2 Thess 2:10–12; Rev 7:2–3; 16:13–14

13:11   While the beast from the sea is associated with political power, the second **beast** that comes up **out of the earth** is associated with religious deception and later is referred to simply as "the false prophet" (16:13; 19:20; 20:10). Like the first beast, it is demonic in nature although it operates in human history through human institutions and individuals. Also like the first beast, it is depicted as having a faux resemblance to Jesus, with **two horns like a lamb's**, but it has a voice and message that betray its true character and allegiance: it **spoke like a dragon**. Its deceptive appearance recalls Jesus' warning, "Beware of false prophets, who come to you in sheep's clothing, but underneath are ravenous wolves" (Matt 7:15).

13:12   The second beast functions in close relationship with the first beast: **It wielded all the authority of the first beast in its sight**, or "in his presence" (RSV), or best, "on its behalf" (NIV, NJB, NRSV). Its essential work is summed up in a phrase: it **made the earth and its inhabitants worship the first beast, whose mortal wound had been healed**. Readers of John's Gospel will recognize a perverted analogy to the work of the Spirit, to the Church's witness to Christ's resurrection, and to the Spirit's role in Christian worship (John 4:23–24; 14:16, 26; 16:14–15). Combining these parallels with how the beast parallels the dragon (12:3; 13:1), a kind of anti-Trinity—a diabolical counterfeit of the relationship of the Father, Son, and Spirit—comes into view. R. H. Mounce sums up the likeness: "As Christ received authority from the Father (Matt 11:27), so Antichrist receives authority from the dragon (Rev 13:4), and as the Holy Spirit glorifies Christ (John 16:14), so the false prophet glorifies the Antichrist (Rev 13:12)."[12]

The second beast is a propagandist for the first. In its first-century setting, there is no individual whose conduct is an obvious match to that of the second beast. Consequently, it probably referred corporately to the priesthood of the imperial cult, consisting of local officials who promoted and enforced worship of the emperor or of the goddess Roma as a way of expressing and deepening loyalty to the empire.

13:13–15   The false prophet deceives **the inhabitants of the earth**, those who are not God's people (13:8), and leads them to worship the beast by way of **great signs** it performs publicly on behalf of the beast (see 13:12). These imitate the signs and wonders that the two witnesses perform (11:3–5), even **making fire come down from heaven** like Elijah of old (2 Kings 1:10–12). This accords with Jesus' prediction in his †Olivet discourse: "False messiahs and false prophets will arise, and they will perform signs and wonders so great as to deceive, if that were possible, even the elect" (Matt 24:24). St. Paul predicts deceptive miracles on the part of "the one whose coming springs from the power of Satan in every mighty deed and in signs and wonders that lie" (2 Thess 2:9). What distinguishes John's prophecy in Revelation from Paul's in 2 Thessalonians is

---

12. R. H. Mounce, *The Book of Revelation* (Grand Rapids: Eerdmans, 1998), 255.

that John describes two end-time adversaries through whom Satan works, while Paul mentions only one.

To promote worship of the first beast, the second beast directs the people to make **an image** in its honor and breathes **life into the beast's image** so that it can **speak**. At the end of the first century there was a tremendous proliferation of temples and images for the †imperial cult, especially in Asia Minor, including all seven of the cities to which Revelation is addressed. At Ephesus was a temple to the emperor Domitian, featuring a colossal statue over twenty-two feet high. The idea of making an image speak was well known in the ancient world. After an idol was made, it was customary to "animate" it by means of a magical ritual to cause the god to inhabit it and to "speak" through casting lots to obtain answers to questions, through prophetic oracles by a priest, or through a ventriloquist's trick.

The additional consequence—to **have anyone who did not worship it put to death**—recalls the archetypical biblical example of government-imposed idolatry, the golden image of Nebuchadnezzar that the three young men were commanded to worship on pain of death (Dan 3). Revelation 13:3, 12, and 14 emphasize the seeming "resurrection" of the first beast by mentioning its recovery from a **mortal wound**. Verse 14 adds the detail that the wound came **by the sword**, perhaps alluding to Nero's death by a self-inflicted sword wound (see comments on vv. 3, 18).

The second beast introduces some kind of sign that distinguishes those who worship and accept the patronage of the beast from those who do not. It requires **all the people** to receive **a stamped image** of the beast's name or number **on their right hands or their foreheads**. This "mark" (NIV)[13] of the beast mimics the "seal of the living God" (7:2–4) and the names of God and the Lamb written on the foreheads of the one hundred and forty-four thousand (14:1) and of the redeemed (22:4). The stamped image, like the seal, denotes allegiance and ownership. Livestock, slaves, and soldiers in the first century often bore a tattoo or brand indicating to whom they belonged or under whose patronage and protection they lived. The stamped image bears **the beast's name or the number that stood for its name**. The false prophet makes this mark a condition of participation in the economic life of society; only those having it can **buy or sell**. In other words, the second beast subjects Christians who refuse the mark of the beast to economic discrimination.

13:16–17

We do not have direct evidence of economic restrictions on Christians in the first century, although it is possible that this took place locally in one or more

---

13. Greek *charagma*. The NABRE offers the most literal translation ("to be branded," NJB; "to be marked," RSV; Vulgate, *habere caracter*).

Attributes of the Second Beast, the False Prophet

Here is a summary of the attributes and activity of the second beast, the false prophet. As with the rest of Revelation, readers should be alert to figurative fulfillments.

- Like the first beast, it is a superhuman entity that advances Satan's goals in human history.
- It gives the appearance of being good, even Christlike, yet its message is from the devil (13:11).
- It collaborates closely with the first beast, which wields political power, exercising a delegated authority and promoting idolatrous submission to it (13:12).
- It deceives people to worship the first beast by performing seemingly miraculous signs and by setting up an image of the first beast that can speak (13:13–15).
- It also compels worship of the beast by putting to death those who refuse to worship and by excluding from economic life all who do not express allegiance to the beast by accepting its "stamped image" (13:16–17).
- It propagandizes, performing signs through its agents, to persuade "the kings of the whole world" to battle against God and his people (16:13–16).

of the seven cities where the churches were located. For instance, it is likely that the requirement of participation in pagan rites excluded Christians from guilds, which were an important part of economic life in Pergamum and Thyatira.

13:18   With the statement that **the number of the beast** is **six hundred and sixty-six** we have arrived at the verse in Revelation that has probably aroused more speculation than any other. To avoid being led astray, the first words of the verse are important: **Wisdom is needed here**. A clue is offered regarding the identity of the beast-antichrist, but understanding must be brought to bear. That discernment should take into account the other attributes of the beast-antichrist and the characteristics of its work as described in Revelation and elsewhere in the New Testament (see comments on 13:1–10 and sidebar, "The Antichrist in the New Testament," pp. 226–27). Among its traits, the *number* of the beast is probably the least important and may pertain primarily to its manifestation in the first century. What should be sought in discerning the presence of the beast at any time in Christian history is a "family resemblance" between its biblical portrait and a contemporary reality.

What does the number signify? At the most basic level of biblical symbolism, if seven represents perfection, six signifies imperfection. When there are three sixes, we have the superlative form of imperfection. However, it is likely that John has in mind a more precise meaning since he says that it is possible to **calculate** (literally, "count") the number of the beast and that it **stands for a person** (literally, "is the number of a man"). This suggests the ancient practice of †gematria (guh-MAY-tree-uh). Both in Hebrew and in Greek the letters of the alphabet were also used as numbers (in Hebrew, the first nine letters signify one to nine; the next nine letters signify ten to ninety, and so on). It is therefore possible to add up the numerical value of the letters and to ascertain a number for a word or phrase. According to gematria, if the numerical value of two words or phrases is the same, there is a relationship between them. When the Greek word for "beast," *thērion*,

Bibi Saint-Pol/Wikimedia Commons

Fig. 12. The bust of the emperor Nero (AD 54–68), the first to aggressively persecute the Church. The letters of his name, Neron Caesar, add up to 666 (see 13:18).

is transliterated into Hebrew (i.e., written with Hebrew letters), the numerical value of the letters is 666. When the Greek version of Nero's name, Caesar Neron, is transliterated into Hebrew, it also totals 666.[14] Many scholars believe that John identifies Nero with the number of the beast.

This interpretation gains support from the fact that some ancient manuscripts give the number of the beast as six hundred and sixteen, which is the sum of the letters in Nero's name if it is transliterated from *Latin* into Hebrew.[15] Given the highly symbolic nature of Revelation, if John understood the number to represent Nero's name, it does not mean that he literally identified Nero with the beast, but it might mean that he understood the beast to be a Nero-like figure and Nero to have been a historical embodiment of the beast.

14. The English letters for the Hebrew are QSR NRWN. Here are the numeric values of the Hebrew letters: Q = 100 + S = 60 + R = 200 + N = 50 + R = 200 + W = 6 + N = 50, totaling 666.
15. Gematria can yield a wide variety of results depending on which name, spelling, and language is used. The emperors Caligula and Domitian can also total 666 (when the abbreviation of the latter's titles printed on coins and inscriptions is used). Modern applications of gematria to 666 have identified Adolf Hitler, Henry Kissinger, Ronald Wilson Reagan, Bill Clinton, and Barack Obama (Michael J. Gorman, *Reading Revelation Responsibly: Uncivil Worship and Witness; Following the Lamb into the New Creation* [Eugene: OR: Cascade Books, 2011], 126–28).

What is the meaning today of John's vision of the two beasts, long after the death of Nero and the end of the Roman Empire? †Preterist interpreters say that the primary meaning of Revelation lies in the past, in first-century events. †Futurists answer that because Rev 16–19 depicts the activity of the beast immediately before the return of Christ, these visions refer to a period of trial at the end of history. However, a strict futurist interpretation fails to do justice to the book's clear references to Rome and circumstances of the first century. The interpretation that seems most consistent with the pattern of biblical prophecy is that Revelation speaks about history's end while directly addressing challenges its original readers faced in the first century, and at the same time speaks to God's people about analogous challenges that arise throughout the course of history.

By associating first-century adversaries of God's people (Rome, the emperor, and the enforcers of the imperial cult) with ancient adversaries (e.g., Egypt, Babylon, Antiochus Epiphanes), Revelation itself points toward a †typological mode of interpreting Scripture and history. History repeats itself: enemies arise, and in a similar manner God intervenes to save his people again and again. The end of history will be marked by a climactic struggle and salvation resembling struggles and salvation that have taken place earlier.

Reflection and Application (13:1–18)

Discerning the beast. It is incumbent upon Christians to discern the spiritual dynamics of the times in which they live. Already in the first century, church leaders discerned that "the spirit of the antichrist . . . is already in the world" (1 John 4:3) and that "the mystery of lawlessness is already at work" (2 Thess 2:7). In a similar way it is sometimes possible to discern the spirit of the first or second beast in historical movements that manifest a family resemblance to the antichrist or the false prophet. For instance, at the end of the eighteenth century, the French Revolution tried to destroy the Church in France. Its leaders seized the Cathedral of Notre Dame in Paris, set up an image of the goddess Reason, and established worship of it. In the twentieth century, National Socialism in Germany rejected Christianity, proclaimed the Führer and the Nazi party as the nation's hope, and persecuted Christians who rejected Nazi ideology, while killing millions of Jews and Christians and starting a world war. Communist regimes of the twentieth century taught atheism, held up the party and some of its leaders as saviors, persecuted religion, and pressured clergy and lay leaders to make the Church a tool of the government.[16]

History provides analogies to the second beast's economic discrimination against those who do not bear the stamped image of the beast. People who attended church or had their children baptized in the Soviet Union often lost their jobs or saw their children denied a university education. Similar persecution has been carried out in Muslim states where, in addition to violent persecution, social, legal, and economic restrictions, and the *jizya* (a tax on non-Muslims), have tempted Christians to renounce their faith in exchange for greater opportunity in society (Mark 8:36).

Although in Revelation the second beast, the false prophet, wields political power to persecute Christians, its primary tool is deception. Revelation unmasks the deceptive ideology of the Roman Empire, which appeared noble and beneficial in some respects, but was in fact idolatrous, violent, immoral, and greedy (see chap. 18), a tool of Satan. Similar deception exists in more recent ideologies. Both socialism and capitalism have led to grave evils when practiced without due regard to fundamental moral principles. The gay rights movement claims to promote justice, freedom, and love yet rejects God's teaching about love, sex, and marriage that is inscribed in our nature and explicitly taught in Scripture. In addition, the movement often persecutes those who refuse to bow to its ideology. False ideologies undergird other evil practices. Abortion is defended on the basis of freedom of choice, privacy, the welfare of women, and quality of life. Pornography is defended in the name of freedom and art, while euthanasia is presented as kindness to the sick and elderly, and so on.

What would you do? Although some Christians face severe persecution at the time of this writing, many do not. However, as St. Paul learned, circumstances can change rapidly. After many positive experiences with Roman officials (see, e.g., Acts 18:14–16; 19:35–40), Paul wrote, "Rulers are not a cause of fear to good conduct, but to evil," and referred to civil authorities as "ministers of God" for justice (Rom 13:3, 6). However, only ten years later the emperor Nero beheaded Paul for his Christian faith. The possibility of abrupt social change and persecution is always present, and Jesus prepared his disciples for this eventuality (Matt 10:16–39; John 15:18–19).

So, what would you do if the government of your country placed economic burdens on Christians who do not subscribe to the prevailing ideology? What if the government would deny your children a university education if you would

---

16. See A. H. and A. K., "State Policy toward the Church in Czechoslovakia," January 4, 1964, http://www.osaarchivum.org/greenfield/repository/osa:af03df66-f66e-4ddf-b12a-c0ec67c77ed4.

not subscribe to its policies about religion, politics, or sexual morality? What if the mass media, the system of public education, and the society around you were pressuring you and your children to accept beliefs and behaviors that contradict the teaching of Scripture and the Church? What if the government succeeded in dividing the Church and some priests and bishops were encouraging Catholics to accept what is contrary to the teaching of Christ and the Church?

Even if you are clear about how to respond, what about your family members or fellow parishioners? It is essential to effectively evangelize, catechize, and lead the next generation of Christians to be faithful witnesses, to form Catholics who are able to meet the test. Cultural Catholicism, even weekly participation in Sunday Mass, is not enough. Temptations assault Christians today through the mass media in ways John's readers never experienced. Satan is still at work through his agents to conform believers not only to the surrounding society and its worldview but to what it worships (its ultimate values), its moral standards, and ultimately its fate.

Mark of the beast. Some Christians have speculated that the beast's exclusion of Christ's faithful from commerce for not accepting "the stamped image of the beast's name or the number that stood for its name" could be implemented literally by means of a surgically implanted electronic chip that identifies a person and his or her financial information in a cashless economy. While such a scenario is possible, the "stamped image" or mark of the beast need not be physical. After all, the seal of the living God and the names of God and the Lamb (7:2–3; 14:1) that mark the faithful are spiritual rather than physical. Whatever one thinks of the use of "implanted" electronic means of managing financial transactions, the fundamental problem with the mark of the beast is a spiritual compromise with evil. To focus on a literal physical mark could lead Christians to fail to notice and refuse marks of collaboration with the beast that come in subtler forms.

The Lamb's Companions, the Eternal Gospel, and the Harvest of the Earth

Revelation 14:1–20

After John's visions of the dragon, the beast, and the second beast, his readers are ready for a consoling message that will sustain their hope. The visions of this chapter do precisely that by revealing the intimate relationship with Christ available to God's people now, by indicating that God is now calling the whole world to repentance, and by giving a glimpse of the final destiny of the just and the wicked that lies just over the horizon.

Revelation's structure is characterized by scenes of fear and danger alternating with scenes showing God's salvation and joy. At the same time this alternation likewise reveals the structure of reality. In the present age, evil forces are still at large; nevertheless, the Lamb's power is greater and his people are united to him and under his protection. Final victory and salvation are assured and can even be experienced now in the midst of trials.

The Lamb and His Companions (14:1–5)

¹Then I looked and there was the Lamb standing on Mount †Zion, and with him a hundred and forty-four thousand who had his name and his Father's name written on their foreheads. ²I heard a sound from heaven like the sound of rushing water or a loud peal of thunder. The sound I heard was like that of harpists playing their harps. ³They were singing [what seemed to be] a new hymn before the throne, before the four living

creatures and the elders. No one could learn this hymn except the hundred and forty-four thousand who had been ransomed from the earth. ⁴These are they who were not defiled with women; they are virgins and these are the ones who follow the Lamb wherever he goes. They have been ransomed as the firstfruits of the human race for God and the Lamb. ⁵On their lips no deceit has been found; they are unblemished.

OT: 1 Sam 21:5–6; Ps 15:1–3; Zeph 3:11–15
NT: 1 Cor 7:25–35; 2 Tim 2:3–4; Heb 12:22–24; Jude 1:24; Rev 7:3–8; 11:1–2
Catechism: celibacy, 1618

This first vision in this chapter relates to two earlier visions. The hundred and forty-four thousand virgins who follow the Lamb almost certainly depicts the army of one hundred and forty-four thousand servants of God whom an angel marked with the seal of the living God (7:1–8). At the same time their singing on Mount Zion before the throne recalls "those who are worshiping" in the temple of God, whom John was told to count (11:1).

14:1   The appearance of **the Lamb**, last seen opening the scroll in God's throne room (5:6–13; 6:1–12; 8:1), is a sight for sore eyes. The fact that he is **standing** undisturbed demonstrates that all the evils the beasts have been allowed to carry out are ultimately powerless against him and his companions. **Mount Zion** is the hill of Jerusalem on which both the temple, God's dwelling, and the palace of the king were located. The Old Testament speaks of Mount Zion as the place of God's presence and salvation, both in the past and at the end of history.[1] This vision of the Lamb on Mount Zion thus functions as an answer to the vision of the two beasts in chapter 13. According to Ps 2, Mount Zion is the place where God has established his king, his Son, who will deal decisively with the rebellion of the kings and rulers of the earth "against the LORD and against his anointed one" (v. 2).

Besides this verse in Revelation, the only other New Testament passage that mentions Mount Zion describes it as a spiritual reality already experienced by Christians in the present: "You have come to Mount Zion and to the city of the living God, the heavenly Jerusalem, and to innumerable angels in festal gathering, and to the assembly of the firstborn who are enrolled in heaven, and to God the judge of all, and to the spirits of the righteous made perfect, and to Jesus, the mediator of a new covenant, and to the sprinkled blood . . ." (Heb 12:22–24 NRSV). According to the author of Hebrews, Christians on earth already have access to and are in some sense present at Mount Zion, which he

---

1. Exod 15:17; 2 Kings 19:31; Ps 2; 48; Isa 4:2–3; 57:13; Joel 3:5; Mic 4:6–8.

identifies with the heavenly Jerusalem. There Christians are surrounded by angels and saints and stand in the presence of God and of Jesus, and in the presence of his "sprinkled blood." Hebrews suggests that Christians enjoy communion with these heavenly realities when the Church is gathered for worship (see Heb 10:19–22). Intimacy with Christ, especially in worship, seems also to be what this vision (14:1–5) portrays.[2] Thus Mount Zion refers to the life of heaven to which baptized believers, united to Christ and indwelt by the Holy Spirit, have access while still on earth.

The Lamb is not alone on Mount Zion but is accompanied by a group of **a hundred and forty-four thousand** people. John's audience has already heard about the large company of the same number that were protected with the seal of the living God before the trials could begin (7:4; see comments there). The fact that the present group has the Lamb's **name and his Father's name written on their foreheads** confirms that this is the same group, since "the seal of the living God" in 7:2, like most seals, can be assumed to bear the name of its owner. In chapter 7 we interpreted one hundred and forty-four thousand as a symbolic number representing the totality of God's faithful people, sealed with the Holy Spirit and summoned to engage in spiritual battle. Here the vision of the same group standing with the Lamb and bearing the name of Jesus and the Father on their foreheads provides both a parallel and a stark contrast to the "inhabitants of the earth" in the preceding vision (13:14–17), who worship the beast and bear the "stamped image" of its name or number (13:17). It reassures readers that although the two beasts deceive and coerce many, those who belong to the Lamb continue to enjoy his presence and protection.

14:2–3 This vision is no silent movie but rather features the most extraordinary music imaginable. John gazes on Mount Zion and hears music from heaven. His perception of it is gradual. First he hears a very loud **sound from heaven like . . . rushing water or a loud peal of thunder**—sounds that indicate a †theophany (1:15; 4:5; 8:5; 11:19). Next he recognizes the sound of musical instruments: **harpists playing their harps**. The harp (Greek *kithara*, from which "guitar" is derived), a stringed instrument, was used in temple worship (Ps 33:2; 57:8) and is mentioned three times in Revelation in connection with heavenly worship (5:8; 15:2). Finally he distinguishes singing. It turns out that the harp music is accompaniment to a **new hymn**, an Old Testament term for a song sung in gratitude to God for new acts of salvation. The phrase was used to describe the

---

2. This is not to say that the author of Revelation was familiar with Hebrews, although it is possible. Rather, both authors reflect a common early Christian perspective that Christian life and worship on earth are already a participation in the life of heaven (Eph 1:3; 2:4; Col 3:1–4).

praise offered to the Lamb: "You were slain and with your blood you purchased for God / those from every tribe and tongue, people and nation" (see 5:9).

No ordinary audience listens to this hymn: it is performed **before the throne, before the four living creatures and the elders**—that is, before God himself and his most exalted ministers. Nor can just anyone sing this song: **No one could learn** it **except the hundred and forty-four thousand** who had been **ransomed.** The verb translated "ransomed" here is the same word used in 5:9, translated literally there as "purchased"; other translations render it "redeemed" (e.g., ESV, NRSV). The scene is reminiscent of a prophetic promise: "Those whom the LORD has ransomed will return / and enter Zion singing" (Isa 51:11). Thus a unique intimacy with the Lamb and a unique role in worship belong to this group whom the Lamb has ransomed **from the earth,** the place where people worship the beast and bear his mark on their foreheads. The contrast continues between those who inhabit the earth and those who commune with heaven (13:6–8).

14:4–5   Now John provides a close-up of the character and conduct of the people who comprise the hundred and forty-four thousand. They are those **who were not defiled with women** because **they are virgins**.

The early Christian esteem for celibacy[3] has led some ancient and modern commentators to interpret these virgins literally as celibates who enjoy a special closeness to the Lord. While the "undivided devotion" that celibacy makes possible (1 Cor 7:35 RSV) harmonizes well with the message of this text, there are stronger reasons not to interpret this group as comprised literally of celibate virgins. First, this vision seems to depict the same hundred and forty-four thousand that was sealed in chapter 7, symbolizing the people of God (see comments on 7:3–8). Second, if the intention of the text is to commend celibacy, it is strange that all the virgins would be male, as "not defiled with women" implies. Finally, this last phrase contradicts other passages of the New Testament (Matt 19:12; 1 Cor 7), whose teaching on celibacy does not speak of marital relations as defiling. On the contrary, it is false teachers who hold a negative view of marriage (1 Tim 4:3).

It makes better sense to understand the "virgins" metaphorically as representing those who are faithful to the Lord. Saint Paul uses "virgin" this way in his exhortation to the church of Corinth: "I am jealous of you with the jealousy of God, since I betrothed you to one husband to present you as a chaste virgin to Christ" (2 Cor 11:2). Conversely, defilement through illicit sexual relations

3. See Matt 19:12; 22:30; Luke 18:29; Acts 21:9; 1 Cor 7:7–9, 25–28, 32–38. The example of Jesus, Mary, John the Baptist, Paul, and others undoubtedly contributed to this development.

is a common prophetic metaphor for idolatry in Revelation (e.g., 2:20–21; 14:8; see Ezek 23).

There is one more reason why the hundred and forty-four thousand servants of God are depicted as male. When this number was first introduced (7:4–8), Old Testament census language was used to allude to males twenty years or older from all Israel fit for military service (Num 1:20). When engaged in a campaign, Israel's soldiers were required to keep their camp holy so that the Lord would remain among them; this involved observing various rules of ritual purity, including abstinence from sexual relations.[4] Here the whole people of God, male and female, young and old, is represented symbolically as soldiers who keep themselves pure and the camp holy while engaged in a very different kind of warfare: worshiping,

Fig. 13. Virgins adore the Lamb who stands on Mount Zion. They sing a new hymn to the music of harps before the throne, the four living creatures, and the elders (14:1–5).

witnessing, and remaining faithful unto death. While ancient Israel's soldiers abstained temporarily from sexual relations, the Lamb's companions are virgins who abstain permanently from the defilement of idols.

These virgins, the Church militant, enjoy a privileged intimacy with Jesus. They **follow the Lamb**. The Greek for "follow" is the same word used seventy times in the Gospels to refer to how disciples relate to Jesus. He is their captain, and they conquer in the same way he did, by love, obedience to God, and laying down their lives. They have the privilege of being with Jesus **wherever he goes**, including the way of the cross (see John 12:24–26).

They are themselves a sacred offering. Not only have they been ransomed "from the earth" (14:3); they have been **ransomed . . . for God and the Lamb** as **the firstfruits**. In the Old Testament, the first fruits are the first and best part of the harvest, given to God as his portion (Exod 34:26). In this case, the Lamb's companions are the first fruits **of the human race**. As usual in the New Testament, ritual purity symbolizes ethical purity: **no deceit**, "no lie,"

---

4. Deut 23:10–15; 1 Sam 21:5–6; 2 Sam 11:9–13.

is found in them, in contrast to the deception and lying of the false teachers, the devil (12:9; 20:3, 8), the beast (see 2 Thess 2:9–12), the false prophet (Rev 13:14; 19:20), and the whore of Babylon (18:23). They therefore are **unblemished**, a word used in the Old Testament to describe something worthy to be offered to God (e.g. Num 28:19). With these traits they resemble Israel's faithful (Ps 32:2; Zeph 3:13; Mal 2:6) and the Lamb himself (Isa 53:9; Heb 9:14; 1 Pet 1:19; 2:22).

Some understand this vision as a promise to suffering Christians of the *future* intimacy with Christ that will be theirs in heaven. However, nothing in John's account indicates that it occurs at a period different from the time of the beasts' waging war against God's people in the previous chapter. Rather, the contrasting parallel between the "inhabitants of the earth" who worship the beast and bear a stamped image of his name on their foreheads (13:8, 16) and the virgin companions of the Lamb who have been "ransomed from the earth" and bear the name of the Lamb and his Father on their foreheads (14:1, 3) suggests that the two visions depict simultaneous realities. Furthermore, the hundred and forty-four thousand following the Lamb wherever he goes present a picture of Christian discipleship in this world.

How are we to interpret the moral excellence of the hundred and forty-four thousand that so clearly exceeds the faithfulness of many Christians both now and when Revelation was written (e.g., the churches of Sardis and Laodicea, 3:1–4, 14–18)? Rather than aiming to show the Church as it is, this vision indicates the purity and faithfulness to which the Lord calls all his disciples and for which he gives them the Holy Spirit (Gal 5:22–23).

Reflection and Application (14:1–5)

A striking feature of Revelation is its presentation of two radically opposed possibilities for human beings: on the one hand, to keep God's commandments, bear witness to Jesus, worship the Lamb and follow him wherever he goes; on the other hand, to worship the beast, go along with those around us who reject God's teaching, and end up on the side of those persecuting God's people.

Ultimately, there are two ways and no middle ground. In our daily choices each of us is progressing toward belonging definitively to one or the other of these two groups. If the compromising Christians of the churches of Asia repent, they will belong to the one hundred and forty-four thousand virgins. If they do not, they will be assimilated to the inhabitants of the earth and followers of the beast who will be destroyed.

Church teaching adds that those who choose deep down to obey God and to follow Christ, but do not purify themselves of attachment to sin in this life, will need to be purified after death (see Catechism 1030–32 and "Reflection and Application" on 20:4–6). Only saints, transformed people, will live with God forever.

Three Angel Heralds (14:6–13)

[6]Then I saw another angel flying high overhead, with everlasting good news to announce to those who dwell on earth, to every nation, tribe, tongue, and people. [7]He said in a loud voice, "Fear God and give him glory, for his time has come to sit in judgment. Worship him who made heaven and earth and sea and springs of water."

[8]A second angel followed, saying:

> "Fallen, fallen is Babylon the great,
> that made all the nations drink
> the wine of her licentious passion."

[9]A third angel followed them and said in a loud voice, "Anyone who worships the beast or its image, or accepts its mark on forehead or hand, [10]will also drink the wine of God's fury, poured full strength into the cup of his wrath, and will be tormented in burning sulfur before the holy angels and before the Lamb. [11]The smoke of the fire that torments them will rise forever and ever, and there will be no relief day or night for those who worship the beast or its image or accept the mark of its name." [12]Here is what sustains the holy ones who keep God's commandments and their faith in Jesus.

[13]I heard a voice from heaven say, "Write this: Blessed are the dead who die in the Lord from now on." "Yes," said the Spirit, "let them find rest from their labors, for their works accompany them."

OT: Isa 21:9; Jer 51:49
NT: Mark 9:43–48
Catechism: accepting the gospel, 1229; hell, 1033–37

Now that all the actors in the final drama of human history have been introduced (except the harlot, 17:1), this vision symbolically depicts the proclamation of the gospel to the †nations. We may suppose that the proclamation of the gospel and the warnings of judgment occur during the same period as the deceiving and persecuting activity of the beasts (chap. 13) and the worship and discipleship of the one hundred and forty-four thousand virgins (14:1–5).

Just as the work of the dragon and the beasts is carried out by human agents (rulers, the empire, officials of the †imperial cult, and false teachers), it is likely that the proclamations of the three angels symbolize the testimony of the Church up to the time when history reaches its climax.

14:6–7   John sees **another angel**, probably meaning one in addition to the seven angels who announced judgments with trumpet blasts (9:1–21; 11:15–19). The fact that it is **flying high overhead** (literally, "in midheaven," NRSV), like the eagle who announced the three woes in 8:13, underscores that its message is directed to everyone, **every nation, tribe, tongue, and people**. It is significant that John does not say "inhabitants of the earth," his term for those fixed in their opposition to God. The angel announces **everlasting good news**, or an "eternal gospel," loudly, so all can hear.

Contemporary Christians may be surprised at the angel's version of the gospel. Where's the part about Jesus? About faith and baptism? In fact the angel's summary is similar to the message proclaimed by John the Baptist and Jesus himself: "Repent, for the kingdom of heaven is at hand" (Matt 3:2; 4:17). In the context of this book, **Fear God and give him glory** means to repent, worship God, and be joined to God's people (15:4; 16:9; 19:5–7). God's coming **to sit in judgment** is equivalent to the arrival of his kingdom (Ps 96:13; 98:9). The message summons the †nations to come and **worship** the one **who made heaven and earth**. Human beings owe obedience and thanksgiving to their creator (Rom 1:20–21, 28). This invitation to turn from idols to the one Creator God is the message the apostles preached to †Gentiles (Acts 14:15–17; 17:24–31).

14:8   The **second angel** echoes a prophecy against the pagan nations in Isa 21:9 and anticipates the lengthy description of Babylon's fall in Rev 17–18: **Fallen, fallen is Babylon**. The declaration of judgment is spoken in the prophetic past tense, as though it has already happened, to indicate its certainty. This is the first of six mentions of **Babylon the great**.[5] Since no explanation occurs here, it is likely that John presupposes his readers already know of Babylon from the Old Testament and its counterpart in their own day. Babylon was the capitol of the empire that destroyed Jerusalem and the temple of Solomon and thus stood as an archetype both of the enemy of God's people and of the land of exile. The ancient inhabitants of Babel—meaning Babylon—who built a tower reaching to heaven to make a name for themselves (Gen 11:1–9) epitomize proud ambition and independence from God. To both Jews and Christians of the first

5. The others are 16:19; 17:5; 18:2, 10, 21.

century, ancient Babylon was a †type of Rome, both as a persecuting power and as the place of their exile (1 Pet 5:13). Here Revelation uses "Babylon" to accuse a society that corrupts the world, adding the image of a prostitute: she **made all the nations drink / the wine of her licentious passion** (literally, "the wine of the passion of her fornication"). As mentioned earlier (see comments on 2:20–22), in Revelation "fornication" can refer literally to sexual immorality, figuratively to idolatry, or both. The vision of Babylon's destruction in chapter 18 highlights its passion for material goods.

Like the previous two angels, the **third angel** speaks in **a loud voice** so that   14:9–11
everyone can hear. His message is a solemn warning against worshiping the beast or accepting a token of allegiance to the beast, **its mark on forehead or hand**. To worship the beast is to accept the claims of a ruler, government, or party to an authority that belongs uniquely to God, or to give the appearance of doing so, by accepting its mark.[6] The consequence of unfaithfulness is unthinkable: to **drink the wine of God's fury** (the same word translated "passion" in 14:8) **poured** unmixed[7] into **the cup of his wrath**, a metaphor for God's fierce judgment (Isa 51:17; Jer 25:15–38). The phrase **tormented in burning sulfur** (literally, "fire and sulfur"; "fire and brimstone," NJB) recalls the description of God's judgment on Sodom and Gomorrah (Gen 19:24) and other prophecies of judgment by divine fire (e.g., Isa 30:33; Ezek 38:22).[8] The fact that their torment occurs **before the holy angels and before the Lamb** may refer simply to the court where the judgment is pronounced (Luke 12:8–9; Rev 3:5), to the manifestation of how wrong they were, or perhaps to the perverse misery of those who hate the Lamb. If the presence of the just is torment to the wicked (Wis 2:12–15), how much more so the presence of the Lamb and his angels? In any case, the **smoke of the fire . . . will rise forever and ever**—an echo of Isa 34:8–10, which promises God's "requital for the cause of Zion" against the nation of Edom, characterized by perpetual burning, sulfur, and rising smoke. Thus there is **no relief** ("rest," RSV; "respite," NJB) for those worshiping the beast or its image or accepting its mark, "no peace for the wicked" (Isa 48:22). This imagery is reminiscent of the unquenchable fire and perpetual torment of Gehenna in Jesus' warnings about sin in the Gospels (e.g., Mark 9:43–48). As in the case of Jesus' words, the purpose of this announcement is to motivate

---

6. In the time of the early Church, as in the period of the Maccabees (see 2 Macc 6:21–28), faithful Christians firmly rejected feigning participation in idolatrous worship in order to escape death (see sidebar, "St. Polycarp, the Church of Smyrna's Most Illustrious Martyr," p. 65).

7. It was customary to mix water with wine at a 1:1 or 2:1 ratio. Only if one wanted to get drunk would one drink wine full strength.

8. Revelation 19:20 and 20:10 depict the two beasts and the devil cast into the lake of fire and sulfur.

The Catechism on Hell

The reality of hell and the consequent urgency of repentance has been a consistent teaching of the Church. Here are excerpts of what the Catechism says in 1033, 1036, and 1037.

> To die in mortal sin without repenting and accepting God's merciful love means remaining separated from him for ever by our own free choice. This state of definitive self-exclusion from communion with God and the blessed is called "hell."
>
> The affirmations of Sacred Scripture and the teachings of the Church on the subject of hell are a *call to the responsibility* incumbent upon man to make use of his freedom in view of his eternal destiny. They are at the same time an urgent *call to conversion*....
>
> In the Eucharistic liturgy and in the daily prayers of her faithful, the Church implores the mercy of God, who does not want "any to perish, but all to come to repentance" (2 Pet 3:9).

the half-hearted to make every effort to avoid such a terrible fate by rejecting worship of the beast or acceptance of its mark.

14:12–13   The NABRE attaches 14:12 to the paragraph with the messages of the three angels, as an explanation of their impact on Christians: this message is **what sustains the holy ones**. However, it makes more sense to take it as a separate exhortation, as other translations do: "Here is a call for the endurance of the saints, those who keep the commandments of God and the faith of Jesus" (RSV). Three essential responses of Christians are thus identified: faith, obedience to God's commandments, and perseverance. The phrase "keep the faith of Jesus" here means either to keep believing in Jesus or to imitate his faithfulness.

Next John hears **a voice from heaven**, presumably the angel who speaks on behalf of Jesus, commanding him, **Write this**. What follows is the second of seven †beatitudes in the book of Revelation, all of which focus on the proper response of readers to the message of the book (see sidebar below). To **die in the Lord** is to die as a faithful follower of Christ, united to him through faith and baptism. The addition of **from now on** refers to the difficult times faced by those who struggle against the beasts and Babylon, in whatever period of history they live. The **Spirit**, perhaps responding interiorly within the prophet John, confirms the message of the heavenly voice and explains the reasons these dead may be regarded as blessed. First, they will **find rest from their labors**— the fulfillment of many prophetic promises (Isa 57:1–2; Jer 46:27; 50:34) and a direct contrast to the fate of those who follow the beast and will experience

The Seven Beatitudes of the Apocalypse

BIBLICAL BACKGROUND

The seven beatitudes sprinkled through the book point readers to their final goal and to the conduct in the present that will lead them there.

1. Blessed is the one who reads aloud and blessed are those who listen to this prophetic message and heed what is written in it, for the appointed time is near (1:3).
2. Blessed are the dead who die in the Lord from now on. They will "find rest from their labors, for their works accompany them" (14:13).
3. "Behold, I am coming like a thief." Blessed is the one who watches and keeps his clothes ready (16:15).
4. Blessed are those who have been called to the wedding feast of the Lamb (19:9).
5. Blessed and holy are those who share in the first resurrection, who will be priests of God and of Christ and will reign with him for a thousand years (20:6).
6. Blessed is the one who keeps the prophetic message of this book (22:7).
7. Blessed are they who wash their robes so as to have the right to the tree of life and enter the city through its gates (22:14).

torment with "no relief" (14:11). Second, they can expect a reward for their pains, since **their works accompany them** (literally, "follow them"). The good deeds and faithful testimony of Christians on earth have a value and obtain a reward that continues beyond the grave.

In these verses God is encouraging Christians to have courage and endurance through his prophet, saying, Do not fear dying in the Lord, whether as a martyr or in any other way, since you are blessed. Your good works, your faithfulness, your loyalty to your Lord will be remembered and rewarded.

Reflection and Application (14:6–13)

The content of our evangelization. John's visionary depiction of the Church's proclamation of the gospel contains a warning of judgment that is missing from many contemporary proclamations of the gospel. In reaction to earlier overemphasis on the fear of judgment, many Catholics since Vatican II have tended to present only Jesus' love and grace and to pass over human accountability to God and the grave consequences of disobedience. To some degree this lacuna in the message that Catholics preach is due to a misunderstanding of what the Council said about the possibility of salvation apart from explicit faith in Christ. The result is that many Catholics have come to regard the gospel as optional—spiritually enriching but not necessary for salvation. Immediately following the nuanced discussion of the possibility of salvation for those who have not heard the gospel, *Lumen Gentium* 16 states:

> But very often, deceived by the Evil One, men have become vain in their reasonings, have exchanged the truth of God for a lie and served the world rather than the Creator (cf. Rom 1:21, 25). Or else, living and dying in this world without God, they are exposed to ultimate despair. Hence, to procure the glory of God and the salvation of all these, the Church, mindful of the Lord's command, "preach the Gospel to every creature" (Mk 16:16), takes zealous care to foster the missions.

In other words, while God may make it possible for some people who have not heard the gospel to be saved, this cannot be presumed.[9]

This does not mean that the Church's message should primarily be fire and brimstone. The gospel's emphasis is always God's grace and the love of Christ. Besides being true, it is generally more effective. Nevertheless, to explain human accountability to God for our conduct and the certainty of future judgment is nothing less than telling the truth. Evangelization must be a matter not of preaching *either* grace or judgment but of preaching *both*. Advance knowledge of impending judgment is a mercy if there is opportunity to avoid a negative outcome. Students benefit from knowing the topics they must master for the final exam; taxpayers are more careful if they know in advance that their tax return will be audited.

A medical doctor who failed to inform at-risk patients of the potentially fatal consequences of smoking, poor diet, or unsafe sexual practices could be guilty of malpractice. Pastors and evangelists would do well to imitate the sober, factual way physicians communicate such information, even if sometimes more impassioned warnings about eternal consequences are necessary.

The Harvest of the Earth (14:14–20)

---

[14]**Then I looked and there was a white cloud, and sitting on the cloud one who looked like a son of man, with a gold crown on his head and a sharp**

---

9. See Ralph Martin, *Will Many Be Saved? What Vatican II Actually Teaches and Its Implications for the New Evangelization* (Grand Rapids: Eerdmans, 2012).

sickle in his hand. [15]Another angel came out of the temple, crying out in a loud voice to the one sitting on the cloud, "Use your sickle and reap the harvest, for the time to reap has come, because the earth's harvest is fully ripe." [16]So the one who was sitting on the cloud swung his sickle over the earth, and the earth was harvested.

[17]Then another angel came out of the temple in heaven who also had a sharp sickle. [18]Then another angel [came] from the altar, [who] was in charge of the fire, and cried out in a loud voice to the one who had the sharp sickle, "Use your sharp sickle and cut the clusters from the earth's vines, for its grapes are ripe." [19]So the angel swung his sickle over the earth and cut the earth's vintage. He threw it into the great wine press of God's fury. [20]The wine press was trodden outside the city and blood poured out of the wine press to the height of a horse's bridle for two hundred miles.

OT: Isa 63:1–6; Joel 3:11–14
NT: Matt 13:24–30, 36–43; 26:64; Mark 13:26–27; 1 Thess 4:15–17; Rev 19:11–15

The three angels' proclamations of the gospel and of impending judgment set the stage for this vision of the end of human history. It concisely depicts the final judgment in harvest imagery familiar to John's readers from the Old Testament and the sayings of Jesus (Matt 13:37–41). In this vision the grain harvest symbolizes the gathering in of the just and the grape harvest symbolizes the gathering of the unjust.

The figure **on the cloud . . . who looked like a son of man, with a gold crown**, represents Christ, already described as "like a son of man" in 1:13. The return of Christ on the clouds is what Christians have been taught to expect.[10] His gold crown represents kingship and victory, while the **sickle in his hand**, the ordinary tool for harvesting grain, signals the end of the age, symbolized as a harvest (Matt 13:30).

14:14

The fact that **another angel** issues from the heavenly **temple** to tell the one like a son of man that **the time to reap has come** has led some interpreters to think that this figure like a son of man is someone other than Christ. But the phrase "another angel" occurs throughout the chapter and elsewhere in Revelation and need not imply that the "one like a son of man" is an angel.[11] The idea that God should inform Christ of the time when **earth's harvest is fully ripe** is consistent with Jesus' teaching that the timing of the end is fixed

14:15–16

---

10. Matt 24:30–31; 26:64; Acts 1:9–11; 1 Thess 4:17.
11. See Rev 7:2; 8:3; 14:6, 8–9, 17–18. Some take the "one who looked like a son of man" to be an angel and yet regard him as representing Christ in the vision (Charles Homer Giblin, *The Book of Revelation* [Collegeville, MN: Liturgical Press, 1991], 143).

by the Father (Acts 1:7; see Matt 24:36). When **the one who was sitting on the cloud** hears this word, he swings his **sickle** once, **and the earth** is **harvested**. Wrapping up human history at the final judgment will be neither difficult nor time-consuming for the one like a son of man. In a moment, in a single act, it will be accomplished.

In the Gospels the harvest as an image of the final judgment has both a positive and a negative connotation. On the one hand, it is the time when God will gather his own into his barn; on the other, it is the time when the wicked will be destroyed (Matt 3:12; 13:30, 37–42).

Joel 4:12–13 furnishes this vision's structure, in which judgment follows the pattern of the grain and grape harvests:

> Let the †nations rouse themselves up and come up
> to the Valley of Jehoshaphat;
> For there I will sit in judgment
> upon all the neighboring nations.
>
> Wield the sickle,
> for the harvest is ripe;
> Come in and tread,
> for the wine press is full;
> The vats overflow,
> for their crimes are numerous. [12]

14:17–18 In Jesus' parable about the harvest in Matt 13:37–43, the angels serve as reapers who gather evildoers for destruction. Here also **another angel** comes **out of the temple in heaven** and is instructed to **cut the clusters of earth's vines** by yet **another angel** coming **from the altar** who is **in charge of the fire**. Fire is often linked to judgment in biblical prophecy (8:5–9; 18:8; 19:20; Amos 1:1–2:5).

14:19–20 The judgment of the wicked is also achieved at a single stroke. The **angel** swings **his sickle** and cuts **the earth's vintage** (literally, "harvests the earth's grapevine") and throws it **into the great wine press of God's †fury**. This imagery of trampling the wicked in a winepress from which their blood flows out like the juice of grapes (used again in 19:11–16) is drawn from Isa 63:1–6, which describes God's intervention to bring judgment on pagan nations in order to redeem his people. This act of judgment takes place **outside the city**. The law of Moses directs that certain objects and activities connected with sin and

---

12. In some other translations these verses are found at Joel 3:12–13.

death be symbolically excluded from the community by being placed outside the camp where God's holy people live.[13] The large number of people subject to this judgment is indicated by the amount of **blood**, signifying the lives of the wicked, that pours out of the winepress of God's †wrath: to **the height of a horse's bridle for two hundred miles**. The NABRE's conversion of the distance to miles obscures the symbolic significance of the number used in the text, sixteen hundred stadia.[14] The number sixteen hundred, whether calculated as forty squared or four squared times ten squared, indicates that this judgment is complete and worldwide in scope. This distance was also regarded as the length of the land of Palestine. It is likely that here "the city" is Jerusalem, symbolizing God's people, referred to later as "the camp of the holy ones and the beloved city" (20:9). The blood that fills the land outside the holy city refers to God's judgment on the wicked in the final battle at the end of history, reported again with different emphases in 19:19–21 and 20:7–10. The sea of blood surrounding Jerusalem and the perpetual torment in burning sulfur (14:10–11) are horrifying images, but intentionally so. It is not possible to overstate the horror of rejecting God's gracious offer of salvation.

Although John's vision of the harvest of the earth provides a vivid picture of the salvation of the just and the destruction of the wicked at the final judgment, it focuses exclusively on the judgment of those living on the earth and makes no mention of the judgment of the dead. The judgment of the dead is depicted in another final judgment vision (20:11–15), after visions of the last battle and the defeat of Satan. It is typical of the visions of Revelation to provide complementary perspectives on an event, rather than to present a single comprehensive picture.

---

13. See, e.g., Exod 29:14; Lev 14:40–45; Num 15:35.
14. One *stadion* (Latin *stadium*) equals about 607 to 738 feet (= 185 to 225 meters).

Seven Angels with Seven Plagues; the Song of Moses and the Lamb

Revelation 15:1–8

After the sounding of the seventh trumpet (11:15), an interlude of visions in chapters 12 to 14 †recapitulated the history of salvation. The visions began with Israel before the birth of Christ, continued through Satan's war on the Church by means of the beasts, recounted the worship and witness of the Lamb's faithful followers, and arrived at the final judgment. Now chapters 15 and 16 return to an earlier point in the story, resuming immediately after the seventh trumpet has sounded. They depict the preparation and pouring out of seven bowls that contain the seven last plagues that complete God's judgment on evil (15:1).

This sequence illustrates the intricate structure of Revelation. Just as it seemed that the seventh seal (8:1) would bring the culminating act of judgment but turned out to contain another series of chastisements, so the seventh trumpet is found to contain seven bowls of God's wrath (chap. 16). After the quasi-liturgical pouring out of the seven bowls, four chapters (Rev 17–20) will narrate a bit more concretely, though still quite elusively, how God will bring judgment upon his adversaries and salvation for his people.

The Song of the Victors in Heaven (15:1–4)

¹Then I saw in heaven another sign, great and awe-inspiring: seven angels with the seven last plagues, for through them God's fury is accomplished.

²Then I saw something like a sea of glass mingled with fire. On the sea of glass were standing those who had won the victory over the beast and its image and the number that signified its name. They were holding God's harps, ³and they sang the song of Moses, the servant of God, and the song of the Lamb:

> "Great and wonderful are your works,
>> Lord God almighty.
> Just and true are your ways,
>> O king of the nations.
> ⁴Who will not fear you, Lord,
>> or glorify your name?
> For you alone are holy.
>> All the nations will come
>> and worship before you,
>> for your righteous acts have been revealed."

OT: Exod 15:1–21; Ps 86:9–10; 111:2; Jer 10:7
Catechism: victors in the heavenly liturgy, 2642

The opening verse serves as an introductory summary of what John will see **15:1** in chapters 15 and 16. This is the third and final **sign** that John sees **in heaven** after the visions of the woman clothed with the sun (12:1) and of the huge red dragon (12:3). This sign alone is called **great and awe-inspiring**, the same Greek words used to describe God's acts of judgment in 15:3–4 (although there translated "great and wonderful"). The content of this sign is summarized as **seven angels with the seven last plagues**, bringing the number of plagues (after the three of 9:18) to a total of ten, the same number that struck Egypt when God delivered Israel through Moses. These are the "last," since **through them God's fury is accomplished** (literally, "completed"; "ended," RSV).

Although it is common to describe the events accompanying the first six seals and trumpets as judgments or expressions of God's wrath, the book of Revelation does not (see sidebar, "Judgment and Wrath in Revelation," p. 135). Instead it reserves the words "judgment," "wrath," and here "fury" to describe God's final response to those who refuse to repent despite the testimony of Christians and the chastisements that accompany the seals and the trumpets that function as divine warnings. At last God's response to evil is going to be revealed.

After recounting visions of events on earth in chapters 12–14, John now **15:2–3a** reports another vision of heaven. He sees **something like a sea of glass**, mentioned in his original vision of heaven in 4:6. In the Old Testament understanding of the cosmos, the translucent floor of heaven forms the firmament or sky of our world, separating the waters above and below it (Gen 1:7). Now, however, the crystal sea is **mingled with fire**, a biblical image of divine judgment, foreshadowing what is about to happen. In this vision of heaven, John sees **those who had won the victory over the beast**; they are standing **on** (many translations say "beside") the sea. After the deliver-

Fig. 14. This Jewish coin from the time of the Bar Kochba revolt (132–136) against Rome shows the kind of harp and trumpets used in temple worship, quite probably influencing John's vision.

ance from Egypt and the defeat of Pharaoh and his army, Moses led all Israel in singing a song of celebration beside the Red Sea (Exod 15:1–21). Here the martyrs and all God's holy people who have remained faithful unto death in the great trial, who have "conquered by the blood of the Lamb / and by the word of their testimony" (12:11), sing God's praises. They are the victors whom the messages to the churches summon readers to join (chaps. 2–3). They are the great multitude of every nation "coming out of the great tribulation" (7:14 ESV), the faithful who have attained to "the first resurrection" (20:5–6). They hold **God's harps** ("harps given them by God," NIV; see 14:2) and sing **the song of Moses, the servant of God**. This vision shows worship in heaven shortly before history's end. Their song celebrates the deliverance of those among the nations who will yet come to worship (15:4) and celebrates God's triumph over his adversaries that is about to unfold through the angels with the seven last plagues. It is called **the song of the Lamb** because it is about the victory achieved through the blood of the Lamb, who ransomed human beings for God (5:9; see also 12:11).

15:3b–4   The **works** of the **Lord God almighty** (the last word translates God's most solemn title, *pantokratōr*, "ruler of all") are amazing, awe-inspiring (15:1). Moreover his **ways**, his habitual paths, are **just and true**, righteous and reliable. He is the true **king of the nations**, a title ascribed to God in Jer 10:7 to contrast him with the idols of the †Gentiles. The appropriate response is to **fear** and **glorify** his **name,** meaning God himself. The fitting reason, according to this hymn, is that **you alone are holy** (a phrase taken up in the Gloria in the Mass). The word translated "holy" is not the usual one, but a word meaning "without fault," drawn from one of the two Old Testament hymns called the Song of Moses.[1]

The hymn celebrates the fact that **all the nations will come / and worship** God. As M. Eugene Boring explains,

1. See Deut 32:4. The hymns are Exod 15:1–18 and Deut 32:1–43.

Biblical and apocalyptic traditions pictured the final triumph of God's kingdom in two contrasting ways. In one picture, the pagan nations are defeated and destroyed in a climactic last battle [see Ps 2; Ezek 38–39; Joel 3:1–2, 12–13; 4:1–2, 12–13 NRSV]. In the other picture, the pagan nations are converted and become worshipers of the one God (Ps 86:9–10; Isa 2:1–4; 19:24–25; . . . Mic 4:1–4).[2]

In Revelation both expectations come to pass. Many from the nations are converted (5:9; 11:13); those who wage war on the Lamb and God's people are destroyed (17:14; 19:11–21; 20:8–9). What brings the nations to worship God is the fact that his **righteous acts** (or "judgments," NRSV, RSV) **have been revealed**. God's righteous act par excellence was the Lamb's atoning death on the cross (Rom 3:21–25); God's other righteous acts of judgment in history also lead people to conversion. Like other texts in Revelation (1:7; 7:9; 11:13), this verse declares the effectiveness of God's interventions in history to draw the nations to himself, which is his long-standing purpose (Gen 12:3).

The Heavenly Temple before the Last Plagues (15:5–8)

---

[5]**After this I had another vision. The temple that is the heavenly tent of testimony opened,** [6]**and the seven angels with the seven plagues came out of the temple. They were dressed in clean white linen, with a gold sash around their chests.** [7]**One of the four living creatures gave the seven angels seven gold bowls filled with the fury of God, who lives forever and ever.** [8]**Then the temple became so filled with the smoke from God's glory and might that no one could enter it until the seven plagues of the seven angels had been accomplished.**

OT: Exod 40:34–35; 1 Kings 8:10–11
NT: Rev 1:13; 19:14

Now John receives **another vision** of a solemn liturgy in God's temple in heaven, identified as **the heavenly tent of testimony**. The tent of testimony is one of the names[3] used in the Old Testament for the tabernacle where the ark of the covenant was kept and where God dwelt among his people (see sidebar, "God's Temple," pp. 186–87). Since the earthly tabernacle was modeled on Moses' vision of the heavenly tabernacle (Exod 25:9; Heb 8:5), the existence of this "heavenly tent" and its basic characteristics are known: it is the most holy

15:5–6

---

2. In Walter J. Harrelson, ed., *The New Interpreter's Study Bible* (Nashville: Abingdon, 2003), 2232.
3. The NABRE renders it "tabernacle of the covenant" (e.g., Exod 38:21).

place, where God resides. Readers will remember that after the sounding of the seventh trumpet, God's temple in heaven was opened, revealing the ark of the covenant, followed by a storm †theophany: lightning, thunder, an earthquake, and so on (Rev 11:15–19). This vision, depicting the same sacred location, resumes the narrative, explaining the events that follow the seventh trumpet blast and the manifestation of the ark in heaven.

The heavenly **temple** opens and **the seven angels with the seven plagues** process out. The angels wear liturgical vestments, clean white linen (linen was worn by priests or angels: Lev 16:4, 23; Ezek 9:2–3; Dan 12:6–7), **with a gold sash** around their chests, like the gold

Fig. 15. "One of the four living creatures gave the seven angels seven gold bowls filled with the fury of God, who lives forever and ever" (15:7).

sash worn by the "one like a son of man" in 1:13, indicating they bear a special authority.

15:7   The **four living creatures** form the inner circle around the throne and seem to lead the heavenly worship (4:8–9; 5:8–10, 14). Just as they initiated the first four seal judgments in chapter 6, so now one of them initiates the bowl judgments by giving **seven gold bowls filled with the fury of God** to the seven angels. The word translated "fury" occurred three times in the previous chapter (translated as "passion" in 14:8 and "fury" in 14:10, 19). This description of divine judgment attributes the human emotion of passionate anger to God, thus helping readers grasp its severity. God's wrath differs from human anger in that it is motivated not by emotional reaction but by perfect justice and the radical incompatibility between God's holiness and evil of every kind. This judgment is definitive because it comes from God, **who lives forever and ever**. The final series of judgments, like the warning chastisements that preceded them, advance as the consequence of an unhurried liturgy in heaven.

15:8   The report that **the temple became so filled with . . . God's glory and might that no one could enter** recalls two previous moments in biblical history when the same thing occurred. When the cloud of God's †glory first descended on the tabernacle in the wilderness, Moses was unable to enter it (Exod 40:35);

when the glory of God filled Solomon's newly built temple, the priests could not enter it (1 Kings 8:11). The mention of **smoke** echoes Old Testament texts that describe the cloud of God's glory as smoke (Isa 6:3–4). The impossibility of entering the temple indicates an overwhelmingly powerful manifestation of God's presence. While on the previous occasions the theophany marked the dedication of the tabernacle and temple, here it points to the completion of God's judgment, **the seven plagues**. The first and last verses of this chapter contain the same word, **accomplished** (Greek *teleō*, to finish or complete), indicating that God's judgment is about to make a complete end of evil.

The Bowls of God's Wrath

Revelation 16:1–21

After the frightening events that accompanied the opening of the seals and the sounding of the trumpets (Rev 6; 8–9), intended as invitations to conversion, John now reports a vision of God's final judgment on evil in the world, depicted symbolically as the pouring out of seven bowls of †wrath.

If the events following the opening of the seals depict tragedies typical of human history—conquest, violence, famine, pestilence—and the events following the sounding of the trumpets represent an escalation in which natural disasters and demonic torments strike the people of earth, to press them toward repentance, the seventh trumpet and the ensuing seven bowls bring final judgment on those who persist in doing evil. The seven bowls, like the fire, smoke, and sulfur that issue from the mouths of the demonic cavalry at the sixth trumpet (9:17–18), are described as "plagues," and several of them bear similarities to the plagues that God brought on Pharaoh and Egypt at the exodus. They manifest God's overwhelming power applied with ever-increasing force against those who resist his will, refusing to repent.

Although some interpreters have tried to link the seven seals, trumpets, and bowls with particular events, none of these historical interpretations maps to the text convincingly. Rather than seeking a detailed correspondence between events and individual seals, trumpets, and bowls, it makes better sense to understand the first two series as symbolizing calamities that have struck and will strike the human race in various times and places from the coming of Christ to his return. The progression from seals, to trumpets, to bowls reflects an intensification of troubles affecting more and more people as history tends toward its climax, just as Jesus' prophecy in his †eschatological discourse on the Mount of †Olives also describes a worsening of conditions before the end (Matt 24:22–30).

While the first five bowls entail natural calamities that affect the whole world, the sixth bowl depicts events leading up to a final assault by God's enemies against his people, and the seventh depicts God's intervention with overwhelming power to judge Babylon. Chapters 17 to 20 zoom in to reveal more about the judgment of Babylon, the defeat of the beast and its armies, and the final defeat of Satan.

The First Four Bowls of Wrath (16:1–9)

¹I heard a loud voice speaking from the temple to the seven angels, "Go and pour out the seven bowls of God's fury upon the earth."

²The first angel went and poured out his bowl on the earth. Festering and ugly sores broke out on those who had the mark of the beast or worshiped its image.

³The second angel poured out his bowl on the sea. The sea turned to blood like that from a corpse; every creature living in the sea died.

⁴The third angel poured out his bowl on the rivers and springs of water. These also turned to blood. ⁵Then I heard the angel in charge of the waters say:

> "You are just, O Holy One,
>   who are and who were,
>   in passing this sentence.
> ⁶For they have shed the blood of the holy ones and the prophets,
>   and you [have] given them blood to drink;
>   it is what they deserve."

⁷Then I heard the altar cry out,

> "Yes, Lord God almighty,
>   your judgments are true and just."

⁸The fourth angel poured out his bowl on the sun. It was given the power to burn people with fire. ⁹People were burned by the scorching heat and blasphemed the name of God who had power over these plagues, but they did not repent or give him glory.

OT: Exod 7:19–21; 9:9–11; Ps 79:9–12; Wis 11:16
NT: Rev 8:8–11; 11:17–18; 17:6; 18:24

16:1–2   The first four bowl judgments form a set, like the events that accompanied the first four seals and the first four trumpets. However, the bowl judgments are all-encompassing, in contrast to the seals and trumpets, which only affected one-fourth and one-third of the earth, respectively. Like the first four trumpet judgments (8:7–12), these four bowl judgments strike each part of a fourfold division of creation: earth, sea, springs and rivers, and heaven. The visions of seven bowls are pictures painted in broad strokes; they are impressionist vignettes rather than renderings in photographic detail. Although I will comment on the possible significance of each bowl individually, it is possible that these †cosmic disasters that completely devastate all four of the aspects of earthly life should be interpreted together as depicting the end of this world, as some other eschatological texts do (e.g., 2 Pet 3:10–11).

A **loud voice . . . from the temple**, perhaps that of the living creature who gave the **seven angels** their bowls (15:7), gives the command to **pour out** the bowls of **God's fury** on the earth. The wrath of God manifests the destructive effects of God's holiness and love on evil, "like the effect of light on darkness."[1] The pouring out of the first bowl results in **festering and ugly sores** like the plague of boils that struck the Egyptians (Exod 9:9–11).[2] This plague is discriminating, afflicting only **those who had the mark of the beast or who worshiped its image**. Experience teaches that spiritual and psychological pains often afflict people who live contrary to God's law, suggesting the possibility that these sores are a consequence of wrongdoing. Some physical maladies also, such as sexually transmitted diseases, follow from immoral conduct, although there are also innocent victims. It is not surprising that those who ally themselves with the antichrist and worship its image would suffer negative effects in their lives.

16:3–7   The pouring out of the second bowl results in the **sea** turning **to blood** and **every creature** in it dying, while the third bowl converts the **rivers and springs of water** into **blood**. These disasters recall the first Egyptian plague, when God turned the Nile and Egypt's drinking water to blood through Moses and Aaron (Exod 7:17–21), and suggest the possibility of an ecological catastrophe of unprecedented proportions.

The declaration of God's justice proclaimed by **the angel . . . of the waters** manifest a fascinating perspective on nature. Rather than understanding the earth's freshwater in rivers and streams as merely natural entities governed by

1. Donal A. McIlraith, *Everyone's Apocalypse* (Suva, Fiji: Pacific Regional Seminary, 1995), 75.
2. The NRSV translation, "a foul and painful sore," reflects the singular form of the Greek word *helkos*.

the laws of physics, Revelation depicts them poetically as animated or supervised by an angel.

The angel addresses God as **just** and **holy, you who are and who were**. He does not include the future element found earlier, "who is to come" (1:4, 8; 4:8), since, beginning with the sounding of the seventh trumpet (11:15–18) and continuing with these seven bowls, God has now come to judge. The angel affirms the justice of God's **sentence** that the inhabitants of the earth must drink blood, since **they have shed the blood of the holy ones and the prophets**: the penalty corresponds to their crime. However, this is not true retribution. According to Gen 9:5–6, the just retribution for taking a life is to have one's life taken away. By making the wicked drink blood rather than have their blood be shed, God executes poetic rather than final justice.

In God's heavenly temple everything is alive: **the altar** itself cries out, confirming that God's judgments are **true and just**. This word pair occurs three times in heaven's praises of God's judgments (here and 19:2) and his "ways" (15:3).

The bowl of the **fourth angel** continues the assault on the order of nature, now on **the sun**, causing it to burn earth's inhabitants **with fire** and **scorching heat**. Although the metaphor of fire can refer to various kinds of divine judgment (e.g., Amos 1–2; Matt 18:9), and the meaning of all the first four bowl judgments remains obscure, science tells us that it is literally possible for the sun's **power to burn people**. The earth's atmosphere shields us from the powerful ultraviolet and infrared rays of the sun. If that atmosphere were to be drastically damaged, either by human interference or by a natural disaster, the consequences could be deadly.

16:8–9

However, the invitation to conversion goes unheeded, at least by the vast majority of the human race (not necessarily every individual; see comments on 9:20–21). Instead, they **blasphemed**, that is, spoke abusively against, **the name of God**.[3] They failed to **repent or give him glory**, precisely the response that all human beings are summoned to make but that idolaters refuse (Ps 66:2–4; Rom 1:21–25; Rev 14:7).

Revelation does not say what happens to faithful Christians when plagues strike the sea, springs of water, and the sun. Only in the case of the first bowl, the sores, does John say that the judgment strikes only those affiliated with the beast. It often happens that God's people suffer sin's temporal consequences that fall on the nation where they live (Jer 45:5; see reflection on 6:1–8). But God is faithful. To die in the Lord is ultimately no tragedy (14:13); the lives of those who die as faithful Christians are safe, as Revelation attests again and again.[4]

---

3. Other English translations render *blasphēmeō* as "cursed" instead of "blasphemed" in 16:9, 11, 21.
4. See Rev 6:9–11; 7:13–17; 14:13; 15:2–4; also Wis 3:1–9; Luke 21:18.

The Fifth and Sixth Bowls (16:10–16)

[10]The fifth angel poured out his bowl on the throne of the beast. Its kingdom was plunged into darkness, and people bit their tongues in pain [11]and blasphemed the God of heaven because of their pains and sores. But they did not repent of their works.

[12]The sixth angel emptied his bowl on the great river Euphrates. Its water was dried up to prepare the way for the kings of the East. [13]I saw three unclean spirits like frogs come from the mouth of the dragon, from the mouth of the beast, and from the mouth of the false prophet. [14]These were demonic spirits who performed signs. They went out to the kings of the whole world to assemble them for the battle on the great day of God the almighty. [15]("Behold, I am coming like a thief." Blessed is the one who watches and keeps his clothes ready, so that he may not go naked and people see him exposed.) [16]They then assembled the kings in the place that is named Armageddon in Hebrew.

OT: Judg 5:19–20; Ezek 38; Wis 17
NT: Matt 24:43–44; 1 Thess 5:2

16:10–11

A plague of supernatural darkness strikes **the throne of the beast**, which Revelation's first readers probably identified as the city of Rome. Like the first four bowls, it replicates a plague God brought to bear on Egypt before the exodus (Exod 10:21–22). Like Wis 17, it depicts the terror that those who had oppressed God's people suffer in the plague of darkness.[5] The anguish is palpable: **people bit their tongues in pain** ("gnawed their tongues in agony," NRSV). The **pains and sores** that resulted from the first bowl are mentioned along with the darkness. Perhaps all three refer to spiritual rather than physical torments. Nevertheless, suffering does not lead those belonging to the beast

Fig. 16. "The fifth angel poured out his bowl on the throne of the beast" (16:10).

5. Wilfred J. Harrington, *Revelation*, Sacra Pagina (Collegeville, MN: Liturgical Press, 1993), 165.

to **repent of their works**—their evil and idolatrous conduct—but rather, like their master the beast (13:5–6), they **blasphemed** ("cursed," NJB, NRSV, RSV) **the God of heaven**. Their hearts are hardened like Pharaoh of old.

The sixth bowl judgment, like the fifth and sixth trumpet judgments (chap. **16:12** 9), does not consist of divine intervention but rather consists of the activity of the evil powers, which God allows and uses to achieve his ultimate purpose. While the earlier fifth and sixth trumpets depict demonic torment experienced by individuals who worship the image of the beast and accept its mark (Rev 9), the action here of **the sixth angel** allows the forces of evil to mount a final attack, an assault that will lead to their final defeat (19:19–21; 20:7–10). The drying up of the **great river Euphrates** opens the way for the **kings of the East**. The Euphrates was the ancient boundary separating East from West (Ezra 4:9–10; Neh 2:9) and marking the eastern edge of the Roman Empire. Israel's worst destruction had come at the hands of kingdoms from the east, Assyria (721 BC) and Babylon (586 BC). In the first century, the lone threat to Roman security and military might came from the †Parthians, who resided across the Euphrates. However, the next few verses reveal that these ancient enemies of God's people and the military threat to Rome are only symbols of something worse. Place names in Revelation are almost always primarily important for what they symbolize.

In the sixth bowl judgment, John sees three **unclean spirits**, a term used **16:13–14** frequently of demons in the Gospels. The comparison to **frogs** indicates that they are in some sense a plague sent by God, like the plague of frogs imposed on Egypt (Exod 7:26–8:11).[6] These frogs emerge from the mouths of the satanic trinity, **the dragon**, **the beast**, and the second beast (13:11–17), hereafter called **the false prophet**. The role of these **demonic spirits** is propagandistic: they are to persuade **the kings of the whole world to assemble** for war. Like Pharaoh's magicians who opposed Moses and Aaron, these demons **performed signs**. When the second beast was introduced in 13:11–17, deceptive signs were attributed to it, just as Jesus foretold of false prophets (Matt 24:24) and Paul foretold of the "lawless one" who is to come (2 Thess 2:8–9). Satan, the beast, and the prophet gather the rulers of the whole †world to **the battle on the great day of God the almighty**, in other words, to the great eschatological conflict, the last battle, the day of judgment, when evil will be defeated at the return of Christ.

This begins the fulfillment of Ezekiel's prophecy that before the final restoration of Israel and the establishment of a new temple (Ezek 39:25–29; 40–48) the

---

6. According to the †Torah, frogs are ritually unclean animals (Lev 11:10–11). Perhaps because of this text they, like serpents and scorpions (Luke 10:19), are associated with evil spirits in some medieval folklore.

Lord would incite the pagan nations to assemble for battle against his people (Ezek 38) so they could be completely defeated, allowing his people to live in peace.

16:15   The opening of the sixth seal and the blowing of the sixth trumpet (9:13–19) were followed by visions that delayed the seventh and final judgment (11:15–19). Here, after the sixth bowl, there is no such delay, but rather a brief message from the risen Lord to his people, emphasizing the imminence and suddenness of his coming to save and to judge. Christ uses familiar imagery for the unknowable moment of his arrival: **Behold, I am coming like a thief** (see Matt 24:43; 1 Thess 5:2). The third of seven †beatitudes follows,[7] intended to guide the readers of Revelation to an attitude of readiness: **Blessed is the one who watches** (literally, "stays awake") **and keeps his clothes ready**. The wording is ambiguous as to whether the person should stay clothed or keep his clothes at hand. The meaning is the same: be ready for the return of the Lord so you are not put to shame by being **naked** and **exposed**, lacking the garment of upright conduct. It is essentially the same message about watchfulness found in some of Jesus' parables (Matt 24:42; 25:13; Mark 13:34–37) and Paul's exhortations (Rom 13:11–14; 1 Thess 5:2–8): stay on guard against temptation, since you do not know when you will need to give an account.

16:16   Verse 16 resumes the explanation of the coming battle, to which the demons are assembling **the kings** by specifying its staging ground: **the place that is named Armageddon,** which in **Hebrew** means "mountain of Megiddo." Megiddo was an ancient city located on a small mound in the Jezreel Valley overlooking an important trade route in north-central Israel.[8] It was the site of a number of important battles. Despite all the ink spilled on the subject, this is the only instance of the name Armageddon in the Bible. The other Hebrew names in Revelation bear figurative rather than literal meanings, usually showing the likeness of present realities to what happened in Israel's history (thus Balak, Balaam, Jezebel, Abaddon, Jerusalem, Babylon). In this case, the allusion to Megiddo may refer to the Song of Deborah that celebrates God's victory through Deborah and Barak over a coalition of Canaanite kings near Megiddo. This was a battle in which, at God's command, the stars fought from the heavens for Israel (Judg 5:19–20), perhaps a †type of the "armies of heaven" in 19:14.[9]

---

7. See sidebar, "The Seven Beatitudes of the Apocalypse," p. 249, for a list of the others. Many translations place this beatitude in quotation marks as words of the risen Lord. Biblical Greek does not use quotation marks, so it is a matter of interpretation.

8. †Dispensationalists have interpreted this as identifying the location of a future battle against the State of Israel by a coalition of enemies (see "Reflection and Application" on 19:11–21 and footnote 14 on p. 316).

9. For a list of other possible meanings of Armageddon, see Osborne, *Revelation*, 594–96.

One of the defining literary features of Revelation is †recapitulation, retelling the same story from different angles. Here the story is about escalating satanic-inspired opposition to Christians and about God's future salvation. The sixth bowl judgment about assembling the kings for battle (16:12–16) is similar in some respects to the demonic invasion that followed the sixth trumpet (9:13–21). Both events depict a period immediately before a seventh decisive judgment. Both speak of enemies from east of the Euphrates and of demonic activity (9:14–19; 16:12–14). Both depict threefold evils issuing from the mouths of the superhuman enemies: fire, smoke, and sulfur from the demonic cavalry (9:17); frog-like demonic spirits from the dragon, beast, and false prophet (16:13–14). The sixth trumpet is met by unrepentant wrongdoing (9:20–21), and the sixth bowl follows persistent unrepentance (16:11). While the plague of the sixth trumpet kills a third of the wicked (9:18), the plague of the sixth bowl assembles the kings of the whole world to the final battle, in which all the beast's followers will be destroyed (19:19–21; 20:7–10).

In the run-up to evil's definitive defeat, to all appearances evil is triumphing and will prevail. In chapter 11, the beast wages war against the two witnesses, conquers, and kills them, and the inhabitants of the earth gloat over them (11:7–10). In chapter 13, the whole world follows the beast, who blasphemes God and is allowed to wage war and conquer the holy ones, subjecting them to captivity and the sword (13:7–10). The second beast deceives the inhabitants of the earth with signs (13:14) and compels everyone to worship the beast's image and accept its stamped image, on pain of exclusion from economic life in society (13:16–17). Here (16:14) the demonic spirits perform signs and mobilize the whole world to attack.

It seems to me that the visions of 11:7–10, chapter 13, and 16:13–14 do not describe separate events but refer in different ways to the final phase of the war of the dragon against the woman and her children (12:17), the war of Satan against the Church, which has been taking place since Jesus ascended into heaven (12:5). Although the conflict ebbs and flows in intensity throughout history, Revelation indicates—in agreement with Jesus' eschatological discourse and with Jewish apocalyptic literature—that it will become especially fierce immediately before the end of the age.

The Final Bowl of Wrath (16:17–21)

[17]The seventh angel poured out his bowl into the air. A loud voice came out of the temple from the throne, saying, "It is done." [18]Then there were

lightning flashes, rumblings, and peals of thunder, and a great earthquake. It was such a violent earthquake that there has never been one like it since the human race began on earth. [19]The great city was split into three parts, and the gentile cities fell. But God remembered great Babylon, giving it the cup filled with the wine of his fury and wrath. [20]Every island fled, and mountains disappeared. [21]Large hailstones like huge weights came down from the sky on people, and they blasphemed God for the plague of hail because this plague was so severe.

OT: Exod 9:22–25; 19:16–18; Isa 66:6

The seventh bowl symbolizes God's final judgment on the part of the human race that persists in rebellion against him. The next three chapters, 17–20, unpack this judgment and give us a more complete picture, although not one that answers all our questions.

16:17   The fact that the seventh angel pours out his bowl **into the air**, above everything else, indicates that the final act of judgment will strike everything.[10] Greek science understood the world to be composed of four elements, and the bowls have now struck all four: earth (16:2), water (16:3–6), fire (16:8), and air. The voice **from the throne** that says, **It is done**, must be the voice of an angel, speaking on God's behalf.[11] Here it speaks before the vision of the harlot Babylon, announcing God's judgment on evil in a prophetic past tense, to indicate the arrival of divine judgment and the certainty of its completion.

16:18   This is the fourth, final, and most severe storm †theophany in Revelation, echoing God's appearance on Sinai.[12] The seventh plague in Egypt was a great hailstorm "so fierce that nothing like it had been seen in Egypt since it became a nation" (Exod 9:24). Here it is **a violent earthquake** that is unprecedented in severity **since the human race began on earth**. To John's readers in Asia, who knew of earthquakes that destroyed cities, this was a frightening prospect.

16:19–21   However, the object of God's judgment is not his people but their persecutor, **Babylon**, which will be the topic of the next two chapters. It is called a **great city** since it is the capital of an empire. To John's first readers, Babylon was the pagan nation that conquered Judah, destroyed the temple, and became the place

10. Another possibility is that the air represents the place of demons and the pouring out of the bowl means their downfall (McIlraith, *Apocalypse*, 79).

11. The voice from the throne will speak again to lead the praises in 19:5 and to explain the meaning of the new Jerusalem's descent from heaven in 21:3–4. The voice says something very similar to "It is done" before the vision of the Bride, the new Jerusalem (21:6).

12. See 4:5; 8:5; 11:19; 16:18. The last three are accompanied by earthquakes, the last two also by hailstorms.

of Israel's exile (see comments on 14:8). Through the prophets, God promised to destroy Babylon for its crimes against his people. Jews and early Christians referred to Rome as Babylon (1 Pet 5:13). Nevertheless, in Revelation, Babylon assumes a symbolic significance as the city of those who reject God, "the dragon's covenant people" who bear the mark of the beast.[13]

Now, John tells us, **God remembered great Babylon**. In the Bible when God remembers someone, it means that he turns his attention to that person or people, either to save (Exod 2:24; Luke 1:72) or, as in this case, to judge. God gives Babylon **the cup . . . of his fury and wrath**, a familiar image from Isa 51:17–23 and Jer 25:15–26. In the writings of both of those prophets, the cup of God's wrath refers to judgment, given first to Israel in punishment for its sins, and then to Israel's enemies, above all, to Babylon.

John uses †cosmic and apocalyptic imagery to describe the judgment God will bring. Babylon will be **split into three parts**, and **the gentile cities** will fall. Other translations of this last phrase are more helpful: "the cities of the nations" (NRSV) or "the cities of the world" (NJB). The point is not their ethnicity; destruction comes to the †nations of the world allied with Babylon against God's people. The flight of **every island** and the disappearance of the **mountains** demonstrate God's surpassing power and greatness in comparison with created things, a point made with similar imagery in the Old Testament (Ps 97:5; Isa 2:12–18; 40:4; 45:2). Immense **hailstones like huge weights**[14] came down **from the sky**; the word for "sky" is elsewhere translated "heaven." Nevertheless, even this overwhelming show of divine power is not enough to convince the inhabitants of Babylon and its allies: **they blasphemed God for the plague of hail**. For the third time, people respond to the bowl judgments by blaspheming God, indicating a definitive choice (16:9, 11, 21). Like Pharaoh of old (Exod 8:15), they harden their hearts and do not repent. Instead, like the beast (13:1, 5–6), they revile God.

John recounts his vision in the prophetic past tense: it is what he *saw*, but it refers to the future. The figurative rather than literal nature of this description of Babylon's demise is confirmed in 17:16–18 and chapter 18, where we learn that the fall of Babylon comes about through an act of war rather than an actual earthquake. Once again we have climbed what seemed like the final ascent only to discover that we have not arrived at our journey's end. Judgment is still raining down, and God's enemies are still shouting their defiance.

---

13. McIlraith, *Apocalypse*, 77.

14. Literally, "weighing a talent"; a talent was about one hundred pounds (roughly forty kilograms). By comparison, the largest hailstones recorded in the United States weighed slightly less than two pounds, a little less than one kilogram.

Reflection and Application (16:1–21)

It was possible at the end of the first century, and also today, to identify events in history that resemble the human-caused catastrophes of the first four seal judgments and the natural catastrophes of the first four trumpets, both of which are partial, that is, localized, in their effects. Yet it does not seem that any worldwide disruption of the natural order like those described in bowls two to five has occurred as of this writing. Either such disasters lie in the future near history's end or John's vision depicts the end of the world figuratively and presents each element of creation being struck one after another for dramatic effect.

What is the message of the seven bowls? No matter how powerful the worldly forces arrayed against God and his people appear, their sudden and irreversible destruction is certain. God is in charge. He is just and brings judgment. He will vindicate his people. He will pay back evildoers for what they have done to others. God is patient and deliberate in his administration of justice, but in the end, calamity descends on those who refuse to repent.

This certainty summons us, in our words and in our deeds, to be faithful witnesses to all around us, fulfilling our mission while God grants more time, "not wishing that any should perish, but that all should come to repentance" (2 Pet 3:9). It summons us to pray for our family, friends, and neighbors who do not know God, as well as for those whose conduct at the present moment indicates they are headed in the wrong direction. Our prayer is that they may know the truth, turn from evil, turn to the Lord, and so be saved (1 Tim 2:4).

The Harlot and the Beast

Revelation 17:1–18

This chapter begins the conclusion of the book of Revelation. John divides the last part of the book into three well-defined sections before a final epilogue. In the first section (17:1–19:10) a glorious angel shows John a vision of a city depicted as a woman, the great whore Babylon, that goes down to utter destruction. The second section (19:11–21:8), consisting of four visions, tells how God routs his enemies, judges the dead, renews creation, and establishes the new Jerusalem. In the third section (21:9–22:9), which is parallel to the first, another glorious angel shows John another city depicted as a woman, the new Jerusalem, the Bride of the Lamb that continues for ever and ever.

To this point Babylon has been mentioned only twice, once by an angel foretelling its destruction (14:8) and again at the end of the chapter 16, where its demise is depicted in the pouring out of the seventh and final bowl of God's wrath (16:19). In the visions of chapters 17 and 18, Babylon's true character will be unveiled. Until now the relationship between Babylon and the two beasts of chapter 13 has not been clear. This vision explains that relationship with fantastic imagery. Then in a surprising turn of events, it reveals how God will turn evil against itself to destroy the "great city" (17:18) that corrupts the earth and sheds the blood of his people.

Babylon, the Great Whore (17:1–6a)

¹Then one of the seven angels who were holding the seven bowls came and said to me, "Come here. I will show you the judgment on the great

271

harlot who lives near the many waters. ²The kings of the earth have had intercourse with her, and the inhabitants of the earth became drunk on the wine of her harlotry." ³Then he carried me away in spirit to a deserted place where I saw a woman seated on a scarlet beast that was covered with blasphemous names, with seven heads and ten horns. ⁴The woman was wearing purple and scarlet and adorned with gold, precious stones, and pearls. She held in her hand a gold cup that was filled with the abominable and sordid deeds of her harlotry. ⁵On her forehead was written a name, which is a mystery, "Babylon the great, the mother of harlots and of the abominations of the earth." ⁶I saw that the woman was drunk on the blood of the holy ones and on the blood of the witnesses to Jesus.

OT: Isa 21:1–2; Jer 51:13; Dan 4:27
NT: Matt 24:15; 2 Thess 2:7

17:1–2   The fact that **one of the seven angels** who held the bowls of wrath shows John the **judgment** coming on **the great harlot** links the judgment on Babylon announced in the previous chapter (16:17–21) to the judgment that will be reported in this one (17:16) and lamented in chapter 18. The identity of the prostitute as Babylon is suggested by the fact that she **lives near the many waters**. Ancient Babylon was located on the Euphrates River, known for its impressive network of irrigation canals. Jeremiah used this exact phrase in a lengthy †oracle foretelling Babylon's destruction (Jer 50–51; see especially 51:13).

Why is Babylon called a harlot? The image of a prostitute is drawn from Israel's prophets, who used the term to describe pagan capitals, such as Tyre and Nineveh, that became exceedingly wealthy and powerful through trade and seduced other nations into corrupt economic, political, or religious relationships (Isa 23:15–17; Ezek 27:2–4; Nah 3:4).[1] Thus **the kings of the earth**, political leaders, **have had intercourse**, or "have committed fornication" (NRSV), with Babylon. In its first-century context, this criticism may have referred to client kings or Roman governors who purchased their offices, enriched themselves, oppressed their people, or otherwise acted unjustly because of their relationship to Rome. Likewise **the inhabitants of the earth**—that is, those not in a relationship with God—become intoxicated with **the wine of her harlotry**. They are thrilled with the luxurious lifestyle she pays for, wealth obtained through her corrupt conduct (see Rev 18:11–13).

---

1. The prophets also use prostitute imagery for Israel or Judah because of idolatry, immorality, and illicit alliances with other nations (Hosea 2:1–5; 4:10–18; 5:3–4; Jer 3:1–13; Ezek 16:15–61; 23). Israel's idolatry is spoken of in terms of adultery, since she sins against her spousal covenant relationship with God. In contrast, Babylon is never charged with violating a marriage covenant with God.

John is then **carried . . . away in spirit**. Other translations validly say "in   **17:3**
the Spirit" (NIV, RSV); John is in a prophetic state under the influence of the
Holy Spirit (as in 1:10 and 4:2). He is taken **to a deserted place** ("wilderness"
or "desert"), echoing language from
Isa 21:1, the beginning of an oracle
of judgment against Babylon. When
John says he **saw a woman**, readers are meant to recall the heavenly
woman of chapter 12, who symbolizes the people of God. This woman
in the wilderness, however, is the
exact opposite, representing "the inhabitants of the earth," the people
who do not belong to God. She is
seated on a scarlet beast. Her posture suggests both a superiority over
and a dependence upon her mount.

Fig. 17. "I saw a woman seated on a scarlet beast. . . . The
woman was wearing purple and scarlet. . . . She held in her
hand a gold cup that was filled with the abominable and sordid deeds of her harlotry" (17:3–4).

The beast's **blasphemous names**
and its **seven heads and ten horns**
and its scarlet color make plain that
this is the same grotesque creature of 13:1–10,[2] authorized by "the huge red
dragon" (12:3) to receive idolatrous worship from the whole world and to wage
war against God's people.

The spotlight now shifts to the woman, who is described in ways that reveal   **17:4–6a**
her character, conduct, and identity. First, she is luxuriously attired in **purple
and scarlet** material that required expensive dyes and implied pretensions of
royalty and wealth; she is **adorned** with jewelry of the finest materials, **gold,
precious stones, and pearls**. The overall impression is that of a high-class
courtesan, enriched by the gifts of her wealthy clients. In her hand she holds **a
gold cup**. At first glance she appears rich and beautiful. However, the cup she
holds is filled with **the abominable and sordid deeds of her harlotry**. The NJB
is more vivid: "the disgusting filth of her prostitution"; and the RSV more literal:
"abominations and the impurities of her fornication." The word "abomination"
refers to something detestable to God, often immorality or idolatry (see Lev
18:22–29; Deut 7:25–26; 18:9–12). The words "abomination" and "impurities"
(Greek *akatharta*; literally, "unclean things") belong to the Jewish language of
worship and refer to what is unclean and unfit for God's presence.

---

2. For explanation of the symbolism and OT antecedents of the beast, see comments on Rev 13:1–10.

Although some say that Roman prostitutes wore headbands indicating their names, it is more likely that the name on **her forehead**, like that of the people of God (7:3; 9:4; 14:1; 22:4) and the followers of the beast (13:16; 14:9; 17:5; 20:4), is primarily a literary device to indicate her identity, like a label on a figure in a political cartoon. Calling the name **a mystery** is a way of emphasizing that it is symbolic rather than literal (like the use of "mystery" in 1:20). **Babylon the great** is a phrase first used in the Bible by Nebuchadnezzar, king of Babylon (Dan 4:27), immediately before he is brought low by his pride. It appears five times in Revelation (14:8; 16:19; 17:5; 18:2, 21). To give Babylon the title **the mother of harlots** and of earth's **abominations** is to say that she is their origin and archetype, their quintessential expression. In his vision John sees that the woman was **drunk** on **blood**, a metaphor for violence and bloodthirstiness (Isa 34:5–7; 49:26; Jer 46:10).[3] Not only is Babylon murderous, but she has killed those who are **the holy ones** and **the witnesses to Jesus**. A picture of greater wickedness could not be painted. The worst crimes of idolatry, murder, immorality, and sacrilege belong to Babylon.

So exactly what does Babylon represent? Although Babylon is closely allied to the seven-headed beast, this vision (especially 17:16) indicates that they are distinct. Though in their first-century manifestation both are undoubtedly to be associated with Rome (17:18), they embody different dimensions of that reality (see sidebars, "Attributes of the Whore Babylon," p. 293; and "Attributes of the Beast," p. 284). The beast represents political power opposed to Christ and his Church, while the whore represents the empire as a socioeconomic and cultural whole that is corrupt and displeasing to God. Just as the woman of chapter 12 represents the people of God and the Bride of the Lamb, the whore represents human society that is closed to and in rebellion against God, the culture of "the world" (John 15:19; 1 John 2:15–17).

Reflection and Application (17:1–6a)

Misogynist? The repulsive image of the whore of Babylon, the allusion to Jezebel in 2:20–23, and the mention of one hundred and forty-four thousand virgins who "were not defiled with women" (14:4) have led some to regard Revelation as being antiwoman. But this criticism fails to take into account the villains of masculine gender in Revelation: Balaam, the false prophet who promotes idolatry and immorality (2:14), the devil, the kings of the earth who are the beast's allies, and the beast, who is depicted as masculine (13:18). It

---

3. See also Josephus, *Jewish War* 5.8.2, par. 344; and Suetonius, *Tiberius* 59.

also fails to consider the very positive image of the woman in chapter 12 and of the Bride, clothed in "fine linen, bright and pure" (19:8 RSV), the wife of the Lamb, in chapters 19–22.[4]

A wake-up call. What is the point of the depiction of Babylon as a prostitute? According to Craig Koester, the image of the harlot was a wake-up call for first-century Christians, meant to jolt them into a radical reevaluation of the world around them and their participation in it.[5] Identifying the idolatrous, immoral, and materialistic surrounding culture as a whore helped Christians realize that it was a good thing when their faithfulness to Christ placed them outside the social mainstream. In every age Christians need to evaluate the values and customs of their culture and nation in the light of the gospel. In that bright light they will often discern the tawdry outlines of the harlot Babylon and recognize their need to distance themselves from it (18:4; 2 Cor 6:17).

The Beast and the Whore Explained (17:6b–14)

When I saw her I was greatly amazed. [7]The angel said to me, "Why are you amazed? I will explain to you the mystery of the woman and of the beast that carries her, the beast with the seven heads and the ten horns. [8]The beast that you saw existed once but now exists no longer. It will come up from the abyss and is headed for destruction. The inhabitants of the earth whose names have not been written in the book of life from the foundation of the world shall be amazed when they see the beast, because it existed once but exists no longer, and yet it will come again. [9]Here is a clue for one who has wisdom. The seven heads represent seven hills upon which the woman sits. They also represent seven kings: [10]five have already fallen, one still lives, and the last has not yet come, and when he comes he must remain only a short while. [11]The beast that existed once but exists no longer is an eighth king, but really belongs to the seven and is headed for destruction. [12]The ten horns that you saw represent ten kings who have not yet been crowned; they will receive royal authority along with the beast for one hour. [13]They are of one mind and will give their power and authority to the beast. [14]They will fight with the Lamb, but the Lamb will conquer them, for he is Lord of lords and king of kings, and those with him are called, chosen, and faithful."

OT: Dan 7, especially 7:20–27

4. For more, see Osborne, *Revelation*, 630.
5. Craig R. Koester, *Revelation and the End of All Things* (Grand Rapids: Eerdmans, 2001), 155.

Interpreting Revelation for the Past, Present, and Ultimate Future

BIBLICAL BACKGROUND

While [†]preterist interpreters confine their explanation of this text to people and events in the first century, the vision of chapter 17 leads those who regard the book of Revelation as Christian prophecy to look to a future eschatological fulfillment, without denying an original application of the prophecy to the time in which it was written.

A precedent for understanding Revelation as a book that speaks about the circumstances of its own time yet also about the ultimate future is found in traditional Christian interpretation of Daniel's visions (Dan 2; 7–12). Many contemporary scholars think that the ten horns of the "fourth beast" (Dan 7:7–8, 19–20) originally referred to the kings of the Seleucid dynasty; the "little horn" that spoke arrogantly and waged war against the holy ones (Dan 7:8, 21; 8:9) symbolized the Seleucid king Antiochus IV Epiphanes (175–163 BC), who tried to force pagan customs and religion on the Jews.[a] However, the end of that crisis did not usher in the kingdom of God as the prophecy seemed to predict (e.g., Dan 7:27), so Jewish tradition looked for a future fulfillment. New Testament writings interpret Dan 7:13–14 as partly fulfilled in the coming of Jesus as "the Son of Man," and in his resurrection and ascension, while awaiting a future fulfillment at Christ's return when the kingdom "shall be given to the people of the holy ones of the Most High, / Whose kingship shall be an everlasting kingship" (Dan 7:27).[b]

Similarly, Revelation's depiction of the beast and of Babylon clearly reflect the challenge that Rome presented to first-century Christians. However, the beast, false prophet, and Babylon cannot simply be reduced to first-century realities, for at least three reasons. First, the language used to depict these figures is [†]typological, referring back to adversaries through all of biblical history, such as Pharaoh, Egypt, Babylon, Leviathan, and the Serpent. It therefore probably prefigures more than a single future fulfillment. Second, some of the specifics in John's visions resist simple identification with first-century history.[c] Third, as in Daniel so in Revelation, the

---

This paragraph of Rev 17 and the one that follows it are among the most difficult to interpret in the book of Revelation. Like some passages from the prophets and other apocalyptic literature, an angel explains the meaning of the vision that John is beholding—though in a rather cryptic way! After explaining the identity of the figures in the vision, the angel proceeds to tell future events involving those figures. Like similar texts in Daniel (e.g., Dan 7–8), the vision probably refers to specific persons and events at the time it was written. In the

destruction of these adversaries is depicted as occurring at the end, when God arrives to judge and the kingdom comes in its fullness.

The authors of Daniel and Revelation understood their works as revelatory both about the situation of the people of God in their own time and about the end of history, whether or not they distinguished these two periods. Grant Osborne reflects this dual perspective by describing apocalyptic literature as "the present addressed through parallels with the future."[d] Apocalyptic could also be described the other way: the future addressed through parallels with the present.

This way of interpreting Daniel and Revelation accords with the recognition that there are types, recurring patterns, running through the Bible and salvation history. The plots of the evil powers against God and his people, the diverse responses of human beings, and God's interventions to judge and to save recur time and again, even though they will have a final manifestation. The visions of Daniel and Revelation speak of the circumstances of the times in which they were written and of history's final hour, even as they offer prophetic guidance and encouragement that apply to times of trial through history (see "Interpretation of Revelation and History" in the introduction, pp. 29–32).

a. See, e.g., the footnotes of the JB, NABRE, or NJB.
b. See Matt 24:15–31; 26:64; Mark 13:14–27; 14:62; Acts 1:9–11; 7:56; Eph 1:20–22; 2 Thess 2:3–10.
c. For example, the persecutions by the two beasts depicted in Rev 13 exceed what we know of persecutions of Christians in the first and second century.
d. Osborne, *Revelation*, 22.

case of Revelation it is more difficult than in Daniel to identify the rulers and events that the angel refers to in his explanation. The obscurity of the references has only encouraged scholars to try to identify them, but no consensus has been reached.

John is **greatly amazed** at the vision of the great harlot seated on the beast,   17:6b–8
and the angel promises to explain **the mystery**, the meaning of these symbols. While the previous paragraph focused on the woman, the present paragraph focuses on **the beast that carries her**, with its **seven heads and ten horns**, first introduced in 13:1–8 (see comments there).

This description of the beast †recapitulates much of what was said before but adds more details—a literary technique common in Revelation, called augmentation. The angel describes the beast cryptically: it **existed once but now exists no longer** ("was, and is not," RSV). At the time John is writing, he understands the beast to be a past and future threat, rather than a present one, thus echoing the earlier vision of the beast seeming to be "mortally wounded" and then "healed" (13:3, 12, 14). **It will come up from the abyss**.

This repeats in the future tense and with different vocabulary what was described in chapter 13 about the beast's place of origin (13:1, sea = abyss, see sidebar, "The Abyss," p. 167). In Rev 13 "the whole world" is fascinated by, follows after, and worships it (13:3; see vv. 8, 12). The present text refers to the same group of people and retells the same story: **The inhabitants of the earth . . . shall be amazed** ("astonished," NIV, NJB) at the beast, because **it will come again.** As John's first vision of the beast hinted three times that the beast imitates Christ's death and resurrection (13:3, 12, 14), this vision hints that the beast counterfeits Christ's resurrection (17:8, 11). What is added is the welcome news that the fate of the beast will be the opposite of that of the Lamb: it **is headed for destruction.**[6] The fate of the beast was foreshadowed in the fifth bowl judgment, the plague that brought darkness on his throne (16:10).

John clarifies whom he means by "the inhabitants of the earth" who so admire the beast: they are those **whose names have not been written in the book of life from the foundation of the world** (also mentioned in 13:8). According to John's vision, the human race is divided into two groups: those who are in awe of the beast and "worship it" (13:8), and those whose names are "written . . . in the book of life," that is, those who were chosen by God from before the foundation of the world (Eph 1:4) and who belong "to the Lamb who was slain."[7]

17:9–11   As in 13:18, where the beast's number is revealed, a puzzling word to the wise is given about the identity of the beast: **The seven heads represent seven hills upon which the woman sits.** This description would have immediately resonated with John's first-century readers since Rome was known as the city on seven hills. The goddess Roma, reclining on seven hills, appeared on coins of that period.[8] But lest the audience think prematurely that they understand, a second meaning is added: the seven heads of the beast **also represent seven kings: five have already fallen, one still lives, and the last has not yet come,** but when it does, it will last only **a short while.** Whatever the angel is referring to, he indicates that the time of the revelation to John is somehow in the middle of the story. Five kings have come and gone, one lives, but the climactic moment lies in the future. For **the beast** that was present in the past, is not present

---

6. The pattern of the beast's rising to a position of dominance over God's people and then being destroyed echoes what is said about the fourth beast and the little horn in Dan 7:7–8, 11, 19–26.

7. Rev 17:8 clarifies 13:8 since it indicates that what took place at "the foundation of the world" was the writing of names in the book of life, not the slaying of the Lamb. For consideration of what this text implies about predestination, see comments on 13:8.

8. For example, a sesterce minted under Vespasian bears this image.

now, and is going to be destroyed **is an eighth king** who **really belongs to the seven**.[9] Writing like this seems intended to confound the reader, to make the reader think hard, to conceal at the same time as it reveals. Again, as in 13:18, the supernatural beast (13:1–4; 19:20) is identified with a human ruler.

Scholars have expended a tremendous amount of effort to understand what John was referring to. Many have identified the seven kings with a series of Roman emperors. Yet there is no consensus regarding which emperor to begin with, whether all should be counted or only those whose reign lasted for some time or only those who made divine claims, and whether to count as "fallen" only those who died violently.[10] Other scholars suggest that the "kings" should be understood as "kingdoms" (the terms are sometimes used interchangeably in Daniel, as in 2:44; 7:17, 23) and that Rome is the sixth kingdom or empire in this series.[11] Many suggest that the eighth king who "really belongs to the seven" (Rev 17:11) refers to the legend of Nero's return. At this distance in time it is impossible to know for certain which contemporary kings or kingdoms John understood his vision to refer to, if any.

Another solution to these difficult verses is to take the numbers of kings here as symbolic rather than literal, like other numbers in Revelation. The text of Revelation itself leads away from a simple decoding of the seven heads of the beast by saying they refer both to seven hills and to seven kings. According to a symbolic interpretation of the numbers, John and his contemporaries live in the penultimate period, the time of the sixth oppressive king or kingdom. A seventh king or kingdom will come and last "only a short while," the number seven signifying completion. After "only a short while" the beast, who existed before, will come back, and the final battle will take place.

Now the identity of the **ten horns** is revealed; they **represent ten kings** who   **17:12–13**
have not yet come to power, who will **receive royal authority along with the beast** for a brief period of time, **one hour**. Again, this alludes to Daniel, where the fourth beast, explained to be a fourth kingdom, has ten horns representing ten kings (Dan 7:7–8, 20, 24). Another "little horn" arises, more powerful

9. The use of the number eight for the beast may refer to the fact that it counterfeits the resurrection, since eight was the number associated with Jesus' resurrection, which occurred on the first day of the week (Matt 28:1), the eighth day.

10. The emperors that might be counted include Julius Caesar (44 BC), Augustus (27 BC–AD 14), Tiberius (AD 14–37), Caligula (37–41), Claudius (41–54), Nero (54–68), Galba (June 68–January 69), Otho (January–April 69), Vitellius (April–December 69), Vespasian (69–79), Titus (79–81), Domitian (81–96), Nerva (96–98), and Trajan (98–117). For more detailed information about the possible kings or kingdoms, see G. K. Beale, *The Book of Revelation*, NIGTC (Grand Rapids: Eerdmans, 1999), 870–78; Osborne, *Revelation*, 617–21; Judith Kovacs and Christopher Rowland, *Revelation* (Oxford: Blackwell, 2004), 187–88.

11. Possible earlier kingdoms include Egypt, Assyria, Babylon, Persia, Media, and Greece.

than the others, who defeats three kings and then makes war against the holy ones and is victorious (7:21). This ruler "shall speak against the Most High / and wear down the holy ones of the Most High" for three and a half years, until God comes to judge and give the kingdom to his people forever (see 7:20–27, esp. v. 25).

17:14   In Revelation, these ten kings are the beast's allies, who unite their power and authority under the beast to **fight with the Lamb**. First-century Christians might have interpreted these as Rome's client kings in various subject lands, who did the emperor's bidding, or as the governors of Rome's ten provinces. However, if the number ten is symbolic, it means fullness or completeness (see "Figurative Language and Symbolism" in the introduction, p. 28), like the number seven, with which it is always paired in descriptions of the dragon or beast. Understood qualitatively rather than quantitatively, "ten kings" could imply either a full contingent of kings allied with the beast or perhaps that all the rulers of nations are on its side.

But how can the beast and earthly kings fight with the Lamb who is in heaven (5:6)? Readers will recall that the beast will "wage war against the holy ones and conquer them" (13:5–7). Whatever is done to Christ's disciples is done to Christ (Matt 25:40, 45; Acts 9:4–5). The war of the beast and its allies against the Lamb is waged against the members of Christ's body.

Fig. 18. Victory of the Lamb over the two beasts, the serpent, and the kings of the earth (see 17:13–14; 19:20–21; 20:10).

However, there is a difference between the account here of the beast's warfare and the earlier accounts of the beast's warfare against the witnesses (11:7) and against the holy ones (13:5–7). In both earlier accounts, as in Dan 7:25, the beast's persecution lasts three and a half years, a substantial but limited period. This prophecy speaks of the ten horns receiving "authority as kings" (RSV) for only "one hour," during which they fight (Rev 17:12). And this time the outcome is dramatically different, since the one they have been attacking now comes to do battle: **the**

Lamb will conquer them. The reason given for his victory is the Lamb's supreme power and authority: **for he is Lord of lords and king of kings**. The Roman emperors claimed the title "king of kings," as did the kings of ancient Babylon and Persia (Ezra 7:12; Ezek 26:7; Dan 2:37). In the Old Testament, only God is called "Lord of lords" (Deut 10:17; Ps 136:3). Here, and again in the description of the final battle in 19:16 (as in 1 Tim 6:15), both titles belong to Jesus.

The Lamb is not alone: **those with him are called, chosen, and faithful**—words the New Testament uses to refer to Christians.[12] These are those who "follow the Lamb wherever he goes" (14:4). These are the "holy ones of the Most High," who receive the kingdom with him (Dan 7:18, 22, 27).

Reflection and Application (17:6b–14)

Identifying figures from Revelation in our world. Although we cannot rule out that the number ten will have literal significance in the fulfillment of the prophecies of Revelation, previous mistaken identifications should make us cautious. In *The Late Great Planet Earth*, Hal Lindsey said that the ten nations of the European Common Market were the allies of the beast. Now that the Common Market has evolved into the European Economic Union and grown to twenty-eight member nations, †dispensationalist Christians have speculated that the United Nations Security Council might be expanded to ten nations that will rule the world.[13]

In attempting to discern parallels in our day to the figures in Revelation, we do better to focus on similarities in attitude and action, rather than in details that may be symbolic or may pertain to its first-century manifestation. For instance, to identify what in our day resembles the beast, we could look for a government that uses its authority to persecute Christians. We might also consider whether that government or world leader claims for itself prerogatives that belong to God. All the details do not have to correspond perfectly. A family resemblance should be sufficient to put Christians on guard (see sidebars, "Attributes of the Beast," p. 284; "Attributes of the Second Beast, the False Prophet," p. 234; and "Attributes of the Whore Babylon," p. 293).

Throughout history many rulers and governments have arisen whose conduct has resembled that of the beast. Nero was such a figure in the first century; Hitler and Stalin were two of several such figures in the twentieth century.

---

12. See, e.g., Rom 8:30; 1 Cor 1:2, 9; 1 Pet 2:9; 5:13.

13. Tim LaHaye and Jerry B. Jenkins, *Are We Living in the End Times?* (Wheaton, IL: Tyndale, 1999), 169–70; see Koester, *Revelation*, 160.

Some Christians who lived under the rule of these oppressors thought they were dealing with the antichrist. If these Christians remained faithful to Jesus, refused compromise with evil, and preserved faith and hope, they interpreted and applied Revelation correctly. These political figures manifested the spirit of the beast in their time, even though it is now clear they were not its definitive and final manifestation.

Similarly, many false religious leaders, movements, and institutions have arisen that share in the spirit of the false prophet either by false teaching, by promoting idolatrous devotion to a nation or government, or by persecuting Christians. The Fathers of the Church sometimes identified heretics and heresies of their day with the antichrist or the false prophet.[14] At various points in history, Christians have discerned the spirit of the antichrist or the false prophet in Islam. In the Qur'an Muhammad denied central truths of the Christian faith, including the Trinity (Surah 4:171), the incarnation (Surah 5:72; 5:75), Jesus' divine sonship (Surah 4:171; 5:116; 6:101), and his death on the cross (Surah 4:157). The Qur'an commands extra taxation for Christians (Surah 9:29), and Muslim countries normally do not allow Christians to fulfill Christ's command to proclaim the gospel; Muslims who accept the gospel are sometimes killed as apostates (Surah 4:89). In recent times Muslim extremists have destroyed churches and murdered Christians.

Thankfully, that is not the whole story. Many Muslims demonstrate tolerance, kindness, and respect toward Christians.[15] Some live lives of outstanding moral virtue and faithfully practice prayer, fasting, and almsgiving in a way that Christians would do well to imitate. For those raised in Islam who have not heard the gospel, Islam may be the best way they know to serve God. The Catholic Church desires dialogue and good relations with Muslims.[16] Because Christians and Muslims hold some beliefs and moral values in common, we can sometimes work together against secularism.

Persecution of Christians characterizes the beast, the false prophet (13:6–7, 15–17), and Babylon, so that is a telltale sign of the dragon's work. For more on discerning present-day temptations in the figures of Revelation, see "Reflection and Application" on 13:1–18 and the reflections on Babylon throughout the next chapter.

14. For instance, Caesarius of Arles (d. 543) referred to Arians and semi-Pelagians in these terms (ACCS 12:xxv, 196–201).

15. Some texts in the Qur'an are more positive toward Christians, teaching respect for Christians and Jews as "people of the book" (e.g., Surah 2:62; 3:113–15; 10:94; 21:7; 28:52).

16. See *Lumen Gentium* 16; *Nostra Aetate* (Declaration on the Relation of the Church to Non-Christian Religions) 3.

Destruction of the Whore by the Beast (17:15–18)

---

[15]Then he said to me, "The waters that you saw where the harlot lives represent large numbers of peoples, nations, and tongues. [16]The ten horns that you saw and the beast will hate the harlot; they will leave her desolate and naked; they will eat her flesh and consume her with fire. [17]For God has put it into their minds to carry out his purpose and to make them come to an agreement to give their kingdom to the beast until the words of God are accomplished. [18]The woman whom you saw represents the great city that has sovereignty over the kings of the earth."

OT: Ezek 23:22–35

This conclusion of the chapter prophesies a startling fact about the demise of the harlot Babylon, a fact not even hinted at earlier in the book. Babylon is destroyed by the very beast (and its allies) on which she is seated. Although in some way the beast and the ten kings supported or sustained her to this point, and like her, were persecutors of God's people, the true attitude of the beast and its allies toward Babylon is revealed to be hatred, a hatred finally expressed in a sudden, horrific, and devastating attack. God inspires evil to destroy evil.

The many **waters** that **represent** large numbers of peoples indicate the harlot's   **17:15–16**
influence over many †nations through commerce, using words that Jeremiah used when speaking of the end of Babylon and her wealth (Jer 51:13). The reasons that lead the beast and ten kings to **hate the harlot** are not stated. Perhaps they despise her decadent luxury as soft and self-indulgent. Perhaps they envy her immense wealth, power, and prominence. Or perhaps the beast, as the dragon's servant (13:1–3), simply manifests the diabolical hostility toward the human race that characterizes the devil. Whatever the motives of their hatred, the beast and ten kings **eat** the **flesh** of Babylon and **leave her desolate and naked**, that is, plunder her wealth. So much for her proud appearance. They destroy Babylon by **fire**, the ultimate stroke against hated enemy cities in the ancient world. The lament of chapter 18 catalogs Babylon's losses.

The next verse explains what is really going on: **For God has put it into**   **17:17**
their minds to carry out his purpose by uniting their royal power under the beast until **the words of God** through the prophets about Babylon's destiny **are accomplished**. Despite the seeming power of evil in the world, God is in control. In God's wisdom, it is evil that will bring judgment on evil—an event that will signal the beginning of the end. This prediction of the angel recalls Jesus' words: "If a kingdom is divided against itself, that kingdom cannot stand.

Attributes of the Beast

BIBLICAL
BACKGROUND

Putting together the texts that speak of the beast, here is what
Revelation says about the beast's identity, attitudes, and actions:

- The beast is a demonic spirit embodied in an empire and in
  a human ruler. It receives its power and authority from the
  dragon, Satan, whom it resembles (13:1–2).
- It mimics Christ by appearing to have come back from the
  dead or recovered from a mortal wound (13:3, 12, 14; 17:8,
  11). This feat and the beast's extraordinary power evoke the
  admiration and worship of those whose names are not written in the
  book of life (13:3–4, 8; 17:8).
- The beast blasphemes God and his people, in part by making divine
  claims for itself (13:1, 5–6; 17:3).
- It is allowed to persecute and seemingly triumph over "the holy ones,"
  imprisoning and killing many of them (11:7; 13:7, 10).
- It is served by a second beast, the false prophet, who persuades people
  to worship it (13:11–17).
- The beast collaborates with the harlot Babylon until shortly before the
  end, when it turns on her (17:16).
- All that the beast does against God's people and against Babylon is
  subject to God's control over history (13:7; 17:17). The beast and its allies fight against the Lamb, but Christ ultimately defeats and destroys
  them (16:14; 17:14; 19:19–20).

See also the sidebars "The Antichrist in the New Testament," pp. 226–27;
"The Catechism on the Antichrist," p. 229; "Attributes of the Second Beast, the
False Prophet," p. 234; and "Attributes of the Whore Babylon," p. 293.

... And if Satan has risen up against himself and is divided, he cannot stand;
that is the end of him" (Mark 3:24, 26). God is wise and powerful enough to
accomplish his will even by means of Satan's malice (1 Cor 2:7–8; Col 2:14–15).

17:18   A final explanation from the angel confirms the identity of the harlot. She
is **the great city** that exercises **sovereignty over the kings of the earth**. To a
first-century reader, this would bring to mind no other city than Rome, an
identification confirmed by the details in the lament over Babylon in the next
chapter.[17] Nevertheless, as we shall see, the meaning of Babylon cannot be
confined to a single city or empire.

17. Although this description of Babylon's destruction uses imagery similar to Ezekiel's about the
judgment coming on Jerusalem in 586 BC (see Ezek 23:22–35, especially vv. 25, 29), it is not likely that

Reflection and Application (17:15–18)

Revelation and the history of Rome. If Revelation's first-century readers thought the beast was a future emperor and Babylon was Rome, they possibly imagined that John's visions would be fulfilled by a future claimant to the imperial throne, a *Nero redivivus*, who would gather Rome's client kings and attack and destroy Rome in a civil war. What actually did happen would have surprised them.

The Lamb did indeed conquer the Roman beast that had previously persecuted and been victorious over the holy ones, but not soon or suddenly by military action. Gradually, despite periodic persecutions, the testimony of the early Church prevailed, and many pagans responded. From an extremely small group at the end of the first century, the Church's membership grew over two centuries to nearly 10 percent of the empire's population.[18] Then the unimaginable happened: the emperor Constantine issued the Edict of Milan, making Christianity legal in the year 313, and was baptized on his deathbed in 337. In the century that followed, a majority of the population became Christian, although the sincerity of some of this large influx of converts was questionable and the instruction they received was often inadequate. Meanwhile Rome had declined and continued to decline politically and economically through internal decadence, political infighting, and foreign enemies. By the time Rome was sacked by Alaric and his hordes of Goths in AD 410, Christians had come to regard Rome as their own, and some were shaken by its defeat. Rome continued to decline for the next few centuries. Augustine felt it necessary to explain Rome's demise in *The City of God*, countering the claims of pagans, who blamed Rome's decline on its abandonment of pagan worship. After answering the pagans, Augustine taught that the City of God cannot be identified with any earthly kingdom, nor even with the Church on earth. The City of Man, comprised of those who live for love of self and what is earthly, passes away. The City of God, comprised of those who love God, deny themselves, and seek the kingdom of heaven, is eternal, regardless of the trials it may suffer on its earthly pilgrimage.[19] In fact, the City of God proved stronger than Rome's barbarian

---

Revelation refers here to the Roman destruction of Jerusalem in AD 70. Babylon is described as the city that exercises "sovereignty over the kings of the earth." When Rome destroyed Jerusalem in AD 70, Jerusalem had been subject to Rome for more than 130 years and exercised no such sovereignty.

18. Charles Freeman, *A New History of Early Christianity* (New Haven: Yale University Press, 2009), 215.

19. "The two cities were created by two kinds of love: the earthly city was created by self-love reaching the point of contempt for God, the Heavenly City by the love of God carried as far as contempt of self" (Augustine, *The City of God*, 14.28, trans. Henry Bettenson [London: Penguin, 1972], 593).

conquerors. One after another they succumbed to the faith of the Christians they had conquered. After the fall of the city of Rome, the eastern part of the Roman Empire—the Byzantine Christian empire—continued in some form for another thousand years.

In John's vision, Babylon refers both to Rome and to the City of Man of which Augustine wrote, especially when it opposes God by leading people astray or persecuting the Church. The next chapter, a revelation of Babylon's final destruction, sheds more light on its nature and can help us to recognize its presence in our world and in our lives.

Judgment of Babylon

Revelation 18:1–24

The destruction of Babylon has already been briefly foretold three times in Revelation (14:8; 16:19; 17:16). Now comes a vision of Babylon's demise that fills an entire chapter.

The description of Babylon's fall prophesied in this chapter echoes motifs from Old Testament prophecies of judgment against pagan nations: ancient Babylon (Isa 13–14; 47; Jer 50–51), Edom (Isa 34), and Tyre (Ezek 26–28). Insofar as these ancient prophecies were fulfilled in the past, those judgments serve as †types of what will happen to this Babylon. Insofar as the ancient prophecies had not yet been fulfilled in John's day, for example, the prediction of Babylon's complete and perpetual destruction (e.g., Jer 50–51), the biblical prophecies foretell the doom that still awaits all that ancient Babylon symbolically represents.[1]

The depiction of Babylon's judgment in Rev 18 has the air of a solemn drama enacted before the eyes of John and his readers. First, a luminous angel appears center stage to announce in a prophetic past tense what will become of Babylon. Next a voice from heaven warns God's people to separate themselves from her sins in order to avoid her punishments. The voice then cries out for judgment, enumerating her crimes, and foretells that her doom will "come in one day" and that "she will be consumed by fire" (18:8). Then,

---

1. The fall of Babylon to Cyrus, king of Medo-Persia, in 539 BC resulted in the death of Babylon's king and the end of the city's prominence as a world power. Nevertheless, Babylon was not totally destroyed as Isaiah and Jeremiah had prophesied, and the city remained as a major center in the Persian Empire, declining gradually after its conquest by Alexander the Great in 331 BC. Revelation reveals Babylon as a spiritual reality that continues to exist and prophesies its destruction at history's end.

like a chorus in a Greek tragedy, the kings, merchants, and seafarers who had profited from Babylon's power and wealth stand and eulogize her as if at a funeral, mourning their loss, while heaven's inhabitants are invited to rejoice. Finally, a mighty angel appears, declares with a dramatic symbolic gesture the certainty and absolute finality of Babylon's destruction, and reiterates the crimes that led to her demise.

A Shining Angel Proclaims Babylon's Fall (18:1–3)

¹After this I saw another angel coming down from heaven, having great authority, and the earth became illumined by his splendor. ²He cried out in a mighty voice:

"Fallen, fallen is Babylon the great.
    She has become a haunt for demons.
She is a cage for every unclean spirit,
    a cage for every unclean bird,
    [a cage for every unclean] and disgusting [beast].
³For all the nations have drunk
    the wine of her licentious passion.
The kings of the earth had intercourse with her,
    and the merchants of the earth grew rich from her drive for
    luxury."

OT: Isa 13:19–22; 34:9–15

18:1–2   Still accompanied by one of the seven angels of the bowl judgments (17:1; 19:9–10), John sees **another angel** descend **from heaven** to solemnly announce God's judgment on Babylon. This messenger, whose **splendor** lights up **the earth**, has **great authority** and speaks with a **mighty voice,** underscoring the importance and divine authorization of his decree.

The angel's message repeats and expands on the words announced in the first prophecy of Babylon's destruction in 14:8: The repetition, **Fallen, fallen**— another prophetic past tense—conveys a solemn finality. The devastation is so complete that the formerly rich and exquisitely adorned city has become a total ruin, inhabited only by wild animals—**every unclean bird** and **disgusting [beast]**,[2] imagery drawn from Isaiah's prophecies of judgment on Babylon and Edom (Isa 13:21; 34:11, 14). Later Jewish tradition understood the unclean

2. Brackets in the NABRE indicate words that are missing in some manuscripts.

birds and beasts mentioned in Isaiah to symbolize demons.[3] Revelation agrees, describing desolate Babylon as a **haunt** (literally, "dwelling place") **for demons**. In the short run, surrendering oneself to evil as Babylon did may lead to wealth, power, and pleasure, but in the long run, all that the evil produces is desolation and death. Perhaps even the demons would prefer not to live there; it is their **cage**, or their "prison," as some other versions correctly render it.

18:3

The reason for Babylon's judgment is now briefly stated: the harlot has corrupted the whole world by seducing three groups into her immorality. First, **all the nations have drunk / the wine of her licentious passion** (literally, "the wine of the passion of her fornication"). Second, **the kings of the earth**, political leaders, **had intercourse with her**, that is, had some kind of illicit relationship with Babylon. Finally, **the merchants of the earth**, the businesspeople, have become **rich from her drive for luxury**.[4]

What do these graphic images of sexual immorality mean in relation to Babylon? Literal immorality was certainly a prominent characteristic of pagan culture and religion. Immorality as a metaphor for idolatry is often mentioned both in the Old Testament (e.g., Hosea 2:4–15) and in Revelation (e.g., 2:20–22). However, the resemblance of Rev 18 (e.g., vv. 3–9) to prophecies about the merchant kingdom of Tyre (cf. Isa 23:16–17; Ezek 26–28) suggests that the primary focus is on an inordinate desire for material goods that leads to doing anything for money. In Isa 23:16–17, Tyre is a harlot who "will return to her trade, and will prostitute herself with all the kingdoms of the world on the face of the earth" (NRSV). The †Septuagint translates Isa 23:17b, "She will become a market to all the kingdoms of the world." Commerce is a necessary part of human culture and not intrinsically sinful, even if Scripture counsels caution (e.g., Sir 27:1–2; Matt 6:24; 21:12–13; 1 Tim 6:9–10). But Babylon and her clients exercise no restraint.

A Voice from Heaven Warns God's People (18:4–8)

---

[4]Then I heard another voice from heaven say:

> "Depart from her, my people,
>   so as not to take part in her sins
>   and receive a share in her plagues,

---

3. *Targum Isaiah* 13:21; *Leviticus Rabbah* 5:1–2; 22:8; *Genesis Rabbah* 65:15 (Beale and McDonough, 1140).

4. The Greek word can mean either luxury or sensuality; in this context a passion for luxury best explains how the merchants became rich.

⁵for her sins are piled up to the sky,
     and God remembers her crimes.
⁶Pay her back as she has paid others.
   Pay her back double for her deeds.
   Into her cup pour double what she poured.
⁷To the measure of her boasting and wantonness
     repay her in torment and grief;
   for she said to herself,
     'I sit enthroned as queen;
     I am no widow,
     and I will never know grief.'
⁸Therefore, her plagues will come in one day,
     pestilence, grief, and famine;
   she will be consumed by fire.
   For mighty is the Lord God who judges her."

OT: Isa 47:7–11; 52:11; Jer 50–51, especially 50:8, 29, 34; 51:6, 9, 45
NT: 2 Cor 6:14–17

18:4–5   The first verse of this section is very important since it contains the only specific instruction that God gives to his people in the context of Babylon's impending destruction. It is either God the Father or Christ who speaks to his people through **another voice from heaven**, as in the previous occasions when this phrase was used (10:4, 8; 14:13). The message—**Depart from her, my people**—echoes several Old Testament prophecies to Israelites in exile in Babylon, such as Isa 52:11: "Depart, depart, go out from there, / touch nothing unclean! / Out from there!"⁵ Although there are differences among these ⁺oracles, they summon the Jews to physically leave Babylon before God's judgment falls on it and to return to Jerusalem, where God is bringing salvation to his people. Here in Revelation the Lord is not issuing a command to physically leave the Greco-Roman cities of Asia Minor. Instead, he is summoning John's audience to keep a spiritual distance from the corruption of the society in which they live, "Babylon," **so as not to take part in her sins / and receive a share in her plagues**.

Other New Testament texts convey the same message. Citing the same text from Isaiah, Paul exhorts the Corinthians not to enter into partnerships with unbelievers, but rather, "come forth from them / and be separate . . . and touch nothing unclean; / then I will receive you" (2 Cor 6:14–17, quoting Isa 52:11).⁶

---

5. Similar texts include Isa 48:20; Jer 50:8; 51:45, 50.
6. See Rom 12:2; Eph 5:3–5; James 4:4; 1 John 2:15–16.

This is a warning for John's readers to avoid the sins mentioned in this prophecy that characterize the society in which they live: idolatry, sorcery, murder, sexual immorality, theft, lying, the love of wealth, excessive consumption, and the slave trade.[7]

The reason Babylon is to be judged is explained in an image that comes from Jer 51:9: **her sins are piled up to the sky**, that is, to heaven. When it says in Scripture that God **remembers**, it means he focuses his attention so as to take the appropriate action, in this case to render judgment on Babylon's **crimes** (literally, her "acts of injustice").

The voice from heaven now announces the sentence to be executed on Babylon, and the principle on which it is based: **Pay her back as she has paid others.** This is the ancient principle of justice declared in Jeremiah's prophecy about Babylon's judgment (Jer 50:29) and in many other places in the Old and New Testaments.[8] Although Jesus teaches his disciples to imitate God's patience and magnanimity and not to exact an eye for an eye and a tooth for a tooth (Matt 5:38–45), he also warns that in the future God will pay back evildoers who refuse to repent according to what they have done (Matt 13:39–42; John 5:29).

18:6–7

Moreover, punitive damages will be exacted from Babylon: **Pay her back double for her deeds.** Some scholars interpret these words as a metaphor for complete recompense, rather than a double portion, although some Old Testament texts may speak of double recompense in a literal sense.[9] In the end the matter is moot since Babylon is guilty of capital crimes—idolatry, immorality, and murder (17:4–6)—and to double capital punishment makes no difference in the outcome. Besides that, Babylon is guilty of leading all the nations into idolatry, immorality, and greed for excessive consumption (18:3). Jesus teaches that a greater punishment awaits those who corrupt others: "It would be better for him if a millstone were put around his neck and he be thrown into the sea than for him to cause one of these little ones to sin" (Luke 17:2). The harlot Babylon holds a gold cup filled with "the abominable and sordid deeds of her harlotry" (17:4), which "all the nations have drunk" (18:3). Now judgment is decreed: **Into her cup pour double what she has poured.** She will drink the cup of divine †wrath.

The retribution coming to Babylon is precise and appropriate. **To the measure of her boasting and wantonness** ("as much as she exalted herself and lived in sensual luxury," NET) / **repay her in torment and grief**. The word the NABRE

---

7. See Rev 9:20–21; 18:3, 11–14; 21:8; 22:15.
8. See, e.g., Ps 28:4; 137:8; Prov 24:12; Isa 3:11; Sir 16:12; Rom 2:6–12; 2 Tim 4:14.
9. See Exod 22:4, 7, 9; Isa 40:2; Jer 16:18; 17:18.

translates "wantonness," related to "luxury" in 18:3, connotes either living in wealth and comfort or living sensually. The word translated "torment" literally means "torture" and in the Bible is found only in Revelation, always in reference to the punishment of the wicked.[10] Babylon's boast—I am a **queen; / ... no widow, / and I will never know grief**—along with the penalty announced in the next verse, comes directly from an ancient prophecy about God's judgment of Babylon (Isa 47:7–11).

18:8   Because of her arrogance, Babylon's humiliation and destruction will be sudden and swift: her divine requital **will come in one day**. The **plagues** with which God punishes her are familiar from prior divine judgments in Revelation and in biblical history: **pestilence**, **grief** (or "mourning," as in 21:4), **famine**.

Finally, she will be **consumed** (literally, "burned down") with **fire**. Fire was the means by which conquered enemy cities were destroyed in the ancient world (see Amos 1–2) and is a frequent image for the destruction of the wicked in the Gospels and throughout the New Testament.[11] Babylon's complete destruction demonstrates that the **Lord God who judges her** has overwhelming power.

Reflection and Application (18:4–8)

What is wrong with luxury? A luxury is a costly, nonessential expenditure that brings pleasure or comfort. Luxury is sometimes appropriate, for example, when intended to honor a worthy person or an important occasion. Gospel examples of luxury that Jesus approves

Fig. 19. Flames descend on Babylon: "Therefore, her plagues will come in one day, pestilence, grief, and famine; she will be consumed by fire. For mighty is the Lord God who judges her" (18:8).

Wikimedia Commons

include the surplus of wine at the wedding feast of Cana (John 2:6–10), the fatted calf slaughtered to celebrate the prodigal's return (Luke 15:23), and the perfumed oil worth a year's wages with which a woman anointed Jesus before his death (Matt 26:8–13).

10. See Rev 9:5; 14:11; 18:7, 10, 15.
11. See, e.g., Matt 3:10; 18:8; 25:41; 2 Thess 1:8; Heb 10:27; 2 Pet 3:7.

Attributes of the Whore Babylon

BIBLICAL BACKGROUND

Pulling together the texts that speak of Babylon, here is a summary of the harlot's identity, attitudes, and actions:

- Babylon was the capital city of the pagan empire that destroyed Jerusalem and the temple in 586 BC and became the place of Judah's exile. Figuratively, it alludes both to the Roman Empire, an immoral and idolatrous society that scorns God's law and persecutes his people, and to other societies that do the same.
- Babylon especially symbolizes an arrogant center of international economic and cultural power that consumes goods from all over the world (18:11–13), whose leading merchants are among the most influential people on earth (18:23).
- The harlot Babylon corrupts the world, inducing rulers and people of all the nations to drink of "the wine of her licentious passion" (14:8)—that is, to share in her idolatry, lust, greed, and excessive consumption of material goods. As the "mother of harlots" and of earth's abominations (17:5), Babylon is the source par excellence of idolatry, of making a god of created things.
- Babylon is allied with the beast (17:3), political power that is opposed to God and his people (13:1–8).
- She is a persecutor of Christians, "drunk on the blood" of God's people, especially prophets and witnesses to Jesus (17:6; 18:24; 19:2).

For more on Babylon, see sidebar, "The Interpretation of Babylon in Christian Tradition," pp. 296–97.

The problem with Babylon, however, is an inordinate desire for fine things that is idolatrous (18:3; Col 3:5). Judging from its imports (18:12–13), Babylon's way of life resembles that of the rich man in Jesus' parable, "who dressed in purple garments and fine linen and dined sumptuously each day" (Luke 16:19). Not only is such a lifestyle intemperate and self-indulgent, but it fails to use its wealth to meet the needs of the poor at its door (Luke 16:20–21).

What does it mean to depart from Babylon? Like Revelation's first-century readers, Christians today need to hear the warning of the voice from heaven, "Depart from her, my people, / so as not to take part in her sins / and receive a share in her plagues." Twenty centuries after Revelation was written, the temptations to conform to a surrounding culture that is idolatrous, materialistic, and immoral may well be stronger than in the first century. Not a few people have been seduced by what the world offers and have neglected and lost their faith; Christian youth seem especially vulnerable to its allurements.

What does it mean to separate oneself from the corruption of the society in which we live? It does not require a monastic or Amish retreat from the world, nor does it mean absenting ourselves from responsibility to do what is in our power to improve the world, to make it reflect the justice of the coming kingdom of God. Rather, departing from Babylon means avoiding the secular worldview, the materialistic values, drugs, drunkenness, sexual immorality, and proud and self-centered attitudes of the society in which we live. This entails being discerning about our involvement with the carriers of the culture of contemporary Babylon: the mass media, the internet, popular entertainment and music, public education, and people who influence us in the wrong direction. Perhaps the best way for Christians to resist the pull of Babylon is to immerse themselves in the society that is the opposite to Babylon, the community of the Church, and to embrace the worldview, values, morality, and attitudes of Jesus Christ.

It is particularly important for Christian parents to teach their children to discern the difference between the world and the body of Christ, between Babylon and the people of God. At certain ages children are prone to admire undeserving celebrities or to look mainly to their peers for approval. These are times when children require extra parental attention if their young hearts are not to be seduced by Babylon. Spiritually vital Catholic schools, homeschooling, youth groups, and summer camp programs are some vital ways of supplying the godly teaching, example, and peer groups that can help Christian children remain faithful.

Kings, Merchants, and Seafarers Lament the Fall of Babylon (18:9–19)

---

[9]The kings of the earth who had intercourse with her in their wantonness will weep and mourn over her when they see the smoke of her pyre. [10]They will keep their distance for fear of the torment inflicted on her, and they will say:

> "Alas, alas, great city,
>   Babylon, mighty city.
>   In one hour your judgment has come."

[11]The merchants of the earth will weep and mourn for her, because there will be no more markets for their cargo: [12]their cargo of gold, silver, precious stones, and pearls; fine linen, purple silk, and scarlet cloth; fragrant

wood of every kind, all articles of ivory and all articles of the most expensive wood, bronze, iron, and marble; [13]cinnamon, spice, incense, myrrh, and frankincense; wine, olive oil, fine flour, and wheat; cattle and sheep, horses and chariots, and slaves, that is, human beings.

> [14]"The fruit you craved
>   has left you.
> All your luxury and splendor are gone,
>   never again will one find them."

[15]The merchants who deal in these goods, who grew rich from her, will keep their distance for fear of the torment inflicted on her. Weeping and mourning, [16]they cry out:

> "Alas, alas, great city,
>   wearing fine linen, purple and scarlet,
>   adorned [in] gold, precious stones, and pearls.
>   [17]In one hour this great wealth has been ruined."

Every captain of a ship, every traveler at sea, sailors, and seafaring merchants stood at a distance [18]and cried out when they saw the smoke of her pyre, "What city could compare with the great city?" [19]They threw dust on their heads and cried out, weeping and mourning:

> "Alas, alas, great city,
>   in which all who had ships at sea
>   grew rich from her wealth.
> In one hour she has been ruined."

OT: Ezek 26:16–18; 27:7–36; 28:13, 16, 18

The voice from heaven then describes the response to Babylon's destruction by three groups who had profited from her wealth—kings, merchants, and those in the shipping industry. They are amazed at Babylon's fall and mourn over the once-great city. Their three laments share a common pattern. All "keep their distance" for fear of sharing in Babylon's torment; all begin with "Alas, alas, great city"; all "weep and mourn" for their own loss of profit; and all express shock and awe at the suddenness of Babylon's destruction "in one hour."

These verses echo Ezekiel's prophecies announcing God's judgment against Tyre (Ezek 27), a pagan city-state to the north of Israel that had become extremely rich, powerful, and proud through its sea trade.[12] These stanzas reveal

---

12. Ezekiel prophesied the complete and permanent end of Tyre at the hands of Nebuchadnezzar, king of Babylon (Ezek 26:14, 19–21). Although Nebuchadnezzar subdued Tyre by means of a long and

The Interpretation of Babylon in Christian Tradition

LIVING TRADITION

Some Church Fathers, including Tertullian (ca. 160–ca. 220) and Irenaeus (130–202), and early interpreters of Revelation including Victorinus (d. 303) and Oecumenius (late sixth century), identified the whore of Babylon with the city of Rome and its empire because of its world domination, its seven hills, its idolatry, and its persecution of Christians. However, as Rome lost political power, this view faded. Andrew of Caesarea in Cappadocia (563–637) writes, "It is more likely, therefore, that the harlot is the earthly kingdom in general which will be condemned at the end." Tyconius (ca. 380) regarded Babylon and the beast as a kind of mystical body of Satan, consisting of those who do not belong to the body of Christ.ᵃ Gradually Babylon became a symbol of the life of sin and "the world." Bernard of Cluny's hymn, "Jerusalem the Golden" (1146), reflects this perspective:

> And now we watch and struggle, and now we live in hope,
> And Zion in her anguish with Babylon must cope;
> But He whom now we trust in shall then be seen and known,
> And they that know and see Him shall have Him for their own.

In the late Middle Ages some Catholic interpreters, such as the Franciscan theologian Peter Olivi (1248–98), associated "the carnal church" with the harlot Babylon, and money-loving clergy with its "merchants" (18:11–15). In the early fourteenth century in *The Divine Comedy*, Dante's pilgrim speaks out against avaricious popes: "You shepherds it was the Evangelist had in mind / when the vision came to him of her who sits / upon the waters playing whore

---

the grandeur of Babylon and more about what is fatally wrong with it. They describe her wealth and the total destruction that will overtake her. No living person from Babylon is mentioned in their lament or in the rest of Revelation. Babylon will be completely destroyed.

18:9–10   To say that the **kings of the earth . . . had intercourse** (literally, "committed fornication," NRSV) with Babylon **in their wantonness**[13] does not, of course, refer literally to sexually immoral acts but rather refers to another kind of illicit partnership. The context suggests that it refers to corrupt political and com-

---

exhausting siege (29:17–18, written in 571 BC), Tyre was not completely destroyed. It may be that the echoes of Ezek 26–28 in Rev 18 are intended to show the ultimate fulfillment of Ezekiel's prophecies against Tyre in God's †eschatological judgment of a spiritual Babylon that perpetuates its sins.

13. From the same root word translated "luxury" in 18:3, which refers to sensual living.

with the kings. / . . . You have built yourselves a God of gold and silver!"[b] Late medieval Reformist Catholics compared the papacy to Babylon insofar as it continued to manifest Rome's vices and to exercise its political power.

The Protestant Reformation repeated this critique of the papacy and of the Catholic Church. The marginal notes of the Geneva Bible (1560) identify the beast with ancient Rome and the harlot that sits on the beast as the papacy, the empire's successor. Leading Reformers, including Luther and Calvin, identified the pope as the antichrist and the Catholic Church as the whore of Babylon, a view that influenced much subsequent Protestant interpretation. Thankfully, over the last half century many Protestants have set aside that interpretative tradition.

Revelation itself, however, associates Babylon not with corrupt religion but with a socioeconomic system ("your merchants were the great ones of the world," 18:23) that seduces and corrupts through greed and persecutes Christians (18:24). In Revelation, false religion is primarily associated with the second beast, the false prophet, who promotes the worship of the beast and its image (13:11–17).

a. For more on the Church Fathers' interpretation of Babylon, see ACCS 12:265–71, 285–96; for a summary of patristic, medieval, Reformation, and subsequent interpretation, see Judith Kovacs and Christopher Rowland, *Revelation* (Oxford: Blackwell, 2004), 178–88, 191–93.

b. Dante Alighieri, *Inferno* 19.106–8, 112, in *The Divine Comedy*, vol. 1, trans. Mark Musa, rev. ed. (New York: Penguin, 1984), 243–44.

mercial collaboration leading to the enrichment of an elite that holds power through the oppression of others. Throughout history and across cultures, a common ulterior motive guiding the conduct of people holding political power has been lust for wealth. The fact that the kings **weep and mourn** as they watch **the smoke of her pyre** (literally, "burning") does not mean that they loved Babylon. The relationship between the prostitute Babylon and her consorts is one of mutual use—fornication, not marriage. The **fear** of the political leaders is for themselves, lest they share her **torment**. They are amazed at what has happened to Babylon: in only **one hour** her **judgment has come**.

In John's day "Babylon" was embodied in Rome, the wealthiest and largest city the world had known (or would know until eighteenth-century London), boasting a population of close to a million, whose elite, along with Rome's client kings and local aristocracies across the empire, lived luxuriously on the wealth produced by slaves, the poor, and a minuscule middle class. About thirty years before Revelation was written (AD 63), a fire consumed about a quarter of Rome over the course of a week (see sidebar, "The First Martyrs of the Church of Rome," p. 216). Here a voice from heaven foretells Babylon's complete destruction in scarcely an hour. Modern readers, aware of the destructive power of nuclear weapons, know how an entire civilization could be destroyed in a single hour in a way that would scarcely have been imaginable to Revelation's original readers.

18:11–17a   In the same way, the **merchants of the earth** mourn the loss of their **markets** because they grew rich through selling things to Babylon. In the first century, Rome was the center of international trade and the prime destination of merchandise from around the Mediterranean world. For Rome to stop buying would mean great loss for all who did business with her. So the merchants **weep and mourn** since they no longer can sell their **cargo**. The list of goods that the merchants sold to Babylon overlaps those of ancient Tyre mentioned in Ezek 27:12–24 (fifteen of the twenty-eight items),[14] but the list actually names the goods that wealthy elites of Rome and the empire craved and purchased. They belong to seven categories: precious stones and metals, luxurious fabrics, expensive wood and building materials, spices and perfumes, food items, animals, and slaves. The catalog of imports lists mainly luxury items rather than necessities. Many of the items had little utility other than to conspicuously demonstrate the wealth of whoever possessed them. Richard Bauckham shows that "many of the items in the list are specifically mentioned as prime examples of luxury and extravagance by Roman writers critical of the decadence, as they saw it, of the wealthy families of Rome in the early imperial period."[15] Items on the list that are not luxurious, such as oil and wheat, were exported to Rome in such vast quantities that their prices sometimes rose in the provinces, making these staple foods harder for the poor to obtain.[16] This catalog of goods shows that implicit in Revelation's use of prostitution-fornication imagery for Babylon's commercial relationships is a critique of Babylon's ostentatious and luxurious lifestyle as well as its passionate greed.

The final item of Babylon's cargoes is mentioned last to catch the reader's attention: **slaves, that is, human beings** (literally, "bodies—that is, human souls"). This concise description indicates the grave offense to human dignity entailed in the buying and selling of people; many centuries later it was used by Christians advocating the abolition of slavery.[17] John's first readers were well aware of the slave trade, since many of them would have been slaves or former slaves, and

14. G. K. Beale, *The Book of Revelation*, NIGTC (Grand Rapids, Eerdmans, 1999), 909.

15. Richard Bauckham, *The Climax of Prophecy: Studies on the Book of Revelation* (Edinburgh: T&T Clark, 1993), 367. Bauckham provides a detailed study of each item on the list of cargoes, explaining its uses, places of origin, and role in the life of first-century Rome (350–71).

16. According to Bauckham, "There is some evidence of bread riots in the cities of Asia Minor around the time when Revelation was written" (ibid., 363).

17. Craig R. Koester, "Roman Slave Trade and the Critique of Babylon in Revelation 18," in *Catholic Biblical Quarterly* 70, no. 4 (October 2008): 786n56.

because the Roman province of Asia was considered a source of choice slaves. Archaeologists have found the remains of slave markets in the cities of three of these seven churches, in Ephesus, Sardis, and Thyatira. Although the Roman Empire accepted the institution of slavery as a fact of life and a foundation of its economy, the slave trade was generally looked down upon. Slave traders were regarded as greedy and dishonest and were associated with kidnapping and prostitution. Commemorative inscriptions in Ephesus and elsewhere show that slave traders sought to buy social respectability by generous donations to public works.[18]

Continuing to address the now-departed Babylon, the merchants resume their lament in poetic parallelism. The emotive power of the laments (18:10, 14, 16–17, 19) is enhanced by being addressed directly to Babylon and by a three- or four-line structure in which the content of one of the lines is repeated for emphasis. Verse 14 repeats the same idea three times: First, **the fruit you craved / has left you**. There is a play on words here, since literally the text says "the fruit for which your soul longed" (NRSV)—those who traded in human souls (18:13) have lost what *their* soul desired. The merchants repeat a second time, **All your luxury and splendor** (literally, "all your bright and shiny things")[19] **are gone** (literally, "lost to you," NRSV, RSV). And a third time: **never again will one find them**. Continuing to stand at a distance out of fear of her **torment** (see comments on 18:7) and to weep, the merchants **who grew rich from her** bewail the sudden loss of Babylon's former glory. Recalling her lavishly expensive clothing and jewelry in virtually the same words used to describe the clothing of the prostitute in 17:4, they rue the fact that **in one hour this great wealth has been ruined**. They mourn what they have loved and lost, business with Babylon, the source of their wealth, their cash cow.

The third group, who make their living at sea in the shipping industry or 　**18:17b–19**
as merchants or fishermen, **who had ships** and **grew rich from her wealth**, cry out in the same way, **weeping and mourning**. As they watch Babylon burn, they exclaim, **What city could compare with the great city?** For wealth, luxury, and economic power, Babylon has no rival on earth, just as the beast seems to have no rival for political power and authority. The seamen **threw dust on their heads**, a gesture of grief as in Ezek 27:29–30, where sailors and mariners mourn the destruction of Tyre, the leading city of a similar economic empire.

---

18. See ibid., 766–86.

19. Here the Greek does not use either of the words referring to sensual luxury (*strēnos* or *strēniaō*) as found in 18:3, 7, 9, but rather a word whose first meaning is "bright."

Reflection and Application (18:9–19)

The city of Rome was a voracious consumer and the largest market of the ancient world, so it is easy to see why Revelation's first readers would have identified Rome with Babylon. However, the upper class in the wealthiest cities of the Roman Empire, including those where the seven churches were located, belonged to the same economic system and craved and purchased the same consumer goods. Babylon is a symbol and must not be confined to a single location or period, lest its presence be overlooked in other places, including our own lives. At the time of this writing, the United States is the world's largest market, while Europe, Canada, Japan, China, and the wealthy elites of the developing nations join the United States as major consumers and markets for luxury goods.

It is easiest to recognize Babylon in our economic system today when advertising overtly appeals to lust or greed, or when immoral products are bought and sold, as in the drug trade, internet pornography, and human trafficking. What is harder to see and harder to combat is the way the world economic system involves those who buy or sell goods in the exploitation of the poor. How much of the clothing and electronic products that we buy is produced in sweatshops in distant countries? How much of the coffee or the fruits and vegetables that we consume is planted and harvested by people who live at or below subsistence level and are forced to work under harsh conditions?

If corporations operate with profit as their *sole* motive and criterion of success, sooner or later they will abuse those who produce their goods, their customers, society, or the environment. Catholics who own, invest, or work in corporations need to work together with other people of good will to give proper place to human dignity, the common good, principles of justice, and consideration of the poor while engaged in the legitimate effort to run a profitable business. Paul writes, "Do not share in another's sins. Keep yourself pure" (1 Tim 5:22). Christian consumers need to pay attention to the ethical practices of the companies with whom they do business to avoid participating in injustice or promoting values and lifestyles contrary to God's word.

A Mighty Angel Confirms Babylon's Judgment (18:20–24)

> ²⁰"Rejoice over her, heaven,
>   you holy ones, apostles, and prophets.
> For God has judged your case against her."

²¹A mighty angel picked up a stone like a huge millstone and threw it into the sea and said:

> "With such force will Babylon the great city be thrown down,
>   and will never be found again.
> ²²No melodies of harpists and musicians,
>   flutists and trumpeters,
>   will ever be heard in you again.
> No craftsmen in any trade
>   will ever be found in you again.
> No sound of the millstone
>   will ever be heard in you again.
> ²³No light from a lamp
>   will ever be seen in you again.
> No voices of bride and groom
>   will ever be heard in you again.
> Because your merchants were the great ones of the world,
>   all nations were led astray by your magic potion.
> ²⁴In her was found the blood of prophets and holy ones
>   and all who have been slain on the earth."

OT: Jer 25:10–11; 51:59–64

Not everyone is mourning Babylon's demise. The voice from heaven (18:4) that **18:20** has narrated the laments of kings, merchants, and seamen now addresses **heaven** and its inhabitants: **You holy ones, apostles, and prophets.** Babylon's victims are invited to celebrate God's justice: **Rejoice over her. . . . For God has judged your case against her.** The basis of God's judgment against Babylon and in favor of those wronged by her was expressed in 18:6: "Pay her back as she has paid others." One commentator puts it this way: "The whole scene could be likened to a universal courtroom, in which a class-action suit takes place. Plaintiffs in this suit are Christians together with all those killed on earth (18:24); the defendant is Babylon/Rome, who is charged with murder in the interest of power and idolatry; and the presiding judge is God."[20] Heaven rejoices at the termination of the reign of evil and injustice—not at the personal fate of those who fail to repent. God does not take "pleasure in the death of the wicked" (Ezek 18:23) but "wills everyone to be saved and to come to knowledge of the truth" (1 Tim 2:4).

The certainty of Babylon's future destruction is now confirmed by a prophetic **18:21** gesture executed by a **mighty angel** who picks up **a stone** and casts it **into the**

20. Elisabeth Schüssler Fiorenza, *Revelation: Vision of a Just World* (Minneapolis: Fortress, 1991), 99.

sea to announce that Babylon will be **thrown down** with **such force** that it will **never be found again**. While Rev 18:2–20 prophesied Babylon's destruction in the past tense, verses 21–23 foretell that judgment in the future tense. John's vision here recalls a similar scene from the book of Jeremiah in which the prophet writes down all the judgments God is going to bring upon Babylon and instructs Seraiah, a royal official on his way to Babylon, to read aloud these judgments when he arrives. After reading the contents of the scroll, Seraiah is to "tie a stone to it and throw it into the Euphrates, and say: Thus Babylon shall sink. It will never rise, because of the disaster I am bringing upon it" (Jer 51:63–64). In John's vision, however, the stone is much larger, **like a huge millstone** weighing hundreds of pounds, and it is thrown into the sea rather than a river. Besides emphasizing the inevitability of its sinking to the bottom, a millstone recalls Jesus' words about the penalty due to those who lead others into sin (Matt 18:6; Mark 9:42; Luke 17:2), one of Babylon's chief faults (Rev 14:8).

18:22–23a   The poignant words describing the cessation of all that pertains to normal human life reveal that what is happening to Babylon is retribution it deserves. The language is taken from a prophecy of Jeremiah about the destruction that ancient Babylon would bring upon Israel: "an end [to] the song of joy and the song of gladness, the voice of the bridegroom and the voice of the bride, the sound of the millstone and the light of the lamp" (Jer 25:10). What Babylon has given she will receive. Nevertheless, judgment on Babylon does not merely represent judgment on Rome or ancient Babylon or any other particular culture or civilization that attacks God's people. Babylon is a symbol of every nation that has harmed God's people through all of history against which God will render just judgment in favor of his covenant people.

18:23b–24   Lest the reader forget the reason for this devastation, Babylon's crimes are restated: **Because your merchants were the great ones of the world, / all nations were led astray by your magic potion.** Revelation depicts Jezebel, Satan, the false prophet, and now Babylon as deceiving or leading people astray.[21] Babylon's merchants, its leaders of business and industry, are singled out for blame because what they did influenced people to sin. They did this by means of their "magic potion" (Greek *pharmakeia*), which other versions translate as "sorcery" or "magic spells." Literally, the word refers to the misuse of drugs or use of occult power (see comments on related words at 9:21 and 21:8).[22] However, it is likely that "your magic potion" should also be taken as a metaphor

21. See Rev 2:20; 12:9; 13:14; 18:23; 19:20; 20:3, 8, 10.
22. This word is used in the †Septuagint to describe practices in Egypt and Babylon (e.g., Exod 7:11, 22; 8:3, 14; Isa 47:9, 12). It is described as one of the "works of the flesh" in Gal 5:20.

for Babylon's proffered material prosperity, which seduces people to embrace a way of life and values that are idolatrous, greedy, and immoral. And Babylon has committed another terrible crime: **blood** was found in her. In the Bible "blood" is used figuratively to refer to responsibility for murder (see Gen 4:10; Deut 21:1–9). Babylon has murdered not only God's people, **prophets and holy ones** (6:9–11; 16:6; 17:6; 19:2), but also **all who have been slain on the earth**. Since Babylon symbolizes both one particular evil civilization and "the world"— human society insofar as it opposes God's rule—the charge is literally true.

Babylon is embodied wherever cultures and socioeconomic systems draw people away from worshiping God and toward sin and the worship of idols. Rome was one such embodiment, as were Tyre and ancient Babylon before her. Contemporary Western culture with its self-centeredness, materialism, and immorality is another. All of these will eventually meet their end, whether gradually or suddenly. Since Christians live in the world yet "do not belong to the world" (John 17:15–16), we are not immune to the loss of possessions and even earthly life when God brings his judgment on cultures and civilizations that oppose him. But this is not a true or final loss for us, since "our citizenship is in heaven" (Phil 3:20) and "we await new heavens and a new earth" (2 Pet 3:13), where "the former things shall not be remembered / nor come to mind" (Isa 65:17).

In Revelation, the destruction of Babylon comes at the end of history, at the pouring out of the seventh bowl of God's wrath. The fall of Babylon, therefore, represents more than the fall of one particular culture and socioeconomic system. Rather, it is judgment on the entirety of human social and economic life insofar as it is opposed to God. Revelation, however, distinguishes two moments in God's judgment of evil: Babylon's destruction at the hands of the beast and its allies (17:16–18:24) and the destruction of the beast, the false prophet, and their armies when Christ returns (19:11–21). Only God knows how precisely these †eschatological events will unfold.

Reflection and Application (18:1–18)

It is striking how Revelation's lurid depiction of Babylon fits the sordid underbelly of international trade in our day. Besides importing luxuries, those who live in the wealthiest nations import vast quantities of illegal drugs that entrap millions in addiction and corrupt hundreds of thousands who produce, transport, and sell this contraband. Pornography and the sex trade are colossal industries, raking in billions of dollars annually, enslaving users spiritually, and often literally enslaving women and children for sex trafficking. Slavery of all kinds is making a comeback, in part to satisfy the rapacious desire of world markets for goods at low prices. According to the Australian nonprofit Walk Free (walkfree.org), as of 2013 nearly thirty million people worldwide were living in slavery. These evils move us to pray for the destruction of Babylon and the coming of God's kingdom.

Celebration in Heaven, Judgment on Earth

Revelation 19:1–21

While the previous chapter depicts the effects of God's judgment on Babylon, the present chapter presents a glorious vision of Christ's return and his victory over the beast, the false prophet, and their allies in the last battle at the end of history (19:11–21). Before the action resumes, however, John overhears a victory celebration in heaven over the judgment of the great harlot Babylon (19:1–4) and a wonderful announcement about what lies in store for the other woman of Revelation, God's covenant people (19:5–10).

Verses 1–10 of this chapter complete the first section of the conclusion of Revelation that began with chapter 17, the vision of the great harlot Babylon and her fate. Verses 11–21 begin the second section (19:11–21:8), setting forth the first of four visions about how God will bring history to its goal.

Victory Celebration in Heaven (19:1–4)

¹After this I heard what sounded like the loud voice of a great multitude in heaven, saying:

> "Alleluia!
> Salvation, glory, and might belong to our God,
> ²for true and just are his judgments.
> He has condemned the great harlot
> who corrupted the earth with her harlotry.
> He has avenged on her the blood of his servants."

³They said a second time:

"Alleluia! Smoke will rise from her forever and ever."

⁴The twenty-four elders and the four living creatures fell down and worshiped God who sat on the throne, saying, "Amen. Alleluia."

OT: Gen 6:11; Deut 32:43; Isa 34:8–10; Jer 51:48
Catechism: prayer of praise, 2642

19:1   Immediately after learning of Babylon's demise through those who lament her, John hears **a great multitude in heaven** engaged in a heavenly liturgy, praising God in antiphonal worship with those near the throne. This "great multitude" in heaven appeared in 7:9–14 as the white-robed victors emerging from the great †tribulation, praising God for victory and salvation. Just before the seven bowls are poured out, the same congregation sings the song of Moses and the song of the Lamb with harps in their hands, praising God's justice (15:2–4). Here the great multitude celebrates God's judgment of Babylon (19:1–3) and announces the arrival of the marriage of the Lamb (19:6). Twice the heavenly multitude shouts, and once the elders and living creatures answer, **Alleluia**! Here in Rev 19 (vv. 1, 3, 4, 6) are the only instances in the New Testament of the familiar Hebrew acclamation that means "Praise the Lord!" They declare that **salvation** (rescue from death), **glory** (supreme honor), and **might** (sovereign authority) **belong to our God**, emphasizing their relationship to God by the word "our."

19:2–4   As in the Hebrew poetry of the Psalms, the reason for praising God follows the call to praise: because God's **judgments** are **true and just**. Specifically, God **has condemned** (literally, "judged") **the great harlot / who corrupted the earth with her harlotry** (Greek *porneia*, "sexual immorality"). Babylon has been the cause of scandal: "Temptations to sin are sure to come; but woe to him by whom they come!" (Luke 17:1 RSV). The earth suffers harm not only by chemical pollution and toxic waste: it is also ruined by sin (11:18; on moral ecology, see "Reflection and Application" on 8:7–12). Her "harlotry" refers to the entire range of evildoing that Babylon incites. Here is another reason God's judgment of Babylon is just: **he has avenged on her the blood of his servants.** Babylon murdered God's "prophets and holy ones" (18:24). God's retribution is not revenge; it is the heavenly judge imposing a just sentence on murderers (see sidebar, "Vengeance," p. 131). The perpetual **smoke** marks the end of the evil that has emanated from Babylon. The wave of praise that begins from the redeemed multitude moves from the periphery toward the center, through

the twenty-four elders and **the four living creatures**, who prostrate themselves toward God on his throne, saying, **Amen. Alleluia.**

Wedding Announcement of the Lamb and His Bride (19:5–10)

---

[5]A voice coming from the throne said:

> "Praise our God, all you his servants,
>   [and] you who revere him, small and great."

[6]Then I heard something like the sound of a great multitude or the sound of rushing water or mighty peals of thunder, as they said:

> "Alleluia!
> The Lord has established his reign,
>   [our] God, the almighty.
> [7]Let us rejoice and be glad
>   and give him glory.
> For the wedding day of the Lamb has come,
>   his bride has made herself ready.
> [8]She was allowed to wear
>   a bright, clean linen garment."

(The linen represents the righteous deeds of the holy ones.)

[9]Then the angel said to me, "Write this: Blessed are those who have been called to the wedding feast of the Lamb." And he said to me, "These words are true; they come from God." [10]I fell at his feet to worship him. But he said to me, "Don't! I am a fellow servant of yours and of your brothers who bear witness to Jesus. Worship God. Witness to Jesus is the spirit of prophecy."

OT: Isa 61:10–62:5
NT: Matt 9:15; 25:1–13; John 3:29; Eph 5:25–32
Catechism: prayer of praise, 2642; the Bride, 677, 757, 865; implications for marriage, 1612, 1617; the Eucharist as anticipation, 1329
Lectionary: 19:1, 5–9: Common of Virgins during Easter

After the great multitude, the elders, and living creatures have praised God's justice in judging Babylon, a **voice coming from the throne** invites all who fear God to praise him. Because the call to praise comes from the throne, there is no doubt that this heavenly worship leader, probably an angel, is divinely inspired. The response is overwhelming: **a great multitude** that sounds like **rushing water** or **peals of thunder** praises God for having established his kingdom, as the voices in heaven and the elders did at the sounding of the seventh trumpet

19:5–6

307

(11:15, 17).[1] As in the earlier instance (11:17), God is named by his supreme title, **the almighty** (Greek *pantokratōr*).

19:7–8   The victory song of God's servants introduces a new and surprising theme. They exhort one another to celebrate and glorify God in view of an event not mentioned explicitly earlier in this book: **the wedding day of the Lamb has come.**[2] A royal marriage is about to occur, like the one celebrated in Ps 45. As in the literature of many cultures—after all enemies have been defeated, the story of Revelation also ends happily with the marriage of a virtuous and victorious king. This Messiah-king and Bridegroom is the one like a son of man, the slain Lamb, who "loves us and has freed us from our sins by his blood" and has risen and is alive forever (1:5, 13, 18; 5:6).

Marriage is a familiar image of God's relationship with Israel. Isaiah 54:5 says, "Your Maker is your husband" (NRSV); the book of Hosea looks forward to the day when Israel will return to the Lord and again call him "my husband" (Hosea 2:16–25, especially v. 18; Ezek 16:6–14). When that happens, the Lord promises to renew creation, to put an end to war, and to "betroth you to me forever" (Hosea 2:21). Isaiah 61:10 envisions this moment:

> I will rejoice heartily in the LORD,
>> my being exults in my God;
> For he has clothed me with garments of salvation,
>> and wrapped me in a robe of justice,
> Like a bridegroom adorned with a diadem,
>> as a bride adorns herself with her jewels.

The chapter that follows confirms that the Lord is marrying his people; he is reestablishing Jerusalem (see Isa 62, especially v. 5). This proclamation in Revelation announces that the fulfillment of these prophecies is at hand.

Other writings in the New Testament announce the same theme. Jesus speaks of himself as the bridegroom in the †Synoptic Gospels (e.g., Matt 9:15), and John the Baptist refers to Jesus this way (John 3:29).[3] Paul tells the Corinthians, "I betrothed you to one husband to present you as a chaste virgin to Christ" (2 Cor 11:2; see Rom 7:4), and explains the Church's bridal relationship to Christ in Ephesians:

1. This praise echoes psalms about God's reign (e.g., 1 Chron 16:8–36; Ps 93; 96; 97; 99). As in Dan 7, where the defeat of Israel's enemies ushers in the eternal reign of the holy ones, so the defeat of Babylon signals the arrival of God's kingdom. Revelation 19:6 supplies the words of the "Hallelujah Chorus" in George Frideric Handel's *Messiah*.
2. Other translations say "marriage of the Lamb." The phrase "let us rejoice and be glad" comes from the Psalms (40:17; 70:5; 118:24).
3. Jesus himself teaches about the invitation to a king's wedding feast for his son, speaking also of wearing a suitable garment and of readiness for the bridegroom's arrival (Matt 22:1–14; 25:1–13).

Christ loved the church and handed himself over for her to sanctify her, cleansing her by the bath of water with the word, that he might present to himself the church in splendor, without spot or wrinkle or any such thing, that she might be holy and without blemish. (Eph 5:25–27)

Although the prophets emphasize God's initiative in the spousal relationship, and Eph 5:25–27 focuses on Christ's role in preparing his Bride for marriage, Rev 19:7–8 highlights the Bride's contribution: the Lamb's **bride has made herself ready**. How and when did she do this? God made it possible for the Bride to present herself worthily: **She was allowed** (literally, "it was granted to her") **to wear / a bright, clean linen garment** ("dazzling white linen," NJB). **The linen represents** (literally, "is") **the righteous deeds of the holy ones**— the faith and love, the upright conduct, the verbal testimony and faithfulness to Christ of her members. Having been bathed by her heavenly Bridegroom through the word and baptism (Eph 5:26, above), the Bride has responded generously to the point of being radiant. The faithful church has said no to idolatry and yes to holiness. Christ has honored his Bride by enabling her— that is, us—to freely cooperate with divine grace and thus to become worthy of the promises of Christ and enter into all that God has in store for us (see Eph 2:7, 10).

Like the explanation of the symbolism of the Bride's bright linen, the fourth †beatitude that the interpreting **angel** (last mentioned in 17:7) instructs John to write motivates readers to persevere in faithfulness and "righteous deeds" (19:8). **Blessed are those who have been called to the wedding feast of the Lamb**. In ancient Judaism, the wedding feast began the second and definitive stage of marriage after bethrothal, when the bride went to live with the groom (see sidebar, "Jewish Wedding Customs," p. 310). Those "called" or invited to this feast are those who have accepted the gospel of Christ (2 Thess 2:14). The metaphor shifts from the whole Church as the Bride to individual Christians as the invited guests at the Lamb's wedding feast. The liturgy takes these words and applies them to the Eucharist, a foretaste of the messianic banquet:[4] "Behold the Lamb of God, behold him who takes away the sins of the world. Blessed are those called to the supper of the Lamb."[5] The angel attests to the trustworthiness of this beatitude: **These words are true; they come from God**.

19:9

---

4. The messianic banquet in the kingdom of God is a common theme both in Jesus' teaching and in Jewish literature. See Matt 8:11 and parallels; Luke 14:15; 22:30; Isa 25:6; *1 Enoch* 62:14; *2 Baruch* 29:8; 2 Esd 2:38 (see Osborne, *Revelation*, 675–76).

5. From the Communion Rite of the Catholic Mass.

Jewish Wedding Customs

BIBLICAL BACKGROUND

New Testament allusions to marriage, including these in Revelation, presuppose first-century Jewish wedding customs.[a] The first stage of marriage was betrothal, which typically occurred before the woman was of childbearing age and always before the couple began living together. A betrothed couple was understood to be legally married (see Matt 1:18–19); the period before the wedding ceremonies was a time of preparation. This stage of the relationship between Christ and the Church, between Christ and individual Christians, takes place through conversion and baptism and is presupposed in Revelation.

The second stage of marriage, the wedding, began when the bride came to live in the house of the groom and was accompanied by various ceremonies.

- First, the bride was adorned. The end of the betrothal period and the adornment of the bride is announced in 19:7–8.
- Next came the procession when the bride and her friends went to the house of the groom, who went out to meet the bride, and then brought her into his house in a joyous entry.
- Then came the wedding feast, which usually lasted a week. The vision of the new Jerusalem coming down from heaven "prepared as a bride adorned for her husband" (21:2) is analogous to the entry of the bride into the home of her groom (21:2–8) and her arrival at the wedding banquet (announced in 19:9).
- The marriage was consummated on the first day of the celebration, and the bride and groom began living together as a married couple from then on. This final stage, consummation and life together, is revealed in the visions of the new Jerusalem in 21:9–22:5.

a. This description is drawn largely from Donal A. McIlraith, *The Reciprocal Love between Christ and the Church in the Apocalypse*, published doctoral dissertation, Theology Faculty of the Pontifical Gregorian University (Rome: Columban Fathers, 1989), 185–89.

19:10   The awesome greatness of the angel (one of the seven who poured out the bowls of divine wrath, 17:1), combined with the awesome revelation of 17:1–19:9, moves the prophet to fall at the angel's feet **to worship him**. The angel immediately interrupts: **Don't!** Worship belongs to God alone. It seems strange that John would make this mistake (twice! he will do so again in 22:8–10), but the incident is intended to reveal two truths.[6] First, it manifests the extraordinary

6. A somewhat similar angelic rejection of prostration followed by exhortation to worship God is found in Tob 12:16–22 and has parallels in other Jewish and Christian literature.

divine †glory of the heavenly messenger and of the revelation he brings. Second, it underscores the profound difference between the loftiest creature, on the one hand, and God and the Lamb, on the other. Despite his greatness, the glorious angel is only **a fellow servant** (literally, "fellow slave") of John and all his brothers and sisters **who bear witness to Jesus**. The fact that those "who hold the testimony of Jesus" (RSV) are of similar standing to a glorious angel shows the lofty dignity of Christians because **witness to Jesus is the spirit of prophecy**. When Christians give testimony about Jesus, they are prophesying; the Spirit of God is speaking through them (Matt 10:20).

The announcement of the fall of Babylon and of the wedding feast of the Lamb seems to signal the arrival of the kingdom. Readers may think they are about to be treated to a description of the messianic banquet or of the †beatific vision. But some loose ends must be attended to. What happens to the dragon? What happens to the beast and the false prophet? Revelation will now recount the defeat of these enemies in inverse order to their appearance in the book.

Part two of the conclusion of Revelation begins here. It contains three judgment scenes: (1) the judgment of the two beasts and their allies (19:11–21); (2) the judgment of Satan (20:1–10); and (3) the judgment of the dead and of Death itself (20:11–15). It concludes with a glimpse of the new creation and the new Jerusalem (21:1–8).

The King of Kings and Lord of Lords (19:11–16)

---

¹¹Then I saw the heavens opened, and there was a white horse; its rider was [called] "Faithful and True." He judges and wages war in righteousness. ¹²His eyes were [like] a fiery flame, and on his head were many diadems. He had a name inscribed that no one knows except himself. ¹³He wore a cloak that had been dipped in blood, and his name was called the Word of God. ¹⁴The armies of heaven followed him, mounted on white horses and wearing clean white linen. ¹⁵Out of his mouth came a sharp sword to strike the nations. He will rule them with an iron rod, and he himself will tread out in the wine press the wine of the fury and wrath of God the almighty. ¹⁶He has a name written on his cloak and on his thigh, "King of kings and Lord of lords."

OT: Ps 2; 45; Wis 18:14–16; Isa 11:1–5; 63:1–6
NT: Rev 17:14
Catechism: return of Christ, 1040; time of return, 673; defeat of Satan, 550

This paragraph and the next present the second coming of Christ with imagery drawn from the Old Testament. Just as the announcement of the wedding of the Lamb in 19:7–8 indicates that Christ fulfills Isaiah's prophecy about God marrying his people and reestablishing Jerusalem (61:10–62:5), this paragraph tells how Christ will fulfill Isaiah's prophecy about God coming as a warrior to rescue and vindicate his people (63:1–6). This vision, more than other New Testament descriptions of Christ's return, employs imagery that helps us to understand its significance yet does not tell us concretely what it will be like.

19:11   The words **I saw** signal a new vision. As usual in Scripture, this vision provides not a literal description but a symbolic depiction of its subject. When **the heavens opened**, John sees the risen Lord coming as a warrior king to judge—a preview of the return of the Lord. A victorious Roman emperor customarily rode a **white horse** in triumphal processions. Although similar language is used to describe the horse and rider in 6:2, the context is different here. This rider is not merely a conqueror (like the rider of 6:2), but is **Faithful and True**, loyal and trustworthy (3:14). He is a model for Christians summoned to faithfulness[7] and an embodiment of God's judgments, which are "true and just" (16:7; 19:2). The fact that he **judges and wages war in righteousness** confirms that he is the messianic descendant of David who "shall judge the poor with justice, / and decide fairly for the land's afflicted" (Isa 11:4), and who will "ride forth victoriously / for the cause of truth and to defend the right" (Ps 45:4 RSV).[8]

19:12   The **fiery flame** of his eyes indicates penetrating knowledge and the justice of the judgment that follows from his clear view of reality. The **many diadems** are the royal crowns of a ruler who reigns over an empire of many nations. Earlier in Revelation the dragon was depicted as wearing seven diadems and the beast ten (12:3; 13:1). Kingship over the nations is about to be restored to their rightful King. The **name inscribed that no one knows except himself** suggests that his identity is beyond the understanding of any creature, while everyone and everything lies exposed to his fiery eyes (Heb 4:11–12).

19:13   The divine warrior of Isa 63 comes to rescue Jerusalem, wearing clothes stained with the blood of Israel's enemies, whom he defeated all by himself. Here, however, Jesus descends from heaven, not from a foreign battlefield, wearing a **cloak that had been dipped in blood**, a reference to his sacrificial death on

---

7. See Rev 2:10, 13; 13:10; 14:12; 17:14.

8. Other texts that depict God or the Messiah as a divine warrior include Ps 68; 97:3, 10; 98:1–2; Isa 11:4; 59:16–19. The divine warrior motif is reflected also in Eph 6:10–17, where Christians are summoned to unite themselves to their warrior God by putting on God's armor, the attitudes and actions that enable them to draw on his strength (see Peter S. Williamson, *Ephesians*, CCSS [Grand Rapids: Baker Academic, 2009], 190–99).

the cross, the solitary combat in which the Lamb has conquered (5:5–6). The **name** he is **called** is **the Word of God**, bringing to mind several biblical texts. The Old Testament reveals that God's word is his instrument in creation and redemption (e.g., Gen 1:3; Ps 33:6; Isa 55:10–11). The book of Wisdom recalls how God's "all-powerful word from heaven's royal throne / leapt into the doomed land, / a fierce warrior" to bring judgment on Egypt when Israel was enslaved there (18:15–16). Ephesians declares that "the sword of the Spirit . . . is the word of God" (6:17; see Heb 4:12). And the Gospel of John solemnly reveals that in the beginning "the Word was with God, / and the Word was God," and that "the Word became flesh" in Jesus Christ (John 1:1, 14).

Fig. 20. The coming of Christ, Faithful and True, the Word of God, the King of kings and Lord of lords, with the armies of heaven (see 19:11–16).

The book of Revelation portrays Christ in startlingly diverse ways. In chapter 1 he is the awesome son of man and risen one, standing in the midst of the churches, firmly holding their "stars" in his hand. In chapter 5, he stands in the middle of heaven's throne as a Lamb that had been slain, bearing the marks of his crucifixion (v. 6). In chapter 12 he is the male child, born to rule the nations with a rod of iron, "caught up to God and his throne" (v. 5). Here in chapter 19 he is both the bridegroom and the conquering king and judge at history's end. The diversity of these depictions of Christ underscores his multifaceted grandeur.

The divine warrior does not come alone; the **armies of heaven** accompany him. The Old Testament refers to the angels as God's army, and the New Testament speaks of Jesus being accompanied by angels when he comes again,[9] so the presence of angels in this army is clear. There are indications, however, that the victorious people of God also belong to the armies of heaven. The armies **followed** the Word of God, a word often used in the Gospels for what

19:14

---

9. See Matt 13:40–42; 16:27; 24:30–31; 25:31–32; Mark 8:38; Luke 9:26; 2 Thess 1:7; Jude 14–15 (Beale and McDonough, 1143).

disciples do (see 14:4). Earlier in the book, one of the prophecies about this final battle describes those accompanying the conquering Lamb as "called, chosen, and faithful" (17:14), qualities typically attributed to Christians rather than to angels. In any case Christ's victorious army is pictured on **white horses** like his and wearing **white linen**, the dress of angels (John 20:12; Rev 15:6), as well as of victorious human beings (Rev 3:4; 6:11; 7:13–14), and the Bride of the Lamb (19:8).

19:15–16   John returns to describing Christ. As in the opening vision (1:16; 2:16), **a sharp sword** issues from **his mouth**. Its function is judgment of **the nations**, that is, those who are not God's people. The same messianic prophecy (from Ps 2:9) that described the male child born of the woman in 12:5 is ascribed to this warrior king: **He will rule them with an iron rod**. Although Christ **himself** acts to **tread . . . the wine press**, the judgment he renders is not his own (John 5:30), but rather **the wine of the fury and †wrath of God the almighty**. Treading grapes is the image of divine judgment used in Isaiah's vision of the divine warrior (Isa 63:1–6, referenced in Rev 14:19–20 and 16:19). The **name written** on the part of his **cloak** that covers **his thigh** repeats the supreme human and divine title given in the earlier prophecy of the Lamb's victory over the beast, **King of kings and Lord of lords** (see comments on 17:14). Jesus will return with complete authority and irresistible power. This account of the return of the Lord in 19:11–16 depicts Jesus as a divine warrior-king and emphasizes that the risen Messiah's return in power is the fulfillment of Old Testament prophecies about God coming to rescue his people.

A variety of New Testament texts depict the return of Christ in glory,[10] mostly using language from Dan 7:13–14 about his coming on the clouds. These texts all present Christ's return as a dramatic interruption and conclusion of life as we know it on earth. Acts 1:11 is perhaps the gentlest description: after a cloud has taken Jesus from their sight (1:9), an angel tells his disciples, "This Jesus who has been taken up from you into heaven will return in the same way as you have seen him going into heaven."

The Last Battle: Destruction of the Beast and His Allies (19:17–21)

[17]**Then I saw an angel standing on the sun. He cried out [in] a loud voice to all the birds flying high overhead, "Come here. Gather for God's**

10. See Matt 24:27, 30; 26:64; Mark 14:62; Luke 21:27; Acts 1:9–11; 1 Thess 4:15–17; 2 Thess 2:8; Rev 1:7.

great feast, [18]to eat the flesh of kings, the flesh of military officers, and the flesh of warriors, the flesh of horses and of their riders, and the flesh of all, free and slave, small and great." [19]Then I saw the beast and the kings of the earth and their armies gathered to fight against the one riding the horse and against his army. [20]The beast was caught and with it the false prophet who had performed in its sight the signs by which he led astray those who had accepted the mark of the beast and those who had worshiped its image. The two were thrown alive into the fiery pool burning with sulfur. [21]The rest were killed by the sword that came out of the mouth of the one riding the horse, and all the birds gorged themselves on their flesh.

OT: Ps 2:2; Isa 11:4; 66:5–6, 15–18, 24; Ezek 39:1–5, 17–20; Dan 7:11
NT: 2 Thess 2:8
Catechism: defeat of Satan, 550

Just as the fall of Babylon was foretold twice before being described in Rev 18, this chapter also describes what has been twice foretold: the last battle (16:14–16; 17:13–14).

Several Old Testament psalms and prophecies speak of a battle at the end of history, when pagan nations will launch a final assault against God's people.[11] When that happens, God will intervene to save his people, destroy their enemies, and establish his eternal messianic kingdom. Revelation reveals more about that long-prophesied final battle yet remains at the level of symbolic rather than literal description.

The vision in 19:17–21 depicts the final battle in horrifying images drawn from Ezek 38–39.[12] According to Ezek 38, when God's people are dwelling securely, Gog the king of Magog (names of uncertain origin that refer to a pagan ruler and a pagan land) will come up against Israel with a great horde of peoples, a mighty army mounted on horses. As in Rev 16:12–16, however, the attack of Gog is subject to God's control (Ezek 38:16). When the battle comes to pass, the Lord resoundingly defeats Gog and his armies, sends fire on the land of Magog (39:6), and tells Ezekiel to summon the birds of prey and wild beasts to "eat the flesh of warriors and drink the blood of the princes of the earth" (39:18). In Revelation the final conflict prophesied in Ezekiel is depicted very briefly twice. This first depiction reports the defeat of the beast and its allies; the second, in 20:8–10, reports Satan's demise.

11. See Ps 2; 46; 48; Ezek 38; Zech 12; 14.
12. The visions at the end of Revelation provide a prophetic interpretation of the last chapters of Ezekiel and follow the same sequence. In Ezekiel, after the final battle (Ezek 38–39), a new temple is revealed (Ezek 40–48). In Revelation, after God defeats the enemies of his people, the new Jerusalem descends from heaven, a temple-city where God and the Lamb will dwell with their people forever (21:22).

19:17–18   John sees a herald **angel standing on the sun**—too bright to look at, with a commanding view of the world beneath him. Since the outcome of the battle is certain, the angel concerns himself with the cleanup. He issues an invitation to the carrion **birds flying high overhead** (literally, "that fly in midheaven") beneath the sun: **Come here. Gather for God's great feast**. The words are manifestly ironic, since the vultures' food is unspeakably horrible and ritually unclean: **the flesh of kings, the flesh of military officers, . . . and the flesh of all, free and slave, small and great**. No class will be excluded from this judgment. "This grisly scene stresses the awfulness of the fate awaiting those who persevere in opposing God and God's designs."[13]

19:19   The focus of John's vision began in heaven (19:11), moved to the sky (midheaven, 19:17), and now focuses on earth, where **the beast and the kings of the earth and their armies** have mustered **to fight against** Christ, **the one riding the horse, and against his army**. This gathering of enemies has been referred to twice before. In 16:13–16, frog-like demonic spirits from the mouths of the dragon, beast, and false prophet summon world rulers to battle at Armageddon "on the great day of God the Almighty." In 17:12–14 ten kings "will give their power and authority to the beast" in order to "fight with the Lamb, but the Lamb will conquer them." A final recap of this battle will appear in 20:7–10.

Looking beyond the symbolic language, what kind of battle against the Lamb and his followers might this refer to? Acts teaches that those who persecute the members of Christ's body attack Jesus himself (e.g., 22:7–8; see also Matt 25:40, 45; 1 Cor 12:27). What Revelation seems to depict is a Satan-inspired worldwide persecution of Christians at the end of history.[14]

19:20–21   No sooner have the enemies gathered than the war is over. In the end, the beast is no match for the white rider. Christ, the lion of the tribe of Judah, the Lamb with seven eyes and seven horns (5:5–6), triumphs over the beast-antichrist with overwhelming power. Jesus won the victory on the cross, and God exalted him to the place of supreme authority.[15] John describes the outcome since there will be no battle to speak of when Christ returns: **the beast was caught,** or "captured," **and with it the false prophet**, who performed signs and deceived those who accepted the mark of the beast. Both are thrown alive

---

13. Donal A. McIlraith, *Everyone's Apocalypse* (Suva, Fiji: Pacific Regional Seminary, 1995), 93.

14. The †dispensationalist interpretation expects a literal battle against the nation of Israel by the antichrist and an international army on the plain of Megiddo in northern Israel, which is improbable for many reasons. For a discussion of this interpretation, see Revelation Resources at www.Catholic ScriptureCommentary.com.

15. See John 12:31; Eph 1:19–23; Phil 2:9–11; Col 2:13–15; Rev 5:9–10.

into hell, **the fiery pool burning with sulfur**. What other translations refer to as the "lake of fire" is mentioned six times in Revelation and identified as "the second death," the final destination of the devil and evildoers.[16] In the Old Testament fire and foul-smelling sulfur are the judgment that God rains down on the wicked, including Sodom and Gomorrah (Gen 19:24) and Gog and his army (Ezek 38:22).[17] While the beast and the false prophet are thrown alive into the lake of fire, the **rest** are **killed**. This distinction between the immediate fate of the two beasts and their armies confirms the impression that the beasts are superhuman spiritual creatures (see comments on 13:1–2, 18), while their armies are human beings.[18]

The means by which this great victory is accomplished is **the sword that came out of the mouth of the one riding the horse**, the powerful word of Christ. St. Paul describes this battle similarly: "The lawless one will be revealed, whom the Lord [Jesus] will kill with the breath of his mouth and render powerless by the manifestation of his coming" (2 Thess 2:8). God's people do not play any role in the capture of the beast or the destruction of his army. The human allies of the beast and false prophet succumb to the fate foretold of Gog's army in Ezek 39:17–20: **the birds gorged themselves on their flesh**.

The whole battle fulfills the messianic prophecy of Isa 11, which envisions an intervention by a Spirit-anointed descendant of David who wins the decisive battle, after which God's people are gathered from all the nations and nature itself is transformed:

> He shall judge the poor with justice,
>   and decide fairly for the land's afflicted.
> He shall strike the ruthless with the rod of his mouth,
>   and with the breath of his lips he shall slay the wicked. . . .
> Then the wolf shall be a guest of the lamb,
>   and the leopard shall lie down with the young goat;
> The calf and the young lion shall browse together,
>   with a little child to guide them. (Isa 11:4, 6)

Before the new creation begins, however, two more adversaries must be dealt with: Satan and death. Revelation 20 tells the story of their end.

---

16. See Rev 20:10, 14 (twice), 15; 21:8.

17. See also Job 18:14–15; Ps 11:6; Isa 30:33; 34:9. It is described as issuing from the mouths of the demonic horses in Rev 9:17–18, and it characterizes God's judgment of the wicked in 14:10; 19:20; 20:9–10; 21:8.

18. The ultimate fate of the human followers of the beast will also be the lake of fire, but not until after their final judgment (20:12–15).

Reflection and Application (19:11–21)

The portrayal of Jesus in this section is startling and perhaps disturbing. Does Revelation reveal the same Jesus that the Gospels present? Catholic faith in the inspiration, truth, and unity of Scripture tells us that both portrayals faithfully reveal the one Jesus Christ, who is the same yesterday, today, and forever. How can we reconcile these diverse depictions of our Lord?

First, it helps to recall that the Gospels and Revelation employ completely different literary genres to tell us about Jesus. To use an analogy, the four Gospels as ancient biographies are like realistic portraits painted by four different artists. Revelation, belonging to the genre of apocalyptic prophecy, presents Jesus' role in God's plan symbolically through images that vary from vision to vision.

Next we need to distinguish between Jesus' mission in his first coming and his mission in the second. The first time, Jesus came to reveal the face of the Father, to save sinners, to offer himself as a sacrifice for sins, and to draw all people to himself. When he returns, he comes as God's anointed king and judge to save those who are eagerly waiting for him, to destroy evil, to defeat humanity's enemies (including Satan, death, the "beasts," etc.), to judge the living and the dead, and to establish an eternal kingdom of peace.

It is also necessary to set aside any two-dimensional impressions of what either the Gospels or Revelation tell us about Jesus. Although the Gospels show Jesus' mercy toward sinners, they also reveal his severity toward the proud who refuse to repent, toward the rich who hoard their resources, and toward those who refuse to forgive. Jesus' message is not all soft and reassuring; rather, his love moves him more than any other person in the Bible to warn people (especially in the parables) about personal accountability, the danger of hell, and the urgency of repentance.

Similarly, Revelation does show Jesus as the lion of Judah, as judge, warrior, and king; yet by far the most frequent image for Jesus in Revelation (twenty-eight times) is the Lamb who was slain, who has purchased us with his blood and made us a kingdom and priests. From the beginning of the book, Jesus is presented as the one "who loves us and has freed us from our sins by his blood" (1:5). He is the shepherd who leads the thirsty to springs of living water, who leads his one hundred and forty-four thousand close companions wherever he goes; he is the Bridegroom of the Church, and will soon be revealed as the lamp of the new Jerusalem (21:23).

The Millennium, the Dragon's Defeat, and the Final Judgment

Revelation 20:1–15

After the fall of Babylon, Christ's return, and the destruction of the beast and its allies, it would seem that history has finally reached its conclusion. However, the defeat of humanity's most ancient enemy has not yet been told. Rather than simply narrate the devil's end, Rev 20 recounts Satan's story in the context of salvation history (as does Rev 12). First the dragon is bound and confined; then comes the thousand-year reign of the martyrs and saints with Christ; then Satan is released to deceive and lead the nations in a final assault against God's people; finally, the serpent is destroyed forever.

Because the interpretation of the first few paragraphs of Rev 20 is so difficult, I will begin with my conclusions and then explain my reasons as I work through the text. Along with many ancient and modern interpreters, I take the initial binding and confining of Satan to be that which Christ accomplished by his life, death, and resurrection. Furthermore, I interpret the first resurrection and thousand-year reign to refer to the present activity of the martyrs and [†]saints with Christ in heaven during the age of the Church. Finally, I interpret Satan's release at the end of the "thousand years" and the attack of Gog and Magog on "the beloved city" to refer to the same battle of the beast and his allies against the Lamb and his army that is depicted in 19:19–21, symbolizing the Church's final trial.

The concluding part of chapter 20, verses 11–15, depicts the final judgment. With Satan's defeat and the casting of Death and Hades into the lake of fire, all the adversaries of God and his people have met their end, and the way is clear for the full arrival of God's kingdom in chapters 21–22.

The Binding of Satan (20:1–3)

---

[1]Then I saw an angel come down from heaven, holding in his hand the key to the abyss and a heavy chain. [2]He seized the dragon, the ancient serpent, which is the Devil or Satan, and tied it up for a thousand years [3]and threw it into the abyss, which he locked over it and sealed, so that it could no longer lead the nations astray until the thousand years are completed. After this, it is to be released for a short time.

OT: Gen 3:1–15; Isa 24:21–22; 27:1
NT: Matt 12:28–29; John 12:31; Col 2:13–15; Rev 12:7–9
Lectionary: 20:1–4; 20:11–21:2: Friday of the Last Week of the Liturgical Year (Year II)

20:1–3   Like other visions in Revelation (e.g., the sealing of the one hundred and forty-four thousand in 7:1–8 and the birth of the Messiah in 12:1–6), the vision of 20:1–10 does not resume where the vision that immediately preceded it left off—Jesus' second coming and the destruction of the beast and its allies—but rather returns to an earlier point in salvation history, the binding of Satan. The sequence of visions does not mean that the events occur in the order of the visions (the birth of the Messiah in 12:5 is a clear counterexample).

The vision of 20:1–10 [†]recapitulates the vision of Rev 12:7–17 but changes the imagery and completes the story. In Rev 12 the angel Michael throws the dragon down to earth, where in rage he pursues the woman and her children, representing the Church (12:9, 13, 17). His direct attack against the woman and her children is frustrated, so the dragon summons the two beasts (Rev 13), whom he uses to establish a rival kingdom and a deceptive ideology to persecute the Church. Here we learn that **an angel . . . from heaven** carries out God's sentence against **the dragon**, identified again (as in 12:9) as **the ancient serpent . . . the Devil or Satan**. Rather than cast down the dragon from heaven to earth (12:9, 13), in the imagery of the present vision the angel **tied it up** with a **heavy chain** and **threw it into the abyss**, a deep pit metaphorically located beneath the earth (Luke 8:31; see sidebar, "The Abyss," p. 167). With **the key** in his hand, the angel **locked . . . and sealed** the abyss over the serpent, symbolic language indicating the devil's secure restraint.

The *purpose* of the angel imprisoning the dragon in the abyss is **so that it could no longer lead the nations astray**. This phrase is important since back in

Jesus' Victory over Satan through His First Coming

BIBLICAL BACKGROUND

During his earthly ministry, Jesus explained that his power to cast out demons was due to the fact that he had bound the devil: "How can anyone enter a strong man's house and steal his property, unless he first ties up the strong man? Then he can plunder his house" (Matt 12:29).

New Testament texts depict Jesus' victory over demonic power with diverse imagery and emphasize different moments when Jesus' victory was realized:

- Some texts link Jesus' victory over the evil one with his incarnation (John 1:5; 1 John 3:8).
- In the Gospel of John Jesus speaks of conquering the devil through his approaching crucifixion and exaltation: "Now is the time of judgment on this world; now the ruler of this world will be driven out" (John 12:31). Paul echoes this view in Colossians: "Having disarmed the powers and authorities, he made a public spectacle of them, triumphing over them by the cross" (Col 2:15 NIV).[a]
- Ephesians 1:20–21 speaks of Christ seated at God's right hand above all other powers at his resurrection.

These perspectives are complementary rather than contradictory: Jesus conquered the devil through his incarnation, life, death, and resurrection. Nevertheless, these biblical authors all agree that although Satan's power has been defeated, it has not yet been eliminated. The devil is still able to tempt God's people and to oppose God's plan. The complete and final elimination of the devil's influence awaits Christ's glorious return.

a. See also Acts 10:38; 1 Cor 2:6–8; Eph 3:8–10; Heb 2:14.

12:9 the devil is described as the one "who deceived" (same Greek word as "led astray") "the whole world." For **a thousand years** (see explanation in discussion of 20:4–6 below) the devil is no longer able to exercise his former power to deceive **the nations** (*ta ethnē*, a Greek expression equally well translated "the †Gentiles"). The Jews and early Christians recognized the Gentile nations as especially subject to Satan (Acts 26:18; 1 Cor 10:20; Eph 2:1–2; Col 1:13); their worship of idols, in reality offered to demons (1 Cor 10:19–20), showed that they were deceived. Yet through his death and resurrection, Jesus tore open Satan's deceptive web and bound his deceptive powers, rendering the Gentiles receptive to the truth of the gospel. This was the experience of the first Jewish

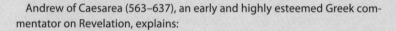

The Binding of Satan in the Abyss according to St. Augustine and Andrew of Caesarea

LIVING TRADITION

St. Augustine (354–430) interprets Rev 20:1–3 in light of Jesus' saying in Matt 19:29 about binding the strong man to plunder his goods:

> By his "goods" that Christ was to "plunder," he means God's future faithful ones whom the devil was keeping for himself because of their ungodliness and various sins. It was for the purpose of binding this strong man that John, in the Apocalypse, saw "an angel coming down out of heaven . . . who bound [the ancient serpent] for a thousand years." The angel, that is, checked and repressed [the devil's] power to seduce and possess those destined to be set free.[a]

Andrew of Caesarea (563–637), an early and highly esteemed Greek commentator on Revelation, explains:

> This passage expresses the destruction of the devil that occurred through the passion of our Lord. For through his passion the one who is stronger than [the devil], namely, Christ our God, bound him who seemed to be strong and freed us, who were his spoils, from his hands and condemned him by throwing him into the pit. . . . The demonstration that the devil is bound is the disappearance of idol worship, the destruction of pagan temples, the abandonment [or] the defilement of [pagan] altars and the knowledge of the will of God throughout the world.[b]

a. *City of God* 20.7, in ACCS 12:322.
b. *Commentary on the Apocalypse* 20:1–3, in ACCS 12:321.

Christian missionaries (Paul and his companions), as Acts recounts. Contrary to their hopes (Rom 9:1–5), the Jewish people as a whole did not embrace the gospel. However, Gentiles in large numbers came to believe in the one true God and in Israel's Messiah. In the centuries that followed, most of the Roman Empire and one Gentile nation after another embraced the good news.

Jesus' victory over Satan did not mean that all satanic opposition ended (Rom 16:20; 2 Cor 12:7; Eph 6:10–17; 1 Thess 2:18).[1] Rather, the binding of Satan in the abyss reflects the change in the overall spiritual situation of the human race that followed Jesus' life, death, and resurrection. Nevertheless, John's vision foresees **a short time** after the thousand years, at the end of the age of the

---

1. According to Beale and McDonough (1145–46), other Jewish writings speak of God or the Messiah binding Satan, preventing him from accusing God's people, or sealing him in the abyss. In each of these cases, the restraint on the devil's activity is not absolute, and Satan is still able to mount some opposition to God's people.

Church, when the devil will **be released** to unleash a final deception on all who dwell on the earth and a final attack on God's people (20:7).

The Thousand-Year Reign of the Martyrs and Saints (20:4–6)

> [4]Then I saw thrones; those who sat on them were entrusted with judgment. I also saw the souls of those who had been beheaded for their witness to Jesus and for the word of God, and who had not worshiped the beast or its image nor had accepted its mark on their foreheads or hands. They came to life and they reigned with Christ for a thousand years. [5]The rest of the dead did not come to life until the thousand years were over. This is the first resurrection. [6]Blessed and holy is the one who shares in the first resurrection. The second death has no power over these; they will be priests of God and of Christ, and they will reign with him for [the] thousand years.

OT: Gen 5:24; 2 Kings 2:11; Dan 7:9–10, 18, 22, 27; 12:1–4
NT: Matt 27:52–53; 1 Cor 6:2–3
Catechism: martyrdom, 2473–74; the saints in heaven, 1023, 1026–28; the blessed share in Christ's rule by interceding, 1029, 1053, 2683; particular judgment, 1021–22; purgatory, 1030–32

This paragraph explains what takes place during the "thousand years" of Satan's confinement in 20:2–3. John begins by saying that he **saw thrones**, seats belonging to individuals exercising authority. Although John does not explicitly say where the thrones are located, heaven is clearly the location, since he is echoing Daniel's statement about seeing heavenly thrones (Dan 7:9), and since the other thrones mentioned in Revelation are not earthly seats of authority. John explains that **those who sat on them were entrusted with judgment**.[2] In the ancient world, judging was part of reigning; there was not a separation of powers between the executive and the judicial functions of government (e.g., Ps 96:10–13; 122:5).

 20:4

The occupants of the thrones are now identified: **the souls of those who had been beheaded for their witness to Jesus and for the word of God**—that is, Christian martyrs (mentioned in 6:9). Although John mentions only those killed by beheading (the common means of executing Roman citizens),[3] the

2. Another way of translating this phrase is "and they sat on them, and judgment was given in their favor," echoing the idea of Dan 7:22 (see Rev 18:20).
3. In the Roman Empire those of lower social standing were usually executed by being crucified, burned alive, or killed in the arena by wild animals.

beheaded stand for all the martyrs by synecdoche, a figure of speech in which one part is named to refer to the whole.

The relationship of the next clause to those beheaded for their testimony is ambiguous in the Greek. Although the NABRE applies it to the martyrs, some interpreters (e.g., the JB and NJB translators) take it to refer to a larger category: faithful Christians who died either by martyrdom or by a natural death but **who had not worshiped the beast or its image nor had accepted its mark**. The difference between these two positions is not as great as it might seem, since most interpreters who think that only the martyrs are explicitly mentioned take them to represent all faithful witnesses to Christ. The martyrs symbolize perfect faithfulness by loving God above everything, including their own lives (12:11). Jesus' promise in the last of the †oracles to the seven churches is directed to *all* who conquer, not only to martyrs: "I will give the victor the right to sit with me on my throne" (3:21).

A special honor awaits these faithful who have died: they **came to life and they reigned with Christ**. The reign of God's people in the future messianic age was a familiar idea in Judaism and early Christianity. It is mentioned three times in Dan 7 (vv. 18, 22, 27) and promised twice in Revelation (5:10 and 22:5). The martyrs and other faithful witnesses who have been raised to life anticipate the blessing promised to all God's people. Although some interpreters take the **thousand years** of Satan's captivity literally, a figurative interpretation better fits the symbolism of the immediate context (key, abyss, heavy chain, dragon, etc.) and of the book as a whole. The Old Testament also often uses the number "thousand" to indicate a very large number rather than a precise quantity (e.g., Deut 7:9; Ps 90:4).

Since the thousand years is followed by the unleashing of Satan and a major assault on the people of God (20:3, 7–9), the †millennium (from the Latin words for "thousand" and "year") cannot symbolize the eternal kingdom of God. Along with others, I understand it to symbolize the age of the Church, during which the martyrs and faithful witnesses who have died reign in heaven with Christ (see "Excursus: Interpretation of 'the Millennium' through History," pp. 329–31, and discussion following 20:10).

20:5   By saying that the **rest of the dead did not come to life** until after this period, John indicates that he is not speaking of the general resurrection that will occur at Christ's return (1 Thess 4:13–17; 1 Cor 15:52). By referring to the experience of "these souls" as the **first resurrection**, John introduces something new, since it is the only place in Scripture that refers to two resurrections.

The Thousand Years according to Andrew of Caesarea

Although some Church Fathers interpreted the thousand years literally, most did not. Andrew of Caesarea (563–637), author of "the standard commentary of the Byzantine tradition,"[a] writes,

> It is in no way good to understand the "thousand years" as referring to a thousand years as such. For when David says "of the word that he commanded for a thousand generations" [Ps 105:8], we ought not to understand this to mean a hundred [generations] times ten. Rather, David means many [generations] taken as a whole. So also in this case, we regard the number "thousand" to signify either many or that which is complete. . . .
>
> Therefore, the "thousand years" are the time from the incarnation of the Lord until the arrival of the antichrist. Whether the matter is as we have interpreted it, or the thousand years are one hundred times ten, as some believe, or the thousand years are less than this, this is known to God alone, who knows how long his patience is beneficial to us, and he determines the continuance of this present life.[b]

a. ACCS 12:xxxi.
b. *Commentary on the Apocalypse* 20.1–3, in ACCS 12:324.

[†]Dispensationalists interpret other biblical passages (e.g., Dan 12:2; John 5:28–29) on the basis of this text to divide the general resurrection of the dead into a resurrection of the just and a resurrection of wicked, separated by a thousand years.[4] However, rather than use a unique and difficult text from a symbolic vision to reinterpret straightforward texts to mean something other than their plain sense, it is better methodology to interpret this obscure text in light of clearer texts.

St. Augustine also struggled with the meaning of "the first resurrection." Drawing on John 5:25—"Amen, amen, I say to you, the hour is coming and is now here when the dead will hear the voice of the Son of God, and those who hear will live"— and baptismal passages from Paul, Augustine concluded that "the first resurrection" refers to the passage from spiritual death to life that takes place in baptism. The problem with Augustine's interpretation is that it fails to

4. See C. I. Scofield, ed., *The New Scofield Reference Bible* (New York: Oxford University Press, 1967), note on 20:5. However, Dan 12:2 and John 5:28–29 do not indicate a time interval between the resurrection of the just and the wicked; rather, they imply that the two groups will rise at the same time. John 5:28–29 is explicit: "the hour is coming in which all who are in the tombs will hear his voice and will come out, those who have done good deeds to the resurrection of life, but those who have done wicked deeds to the resurrection of condemnation."

do justice to the immediate context, 20:4–5a, where Revelation clearly refers to "the souls of those who had been beheaded" coming to life.

The simplest solution is that the first resurrection refers to the life with Christ in heaven that the blessed, including martyrs, experience immediately after death (Luke 23:43; Phil 1:23; see Catechism 954). Although the expressions "came to life" and "resurrection" normally refer to bodily resurrection, in the context of a vision with many symbolic elements, a figurative use of these terms is not surprising.

20:6   John declares this rising a special privilege by holding it up for admiration in a †beatitude: **Blessed . . . is the one who shares in the first resurrection**. Not only are the recipients of this honor blessed, but they are also **holy**—that is, associated with God himself in a special way. Furthermore, they are exempt from the power of the **second death**, later explained as the "pool of fire" (20:14; 21:8). Albert Vanhoye explains that they enjoy "complete and definitive security, something which [they] could not possess before."[5]

Not only are these faithful preserved from the terrifying second death, but **they will be priests of God and of Christ, and they will reign with him for [the] thousand years** of the church age before Christ's return. John has twice affirmed that through the offering of his life, Christ has *already* made Christians on earth "into a kingdom" and consecrated them "priests for his God and Father" (1:6; 5:9–10). This vision of the millennium indicates that the martyrs and other faithful in heaven exercise their priesthood and royalty in an even greater way that anticipates the ultimate destiny of all God's people. Slight changes in wording from previous texts in Revelation highlight the differences. These Christians are not only priests "*for* his God and Father" (1:6, emphasis added; see 5:10), but they are also priests *of* God and *of* Christ, belonging entirely to God and his divine Messiah. Furthermore, their effective sharing in Christ's kingly authority begins before Christ's second coming and the definitive arrival of the kingdom of God: "they will reign with him for [the] thousand years." Other New Testament texts promise that Jesus' disciples who renounce everything or endure trials for his sake will share in his reign (Matt 19:27–28; Luke 22:28–30; 2 Tim 2:12). Vanhoye draws out the implications:

> Since they have participated more intensely in the Passion of Christ they have, without waiting, an effective participation in his reign. The martyrs and the saints "live" (20:5) already with Christ and just as the fruitfulness of the Passion of Christ has been manifested not only by his heavenly glory but also by the extension of

5. Albert Vanhoye, *The Old Testament Priests and the New Priest* (Petersham, MA: St. Bede's Publications, 1980), 300.

his spiritual reign upon the earth, so, in the same way, the martyrs and saints will enjoy power upon the earth in union with him. . . . This reign is closely connected with their priesthood, that is to say, with the privileged relationship which they henceforth enjoy with Christ and with God.[6]

Earlier visions in this book hinted at the priestly and royal role of the martyrs and other faithful in heaven during the Church's earthly pilgrimage. The twenty-four elders, heavenly representatives of the Church and likely participants in the first resurrection, worship God and the Lamb and offer the prayers of God's people on earth (5:8). In 7:9–17 those "coming out of the great tribulation" (7:14 ESV) worship before God and the Lamb in his temple. The word that is used for "temple" (Greek *naos*) refers to the part of Israel's temple that only priests were allowed to enter. In a vision immediately before the seven last plagues, John sees the liturgical worship of "those who had won the victory over the beast" in heaven on "a sea of glass mingled with fire," where they sing the song of Moses and the song of the Lamb (15:2–4). In 19:1–8 the heavenly multitude before the throne offers liturgical praise for the fall of Babylon and the arrival of the wedding day of the Lamb.

These texts indicate that the priestly and royal role of the martyrs and saints in heaven entails their complete, unrestricted, and immediate participation in the worship constantly taking place before God's throne. From there they are in a position to intercede for the Church and the world and to help shape the outcome of human history, reigning with Christ by means of their priestly intercession. What else their reign with Christ might entail in this "thousand years" before his second coming has not been disclosed to us.

Reflection and Application (20:4–6)

Invoking the saints. Vanhoye relates the heavenly reign and priesthood of the martyrs and other blessed in heaven to the ancient Christian tradition of asking them to pray for us:

> And so in this passage of Revelation we are entitled to recognize not only one of the first testimonies which the Church has, from a very early date, accorded to its martyrs and saints, but also the foundation for the piety which has led Christians from the earliest centuries to turn to them for their intercession. If they are priests with Christ and reign with him, it is certainly not useless to address ourselves to them.[7]

6. Ibid., 305.
7. Ibid.

Previous generations of Catholics showed more confidence in the intercessory role of the saints and martyrs than most Christians do today. They manifested their devotion to the martyrs and saints by venerating their relics and imploring their intercession, and their faith was rewarded. St. Augustine recounts many miracles in book 12 of *The City of God*, including a blind man who was healed at the finding of the relics of the martyrs Protasius and Gervasius. Churches dedicated to heavenly patrons across Europe, even in small villages, preserve the memory of miraculous conversions, healings, and deliverances from plague or conquest; they testify to the heavenly reign of the martyrs and saints with Christ.

Aspiring to "the first resurrection." Revelation's seven beatitudes (see sidebar, "Seven Beatitudes of the Apocalypse," p. 249) guide the aspirations of readers to true values by describing a group of people as fortunate or happy and praising the basis of their happiness. The fifth beatitude (20:6) announces the good fortune of those who attain to the first resurrection; they are exempt from the second death, belong to God and Christ as priests, and reign with Christ for a thousand years. This beatitude summons readers to wholeheartedly reject compromise with sin and the power of the world. The encouragement to be counted among the martyrs and others who remain faithful through trials is directed to all who hear the words of this book: it is a universal call to holiness.

Prayers for the dead. Scripture, tradition, and experience suggest that not all who belong to God's people die in a state of readiness to be in God's presence (see, e.g., 2 Macc 12:40–46). Jewish rituals of mourning traditionally included prayers for God's mercy on and forgiveness for the dead. The early Christians assumed this perspective and practice, as inscriptions and graffiti in the catacombs illustrate. The Catechism 1030–31 explains the Catholic understanding:

> All who die in God's grace and friendship, but still imperfectly purified, are indeed assured of their eternal salvation; but after death they undergo purification, so as to achieve the holiness necessary to enter the joy of heaven.
>
> The Church gives the name *Purgatory* to this final purification of the elect [cf. Council of Florence (1439): DS 1304; Council of Trent (1563): DS 1820; (1547): 1580; see also Benedict XII, *Benedictus Deus* (1336): DS 1000].

Since God alone knows the consciences of men and women, the Catholic Church recommends offering Mass, prayers, and other sacrifices on behalf of all who have died (see Catechism 1032).

Excursus: Interpretation of "the Millennium" through History

Christian interpretation of the thousand-year reign of the martyrs and other faithful with Christ, also called the †millennium, has been quite diverse.[8] Some early and highly respected Christian teachers, including Papias (d. 135), Justin Martyr (d. 165), Irenaeus (d. 202), Tertullian (d. ca. 220), and Victorinus (d. 303), expected a literal thousand-year period of an earthly paradise when Christ and the saints would rule the nations and biblical prophecies about a transformed creation (e.g., Isa 65:17–25) would be fulfilled within history—a view called †chiliasm or †millenarianism. A common idea was that history would follow the pattern of creation. After the first six days (each a thousand years in accord with Ps 90:4), a sabbath of one thousand years of Messianic earthly reign would precede the eternal kingdom.

However, belief in a millennial earthly paradise before the eternal kingdom came to be associated with hopes for extraordinary material prosperity and bodily pleasure. In reaction, other ancient writers such as Origen (ca. 185–254), Dionysius of Alexandria (ca. 198–264), and Jerome (ca. 347–420) interpreted the millennium in an allegorical and moral sense: Armageddon became the "triumph of God over sin and vice," and the thousand-year reign became the period when people embraced "obedience and chastity, for Satan is bound whenever people resist evil thoughts."[9]

In the early fifth century, Augustine (354–430), following Tyconius (ca. 380), taught that the thousand-year reign of Christ and the saints began with Christ's first coming and continues in the Church until Christ's second coming—a view called amillennialism.[10] The first resurrection is spiritual and occurs in baptism; the second resurrection is the general physical resurrection of the just and the unjust at the end of history. The thrones of 20:4 are the sees of bishops. The conversion of Constantine and the spread of Christianity through the empire shows that Satan is confined to the hearts of unbelievers, and the reign of the saints has begun. In the present reign of the Church, the wheat and the tares remain mixed together until the last judgment and the beginning of the †eschatological kingdom. Before that occurs, the devil will be released and will test the Church. Augustine's interpretation became the dominant one through the early Middle Ages and beyond.

---

8. For helpful overviews, see Craig R. Koester, *Revelation and the End of All Things* (Grand Rapids: Eerdmans, 2001), 3–8; Judith Kovacs and Christopher Rowland, *Revelation* (Oxford: Blackwell, 2004), 200–214; and ACCS 12:320–36.

9. Koester, *Revelation*, 6.

10. Augustine, *City of God* 20.6–9.

Late medieval interpreters such as Alexander Minorita (d. 1271) and Peter Olivi (1248-98) speculated that the thousand years refers to the Church's ascendancy that began with the conversion of Constantine in the early fourth century, and would end with the release of Satan in the fourteenth century. The occurrence of the Great Western Schism (1348-1417) and the bubonic plague (1346-53), called the Black Death, confirmed this interpretation in the eyes of some. The Reformation period saw various revivals of †millenarianism, as well as revivals of Augustine's interpretation by the leading Reformers. Catholic interpreters of the sixteenth century also inclined toward Augustine's view. The Jesuit commentator Francisco Ribera (1537-91) interpreted the thousand years to be the period between Christ's death and the coming of the antichrist. In contrast to Augustine, however, Ribera held that the millennial rule belongs to the souls of the faithful departed in heaven rather than to the Church on earth.[11]

Some subsequent interpreters expected the millennial kingdom to come gradually as the Church fulfills its mission, culminating in Christ's return—referred to as postmillennialism. Revivalists such as Jonathan Edwards (1703-58) expected the millennium to be inaugurated through outpourings of the Spirit. Likewise, Charles Finney (1792-1875) envisioned the millennium as being inaugurated by evangelism and social reform such as the end of slavery and the promotion of temperance, with the timing of its arrival dependent on people's response (see 2 Pet 3:12). Twentieth-century Protestant advocates of the "social gospel" likewise adopted a postmillennial view. Some Catholics today expect a temporal era of peace, triumph, and unity for the Church before Satan's final assault, the return of Christ, and the eternal kingdom.[12]

The leading interpretation of the millennium among fundamentalist and some evangelical Christians today, premillennial †dispensationalism, arose in the early nineteenth century. According to this interpretation, Christ will return before the great tribulation (see sidebar, "The Great Tribulation," pp. 146-47), raise believers who have died, and †rapture—snatch up—all true Christians to heaven. After seven years Christ will return with the Church and defeat the beast, the false prophet, and their armies. Then the Church will reign with Christ for a thousand years on a transformed earth, fulfilling Isa 65:18-25, "in a time of universal peace, prosperity, long life, and prevailing righteousness."[13] While the faithful Christians whom Christ has raised will live forever, the people who

11. Kenneth G. C. Newport, *Apocalypse and Millennium: Studies in Biblical Eisegesis* (Cambridge: Cambridge University, 2000), 76. My interpretation is similar to Ribera's.

12. For example, Joseph Iannuzzi, OSJ, *The Triumph of God's Kingdom in the Millennium and End Times* (Havertown, PA: St. John the Evangelist Press, 1999).

13. Scofield, *New Scofield Reference Bible*, 1373, notes on 20:2, 4.

survive the tribulation and live during the millennium will enjoy long lives (Isa 65:20). Then Satan will be released for a short time and organize an uprising that takes the form of a military assault against the reign of Christ and the saints in Jerusalem. God will intervene to send fire from heaven to consume the armies of Gog and Magog and to cast Satan into the lake of fire. Then the unrighteous who have died will be raised and judged, and God's eternal reign will begin.

The Catholic Church rejects †millenarianism, interpretations like dispensationalism that expect a visible earthly reign of Christ before the final judgment.[14] The Church also rejects the view that Christ's kingdom will come to pass through a human political program, through a "secular messianism" (Catechism 676), or even through the "progressive ascendancy" of the Church (Catechism 677). Rather, the kingdom will come "only by God's victory over the final unleashing of evil," and the descent of the new Jerusalem from heaven (Catechism 677).

Judgment of the Devil (20:7–10)

[7]When the thousand years are completed, Satan will be released from his prison. [8]He will go out to deceive the nations at the four corners of the earth, Gog and Magog, to gather them for battle; their number is like the sand of the sea. [9]They invaded the breadth of the earth and surrounded the camp of the holy ones and the beloved city. But fire came down from heaven and consumed them. [10]The Devil who had led them astray was thrown into the pool of fire and sulfur, where the beast and the false prophet were. There they will be tormented day and night forever and ever.

OT: 2 Kings 1:10–14; Isa 66:15–17, 24; Ezek 38–39
NT: Rev 16:13–16; 19:17–21
Catechism: the Church's final trial, 675; millenarianism and secular messianism, 676; final unleashing of evil, 677, 680
Lectionary: 20:1–4; 20:11–21:2: Friday of the Last Week of the Liturgical Year (Year II)

Just as 20:4–6 explains the "thousand years" mentioned in 20:2–3, this paragraph explains the release of Satan "for a short time" (end of 20:3). Here the locked and sealed abyss where Satan has been bound is referred to as **his prison**.

20:7–8

14. In 1944 the Holy Office published a decision with the approval of Pope Pius XII that "mitigated millenarianism," which teaches a visible earthly reign of Christ before the final judgment, cannot be safely taught (DS 3839). This is not a definitive denial of that interpretation but an authoritative pastoral directive against teaching it.

St. Augustine on the Final Battle

LIVING TRADITION

St. Augustine interprets Rev 20:8–9:

> This is to be the very last of all persecutions immediately preceding the very last of all judgments—a persecution that holy church, the worldwide city of Christ, is to suffer at the hands of the worldwide city of the devil, in every place where the two cities will then extend. [This] obviously does not mean that they gathered or will gather in some one place where, we must suppose, the camp of the saints and the beloved city is to be. For, of course, this city is Christ's church, which is spread over the whole world. Wherever his church will be (and it will be among all nations, "over the breadth of the earth"), there is to be the camp of the saints and the beloved city of God. There will she be surrounded by all her enemies, intermingled with her as they are and will be in every people, girded with the appalling magnitude of that besetting, hemmed in, straitened and encompassed by the pressures of that mighty affliction.[a]

a. *City of God* 20.11–12, in ACCS 12:339, 341.

As noted in the comment on 20:3, the binding and imprisonment of Satan means that the devil's power has been severely curtailed but not completely eliminated. Jesus explains his ability to perform exorcisms as evidence that he has bound the devil (Matt 12:29; Mark 3:27; Luke 11:21–22), but that binding does not prevent Satan from continuing to oppose Jesus and his disciples (Luke 4:13; 22:3, 31; John 13:27). The dragon was bound and confined "so that it could no longer lead the nations astray" until after the thousand years (20:3). Now he is **released**—a [†]divine passive indicating that even this event is subject to God's divine control—**to deceive the nations** and **to gather them for battle**. The Greek uses the definite article: Satan gathers them for *the* battle, referring to the last battle foretold by the prophets (especially in Ezek 38–39) and by Rev 16:14–16, the battle at Armageddon, and already recounted in Rev 19:17–21. This retelling of the story reveals the destiny of Satan, the ultimate adversary (Gen 3; Rev 12:9; 20:2). The fact that he musters [†]nations **at the four corners of the earth** indicates a worldwide attack; mentioning that **their number is like the sand of the sea** emphasizes the magnitude of the opposition, echoing a simile used of enemies in previous unsuccessful attacks on God's people in the Bible (Josh 11:4; Judg 7:12; 1 Sam 13:5). The reference to **Gog and Magog** indicates that this battle is the fulfillment of Ezekiel's vision (Ezek 38–39, alluded to in Rev 19:17–21) in which Gog, king of Magog, gathers the nations to fight against Israel (Ezek 38:15–18).

In Greek the phrase **they invaded the breadth of the earth** (literally, "they 20:9
went up on the plain of the earth") echoes Ezek 38:11, 16 regarding the army of
Gog and Hab 1:6, which describes the advance of Babylon's army. The **camp of
the holy ones**, that is, the Church, alludes to Israel's camp around the tabernacle
(see Num 2; 10–11; Deut 23:15) during the wilderness journey, a period the
New Testament interprets as prefiguring the age of the Church (1 Cor 10:1–11;
Heb 3:1–4:3; Rev 12:6, 14). Likewise, **the beloved city** refers †typologically to
God's covenant people as Jerusalem, the heavenly city of God already spiritually
present in history (Gal 4:26; Heb 12:22), even though its full arrival as the city
that descends from above awaits the end. The phrase "beloved city" emphasizes
an important theme of Revelation, the spousal love of the Lamb for his Bride,[15]
especially in her hour of trial.

By saying **fire came down from heaven and consumed them**, John echoes
descriptions of God's fiery judgment against Gog and Magog (Ezek 38:22; 39:6),
using a phrase from the story of God's sending fire from heaven to consume
the soldiers who came after Elijah in 2 Kings 1:10–14. Like the account of the
Word of God killing the beast's army with the sword issuing from his mouth
(19:15, 19–20), this is not a literal description but rather imagery that depicts
divine destruction of those who seek to destroy God's people (1 Cor 3:17).

In several places Revelation foretells an extraordinary unleashing of evil
in an attack on the Church of Christ before history's end. The first instance is
the power granted the beast to conquer and kill the two witnesses when their
powerful testimony is completed (11:7). Another is found in the introduction
of the beast who is "allowed to wage war against the holy ones and conquer
them" (13:7; also 13:8–18). Then again, Revelation refers to the final battle when
the sixth bowl is poured out and the kings of the whole world are assembled at
Armageddon (16:13–16), when the ten kings join the beast to make war on the
Lamb (17:12–14), and when the beast, the king, and their armies are gathered
to fight the white rider and his army (19:17–21). The present text is the final
account of evil's assault on the people of God, focusing on God's response and
the defeat of the devil.

Many commentators, ancient and modern, interpret these texts to speak of
the same end-time persecution of Christians. As Augustine argues (see sidebar,
"St. Augustine on the Final Battle," p. 332), these accounts refer not to physical
warfare in one location but rather to a worldwide persecution of God's people.

The Devil, the spiritual being who **led . . . astray,** or "deceived," people from 20:10
all †nations to attack the Church, now receives his requital. One can hardly

15. See Rev 1:5; 3:9, 19; 19:7; 21:2, 9.

imagine committing a greater evil than to lure people into sin that brings about their destruction (Matt 18:6–7). At last the dragon, the ancient serpent, Satan, the one who started it all (Gen 3; Rev 12), is **thrown into the pool of fire and sulfur**. In this punishment he joins his agents, **the beast and the false prophet**. Although the NABRE, like many translations, implies that the two beasts precede the devil in the lake of fire by saying they **were** there, the Greek text does not include a verb indicating sequence: the point of the text is that all three end up in the same place. The terrible fate of the diabolical trinity is not annihilation; rather, **they will be tormented day and night forever**. Since Satan and his agents are spiritual beings that do not have bodies, the torment of the lake of fire and sulfur is imagery that refers to extraordinary spiritual suffering.

Before concluding this consideration of "the thousand years" and the assault on "the beloved city," it is worth offering a few reasons, in addition to what has already been said, why the †dispensationalist interpretation of these events seems improbable.[16] First, Revelation's apocalyptic genre and the fact that visions in the Bible normally convey their message in symbolic terms make it likely that here also the author is speaking in symbolic terms. Second, it is hard to imagine a literal millennial age that is not strange and contradictory. What kind of life would the resurrected martyrs and faithful Christians live during their reign with Christ on earth while sin and death continue to characterize the rest of the population? One would think that Christ and his faithful followers would be well positioned to render persuasive evangelical testimony! At the end of the thousand years, would the wicked think themselves able to defeat the deathless saints and the risen Christ? Would the latter be incapable of dealing with an insurrection before their land is invaded and city surrounded? Finally, the prophecy of Israel's glorious future (Isa 65:18–25) that some ancient and modern interpreters apply to a literal earthly millennium makes better sense as a poetic depiction of life in the eternal kingdom.[17] This is especially true since Isaiah paints that idyllic picture as the situation *after* God creates "new heavens / and a new earth" (Isa 65:17), an event that Revelation places at the beginning of the vision of the new Jerusalem (21:1).

16. For more on this subject, see the online Revelation Resources at www.CatholicScriptureCommentary.com.

17. Although Isa 65:20 mentions death, it does so only as a way of describing extraordinarily long life. Lacking the clearer understanding of eternal life that Christians have as a result of the resurrection of Christ, the Old Testament authors sometimes speak only of long life (see, e.g., Ps 23:6).

Reflection and Application (20:7–9)

Are we living in the last days? Many passages in the New Testament indicate that the life, death, and resurrection of Jesus began the final phase of human history (Acts 2:17; 1 Cor 10:11; Heb 9:26). The question is whether we are living in the period *immediately* before Christ's return. The fact that many Christians in the past have thought they were living near history's end rightly makes us cautious about jumping to conclusions. Nevertheless, it is a legitimate question, since Christ urged us to be watchful, and Scripture and Tradition teach that certain events will precede his return.

In his †Olivet discourse Jesus declares that "this gospel of the kingdom will be preached throughout the world as a witness to all nations, and then the end will come" (Matt 24:14). The Church's testimony to the nations is progressing toward that goal. Almost all nations (cultural-linguistic groups) have heard the gospel, and the number of Christians in Africa and Asia is rapidly increasing. Although the recognition of the Messiah by "all Israel" (Rom 11:26; Catechism 674) has not occurred, since the late twentieth century there has been a marked increase in the number of Jews who recognize Jesus as the Messiah.[18]

The presence of negative signs must also be noted. The millions who died in the wars and natural disasters of the twentieth century recall the warning events that accompany the seals and trumpets in Rev 6 and 8–9 (see "Reflection and Application" on 9:1–21). Some societal trends bring to mind the the "final trial" through which the Church must pass before the end (Catechism 675). Has the abyss been opened and Satan released to deceive the nations (9:1–6; 20:7–8)? Beast-like totalitarian governments, sometimes overseeing vast empires, have demanded the equivalent of worship, requiring absolute submission to leaders, the state, ideologies, or political parties, denying their citizens freedom of religion and conscience. Some of these have launched fierce persecutions of Christians, with the result that the number of twentieth-century martyrs exceeds all the martyrs of previous centuries combined, while the persecution and murder of Christians in many parts of the world continues. Although as of this writing no beast figure (2 Thess 2:3–4, 8–10; Rev 13) comparable to the twentieth-century dictators is in sight, political change can occur rapidly and unexpectedly.

Meanwhile, an international, immoral, and materialistic culture resembling Babylon has arisen and diffuses itself through the world via markets, advertising, the entertainment industry, the mass media, and the elites that control

---

18. For a history of this movement, see Dan Cohn-Sherbok, *Messianic Judaism* (New York: Continuum, 2000).

public education. It seduces people to embrace its values and to abandon faith and obedience to God and his word. The consequent apostasy (2 Thess 2:3) of large numbers from Christianity in Europe and the Americas is historically unprecedented.[19]

So are we living in the last days? Like the Christians who faced great trials in the past, it is impossible to know for certain whether we are living at the end or in a time of crisis that foreshadows it. What is important is to heed what Revelation says about responding to the challenges we face. John's prophecy summons Christians to discern the spiritual forces at work in the world, to love God and to reject idols, to refuse to compromise with greed or lust, to resist evil in the face of political, economic, or social pressures. We are to keep bearing witness to the gospel, persevering in trial, praying, hoping, and rejoicing in anticipation of Christ's glorious return. Jesus' words apply: "When these signs begin to happen, stand erect and raise your heads because your redemption is at hand" (Luke 21:28).

Judgment of the Dead, Death Destroyed (20:11–15)

---

[11]Next I saw a large white throne and the one who was sitting on it. The earth and the sky fled from his presence and there was no place for them. [12]I saw the dead, the great and the lowly, standing before the throne, and scrolls were opened. Then another scroll was opened, the book of life. The dead were judged according to their deeds, by what was written in the scrolls. [13]The sea gave up its dead; then Death and Hades gave up their dead. All the dead were judged according to their deeds. [14]Then Death and Hades were thrown into the pool of fire. (This pool of fire is the second death.) [15]Anyone whose name was not found written in the book of life was thrown into the pool of fire.

OT: Isa 51:6; 66:24; Dan 2:35; 7:9–10; 12:1–2
NT: 1 Cor 15:22–28; 2 Cor 5:10; 2 Pet 3:7, 10
Catechism: Christ's judgment and its basis, 678–79, 682
Lectionary: 20:1–4; 20:11–21:2: Friday of the Last Week of the Liturgical Year (Year II)

Now John sees another vision of the final judgment, this one focusing on the judgment of the dead. An earlier vision of the final judgment, that of the

---

19. The closest historical parallel might be the near disappearance of Christianity in North Africa and parts of the Middle East after the Muslim conquest of the seventh century. The difference is that the apostasy of the West has been voluntary rather than the result of coercion.

harvest of the earth (14:14–20), focused on the judgment of those living on the earth at the end of history.

The first thing John sees is a **throne**; he describes it as **large**, or "great," dis-   20:11
tinguishing it from the thrones of the saints and martyrs mentioned in 20:4. It is **white**, the color of victory, purity, and holiness. The text does not identify **the one who was sitting on it**. The New Testament speaks of God the Father as judge and also of Christ as judge.[20] In John 5 (vv. 22, 27, 30), Jesus indicates that the Father has given judgment to the Son, but that the Son judges accord-ing to the will of the Father.

John's vision that **earth and the sky fled from his presence and there was no place for them** might mean no more than creation's awe before its creator and judge. However, other biblical prophecies speak of the destruction of the present creation before the "new heavens and earth" appear. Isaiah writes, "The heavens will vanish like smoke, the earth will wear out like a garment" (Isa 51:6 RSV; see also 2 Pet 3:7, 10). When the new heaven and new earth appear in the next chapter, John tells us that "the former heaven and the former earth had passed away" (21:1).[21]

Now John reports a vision of the last judgment. He sees **the dead, the great**   20:12
and the lowly, standing before the throne. No one escapes this day of reckon-ing, regardless of rank or social standing, but all await the judge's verdict. Then **scrolls were opened** as in Daniel's vision (Dan 7:10). The scrolls, or "books," represent the divine record of the acts of human beings, whether good or bad: **The dead were judged according to their deeds** in light of God's perfect record of them, **written in the scrolls**. Jesus prophesies about this moment: "There is nothing concealed that will not be revealed, nor secret that will not be known" (Luke 12:2; see 1 Cor 4:5; Heb 4:13).

Although St. Paul stresses that human beings are saved by grace (Eph 2:8–9), he also firmly teaches that we will be judged by our works: "We must all appear before the judgment seat of Christ, so that each one may receive recompense, according to what he did in the body, whether good or evil" (2 Cor 5:10).[22] There will be no escaping the fact that God knows, will bring

---

20. Matt 6:4; 18:35; and Rom 14:10 speak of the Father as judge; Matt 7:22–23; 25:31–46; and 2 Cor 5:10 speak of Christ as judge.

21. Other biblical texts point to elements of continuity between this creation and the next (e.g., Rom 8:19–21). While all agree that the new heaven and new earth entail a radical discontinuity with the present, Christian interpreters differ regarding whether the present order will be destroyed or radically transformed. See Daniel Keating on 2 Pet 3:10–13 in *First and Second Peter, Jude*, CCSS (Grand Rapids: Baker Academic, 2011), 180–85.

22. For more on judgment according to works, see also Matt 16:27; 25:31–46; Rom 2:5–16; 14:12; 1 Cor 3:12–15; 1 Pet 1:17.

to light, and will judge us for what we have done or failed to do, in thought, word, or deed.

The necessity of divine grace is indicated by the next phrase. **Then another scroll was opened, the book of life**. This scroll, mentioned in another of Daniel's visions (12:1–2) and already referred to three times in Revelation (3:5; 13:8, 17:8), contains the names of those who have accepted God's gift of eternal life. The image of a "scroll" or "book" refers to the register of a city's citizens in the ancient world. This register names the citizens of the new Jerusalem. In 13:8 the book of life is described as belonging "to the Lamb who was slain"; it names those whom the Lamb has "purchased for God" with his blood "from every tribe and tongue, people and nation" (5:9; regarding free will, see the comment on 13:8).

Those listed in the book of life are not excused from judgment "according to their deeds." Rather, their conduct confirms their election (2 Pet 1:10), since "they have washed their robes and made them white in the blood of the Lamb" (7:14) through repentance, faith, and baptism. God's grace has produced good works (Titus 2:11–13).

20:13   This verse †recapitulates 20:12 with more detail about how all the dead arrive at the last judgment: **The sea gave up its dead**. In the ancient world it was sometimes thought that those who died at sea were not able to pass to Hades, the place of the dead. John's vision indicates that no one escapes this judgment, wherever they may have died. Then **Death and Hades**, personified together, are compelled to yield **their dead**. How did this come about? In John's opening vision the risen Jesus, revealed as the regal figure of Dan 7:13–14, declares, "I hold the keys to death and the netherworld [literally, Hades]" (1:18). The general resurrection will occur when Jesus summons all the dead: "The hour is coming in which all who are in the tombs will hear his voice and will come out" (John 5:28–29).

20:14–15   The final verses of the chapter report the verdict. First, **Death and Hades were thrown into the pool of fire**. They were the first enemies mentioned in Revelation (1:18) and are the last to be defeated. As St. Paul says, after Christ "has destroyed every sovereignty and every authority and power, . . . the last enemy to be destroyed is death" (1 Cor 15:24, 26). The "fiery pool burning with sulfur" was mentioned in 19:20 as the final destination of the beast and the false prophet, and in 20:10 as the final destination of the devil himself. It is fitting that death, the devil's tool (Wis 2:24; Heb 2:14–15), should share the fate of the one who wielded it. John explains that the lake of fire is the same as **the second death**, from which everyone who "shares in the first resurrection" is safe (20:6).

Tragically, the lake of fire also becomes the final destination of human beings who, despite many warnings, refused to repent of their evildoing (2:21–22; 9:20–21; 16:9–11), rejecting the love and forgiveness available through the blood of the Lamb (1:5). These are the ones whose names are **not found written in the book of life**, indicating that because of their refusal, they do not belong to God's chosen people destined for salvation. The imagery of perpetual fire originates in the last chapter of Isaiah, which speaks of God gathering his people from all the nations to establish his kingdom and of inextinguishable fire as the final punishment of the wicked (Isa 66:24). John the Baptist (Matt 3:10, 12) and Jesus (Matt 7:19; 13:40–42; 18:8–9) invite people to repent, warning of this terrible fire that awaits the wicked. In his parable about the judgment of the nations Jesus foretells what takes place here: the king "will say to those on his left, 'Depart from me, you accursed, into the eternal fire prepared for the devil and his angels'" (Matt 25:41).

Sin is the root of all the evils that have befallen the human race; without this means of access, even Satan would be powerless (Col 2:13–15). After dealing with the root through his sacrificial death (1:5; 5:9), the risen and exalted Lamb relentlessly reverses all of sin's consequences, making forgiveness and the power of his own Spirit available to human beings, proclaiming the gospel to the world through the Church, and judging the demonic powers and human beings who refuse to repent (1 Cor 15:22–28). Revelation 6–20 tells the story of how Christ carries out God's plan inscribed in the scroll that was revealed in chapter 5 and entrusted to the prophet in chapter 10. The final two chapters of Revelation reveal what awaits the human race on the other side of the problem of human sin, which God has solved through Jesus Christ.

Reflection and Application (20:11–15)

Human freedom and the pool of fire. The prospect of eternal suffering in hell is truly disturbing, even though the possibility of rejecting God follows logically from human freedom. People who claim that God will not allow anyone to end up in hell fail to realize that their well-meaning optimism reduces human beings to pets or robots, like the Stepford wives, who cannot help but be pleasing. While repentance and salvation are available until the last second of life, everyday experience and Scripture suggest that many refuse the offer. C. S. Lewis offers a deeper and more realistic explanation than universalism:

> There are only two kinds of people in the end: those who say to God, "Thy will be done," and those to whom God says, in the end, "Thy will be done." All that

are in Hell, choose it. Without that self-choice there could be no Hell. No soul that seriously and constantly desires joy will ever miss it. "Those who seek find. To those who knock it is opened."[23]

The realistic teaching of Scripture about the danger of hell has motivated count-less priests, religious, missionaries, and laypeople to make great sacrifices in order to announce the good news about the Lamb's victory so that as many people as possible may come to the knowledge of the truth and so be saved (1 Tim 2:4). As St. Paul says, "Since we know the fear of the Lord, we try to persuade others. . . . For the love of Christ impels us, once we have come to the conviction that one died for all . . ." (2 Cor 5:11, 14).

23. C. S. Lewis, *The Great Divorce* (New York: Macmillan, 1946), 72–73.

The New Creation and the Bride of the Lamb

Revelation 21:1–27

When all the adversaries of God have been defeated and every human being has rendered an account of his or her life before Christ, then the fulfillment of God's gracious plan will come to pass (Eph 2:7). John provides a preview of what awaits God's people, using Old Testament prophecies and symbolic language. While its exact shape remains hidden behind splendid images, John's vision reveals important truths about our ultimate future.

Two visions that unveil the final phase of God's plan comprise all of Rev 21 and the first paragraph of chapter 22. The first vision here (21:1–8) completes a series of four (starting at 19:11) reporting how God brings history to its goal and provides an overview of the new order. The second (21:9–22:11) parallels the vision of Babylon and its fall (17:1–19:10) and provides a close-up of the Lamb's Bride, the new Jerusalem, the polar opposite of the harlot Babylon. An epilogue concludes the book (22:12–21).

Heaven Comes to Earth, God Comes to Dwell with His People (21:1–4)

¹Then I saw a new heaven and a new earth. The former heaven and the former earth had passed away, and the sea was no more. ²I also saw the holy city, a new Jerusalem, coming down out of heaven from God, prepared as a bride adorned for her husband. ³I heard a loud voice from the throne saying, "Behold, God's dwelling is with the human race. He will dwell

with them and they will be his people and God himself will always be with
them [as their God]. [4]He will wipe every tear from their eyes, and there
shall be no more death or mourning, wailing or pain, [for] the old order
has passed away."

OT: Isa 52:1; 61:10–11; 62:4–5; 65:16–25; 66:22
NT: 2 Pet 3:10–13
Catechism: new heaven and new earth, 1042–50; Church as God's temple and Bride, 756–57, 796
Lectionary: 21:1–5a: Fifth Sunday of Easter (Year C); 20:1–4; 20:11–21:2: Friday of the Last Week
of the Liturgical Year (Year II)

21:1 John's vision of a **new heaven and a new earth** depicts the fulfillment of
the prophecy at the end of the book of Isaiah: "The former things shall not be
remembered / nor come to mind. / Instead, shout for joy and be glad forever /
in what I am creating" (Isa 65:17–18). According to John, **the former heaven
and the former earth had passed away**. Second Peter says that when Christ
returns, "The heavens will pass away with a mighty roar and the elements will be
dissolved by fire, and the earth and everything done on it will be found out," to
clear the way for "new heavens and a new earth in which righteousness dwells"
(2 Pet 3:10, 13). When God completes his redemption of the human race, he
will radically renew creation so it can be "set free from slavery to corruption
and share in the glorious freedom of the children of God" (Rom 8:21).[1] The
statement that **the sea was no more** refers to the sea as a symbol of unruly
chaos (Gen 1:1), the lair of the evil serpent (Isa 27:1), the beast's place of origin
(13:1). These words should not be interpreted as a literal description of the new
creation, indicating there will be no large bodies of water in it. The vision of
the †eschatological temple in Ezek 47 tells how the Dead Sea will be renewed
by the river flowing from the temple. Neither vision aims at literal description;
both communicate truths about the age to come through symbolic descriptions.

21:2 The mention of a **new Jerusalem** is entirely fitting here since the prophecy
that promises a new heaven and earth also promises that God will create "Jerusalem to be a joy / and its people to be a delight" (Isa 65:18). Jerusalem is
called **the holy city** because it was God's own city, where God dwelt among his
people in the temple. John sees this city **coming down out of heaven from God**,
a fact he mentions two other times (3:12; 21:10). Two important implications
follow. First, the eternal home of God's people is the result not of mere human
effort but of God's gracious provision (John 14:2–3). Second, the new Jerusalem

---

1. While Rev 20:1 and 2 Pet 3 leave the impression that the present creation will be completely
obliterated and replaced, Rom 8:21 hints at a radical transformation, like the transformation that will
occur when our bodies are redeemed at the resurrection (Rom 8:23; 1 Cor 15:51–53).

does not remain in heaven, but comes down *out of heaven* and must therefore be located on the new earth. Christians are accustomed to speak of going to heaven, and that is accurate enough until Christ returns. This text indicates that God's ultimate plan for the human race is not that we go to heaven, but that heaven, the dwelling of God, comes to a re-created earth. Revelation tells us less than we would like to know about our ultimate future, but this hint is tantalizing. When the resurrection occurs, besides receiving back real but radically transformed bodies, we will live on a transformed earth.

The idea of another Jerusalem that transcends the historical earthly Jerusalem appears several times in Revelation (11:2; 14:1; 20:9) and is mentioned elsewhere in the New Testament. Paul writes that "the Jerusalem above is free" and is the "mother" of all Christians, Gentile as well as Jew (Gal 4:26). The writer to the Hebrews depicts Abraham and the Old Testament faithful along with Christians "looking forward to the city with foundations, whose architect and maker is God" (11:10), which God "has prepared . . . for them" (11:16; see also 13:14). More than that, Hebrews indicates that in some sense Christians already have access to that city (12:22). In Rev 21, the heavenly Jerusalem, with which the Church on earth already has communion (11:1; 14:1–4), descends and remains forever.

The final phrase is the most intriguing. This new Jerusalem that descends from heaven is **prepared as a bride adorned for her husband**. Before the descent of the Word of God on a white horse (19:11), a heavenly chorus announced that "the wedding day of the Lamb" has come and that "his bride has made herself ready" (19:7). She wears a wedding dress of "bright clean linen, . . . righteous deeds of the holy ones," desiring to please her heavenly Bridegroom (19:8). Now that Christ, the King of kings, has defeated all his enemies, the royal wedding can occur. According to Jewish custom, the second stage of marriage is about to begin (see sidebar, "Jewish Wedding Customs," p. 310): the bride is brought to the home of her groom to begin their married life. The risen Christ has prepared a place for his Bride in a renewed creation, and now she comes to live with him forever (John 14:2–3). If the last chapters of the Bible sound like a fairy tale in which the prince finally weds the maiden whom he rescued, and they live happily ever after, it is because those tales are faint anticipations and foreshadowings of the true story that is God's plan for his beloved, the human race. The new Jerusalem appears as a bride because it symbolizes the Church, the Bride of the Lamb (Eph 5:25–27). At last the marital imagery for the covenant between God and his people found in the Old Testament will find complete fulfillment:

As a young man marries a virgin,
your Builder shall marry you;
And as a bridegroom rejoices in his bride
so shall your God rejoice in you. (Isa 62:5)

21:3   For the third time (16:17; 19:5), John hears a **voice from the throne**. Since the next speaker (21:5–7) is identified as "the one who sat on the throne" and speaks as God in the first person, it is probably the Lamb who shares the throne of his Father (5:6; 22:1, 3) who now speaks. He announces, **God's dwelling is with the human race** (literally, "among human beings," NJB). The word translated "dwelling" literally means "tent" and is used in the Old Testament for the tabernacle in which God dwelt with Israel in the wilderness. The promise that God **will dwell with them** uses the same verb employed in John 1:14 and is derived from the word for "tent": "The Word became flesh and *dwelt* among us" (RSV, emphasis added). The voice thus promises that God's presence will be established in the new Jerusalem, making the city itself a temple (see sidebar, "God's Temple," pp. 186–87). The declaration that **they will be his people and God himself will always be with them [as their God]**[2] uses a phrase that sums up the covenant. The †eschatological promise of Ezek 36:28 is fulfilled: "You will be my people, and I will be your God."

21:4   The announcement that God **will wipe every tear from their eyes, and there shall be no more death or mourning, wailing or pain**, referring to Isa 25:8, signals the imminent fulfillment of the marvelous and mysterious prophecy of Isaiah about the day of the Lord and victory over death (Isa 26:19; see also 35:10; 51:11). By destroying death, God reverses the consequences of sin and the fall (Gen 2:17; 3:16–19; Rom 5:12), bringing an end to **the old order**. This victory over death was made possible through Jesus' death on the cross (Rom 5:18–21).

Reflection and Application (21:1–4)

For many Catholics accustomed to thinking about eternal life in heaven, Revelation's picture of the new Jerusalem descending to a re-created earth may come as a surprise. However, a close look at the Catechism shows that it devotes one section to "Heaven" (1023–29), and after the section on the "Last Judgment" (1038–41) comes a separate section on "The Hope of the New Heaven and the New Earth" (1042–50).

---

2. Some ancient manuscripts say "peoples" instead of "people," reflecting the understanding that, unlike the first tabernacle that belonged to ethnic Israel, this dwelling of God is with the human race as a whole. The brackets around the final words indicate they are missing from some manuscripts.

Summing up the Catechism, heaven is where "those who die in God's grace and friendship" go to live with Christ immediately after death (or after their purification is complete in Purgatory), before the resurrection of their bodies (1023). They live there in a "communion of life and love with the Trinity, with the Virgin Mary, the angels and all the blessed" (1024), a reality beyond human understanding. In heaven, God gives human beings the ability to see him in his heavenly †glory, what theologians describe as "the †beatific vision" (1028).

However, turning now to Catechism 1042–48, the ultimate future of God's people—after the resurrection and the last judgment—is to reign with Christ in a re-created cosmos. Then "the Kingdom of God will come in its fullness. . . . The righteous will reign forever with Christ, glorified in body and soul. The universe itself will be renewed" (1042). "In this new universe, the heavenly Jerusalem, God will have his dwelling among men [cf. Rev 21:5]" (1044). "*We know neither the moment of the consummation* of the earth and of man, nor the way in which the universe will be transformed" (1048, emphasis original).[3]

So what's the difference? When the kingdom of God comes in its fullness, God's people will have new bodies and live on a renewed earth. Nevertheless, there is continuity between heaven now and the new creation in the future age: in both, human beings enjoy the beatific vision; in both, they reign with Christ; in both, they are freed from all suffering and sorrow. If heaven is defined as where God is present and reigns completely, it is clear that when the new heaven and the new earth are created, heaven comes to earth.

For many centuries Christian hope has focused on heaven. In contrast, the hope of the early Christians centered on the return of Christ (Titus 2:13), the resurrection of the dead, and the full establishment of God's kingdom as expressed in the Lord's Prayer: "Thy kingdom come, thy will be done on earth as it is in heaven." Without lessening our desire to go to heaven when we die, we Christians would do well to set our hopes on the full and final establishment of Christ's kingdom on earth.

God Announces a New Order (21:5–8)

---

[5]The one who sat on the throne said, "Behold, I make all things new." Then he said, "Write these words down, for they are trustworthy and true." [6]He said to me, "They are accomplished. I [am] the Alpha and the Omega,

---

3. Catechism 1048, quoting *Gaudium et Spes* (Pastoral Constitution of the Church in the Modern World) 39, par. 1.

the beginning and the end. To the thirsty I will give a gift from the spring of life-giving water. [7]The victor will inherit these gifts, and I shall be his God, and he will be my son. [8]But as for cowards, the unfaithful, the depraved, murderers, the unchaste, sorcerers, idol-worshipers, and deceivers of every sort, their lot is in the burning pool of fire and sulfur, which is the second death."

OT: 2 Sam 7:14; Isa 43:19; 49:10; 55:1
NT: John 4:10–14; 7:37–39

21:5–6   God the Father speaks directly for the second time in Revelation (the first time was in 1:8). His words, **Behold, I make all things new**, echo Isa 43:19 LXX: "Behold, I make new things." God emphasizes the importance of this message by a special command: **Write these words down** because they are **trustworthy and true**—as utterly certain as though already **accomplished**. As in 1:8, God's self-presentation affirms his eternity. He is **the Alpha and the Omega**, the first and last letters of the Greek alphabet, explained as **the beginning and the end**, similar to his declaration in Isaiah, "I am the first, I am the last" (Isa 44:6; see also 41:4; 48:12). God's promise **to the thirsty** that he will give them drink **from the spring of life-giving water** (literally, "water of life") refers both to the Holy Spirit and eternal life (Isa 49:10; John 7:37–39; Rev 22:1, 17). The Greek word order emphasizes that this water is given as **a gift**, freely, without payment.

21:7–8   This promise, however, is conditional on the choices that John's readers make in the present. There are only two ways. As in the oracles to the churches (Rev 2–3), every listener is invited to be a **victor**, one who overcomes the world, the flesh, and the devil to enjoy the extraordinary privilege of being God's **son** or daughter, destined to **inherit these gifts**. Not only is the victorious Church the Bride of the Lamb; each member also has been adopted as a son or daughter of God (Hosea 2:1; Rom 8:23; 2 Cor 6:18). God has chosen the closest human relationships, husband-wife and parent-child, to reveal the kind of relationship that is ours with him and with Christ. We are sons and daughters of God; we are the Bride of the Lamb.

The fearsome alternative is to end up in **the burning pool of fire and sulfur, which is the second death**. What path leads to that horrible destination? Various kinds of evil conduct are named. It might surprise readers to see that **cowards** head the list. To be Jesus' disciples requires that we put him first to the point of readiness to die for him (Mark 8:34–38). Fear that leads to compromising our faith is an evil that must be wholeheartedly rejected. The Greek word translated **unfaithful** can mean either "those who break their word" (NJB) or "unbelievers" (NET), those who refuse the good news. The others excluded from eternal blessedness include those who persist in conduct that violates the Ten Commandments: **murderers, the unchaste, . . . idol-worshipers, and deceivers of every sort** (other translations say "and all liars").[4] Two of the terms are less familiar. The **depraved** (literally, "detestable" or "polluted") was applied to the conduct of the whore in 17:4–5 and has its roots in the †Torah's condemnations of moral conduct that is particularly abhorrent to God and unacceptable among his holy people, especially idolatry and sexual immorality (Lev 18:22–29; Deut 7:25–26; 12:31; 18:9, etc.). The word translated **sorcerers** (Greek *pharmakoi*; "those who practice magic arts," NIV) in its first-century context refers to people who engage in occult practices and use drugs for evil purposes (see comments on 9:21 and 18:23b).

A Close-up of the Lamb's Bride, the Holy City Jerusalem (21:9–14)

[9]**One of the seven angels who held the seven bowls filled with the seven last plagues came and said to me, "Come here. I will show you the bride, the wife of the Lamb."** [10]**He took me in spirit to a great, high mountain and showed me the holy city Jerusalem coming down out of heaven from God.** [11]**It gleamed with the splendor of God. Its radiance was like that of a precious stone, like jasper, clear as crystal.** [12]**It had a massive, high wall, with twelve gates where twelve angels were stationed and on which names were inscribed, [the names] of the twelve tribes of the Israelites.** [13]**There were three gates facing east, three north, three south, and three west.** [14]**The wall of the city had twelve courses of stones as its foundation, on which were inscribed the twelve names of the twelve apostles of the Lamb.**

OT: Ezek 40:1–2
NT: Rev 17:1, 3
Catechism: apostles as foundation stones, 765, 865; Church as Bride, 796
Lectionary: 21:10–14, 22–23: Sixth Sunday of Easter (Year C)

After the introductory panorama of the new creation (21:1–8), John's final vision (21:9–22:5) provides a close-up, a symbolic explanation of the new Jerusalem and of life within it. Just as Scripture uses the term "Jerusalem" to refer to both a place and its inhabitants, so the term "new Jerusalem" refers both to

---

4. Richard Bauckham comments: "From 21:8, 27; 22:15, it is quite clear that unrepentant sinners have no place in the new Jerusalem. Attempts to see Revelation as predicting universal salvation . . . strain the text intolerably" (*Climax of Prophecy* [Edinburgh: T&T Clark, 1993], 313n100). For more on idolatry, see sidebar, "Idolatry: What It Is and What's Wrong with It," p. 175, and "Reflection and Application" on 2:12–17.

the people of God as the Bride of the Lamb (21:2) and to the "place" of their eternal dwelling with God.

John's depiction of the new Jerusalem, the Bride of the Lamb, is intended to draw a contrast with the vision of Babylon, the great harlot in 17:1–19:10. This parallel poses an implicit question for readers: Which city will you choose?

21:9–10   The words **Come here. I will show you** and **He took me in spirit** deliberately repeat the language of 17:1, 3 where **one of the seven angels** shows John the harlot Babylon. But here the content of the vision is diametrically opposite. John sees **the bride, the wife of the Lamb**. John thus presents contrasting paradigms of feminine beauty. Babylon is garish and seductive, corrupt and immoral, the consort of the beast and the kings of the earth; Jerusalem is a radiant and pure bride, now married to the Lamb. According to ancient marriage customs, the marriage is completed and consummated when the bridegroom brings his bride to live with him (see sidebar, "Jewish Wedding Customs," p. 310). God has chosen to draw all those who accept his salvation, the part of humanity that has said "Yes," into a marriage with himself. The Creator has married his creation, fulfilling ancient prophecy, "Your husband is your Maker; / the LORD of hosts is his name" (Isa 54:5).

In what follows, the new Jerusalem is described as a city in symbolic terms that reveal the beauty, glory, holiness, and security of our eternal home, and the relationship between God and his people there, but virtually nothing concrete about ordinary life. The fact that it is described as a city indicates that it is a place of social interaction, a culture, a civilization lived in the presence of God. It does not mean that all are destined to become urban apartment dwellers! The prophetic poetry of Isa 65:21–22—equally symbolic—depicts life on the land.

The prophet is taken **in spirit**, or "in the Spirit" (i.e., under divine inspiration), to **a great high mountain** and is shown a **city**—words taken from Ezek 40:1–2. The final chapters of Ezekiel (40–48) present a mysterious vision in which the prophet sees a city being built and an angel who measures the dimensions of a glorious temple, which would replace the temple of Solomon that was destroyed by Babylon in 586 BC. Allusions to Ezekiel's vision of the future temple indicate that John is gazing on its fulfillment. Many Old Testament prophecies said that the future Jerusalem would be located on a high mountain (Isa 2:2–3; 25:6–26:2; Mic 4:1–2). As in Rev 21:2, its heavenly origin is emphasized: it is **coming down . . . from God.**

21:11–14   This city is brilliant with the **splendor of God**, his glory. Finally, the marriage is consummated; the glory of God, Christ's own presence, fills the temple-city.

God's glory is the visible manifestation of his greatness that was present in the cloud at Sinai (Exod 24:15–16) and filled the tabernacle and temple (Exod 40:34–35; 1 Kings 8:10–12). Isaiah prophesied that it would shine on †Zion (60:1–3), and Ezekiel foresaw it returning to the new temple (43:2–5). In the Bible, the word "glory" connotes radiant light and grandeur. Speaking of the bridal city's beauty, the text says her **radiance** is **like that of a precious stone, like jasper, clear as crystal**. Jasper is opaque rather than transparent, so some scholars think the reference is really to a diamond, sparkling like crystal.[5]

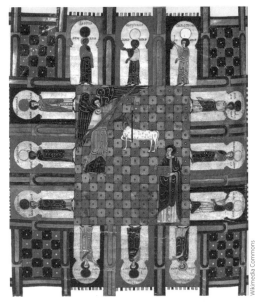

Fig. 21. The new Jerusalem with "twelve courses of stones as its foundation, on which were inscribed the twelve names of the twelve apostles of the Lamb" (21:14).

Like the great cities of the ancient world, the new Jerusalem has **a massive, high wall**. Its divine government and complete security is indicated by the presence of **twelve angels . . . stationed** by its gates. The gates are on all four sides, facing the directions of the compass. The description of the heavenly city is characterized by symbols of God's people throughout both the Old and New Testaments: **twelve gates** named for the **twelve tribes** of Israel, fulfilling Ezek 48:30–35, where the future temple has twelve gates, also three on each side, each named for a tribe. The tribes themselves are named for the patriarchs, the ancestors through whom Israel came into existence. The many promises in the prophets that God will one day gather and restore all his people in the land of Israel attain definitive fulfillment in the new Jerusalem. **Twelve courses of stone**, or "foundations" of the walls (NRSV, RSV, etc.), are inscribed with the **names** of the **twelve apostles of the Lamb** through whose testimony the Christian people came into existence. Ephesians 2:20 expresses a similar idea: the Church is "built upon the foundation of the apostles and prophets, with Christ Jesus himself as the capstone."

---

5. Regarding jasper, "God on his throne 'had the appearance of jasper,' [4:3] and jasper seems to be the major jewel of the book (it was the first jewel mentioned in 4:3–4; it is the material that makes up the walls in 21:18; and it is the first of the foundation jewels of 21:19–20). In all these passages, the jewels primarily symbolize the glory of God in all its radiance and purity" (Osborne, *Revelation*, 749).

Jerusalem the Invincible

BIBLICAL
BACKGROUND

The custom of admiring the physical attributes of Jerusalem as a symbol of its invisible qualities is found in Ps 46; 48; 125. For example,

> Go about Zion, walk all around it,
>   note the number of its towers.
> Consider the ramparts, examine its citadels,
>   that you may tell future generations:
> That this is God,
>   our God for ever and ever. (Ps 48:13–15)

The NABRE footnote says it well: "Israel's God is like Zion in being eternal and invincible. The holy city is therefore a kind of 'sacrament' of God."

The Dimensions and Decoration of the New Jerusalem (21:15–21)

¹⁵The one who spoke to me held a gold measuring rod to measure the city, its gates, and its wall. ¹⁶The city was square, its length the same as [also] its width. He measured the city with the rod and found it fifteen hundred miles in length and width and height. ¹⁷He also measured its wall: one hundred and forty-four cubits according to the standard unit of measurement the angel used. ¹⁸The wall was constructed of jasper, while the city was pure gold, clear as glass. ¹⁹The foundations of the city wall were decorated with every precious stone; the first course of stones was jasper, the second sapphire, the third chalcedony, the fourth emerald, ²⁰the fifth sardonyx, the sixth carnelian, the seventh chrysolite, the eighth beryl, the ninth topaz, the tenth chrysoprase, the eleventh hyacinth, and the twelfth amethyst. ²¹The twelve gates were twelve pearls, each of the gates made from a single pearl; and the street of the city was of pure gold, transparent as glass.

OT: Exod 28:15–21; Isa 54:11–14; Ezek 40–41
NT: Rev 11:1–2

21:15–17   Back in chapter 11 the prophet John was given a measuring rod like a traveler's staff and was told to measure the temple and to count the worshipers—an allusion to Ezek 40–41, where an angel measures the dimensions of the †eschatological temple. John was told to exclude the area outside the sanctuary, destined to be trampled by the nations for forty-two months (11:1–2). In that vision the temple, still under construction, represented the Church before Christ's return. Measuring it and counting those who worshiped in it were ways of indicating that Christians belong to God and enjoy his spiritual protection during the time of their earthly pilgrimage.

Now a powerful angel (21:9, 15) carries out a ceremonial measurement of **the city**, God's true and final temple, with **a gold measuring rod** to celebrate its completion. Besides confirming God's ownership and protection, as the previous measuring did (11:1), this measuring serves as a literary device that reveals the nature of this temple-city through its symbolic dimensions. The city is described as **square**; in fact, it is a perfect cube, since its **length and width and height** are equal. The only other space depicted in the Bible as a perfect cube was the holy of holies—the heart of the temple, where God resides "enthroned on the cherubim" (Isa 37:16)—twenty cubits in each dimension (1 Kings 6:19–20). The cubical shape of the new Jerusalem thus reveals that it *is* the holy of holies, the place of God's presence. In ancient Israel, only the high priest could enter before God in the holy of holies and only once a year, on the Day of Atonement to offer sacrifice. But now that the Lamb has been slain, an eternal and all-sufficient sacrifice (Rev 5:9; Heb 9:11–12; 10:10), and God's people have washed their robes in the blood of the Lamb (Rev 7:14), all have been made priests (1:6; 5:10) and live forever in his presence without interruption.

The city is immense: **fifteen hundred miles in length and width and height**, extending in every direction as far as the Roman Empire did from east to west. The NABRE's conversion of the distance to miles obscures a symbolic number in the Greek text: the city is *twelve thousand* stadia in all directions: twelve, the number of the people of God, times a thousand (ten to the third power), a number signifying immensity. The wall that surrounds the city and manifests its security is extraordinarily high (21:12, 17) compared to the walls that surrounded ancient cities: **one hundred and forty-four cubits** (216 feet).[6] I take this as an allusion to the one hundred and forty-four thousand (7:4; 14:1–5), the number that symbolizes God's army of truly faithful servants. Their heroic testimony (12:11), praise and worship, virginal purity, and discipleship (14:3–4) served as a wall of defense for the Church. Their contribution is as essential to the symbolic architecture of the new Jerusalem as the twelve gates with the

---

6. The Greek behind the NABRE's "according to the standard unit of measurement the angel used" is obscure. The RSV renders it literally: "by a man's measure, that is, an angel's." The NRSV interprets it: "by human measurement, which the angel was using."

names of the tribes (21:12) and the twelve courses of stone with the names of the apostles (21:14).

21:18–21   The wall is **constructed of jasper** while the city itself is transparent **gold**. Besides emphasizing the wealth and beauty of the new Jerusalem, this detail reinforces the temple theme, since Solomon's temple was overlaid with gold (1 Kings 6:20–22) as was the second temple after Herod rebuilt it. The depiction of a city with jewels decorating its foundations and gates fulfills the Lord's promise through Isaiah of a glorious future for his "wife," Jerusalem:

> O afflicted one, storm-battered and unconsoled,
> I lay your pavements in carnelians,
> your foundations in sapphires;
> I will make your battlements of rubies,
> your gates of jewels,
> and all your walls of precious stones.
> All your children shall be taught by the LORD;
> great shall be the peace of your children.
> In justice shall you be established,
> far from oppression, you shall not fear,
> from destruction, it cannot come near. (Isa 54:11–14)

The list of jewels that decorate the foundations is taken from the twelve precious stones inscribed with the names of the twelve tribes on the Israelite high priest's "breastpiece of decision" (Exod 28:15–21).[7] The high priest wore the twelve engraved gems as a symbolic reminder of the people before the Lord, a means of invoking God's blessing on his people. Here, as in the listing of the twelve tribes in 7:5–8 and throughout Revelation, the twelve tribes represent not just the biological descendants of the patriarchs but also †eschatological Israel, comprised of Jews and †Gentiles united in the Messiah (Gal 3:27–29). The twelve gates composed of **twelve pearls** echo an ancient Jewish translation of Isa 54:11.[8] The fact that the new Jerusalem's foundations match the gems of the high priest's breastpiece, and the constant repetition of the number twelve and multiples of twelve in the city's symbolic architecture, forcefully demonstrate that John views the Church in seamless continuity with faithful Israel.

---

7. The names of eight of the jewels are identical to those found in the LXX; the names of the other four are alternate names for the remaining gems. The twelve jewels would also have had significance for pagans, since they are the twelve precious stones of the zodiac.

8. *Targum Isaiah* 54:11, quoted in G. K. Beale, *The Book of Revelation*, NIGTC (Grand Rapids: Eerdmans, 1999), 1083.

More about the New Jerusalem (21:22–27)

²²I saw no temple in the city, for its temple is the Lord God almighty and the Lamb. ²³The city had no need of sun or moon to shine on it, for the glory of God gave it light, and its lamp was the Lamb. ²⁴The nations will walk by its light, and to it the kings of the earth will bring their treasure. ²⁵During the day its gates will never be shut, and there will be no night there. ²⁶The treasure and wealth of the nations will be brought there, ²⁷but nothing unclean will enter it, nor any[one] who does abominable things or tells lies. Only those will enter whose names are written in the Lamb's book of life.

OT: Tob 13:8–18; Ps 72:19; Isa 24:23; 60; Jer 3:16–17; Hab 2:14; Zech 14:7

John radically differentiates the new Jerusalem from the old by saying, **I saw** 21:22
no temple in the city. Here there is no special location or house where God resides and where he may be approached, as in historic Jerusalem. Its walls of gold and its cubical shape have already indicated that the city as a whole is not merely a temple but the holy of holies itself, permeated by God's presence. Now it is stated in a way that stretches logic: **its temple is the Lord God almighty and the Lamb**. God and the Lamb have become the dwelling place; there is no special place to seek them. All of life is lived in their presence. As elsewhere in Revelation, the Lamb manifestly shares the fullness of divinity with the Lord God almighty. The details of Ezekiel's vision of the future temple in Ezek 40–48 are now revealed to have been symbolic, while the new Jerusalem fulfills a prophecy of Jeremiah's in an almost literal manner: "At that time they will call Jerusalem 'the LORD's throne.' All nations will gather together there to honor the name of the LORD at Jerusalem" (Jer 3:17).

The next four verses show the fulfillment of another prophecy: Isaiah's de- 21:23–24
scription of the future restoration of Zion, another name for Jerusalem (Isa 60). In Isaiah's prophecy the arrival of light symbolizes God's radiant presence among his people and the illumination his glory provides to the nations (60:1–3). What follows is the gathering of Zion's children from distant places, the enrichment of the city and adornment of the temple from the wealth of the nations, the destruction of nations that refuse to submit, and service by former enemies (60:4–16). Jerusalem will enjoy perfect security, and her people will be righteous and numerous, possessing the land for all time; God's †glory will be their light forever, making superfluous the light of sun and moon (Isa 60:17–22).⁹

9. The Church reads the beginning of Isa 60 on Epiphany ("Arise! Shine, for your light has come, / the glory of the LORD has dawned upon you") to refer to the manifestation of the light of Christ at his

In the new Jerusalem there is **no need of sun or moon**, for **the glory of God** illuminates the city. The risen Jesus shares in the divine action: **its lamp was the Lamb**. Now **the nations will walk by its light**, meaning the light that emanates from the new Jerusalem. The bride-city has walls of jasper, clear as crystal (21:11, 18), and a "street . . . of pure gold, transparent as glass" (21:21). Donal A. McIlraith explains the transparency of the city: "Thus it can be completely filled with light. And this light is the glory of God. It shines in the city because of the Lamb, the risen Christ, who makes it present as its lamp. . . . The Church starts off as a golden lampstand with Christ outside it. It ends up as a golden city and Christ within."[10] What is enlightened by Christ becomes light (Eph 5:13–14).

When **the kings of the earth bring their treasure** to Jerusalem, they too fulfill ancient prophecies (Isa 60:5, 11; 61:6), although it raises a question. Except for an initial description of Jesus as "ruler of the kings of the earth" in 1:5, the other six times the "kings of the earth" are mentioned in Revelation, they appear in a negative light: consorting with the harlot (17:2, 18; 18:3, 9), allying themselves to the beast (19:19), and trembling at their imminent judgment (6:15). This negative picture corresponds to some prophetic denunciations of the "kings of the earth" (e.g., Ps 2:2; Isa 24:21; Ezek 27:33). However, other Old Testament texts show the "kings of the earth" coming to hear Solomon's wisdom (1 Kings 5:14; 2 Chron 9:23), acknowledging the supremacy of the Davidic king (Ps 89:28), and worshiping the Lord God of Israel (Ps 102:16; 138:4; 148:11). This vision presupposes a division: some kings of the earth (i.e., human rulers and those who follow their lead) will continue in evildoing and will be condemned, while others will repent and acknowledge the Lord and his Messiah—accepting the teaching of the new Solomon—and will enter into his royal city (Isa 60:12). In the course of history many "kings," chiefs, rulers, and leaders of many kinds have embraced Christ's gospel and have entered the new Jerusalem's earthly entrance, the Church, bringing with them thousands and thousands of people, an extraordinary treasure (see also 21:26).

21:25–27   Verses 25–27 elaborate on the absolute security of the new Jerusalem and explain who and what can enter the city that is itself the holy of holies. The gates of an ancient city were an essential element of its defense, open during the day, when an approaching enemy could be seen, and closed at night lest an enemy

---

first coming. This is because Isa 9:1–6 also uses the imagery of light shining in the darkness to refer to the birth of the Messiah. This usage illustrates the inaugurated eschatology of the gospel: the reign of God has already begun in the coming of Christ, yet awaits its definitive fulfillment at the end of history.

10. Donal A. McIlraith, *Everyone's Apocalypse* (Suva, Fiji: Pacific Regional Seminary, 1995), 105.

enter under cover of darkness. The fact that the **gates** of the new Jerusalem **will never be shut** signifies that all threat of evil has been eliminated (Isa 60:11, 18).

The fact that the city is described as having gates and that "the kings bring their treasure" into it (21:24) has caused some readers to wonder if people can come in and out of the new Jerusalem. And if so, where can they go? What lies outside the glorious city?

These questions must be answered in the light of book's visionary symbolic character. The new Jerusalem is not a literal city but, as its immense cubical dimensions suggest, a symbol of the whole, new world where God will dwell with his people. A description of this new world in Isa 11:9 adds perspective: "They shall not harm or destroy on all my holy mountain; / for the earth shall be filled with knowledge of the LORD, / as water covers the sea." The holy mountain, another way of referring to Jerusalem and its temple, exists in a new earth that is filled and transformed by the knowledge of God. The new Jerusalem is not limited to a particular place, even a very large place. The beginning of this chapter (21:2–3, 9–10) says that the new Jerusalem *is* the Bride of the Lamb, the people of God. The description of the city is a symbolic way of depicting a variety of truths about our eternal future, above all, the new intimacy of God with his people that will be ours when the kingdom comes at Christ's return. The visions in Revelation depict symbols of real things, rather than the realities themselves. In order to understand the realities to which the symbols point, we reflect on the meaning of each aspect of each symbol.

John continues his symbolic description of the new Jerusalem: **there will be no night there** (Isa 60:20). Like the sea (Rev 21:1), night serves as a symbol of evil (as in John 11:10; Rom 13:12–13; 1 Thess 5:5), which has now been vanquished. Although **nothing unclean** enters this holy temple-city, **the treasure and wealth of the nations will be brought there**. This echoes several verses in Isa 60 (vv. 5–7, 9, 11, 13, 16–17) that speak of the best products and precious metals that will be brought to future Zion from all over the world. In itself material wealth is a good rather than an evil, even if Babylon and the nations were corrupted by their lust for it (Rev 18:3). In Isa 60, this wealth furnishes "acceptable offerings" on God's altar (v. 7) and adorns his "sanctuary" (v. 13).

What does the "wealth of the nations" that will enter the eternal kingdom signify? Some have speculated that it refers to the best of human culture, of literature and art and science, purified of every defect. Like our physical bodies at the resurrection, life in the new Jerusalem will be characterized both by continuity with what is familiar and excellent (Phil 4:8; Col 3:1–4, 12–17) and by what is so radically new that we cannot now imagine.

Again John reminds his readers that the holiness of the new Jerusalem excludes **any[one] who does abominable things or tells lies** (literally, "anyone who practices abomination or falsehood," NRSV). The word "abominable" is from the same Greek root translated "depraved" in 21:8 (see comments there), referring to moral conduct that is abhorrent to God. In contrast, those privileged to enter the new Jerusalem include **only those . . . whose names are written in the Lamb's book of life.** This refers to those redeemed by Christ (Eph 1:4), who washed their robes in the blood of the Lamb through repentence and baptism and have persevered in faith (7:14).

The River of Life and Concluding Words

Revelation 22:1–21

This chapter continues John's vision of the new Jerusalem, revealing its resemblance both to the garden of Eden before the fall and to the future temple of Ezekiel's vision (Ezek 40–48). Finally, in a solemn epilogue, John reports concluding words from the angel through whom he has received this revelation, from Jesus himself, and a response from the Spirit and the Bride, followed by a final greeting from John.

Life-Giving Water Flows from the Throne, a New World Dawns (22:1–5)

¹Then the angel showed me the river of life-giving water, sparkling like crystal, flowing from the throne of God and of the Lamb ²down the middle of its street. On either side of the river grew the tree of life that produces fruit twelve times a year, once each month; the leaves of the trees serve as medicine for the nations. ³Nothing accursed will be found there anymore. The throne of God and of the Lamb will be in it, and his servants will worship him. ⁴They will look upon his face, and his name will be on their foreheads. ⁵Night will be no more, nor will they need light from lamp or sun, for the Lord God shall give them light, and they shall reign forever and ever.

OT: Gen 2:10; Isa 35:6–9; Ezek 47; Zech 14:6–9, 11
NT: John 4:10–14; 7:37–39; 1 Cor 13:12; 1 John 3:2

Catechism: river of life, 1137; heavenly worship, 1138; humanity in the new Jerusalem, 1044–45; the future life, 2550
Lectionary: 22:1–7: Saturday of the Last Week of the Liturgical Year (Year II)

22:1–3a   John's vision of a **river of life-giving water** flowing **down the middle of its street** draws together a string of biblical images. Genesis 2:10 describes a river that "rises in Eden to water the garden" and sustains various trees that are "delightful to look at and good for food," including "the tree of life in the middle of the garden" (Gen 2:9). God thus creates the ultimate future to be like the beginning, only better.

The prophet Ezekiel saw "water flowing out from under the threshold" of the †eschatological temple (47:1). This water begins as a trickling stream, but soon becomes a deep, impassable river that waters "a great many trees on each side" (47:7). From there it flows through the wilderness to the Dead Sea, where it makes the waters fresh, allowing many kinds of fish to thrive. Ezekiel describes the fruit trees that the river irrigates: "Their leaves will not wither, nor will their fruit fail. Every month they will bear fresh fruit because the waters of the river flow out from the sanctuary. Their fruit is used for food, and their leaves for healing" (47:12).

John's vision, however, indicates something greater than what was previously revealed. Instead of "every kind of fruit tree" (Gen 1:11), **the tree of life**, previously found only in Eden (Gen 2:15–17; 3:22), flourishes on both sides of the river, bearing fruit every month.[1] Since John has already indicated that there is "no more death or . . . wailing or pain" (21:4) in the new Jerusalem, the **medicine for the nations** may symbolize the now-complete healing of body, soul, and spirit that has come to all nations and to every person through the work of the Holy Spirit.

Like Ezekiel, Zechariah prophesied that when the Lord finally restores Jerusalem, "fresh water [literally, 'living waters'] will flow from Jerusalem" toward the east and west (14:8). In the Gospel of John, Jesus presents himself as the source of "living water," which he offers to the Samaritan woman (4:10–14). Later, in the temple during the Feast of Tabernacles, Jesus promises "living water" to anyone who comes to him (7:37–38).[2] The evangelist interprets Jesus' words: "He said this in reference to the Spirit that those who came to believe in him were to receive" (7:39).

---

1. Since the Greek uses a singular form when it speaks of "the tree of life," it is possible to interpret it as a single tree on the bank of the river, although it is likely that John intends a collective singular to refer to trees on both sides of the river, as in Ezek 47:7, 12. The symbolism of a single tree fits well with the ancient Christian interpretation of the cross as the tree of life.

2. The Jewish liturgy for the Feast of Tabernacles featured a water ritual recalling Zechariah's prophecy of a future celebration of Tabernacles in a restored Jerusalem (Zech 14:16).

The river in the prophet John's vision is **flowing from the throne of God and of the Lamb**. God and Christ share one throne, indicating Jesus' full divinity. The Spirit is the one through whom the Father and the Son create and communicate biological life to all living things (Gen 1:2; 2:7; Ps 104:30); he is the one who communicates divine life to human beings and is the one in whom human beings enjoy communion with God and the Lamb (2 Cor 13:13).

Alluding again to Zechariah's prophecy that Jerusalem would be reestablished in security when God assumes kingship over all the earth (Zech 14:9–11), John says, that **nothing accursed will be found there** (literally, "every curse will be no longer"). This is drawn from Zech 14:11, which declares that there will be no decree of destruction in the eschatological Jerusalem. Every

Fig. 22. The angel shows John the new Jerusalem (21:9–10), the river of life flowing from the throne, the tree of life bringing forth twelve fruits, the saints reigning forever (22:1–5).

curse or judgment owing to human sin (Gen 3:16–19), whether Israel's (Deut 28:15–68) or that of the rebellious nations (Isa 34:1–2; Zech 14:2–3), will be absent.

Like other visions in Revelation, John's vision of the new Jerusalem has a timeless quality about it. On the one hand it clearly refers to life in the future when Christ returns and fully establishes God's kingdom on earth. On the other hand, the vision depicts realities from the past (e.g., the twelve tribes of Israel, the twelve apostles of the Lamb), as well as realities Christians presently experience. Already we drink of the water flowing from the throne of God and the Lamb through our present sharing in the life of the Holy Spirit. Already we feed on the fruit from the tree of life, the cross of Jesus, namely, the Eucharist. Even now the nations, those who were previously not God's people, are being healed by the medicine of that tree. Already many kings and whole nations have entered and brought their wealth into the heavenly Jerusalem, a city that already exists (Ps 87; Gal 4:26; Heb 12:22).

22:3b–5   A few pregnant phrases at the close of John's final vision sum up the essential features of life in the new Jerusalem: **The throne of God and of the Lamb** will be there. What was previously hidden in heaven and accessible only "in the Spirit" will be fully revealed on earth. God's **servants**—people who belong to him fully because the Lamb has purchased them for God (Rev 5:9; 1 Cor 6:20)—**will worship him**. They will do what no human being has been able to do for all of history (Exod 33:20), yet was longed for in the Old Testament (Job 33:26; Ps 17:15; 42:3; 84:8) and promised in the New (Matt 5:8; 1 Cor 13:12; 1 John 3:2): **They will look on his face**. Because the Lamb has made them priests for God (Rev 1:6; 5:10), God's **name will be on their foreheads** as the high priest had God's name written on the miter he wore over his forehead, marking him as "Sacred to the LORD" (Exod 28:36–38). This priestly privilege was promised to "the victor" in Rev 3:12 and anticipated in the sealing of the one hundred and forty-four thousand (7:3; 14:1).

Again, the fact that there will be no **night** indicates that the redeemed will live in perfect security. God will be so radiantly present to them—fulfilling Aaron's priestly blessing ("The LORD let his face shine upon you," Num 6:25)—that they will not **need light from lamp or sun**. Finally, since the Lamb has also constituted them a "kingdom" (Rev 1:6; 5:10), a royal family, **they shall reign forever and ever**. In this they fulfill the prophecy of Daniel: "The holy ones of the Most High shall receive the kingship, to possess it forever and ever" (7:18). The blessing first granted to those who attained to the first resurrection for a "thousand years" (Rev 20:6) is shared by all God's people forever. What will they reign over? We are not told, but perhaps this refers to redeemed humanity's fulfilling the role of governance and stewardship over the new creation that God intended for the human race at the beginning (Gen 1:28).

Five biblical images in these visions sum up the blessedness God will bestow on his people: they live in *a new creation*; they are *the Bride of the Lamb*; they inhabit the *new Jerusalem* that has become God's true *temple* on earth; God's original plan reaches fulfillment as the *garden of Eden* is restored.

Reflection and Application (22:1–5)

What will life be like when the kingdom of God comes in fullness? Anyone hoping for a concrete description from Revelation or elsewhere in the Bible will be disappointed. While life in the kingdom will preserve some continuity with what we already know, it will so far transcend anything we have ever experienced that symbols, images, and analogies are as close as we can get.

A baby in the womb is happy and content. The environment is warm and secure; the infant is close to mom although having no idea what that means. Everything seems perfect until the baby is pushed out of the womb into the world. The life the baby enters is a continuation of the life already known in the womb, yet it is incredibly different—more diverse, rich, complex, and beautiful. The difference between life in this world and life in the coming kingdom must be something like that. It is so far beyond us that we can only acquire the barest notion of what it will be like through images from the prophets and the words of Jesus.

The fact that the coming kingdom will be infinitely greater than we can know or imagine should not deter us from reflecting on the the biblical texts that speak of our ultimate future but should rather encourage us to pray them and allow the flame of our desire to be enkindled. At the heart of life in the kingdom is a perfectly complete and full relationship with God our Father, Christ our Lord, and one another in the Holy Spirit, an extension and completion of something we have already begun to taste (Rom 8:23; Eph 1:13–14). Perhaps Paul says it best: "Now we see in a mirror, dimly, but then we will see face to face. Now I know only in part; then I will know fully, even as I have been fully known" (1 Cor 13:12 NRSV).

Sometimes people are put off by descriptions of heaven as perpetual worship, thinking something like, "Mass is great, and heavenly adoration will be infinitely more wonderful, but I'm not convinced it is what I'd like to do forever." That is not surprising, since human beings are embodied spirits created to interact with a physical world and to relate to other embodied spirits. Although nothing is said in Scripture about daily life in the new Jerusalem, it helps to recall that it is a *city*—by definition, a place of human interaction and activity. I find it helpful to reflect on the visions of Isaiah[3] regarding the time of restoration and life in the age to come, which depict human prosperity, joy, celebration, and agricultural and family life in a world like our own but radically renewed. Although they should not be taken as literal descriptions of life in the kingdom (e.g., they speak of long life rather than eternal life), they really do describe it, albeit in picture language. Likewise, Jesus' imagery of the future kingdom bears resemblance to human life as we know it: Jesus speaks of a wedding feast, a banquet (Matt 8:11; 22:2).

The garden of Eden before the fall gives some idea of how God may wish to dwell with human beings, of what we are to do, and how he may wish us to relate to one another. For instance, work was an aspect of the human vocation

---

3. See Isa 2:1–4; 25:6–9; 26:1–4; 27:6; 35; 61–62; 65:17–25; 66:10–14, 22–23.

before the fall (Gen 2:15). On the other hand, the Bible also speaks of a future rest (Heb 4:9–11). The biblical indications of what God has in store for his people defy all attempts at precise description.

John Reports the Angel's Final Words (22:6–11)

⁶And he said to me, "These words are trustworthy and true, and the Lord, the God of prophetic spirits, sent his angel to show his servants what must happen soon." ⁷"Behold, I am coming soon." Blessed is the one who keeps the prophetic message of this book.

⁸It is I, John, who heard and saw these things, and when I heard and saw them I fell down to worship at the feet of the angel who showed them to me. ⁹But he said to me, "Don't! I am a fellow servant of yours and of your brothers the prophets and of those who keep the message of this book. Worship God."

¹⁰Then he said to me, "Do not seal up the prophetic words of this book, for the appointed time is near. ¹¹Let the wicked still act wickedly, and the filthy still be filthy. The righteous must still do right, and the holy still be holy."

OT: Dan 8:26; 12:9–10
NT: 2 Tim 3:12–13; Rev 1:3; 19:10

Verses 6–9 conclude John's final vision, indicating the grandeur of the vision of the new Jerusalem by the intense response it produces in the prophet. At the same time these verses begin the epilogue of the book (22:6–21), a final word that parallels the prologue (1:1–3), framing the book with indications of its authority and importance as a prophetic communication. By way of final reminder, the present verses also sum up many of the ethical implications of the prophecy for its readers.

While that much is clear, the epilogue remains difficult to interpret since there are obviously several speakers, and their identities are not always stated and must be inferred from the content. As with the beginning of the book, some scholars read the words by multiple speakers as a liturgical dialogue.[4] Whether or not the early Christians enacted it as liturgy, John enables his readers to listen in on a conversation between divine, angelic, and human voices at the beginning and the end of this book.

4. See Ugo Vanni, "Liturgical Dialogue as a Literary Form in the Book of Revelation," *New Testament Studies* 37 (1991): 348–72. The phenomenon of an abrupt unexplained change of speakers is found in both the prophetic books and Psalms (e.g., Ps 2; 110; Isa 40).

The angel speaking to John is the one who showed him the vision of "the **22:6–7** bride, the wife of the Lamb," and explained the new Jerusalem (21:9–22:5). This same angel verifies John's report of what he saw, calling it **trustworthy and true**, the same phrase that God spoke earlier from the throne about this vision (21:5). And the angel refers to Jesus as **the Lord, the God of prophetic spirits** (literally, "the God of the spirits of the prophets") and repeats what was said in the first verse of the book, that Jesus sent **his angel to show his servants what must happen soon.** In other words, this message and those of other Christian prophets comes from Jesus. Then Jesus himself speaks, confirming the imminence of his coming: **Behold, I am coming soon.** The double affirmation that all this will happen "soon" reflects Christ's perspective on time, not ours, and communicates urgency (see sidebar, "What Christ Means by 'Soon,'" p. 41, and "Reflection and Application" on 1:1–3). Although the NABRE does not put it in quotation marks, it is likely that Christ himself pronounces the †beatitude on **the one who keeps the prophetic message of this book,** similar to the beatitude pronounced in the prologue (1:3), framing Revelation with an encouragement to give heed. Revelation does not convey mere information but teaching to be put into practice.

Now **John, who heard and saw these things,** reports the impact of the **22:8–9** final vision on himself: he falls prostrate **to worship at the feet of the angel who showed them.** John and his readers realize this is excessive and improper veneration to give to an angel (see Col 2:18), but John's over-the-top response shows the grandeur of the vision: the message is so awesome that it evokes worship of the messenger (compare John's response to the overwhelming vision of Babylon and its demise in 17:1–19:10). The angel responds vigorously, placing himself at the same level—**a fellow servant** (literally, fellow slave) with John and his **brothers,** that is, other Christian **prophets.** On the one hand, this is a humble status, since they are all mere creatures and servants; on the other, it is an exalted status, because they serve the transcendent Creator God. It is striking that those who **keep the message of this book** enjoy the same humble yet exalted standing that belongs to the prophets and this angel from God's temple in heaven (15:6). The common duty of all these servants is to **worship God,** implicitly, God alone.

The angel continues to speak, telling John, **Do not seal up the prophetic** **22:10–11** **words of this book.** This instruction is opposite to what an angel told Daniel about the revelation given him: "Keep secret the message and seal the book until the end time" (12:4). The reason for the different instruction is stated right away: **for the appointed time is near.** John and his readers, including us, already live in the end time: the lion of Judah "has triumphed"; the Lamb has been slain and has "purchased for God / those from every tribe and tongue, people and nation" (5:5, 9); the Lamb has been exalted to the throne of God (3:21; 5:6) and from there is directing history toward its goal. This is the perspective shared by Paul and other New Testament authors (1 Cor 10:11; 15:24–25; Heb 9:26).[5]

Although the end is near, it has not yet arrived. In the meantime, God allows people to make choices just as they did in the time of Daniel, a prophet who used similar words (Dan 12:10, echoed here in Rev 22:12): **Let the wicked still act wickedly, and the filthy still be filthy. The righteous must still do right, and the holy still be holy**. Whatever other people do, those who have washed their robes in the blood of the Lamb must persevere in just and holy conduct (2 Cor 7:1).

Jesus Speaks, the Spirit and the Bride Respond (22:12–17)

[12]"**Behold, I am coming soon. I bring with me the recompense I will give to each according to his deeds. [13]I am the Alpha and the Omega, the first and the last, the beginning and the end."**

[14]**Blessed are they who wash their robes so as to have the right to the tree of life and enter the city through its gates. [15]Outside are the dogs, the sorcerers, the unchaste, the murderers, the idol-worshipers, and all who love and practice deceit.**

[16]"**I, Jesus, sent my angel to give you this testimony for the churches. I am the root and offspring of David, the bright morning star."**

[17]**The Spirit and the bride say, "Come." Let the hearer say, "Come." Let the one who thirsts come forward, and the one who wants it receive the gift of life-giving water.**

OT: Ps 101:3, 7–8; 118:20; Isa 11:1; 55:1; 62:10–11; Mal 3:5
NT: John 7:37; Rev 1:8; 21:6
Catechism: sacrament of penance, 1468–70; desire for second coming, 524, 671
Lectionary: 22:12–14, 16–17, 20: Seventh Sunday of Easter (Year C)

The purpose of this almost-final section is to proclaim the gospel to the audience of this book and invite a response, here and now.

22:12–13   With the exception of Jesus' words in 22:7, the prophet John has been reporting what he saw and heard in his vision. But now the risen Lord himself speaks again to emphasize the imminence of his return (**I am coming soon**)

5. See also Matt 3:2; 4:17; Mark 1:15; Rom 13:12; Phil 4:5; 1 Pet 4:7.

and the certainty of **recompense** or payment (**to each according to his deeds**). This is a call to conversion along the lines of "repent or perish." Everyone must choose to stand either with those who act wickedly, remain filthy, and incur eternal condemnation or with those who do right, seek holiness (22:11), and enjoy eternal life. Christ the judge presents himself here with the same divine title that God the Father used to present himself in the prologue (1:8) and at the announcement of the new creation (21:6): **I am the Alpha and the Omega**. Christ explains the meaning of this title by a phrase he has already applied to himself twice before in this book (1:17; 2:8), **the first and the last**, and by the phrase that God used to explain it in 21:6, **the beginning and the end**. God and the Lamb are both eternal.

The seventh and last †beatitude makes clear that the call to conversion is   22:14–15
truly good news: **Blessed** are those **who wash their robes**. A previous vision revealed people before the throne of God who had "washed their robes and made them white in the blood of the Lamb" (7:14). This blessedness is not the result of a perfect moral record, nor is it available as a result of merely human moral effort. It belongs to those who turn from evil to God and receive cleansing and grace from the sacrifice of Christ through baptism (Acts 22:16; Eph 5:26) and ongoing repentance: "If we walk in the light as he is in the light, then we have fellowship with one another, and the blood of his Son Jesus cleanses us from all sin. . . . If we acknowledge our sins, he is faithful and just and will forgive our sins and cleanse us from every wrongdoing" (1 John 1:7, 9). Jesus explains a twofold **right** that belongs to the blessed as a consequence. First, they have access **to the tree of life**, eternal life, previously kept back from the human race because of the sin of our first parents (Gen 3:22–24). Second, they **enter** the new Jerusalem **through the gates**—they have the right to dwell there as true citizens.

Then comes a warning now repeated for the third time (see 21:8, 27): people who continue in grave wrongdoing are excluded from this right. It says these people are **outside**, but this does not mean that there exists a place for the wicked in the new creation. Since Revelation refers to nothing on the new earth besides the new Jerusalem, where God dwells with his people, we may infer that the new Jerusalem comprises the whole of the re-created earth and that all evil is excluded. The only other location that Revelation mentions is the lake of fire. The categories of conduct excluded from the new Jerusalem in 22:15 were all implied in the list of wrongdoers destined for the "burning pool of fire and sulfur" in 21:8 (see comments there), except **the dogs**, mentioned first here and possibly a catchall term for the categories that follow. In the Bible (as among

Middle Eastern people in recent times), "dogs" may be used as a derogatory term for people considered foolish or slaves of their appetites, especially people regarded as unclean; first-century Jews used it of †Gentiles.[6]

The final category of those who cannot enter the city is another catchall: **all who love and practice deceit** ("falsehood," NRSV). Like the two previous lists of those excluded from the new Jerusalem (21:8, 27), this list concludes with the Greek root *pseudos* (from which English derives "pseudo-"). By this phrase Christ refers to people who justify false belief because it accords with the way they live their lives, or perhaps to people who claim right beliefs yet conceal an opposite way of living. Several passages in the New Testament describe this tendency of fallen humanity toward self-deception and indicate that it will become more widespread in the period before Christ's return (John 3:19–21; Rom 1:18–32; 2 Thess 2:9–12; 2 Tim 3:1–5).

22:16   Echoing the prologue (1:1–2) and thus framing the book, **Jesus** himself ratifies its content, confirming that it was he who **sent** his **angel** with this **testimony**, a solemnly attested message **for the churches**. Jesus addresses his words to a plural **you**, probably meaning John and the other Christian prophets in agreement with him (22:6; 1 Cor 14:29, 37). Christ solemnly declares who he is by an **I am** statement like those that disclose his identity in the Gospel of John.[7] He declares that he is the Messiah, using titles that recall Old Testament promises: he is **the root and offspring of David** (echoing Isa 11:1, 10; see Rev 5:5) and the **bright morning star** (echoing Num 24:17, "a star shall advance from Jacob"), the first light signaling the coming of a new day (2 Pet 1:19). Both Old Testament texts depict a ruler whom God will raise up to be victorious over the wicked.

22:17   The risen Lord has spoken 22:12–16 as an †oracle through the prophet John. Now the Holy Spirit that animates the Church responds on behalf of the Church to Jesus' promise to come (v. 12): **The Spirit and the bride say, "Come."** The Spirit, still speaking through John, next addresses those listening to the book of Revelation as it is being read, inviting them to unite their voices with the prayer of the Spirit and the Bride: **Let the hearer say, "Come."** Heartfelt longing for Jesus' return characterizes Christian faith, hope, and love (e.g., 2 Tim 4:8; 2 Pet 3:11–14). Paul concludes 1 Corinthians with the original Aramaic words that expressed this longing: "*Marana tha*," meaning "Our Lord, come!" (1 Cor 16:22), a way of saying "Thy kingdom come!" to the risen Jesus. At the same

---

6. See Isa 56:10–11; Matt 7:6; Phil 3:2; 2 Pet 2:22. Because it is followed by "the unchaste" (*hoi pornoi*), some have interpreted it to refer to male prostitutes, called dogs in Deut 23:18; others have interpreted "dogs" to refer to unfaithful Christians. However, there is no compelling reason to limit its meaning to either of these possibilities.

7. See, e.g., John 6:48; 8:12; 10:11; 15:1.

time, the prayer expresses a desire in the present that Jesus would come among his people at the Eucharist, which would likely follow a reading of Revelation in the liturgical assembly.

Meanwhile the Spirit invites everyone in the assembly **who thirsts**—that is, who longs for the Lord and longs for life—to **come forward** and **receive the gift of life-giving water**. The word "forward" is not found in the Greek, but the NABRE supplies it to indicate that readers are encouraged to draw near spiritually to the risen Lord who is eager to pour out his Spirit on the Church as she worships. Through Isaiah the Lord promised to satisfy the thirst of Israel without price, freely, as a gift (Isa 55:1). The spring of endless divine life is available to John's readers, not only in the new Jerusalem but also here and now (John 7:37).

A Solemn Warning and Closing Greetings (22:18–21)

> ¹⁸I warn everyone who hears the prophetic words in this book: if anyone adds to them, God will add to him the plagues described in this book, ¹⁹and if anyone takes away from the words in this prophetic book, God will take away his share in the tree of life and in the holy city described in this book.
> ²⁰The one who gives this testimony says, "Yes, I am coming soon." Amen! Come, Lord Jesus!
> ²¹The grace of the Lord Jesus be with all.

OT: Deut 4:2–4; 13:1–6; 29:19–20; Prov 30:6
NT: Rom 16:20; 1 Cor 16:22
Catechism: coming soon, 673; desire for Christ's coming, 1130, 1403

Identifying who is speaking in each of these verses is not easy. Although   **22:18–19** some interpreters attribute to Jesus the solemn warning not to add or subtract from **the prophetic words in this book**, it is probably from John as a prophet, speaking authoritatively on behalf of God. While the NABRE renders the Greek as **I warn**, it literally says, "I testify to." Testifying to the word of God is precisely the role given to John at the beginning of the book (1:2, 9).

The most obvious meaning of these verses is a divine warning against tampering with the text of the book of Revelation, but there is more. John echoes Moses' teaching in Deuteronomy: "You shall not add to what I command you nor subtract from it" (4:2). The context is a reminder of Israel's idolatry and immorality at Peor (Num 25), which Num 31:16 attributes to "the counsel of

Balaam" (RSV; see Rev 2:14). The prohibition against adding to or subtracting from God's word is repeated in Deut 13:1–6, where the context refers to false prophets who will try to lead Israel to follow other gods. Thus Rev 22:18–19 is directed against false teaching and false prophecy, warning that God will punish interpretations of the Christian faith that allow the idolatry, immorality, and compromise with evil that Revelation condemns.

The penalties imposed on anyone who tampers with the message are severe: God will **add** to him **the plagues described in this book**.[8] Similarly, God will **take away his share in the tree of life and in the holy city**. In other words, if such a person once enjoyed the hope of eternal life through faith and baptism, he or she will lose it.

22:20–21   The book concludes with brief words by Jesus, the Church, and John. Jesus identifies himself as the **one who gives this testimony**. Jesus himself is the source of the book of Revelation. The beginning of this book describes its content as the revelation that God gave to Jesus, who sent his angel to John, who bears witness to "the testimony of Jesus Christ by reporting what he saw" (1:1–2). Jesus' final word is **Yes, I am coming soon** (see 1:3; "Reflection and Application" on 1:1–3; and sidebar, "The Timing of Jesus' Return," p. 182). The slight change of wording from "Behold" in 22:12 to "Yes" here makes the repetition emphatic. The response of the Church animated by the Spirit, the Bride of the Lamb, is also an emphatic repetition of what was said in 22:17—**Amen! Come Lord Jesus!**—expressing the earnest longing and prayer of all God's people for that day to come.

Finally, John adds his closing greeting to the churches: **The grace of the Lord Jesus be with all**. While the love between the Lamb and his Bride awaits a future consummation, John prays that in the meantime the Lamb's grace, his efficacious favor, may rest upon all who read his words.

---

8. Revelation identifies the following as plagues: demonic tormentors (9:18, 20), afflictions imposed by the two witnesses (11:6), the seven bowls (15:1, 6, 8; 16:9, 21), and the judgment on Babylon (18:4, 8).

Suggested Resources

Sources from the Christian Tradition

Augustine, St. *The City of God*. Translated by Henry Bettenson, with a new introduction by G. R. Evans. London: Penguin, 2003. Book 20 contains Augustine's interpretation of the eschatological texts in Scripture, including Revelation.

Weinrich, William C., ed. *Revelation*. Ancient Christian Commentary on Scripture: New Testament 12. Downers Grove, IL: InterVarsity, 2005. Selections from Church Fathers on every passage of Revelation.

Scholarly Commentaries

Beale, G. K. *The Book of Revelation*. New International Greek Testament Commentary. Grand Rapids: Eerdmans, 1999. A Reformed scholar's in-depth study.

Harrington, Wilfred J. *Revelation*. Sacra Pagina. Collegeville, MN: Liturgical Press, 1993. Insightful, concise, rich in background information. Nevertheless, it departs from Catholic doctrine, interpreting Satan as merely a symbol of evil (111) and the lake of fire as annihilation (201–2, 205–6).

Osborne, Grant R. *Revelation*. Baker Exegetical Commentary on the New Testament. Grand Rapids: Baker Academic, 2002. A perceptive commentary that summarizes and evaluates recent scholarship, written by an evangelical scholar with a futurist point of view.

Popular and Midlevel Works

Hahn, Scott. *The Lamb's Supper: The Mass as Heaven on Earth*. New York: Doubleday, 1999. Hahn tells how attending Mass before his conversion to

Catholicism helped him understand Revelation; he explains the relationship between the worship of heaven and the sacred liturgy.

Koester, Craig R. *Revelation and the End of All Things*. Grand Rapids: Eerdmans, 2001. Excellent commentary by a Lutheran scholar.

McIlraith, Donal A. *Everyone's Apocalypse: A Reflection Guide*. Suva, Fiji: Pacific Regional Seminary, 1995. An Irish missionary/biblical scholar's concise, insightful guide.

Wright, N. T. *Revelation for Everyone*. Louisville: Westminster John Knox, 2011. An excellent and engaging popular commentary by a renowned Anglican bishop and biblical scholar.

Specialized Resources

Bauckham, Richard. *The Climax of Prophecy*. Edinburgh: T&T Clark, 1993. An Anglican scholar's profound exegetical essays covering most of Revelation.

———. *Theology of the Book of Revelation*. New Testament Theology. Cambridge: Cambridge University, 1993. Excellent summary of the theology of Revelation.

Beale, G. K., and Sean M. McDonough. "Revelation." Pages 1081–1161 in *Commentary on the New Testament Use of the Old Testament*, edited by G. K. Beale and D. A. Carson. Grand Rapids: Baker Academic, 2007. Thorough guide to Revelation's allusions to the Old Testament and Jewish intertestamental literature.

Kovacs, Judith, and Christopher Rowland. *Revelation*. Oxford: Blackwell, 2004. A useful guide to interpretations through history.

Olson, Carl E. *Will Catholics Be "Left Behind"?* San Francisco: Ignatius, 2003. Catholic critique of dispensationalist eschatology.

Resseguie, James L. *The Revelation of John: A Narrative Commentary*. Grand Rapids: Baker Academic, 2009. A commentary focusing on Revelation's literary features.

Vanhoye, Albert. *Old Testament Priests and the New Priest*. Petersham, MA: St. Bede's Publications, 1980. Includes rich section (279–309) on Revelation's teaching that Christ has established Christians as priests.

Glossary

apocalypse, apocalyptic (from Greek *apokalypsis*, "revelation," "unveiling"): a literary genre common in Jewish and Christian circles between 200 BC and AD 200 that employs visions, heavenly journeys, and symbolism to reveal spiritual realities that underlie earthly events or to reveal what will happen at history's end (see "Genre" in the introduction, pp. 18–19).

Apostolic Fathers: Christian teachers of the generation after the apostles—for example, Clement, Ignatius of Antioch, Polycarp.

beatific vision: the contemplation of God face-to-face, a blessing that belongs to God's people in heaven after death in the eternal kingdom (22:4).

beatitude: pronouncement that someone is fortunate or happy, implicitly praising the behavior or circumstance that is the basis of the person's happiness.

chiliasm: *see* **millenarianism**.

cosmic: (1) what has to do with the created order; (2) what has worldwide significance; (3) what pertains to supernatural beings; (4) what is immense in extent.

dispensationalism, dispensationalist: a school of biblical interpretation among conservative Protestants named for the belief that God deals with people differently in different dispensations or epochs of salvation history. Dispensationalism emphasizes literal interpretation, the †rapture, the great †tribulation, Armageddon, discontinuity between Israel and the Church, and a literal thousand-year reign of Christ on earth before a final assault by Satan against Jerusalem.

divine passive: the use of the passive voice to imply that God is the one who is acting. For example, Rev 19:8 says "it was granted her to clothe herself / with fine linen, bright and pure" (ESV), implying that God has granted this grace to the Bride of the Lamb.

doxology: a compact prayer of praise to God.

eschatology, eschatological (from Greek *eschata*, "last things"): theology of what concerns the end of human history, the glorious return of the Christ, the resurrection of the dead, the last judgment, and eternal life in the kingdom. Christian faith is characterized by an inaugurated eschatology: the reign of God has already begun in the coming of Christ yet awaits its definitive fulfillment at the end of history.

fury: *see* **wrath**.

futurist: an approach to interpreting Revelation that understands it as pertaining primarily to the period immediately before the return of Christ.

gematria: a traditional Jewish system of assigning numerical value to the letters of a word, in the belief that words with identical numerical values are related to one another.

Gentiles: *see* **nations**.

glory (Greek *doxa*): (1) honor or praise; (2) majesty or greatness that is manifest; (3) splendor or radiance—God's glory is his radiant presence (15:8; 2 Chron 7:1–3).

Hellenistic: of or relating to Greek history, language, and culture in the ancient world after Alexander the Great (d. 323 BC).

imperial cult: acts of worship directed to living or dead members of the imperial family or to the goddess Roma. These religious practices were encouraged and sometimes required as an expression of loyalty to the Roman empire (see 13:1–4).

inhabitants of the earth: a phrase that means "those who dwell on the earth," but which in Revelation always refers to those who do not belong to God's people (see sidebar, "Who Are the 'Inhabitants of the Earth'?," p. 130).

intertestamental: a period in history between Malachi, the last book of the OT preserved in Hebrew (ca. 445 BC), and the NT.

messiah (from Hebrew *mashiakh*, "anointed one"; Greek *Christos*): Christ, the royal descendant of David promised by God through the prophets, whom many Jews expected to establish the kingdom of God. Christians recognize Jesus as the Messiah, the universal and eternal king. Revelation uses the word "Christ" both as part of Jesus' name (1:1, 2, 5) and as his title (11:15; 12:10; 20:4–6).

millenarianism: (1) belief that there will be a thousand-year reign of Christ on earth before the establishment of God's eternal kingdom (also called millennialism and chiliasm; see "Excursus: Interpretation of 'the Millennium' through History," pp. 329–31); (2) belief in a future utopian age.

millenialism: *see* **millenarianism**.

millennium: a thousand years; in 20:4–6, the thousand-year reign with Christ of the martyrs and other faithful Christians who did not compromise themselves, or accept its mark (see "Excursus: Interpretation of 'the Millennium' through History," pp. 329–31).

nations (Greek *ethnē*), also translated as "Gentiles" (11:2): (1) peoples of non-Jewish descent including those who accept the kingship of God and the light of the Lamb in the new Jerusalem (15:3–4; 21:24, 26); (2) those who do not belong to God's people, including those who oppose him (11:18; 16:19) and those who succumb to Babylon's seduction (18:3) and satanic deception (20:8).

Olivet discourse: Jesus' †eschatological discourse on the Mount of Olives (Matt 24; Mark 13; Luke 21).

oracle: a discrete prophetic message like those collected in the prophetic books of the OT or like the prophecies to the seven churches of Asia in Rev 2–3.

parousia (Greek *parousia*, "presence," "arrival"): the glorious return of Christ at the end of history.

Parthia, Parthians: a warlike federation of tribes on the eastern frontier of the Roman Empire.

preterist: an approach to interpreting Revelation that understands it as mainly pertaining to events of the first century.

rapture: according to dispensationalist interpretation of 1 Thess 4:17, the transporting of believers to heaven before, during, or after the great tribulation (Revelation Resources at www.CatholicScriptureCommentary.com).

recapitulate, recapitulation: to repeat or sum up. Revelation frequently retells portions of the story of salvation that the book as a whole narrates, highlighting different aspects at each retelling (see "Literary Features" in the introduction, p. 26).

saints: (1) the word used in many translations for God's holy people of the Old and New Testaments (Ps 16:3; Dan 7:21–22; 2 Cor 1:1); (2) those of God's people who have died and are with the Lord in heaven; (3) those whom the Church has officially recognized as being in heaven (i.e., canonized saints).

Septuagint: Greek translation of the Hebrew Bible dating from the third and second century BC. The title means "seventy" in Greek, from a tradition that seventy scholars did the translation (the abbreviation is LXX, Latin for "70"). As the Bible used by Greek-speaking Jews and Christians, it is often quoted in the NT.

Synoptic Gospels, Synoptics (from the Greek for "seeing together"): term applied to the Gospels of Matthew, Mark, and Luke because they contain much similar material and view the life of Jesus from a similar perspective.

theophany: a manifestation of God like the one that occurred on Mount Sinai when God bestowed his covenant on Israel (Exod 19:16) or the one that took place by the Chebar canal when God revealed himself to Ezekiel (Ezek 1:13). In Revelation, God manifests his presence through lightning and thunder and other phenomena at the conclusion of each series of divine interventions (8:5; 11:19; 16:18).

Torah (Hebrew for "law" or "instruction"): the first five books of the Bible, also called the law of Moses or the Pentateuch. Torah is also used more broadly to refer to all God's teachings on how to live an upright life in covenant relationship with him.

tribulation (Greek *thlipsis*, also translated as "affliction," "hardship," "distress"): according to the NT, the suffering and trials that Christians can expect to undergo on account of their faith.[1] The "great tribulation" is the period of trial before the final defeat of evil, foretold in Dan 12:1–2 and alluded to in the NT (Matt 24:21; Rev 7:14; see sidebar, "The Great Tribulation," pp. 146–47).

type: a person, place, institution, or event in an earlier stage of God's plan that foreshadows God's action at a later stage. For instance, the exodus from Egypt foreshadows Israel's return from exile (Isa 40:3–5) as well as redemption in Christ (1 Cor 10:1–4; 1 Pet 1:18–19). Revelation also presents evil individuals (Balaam and Jezebel) and cities (Babylon, Sodom) as types of similar entities that appear at the time of its writing and in the eschatological future (see "Interpretation of Revelation and History" in the introduction, pp. 31–32).

typology: a way of interpreting Scripture or history by discerning patterns in God's action, known as †types.

world: (1) Revelation uses the phrase "whole world" (*oikoumenē holē*) to refer negatively to nations and human society insofar as they are opposed to God (3:10; 12:9; 16:14); (2) it uses a different Greek word for "world" (*kosmos*) to refer neutrally to creation (11:15; 13:8; 17:8).

wrath: in Revelation, the final and irresistible judgment of God and the Lamb at the end of history on those who, despite warning judgments and the testimony of Jesus' witnesses, refuse to turn away from evil. God's wrath differs from human anger in that it is motivated not by emotional reaction but by true justice and the radical incompatibility between God's nature and evil of any kind.

Zion: a hill in ancient Jerusalem on which the temple and the palace of the Davidic king stood (Ps 2:6; 76:3). Biblical poetry often uses "Zion" or "daughter of Zion" to refer to Jerusalem or God's people as a whole. Hebrews 12:22 refers to Mount Zion as the heavenly Jerusalem, to which Christians already have access; Mount Zion in Rev 14:1 seems to have the same meaning.

---

1. See Matt 24:21; 2 Cor 1:4, 8; 2:4; Col 1:24; 1 Thess 1:6; Rev 1:9.

Index of Pastoral Topics

This index indicates where topics are mentioned in Revelation that may be useful for evangelization, catechesis, apologetics, or other forms of pastoral ministry.

Index of Sidebars